The Windmill Tilter

Wm X Stet

The Windmill Tilter

Shaping a Life in the Middle of 20th Century
1930–1965

William Kergan Street

To: Susie & Dale
I hope you enjoy this
memoir and that it will
help you revive your own
recollections of times long
past. Warmest,

Bill

iUniverse, Inc.
New York Lincoln Shanghai

The Windmill Tilter
Shaping a Life in the Middle of 20th Century 1930–1965

iUniverse books may be ordered through booksellers or by contacting:

iUniverse
2021 Pine Lake Road, Suite 100
Lincoln, NE 68512
www.iuniverse.com
1-800-Authors (1-800-288-4677)

Because of the dynamic nature of the Internet, any Web addresses or links contained in this book may have changed since publication and may no longer be valid.

The views expressed in this work are solely those of the author and do not necessarily reflect the views of the publisher, and the publisher hereby disclaims any responsibility for them.

ISBN: 978-0-595-43087-1 (pbk)
ISBN: 978-0-595-87428-6 (ebk)

Printed in the United States of America

Contents

Acknowledgements

Writing this memoir has, in itself, been an adventure that could add another chapter to the experiences I have set down here. Rummaging around in boxes of old photos, letters, log books, and journals from years ago has given me an opportunity to review, or better said, relive, many of my youthful adventures. Remembering these in turn has brought back to me, from the deep pool of my consciousness, memories of the pain or pleasure derived from these experiences, and what they meant to me at the time.

Having finished the book I need to acknowledge at being startled by the vast number of actors in my story, a very disparate group to be sure, but the great majority remain unmentioned. I have never met a person I was afraid to gain wisdom from, and all of this troupe have contributed to my life learning process by teaching me something or enlightening me in many other ways. I should very much wish to thank these bit players for participating in my Life Play, but alas, many have already crossed the stage and no longer orbit around my life. Gone, but as they say, not at all forgotten. Luckily for me, a smaller number have stayed as enduring friends throughout my life.

Writing this memoir has taken several years of constant urging from family and friends to finally complete. And I want to thank my many friends, who knowing I was trying to write a memoir, offered useful comments on parts of it, and also for their asking me on many occasions, "How's the book coming along," shaming me into once again getting back to work when I was "all written out."

I especially wish to recognize the help and literary skills my dear Bobby applied to all facets of this enterprise. The dozens of red pens used up, as she diligently corrected my multitudinous mistakes in syntax, punctuation and spelling, are a testament to her determination that I would finish what I started, no matter what. I also need to add that whatever mistakes appear will have been those few times when I overrode her good judgment.

On top of that, without her continuous encouragement and loving support this remembrance would never have been written.

William K. Street
Bliss Landing, B.C
August 21, 2007

Prologue

The Cosmos, the Earth, the Sea, ... and Me

I have set myself a task, I suppose one often asked of folks my age, to set some record down of a life probably not given many more years, or certainly before some wayward gene eases my mind into the smoothness of senility, to record some of my experiences for the entertainment, and possible interest of my family, the better to know some of the history I, and because of me, they, are a part of. I hope to be able to write with honesty about my life and that some may enjoy it as a chronicle of a certain time and place, and in the doing, perhaps I might learn much about myself that was hard to understand during the complexity and demands of daily living.

I sit here with an almost blank piece of paper in front of me, confounded by how to start and how to describe the connection between the experiences that make up my life, and my thoughts, belief systems, and feelings, which are the legacy of my life experience. There is, I know, a correlation between what we think and believe and the actions we choose to undertake during a lifetime. Of course, chance and happenstance assert their impacts on us all, occasionally to a huge degree, but I suspect not as much as we would like to believe as we rationalize our choices and behavior and experiences over time.

I will try hard to make these connections against the background of my time, my upbringing, and the major influences that shaped me, as I begin the long journey of recalling the past....

*   *   *

It is fitting for me to start this project here at the edge of the sea, looking westward from my writing table out across the almost flat sandy beach that barely slopes from the stone seawall a few meters from my window, until it is touched lovingly, caressed I am thinking, by the sea. Today it is calm and I look west between the two islands, one to the north, the other to the south, that break the curve of the unending horizon but not the shallow swells that continue calmly onward to languidly roll up on the sand in the sparkling sunshine one hundred feet from the sea wall. It sets me thinking on connections, not only with the characters populating my story, but of myself to a grander scheme that exists, that I can but partially comprehend.

The sound of the waves breaking seems to set a fundamental rhythm for life near the beach, and perhaps for all life. Those never ending swells that began thousands

1

of miles to the west, moving slowly but inexorably toward the land, makes me sense in their meter that the earth itself is breathing, through the sea, ... in ... and ... out, ... in ... and ... out. Very early in my life I developed a sense about our planet's vast oceans, that everything alive came somehow from the sea and therefore in some wonderful way I am connected with every other living thing on earth. What a gratifying feeling this is if one takes the time to truly engage the thought.

Our two islands break an otherwise perfect view of the edge of our world, this planet whose beautiful curving rim can only be seen when looking across a great and uninterrupted expanse of water. It is then I realize we are truly on a sphere that floats in the vastness of the universe with countless other floating worlds, in seemingly serene isolation, all gently tethered together by gravity. If I concentrate while looking over the western rim where the edge of the world meets the sky, it's then I can sometimes make myself feel that I'm actually on the bottom, or the side of our planet in its drift through the cosmos and this thought almost induces a sense of vertigo in me as the earth and I make our way together through the space and time of our universe.

If you shut your eyes and listen, the sound of the surf as it spreads upward to its apogee over the sand is like wind rustling through aspens in the hills of Wyoming, only to occasionally be broken by the thunk of a larger wave breaking downward instead of unfolding gracefully onto the sand. These sounds, this vista to the West, this sense that all life is connected to the sea, the sea to the sky, the sky, our pathway to the universe and the infinite, all connected.

When I can sit still and relax, perhaps in some form of meditation, I feel within me the soft humming of the starstuff we are made from, not so much the atoms making up our parts, nor their electrons and protons whizzing at light speed within me, but more the soft vibration of the particles of energy that somehow combine to create every single thing in the universe.

Is there a purpose to this life of mine? Did this billion year arc of genes that became Me, carry hidden in their protoplasm a wondrous terminus towards which we all are heading, but which we still cannot know and cannot describe? Perhaps some things will become clearer to me as I rummage around in the past looking for connections, for implications, and for understanding. I invite you to come along with me as I pry loose the memories from the collapsing edifice of my youth, and reconstruct that time past, partly in the search for some lessons, but perhaps also for the sheer joy of remembering the days when I was young and strong and optimistic.

Mazatlan 2006

Setting the Stage

Our hero's foundations: depression, war, family, and the West

I was born in January of 1930, the beginning of a decade that was already enmeshed in the midst of a worldwide economic depression and would end in a colossal world war. A very exciting time to arrive if I do say. Over time, these two great events had a major influence in my life, helping form my later thoughts and attitudes. In my earliest years, life revolved around our parents, grandparents and great grandparents and I was not conscious of the momentous events gathering outside my immediate little boy universe. The significance of this history would only be learned some years later. After passing the midpoint of the decade and starting school in 1935, I began to be more aware of the events my parents were talking about and they often read the headlines to us children and tried to explain what was happening in the world outside our close little family.

My impression today when I think back on those early years, is that indeed, very exciting things were going on all over the world and some even close to home, and often when we were taken downtown we could hear the newsboys, some just kids, hawking their papers with the loud call, "EXTRA! EXTRA! Read all about it," and the headline would be two or three inches high to punctuate the importance of the event. It seemed that almost every day some new and interesting thing was happening somewhere, and life appeared exceedingly exciting to me.

Many of the events in the world outside, we heard on the radio or saw in the morning newspaper headlines during those years, such as the Lindberg kidnapping trial, John Dillinger, shot in 1934, and Pretty Boy Floyd, the war in Spain, Al Capone and the mob, the Japanese rape of Nanking, the Flying Tigers and Gen. Clair Chenault, the 2nd election of Franklin D. Roosevelt, the Hindenberg crash, Amelia Earhart's disappearance, Wiley Post and Will Rogers getting killed taking off from Nome in the Winney Mae in 1935, and the start of World War II in 1939, with the German invasion of Poland.

I also know that the effect of the Great Depression on my parents, and through them on our family, manifested itself into my life as they tried to impart to me and my siblings, Georgann (Jan) and Jack, the hard lessons learned during this period. With no family resources to fall back on, Work, Frugality and Saving became their life mantra and they hoped this would hold back the depression from wrecking our family's financial security as had happened to countless others. As it turned out they were right, or very lucky, because Dad almost always had a job during those years, and his jobs became bigger and better, requiring our family to move from the West Coast several times, before I was fourteen.

In an effort to keep their children aware of the good fortune they enjoyed, and to better understand the desperate straits of other folks, our parents would try to make us understand just how devastating the depression was to those less fortunate. We, it seemed, had actually escaped the effects of the depression scot-free and I well remember their taking us to see the shantytown area south of downtown Seattle in 1939, a hodgepodge of shacks thrown together with corrugated metal, a place to get out of the rain and hold the scanty supply of belongings these people possessed. It was not a pretty sight; rainwater in puddles lying on the uneven ground, smoke coming from metal stovepipes and some laundry undulating in the rain. Evidently overcome by an endless pall of deadening gray, a lack of any color that might have brightened life, and lacking any prospect, people moved slowly about as if there was nothing to do to better their situation. And there wasn't. This would have to wait for the war to overtake America.

During those hard depression years we children often saw men attempting to make a living going door to door offering to sharpen our kitchen knives or chop kindling, for a meal, or to sell Fuller brushes. There seemed to be hundreds of "Fuller brush" salesmen about, so many it must have been terribly hard to make a meager living. As a youngster, not only did I see beggars on the streets of Milwaukee and Seattle, but as well, World War I veterans missing legs or arms, selling yellow pencils held in a cup, with another cup alongside in hope of receiving a kindly offering. There were not many jobs and in most city parks we always saw groups of unemployed men sitting or sleeping under newspapers on benches, or in the summer lying about on the grass. It was a hard time and most families had seen their assets and livelihood diminish dramatically, often to nothing.

I became a Cub Scout in 1940, and a year later went on a troop weekend camping trip, returning home on Sunday December 7, 1941. At mid-morning as we stepped out of the car near the Denny Blaine Episcopal church, the first person we saw excitedly told us that Japan had attacked America's Pearl Harbor naval base in Hawaii and devastated most of our naval military capacity in their sneak attack. This event destroyed forever whatever isolation and safety from world events America had enjoyed in the past. There was no doubt in anyone's mind that we were going headlong into a full scale war where we would show what America was truly made of. We had been badly hurt and we were angry, and everyone was determined to make the enemy pay dearly for this assault on us.

It may have been one of mankind's darkest hours (I'm sure it was!) but to me, not yet a teenager, without a doubt the advent of World War II was the most exciting event a young boy could experience, and I desperately hoped it would last long enough for me to be able to enlist as a fighter pilot and become an ace! Of course, it ended when I was 15 and my dream of ace-hood faded with Japan's surrender.

But the war brought with it many changes in our lives like rationing, with food stamps that strictly limited purchases of many types of foods, especially butter, meat and sugar; and gasoline cards allowing only a few gallons per week; and countless other items gone completely to the war effort. Mother also spent most of her days in war-related efforts mounted by local women's groups, making First Aid supplies, volunteering in hospitals, and knitting afghans to be sent to the troops. I, along with several of my sixth grade boy friends, were pictured in the newspaper knitting afghan squares, and we were not even embarrassed to be seen doing "womans" work. It was for the war effort, and almost everyone tried to be involved one way or another.

Every day the newspapers were full of war headlines, photographs of battles being waged in Africa, Europe, and Asia, and maps showing where each army was confronting the other in places I had never heard of, and of course the claims of both sides as to who was winning. I received the best geography education possible and by the war's end was fully aware of almost every out-of-the way corner of the world.

With Fort Lewis, one of the largest army forts in the west, McChord Army Air Corp base near Tacoma, Sand Point Naval Air Station in Seattle, the large naval base at Bremerton, and the Boeing aircraft plant cranking out B 17's, and later B 29's, there was the presence of a huge military effort everywhere around us. The evening streets in Seattle and Tacoma were always full of servicemen out for a good time, and mothers tried hard to keep their daughters corralled.

But it was the airplanes that were special for me! I studied them in detail. I saw them flying and made many models of them and I knew without looking up which plane it was from the special sound of its engine as it flew over. How they flew over! The new Grummen Avengers low over the rooftops when we lived at the top of 36th Avenue as they headed into Sand Point Naval Air Station, or P38's roaring low-level up past Point-No-Point below Les and me standing on the bluff at Hansville, or the mock dogfights high over the Straits of Juan de Fuca between Hansville and Whidbey island, or P39 Aircobras heading for Alaska and then on to Russia, after refueling at McChord, and later on, B17's and B29's flying out over the city and Lake Washington from Boeing Field!

These two world catastrophes, depression and war, worked their way into my life as they worked their way to conclusion in the world at large, and I know that they affected how I think and feel about the world, and especially this country America, where I am greatly fortunate to have been born and lived most of my life.

A third major influence in my life was our family's Western myth. It was the story of how our family came to California by covered wagon in 1846 and what they did after they arrived. It was not a myth in that it never happened, but a myth in that the story had been told and retold until it carried a certain aura of courageousness, intrepidness, determination and adventure, which was adopted by all of us, enjoyed with a certain fervor, and ultimately contributed to our family's sense of pride and specialness.

This story's main character, "Poppy," my great grandfather George Van-Gorden, was a one year old child when his father and mother and the rest of the Harlan party, made the covered wagon journey to California. It ended when he died at 93 as the last surviving member of the California Pioneer Society. The stories of Poppy's legendary life told to me by my grandmother and mother, included Poppy's job as manager of the Hearst ranch at San Simeon in the 1870's and 1880's, George Hearst's gold and silver mines and vaqueros, Poppy's trip to the Klondike gold rush in 1898, his lifetime around horses and his racehorse breeding, and the story of the golden rivet, all built in me a tremendous sense of our family's part in the history of the West, but more importantly, at a very young age, my sense that Poppy had led an adventurous and exciting life.

It was California that had attracted my ancestors. They arrived before it was a state and before gold was discovered at Sutter's Mill. The family migration ended on the shore of the Pacific in 1846, near what was then called Yerba Buena, before being changed by the Americans on March 10, 1847 to San Francisco.

As a little boy, I watched the Golden Gate Bridge being built from my Aunt Marion's and Uncle Ed's living room on Lake Street, where they had set up a telescope and Poppy was the honored guest, as the last of the California pioneers, at the ceremony of driving the final "golden" rivet signifying completion of construction of the bridge on April 26, 1937.

This Golden Gate was, for me, the entrance to the rest of the world and it beckoned me with a beautiful siren song of adventure and filled my mind with the urge to someday travel through it to the mysterious places and peoples of other lands. This same call had moved my ancestors to leave England and Holland to sail to the new lands of North America, and almost two centuries later, with the energy that comes from being free to choose their own destinies, my more recent forefathers made their trek westward across the plains and mountains to their new lives in California.

The natural beauty of California in its myriad aspects filled my young mind's eye and bonded me to that land in a way that has forever made me feel, when I travel to California, I have come home in some essential way. These beautiful images engraved so long ago in my brain, of the seashore, the mountains, and especially the rolling hills above the Pacific have never left me. In 1934 we lived for a while in Burlingame, south of San Francisco, where I could see the hills that paralleled the coast to San Jose, and although they faded from our sight in the blue Pacific haze past Santa Cruz I came to know they reached to Monterey and Big Sur, past San Simeon and Santa Barbara, south all the way into old Mexico.

These hills turning dry, becoming yellow in early summer as the grass died in the buzzing sun, were broken only by the clumps and spots of dark green oak and cypress. These becoming solid green patches in the now dry creek beds and coulees that fell away towards the ocean, ending abruptly at the edge of the rocky graybrown cliffs that hung high over the green water of the Pacific. Rocks immovable and stoic, completely unconcerned with the relentless swells birthed far out in the Pacific, moving constantly forward to crash against them, only to fall away to nothing but white froth, sliding back to meet and join the next wave.

In 1935 father accepted a new job with the Boston Store, forcing the family to move to Milwaukee. During that long train trip east I remember waking up in my Pullman berth and raising the shade to look out into the western night and every so often seeing a lone light far off, a pinprick of life in the obliterating blackness and wondering how people could bear to live so utterly alone in that immense prairie space. *What kind of people were they … why had they stopped there … how did they live and what did they do … were they cowmen or farmers … and how did they communicate with their kind?* It seemed to me unbearably sad that they were there and so alone. But perhaps I was simply projecting my own feelings and anxiety about moving east, a place I had learned to disdain at a very early age due to my family's overly proud western heritage.

Later, in January of 1938, another new job for father caused us to retrace our steps westward, but this time to the land of low lying clouds, endless forests and beautiful mountains … and water..the timeless running river waters of the Stillaguamish…. Skykomish … Nooksack…. Klickitat…. Snoqualmie.. Nisqually … lovely rolling Salish names so beautiful the newcomers adopted them. A land of fir and cedar, hemlock and spruce, Tamarack and pine … forests unending except where they met the dark salt water and barnacled rust colored rocks of countless quiet coves and curving beaches along Puget Sound or were lost to view in the mist laden distant air of the Pacific Northwest.

This beautiful western land of America … its immense spaces … its manliness … its sense of freedom and lack of pretentiousness … its directness and demands … and perhaps most important, its optimism … all have converged in my mind to sometimes overwhelm me with profound feelings of love … and awe … and instilled in me a lifelong sense of connection to nature in all its manifestations from the awesome mystery of the universe to the brilliant bright liquid yellow of a buttercup found in a field, and a strong sense of optimism that no matter what happened, everything would turn out all right, and deep in my being, a thankfulness for the chance to be alive and a part of it all.

The Little Boy With Wide Eyes

Wherein our hero's eyes are opened
To the awaiting wonders of the world

The house on Lake Street belonged to his aunt and uncle and was westward and higher than downtown and thus afforded an uninterrupted view of the entrance to San Francisco Bay and the Golden Gate Bridge that was under construction at the time. His uncle had set up a telescope in the living room and the boy was engaged in looking through it, probably for the ninth time that morning, no doubt to the concern of the adults, since he had to stand on a footrest to reach the eyepiece.

His mother sat near a table working on a needlepoint project and talking quietly with her sister who was sitting nearby looking at the newspaper, both seemingly indifferent to his activities. The boy kept his eyes to the telescope but his ears kept close attention to the changes in tone or subject of the two women's conversation. At one point he heard his aunt say, "I see in the paper that 'Old Ironsides' the sailing ship, arrived yesterday. It's down at fisherman's dock below the Presidio. Might be fun to see it."

With that the boy jumped down from his perch at the telescope and ran to the table exclaiming "I want to see 'Old Ironsides' Mama, can we go today?" "We'll see", she said. "I really want to go! I DO!" he said, jumping up two legged to land flat footed emphasizing his wish. "PLEASE can we?" "We'll see. If you're a good boy maybe we can go this afternoon," she said, with the firmness of an adult who does not want to be coerced by a child. But he knew then, from her look and tone of voice, that she would grant his wish.

Later in the afternoon she took the boy down to the edge of the bay and holding his hand they walked together in the sunshine along the waterfront for several blocks, past one dock after another, most of which had large warehouses or terminals on them. Gently swaying in the water's constant motion between the long docks, were the ships, rusty freighters of many descriptions tied to the piers with huge ropes, their bows pointing towards the land. Ships that had come into the port from across the ocean, or were about to leave for somewhere far away, and

9

gangs of men were loading or unloading them in a bustle of activity on each dock.

His mother explained to the boy what was happening, that "Most of these steamships came to San Francisco filled with all sorts of things that are from other countries, things that will be taken to stores like where Daddy works, where they'll be sold."

"What kinds of things?" the boy asked his mother. "Well, maybe silk scarves from China, or pineapples from Hawaii, or toy race cars from Japan like you have at home. All of the boats we see tied up at the docks have come into this port from some other land and when they are loaded again, they'll sail away, filled with other things that someone far away wants."

Looking ahead past one of the dock warehouses the boy could see a different kind of ship's bow coming into view as they walked towards it. "Mama, look at that!" he exclaimed excitedly. "I see it," she answered, "that's the old sailing ship you and I have come to see. Isn't it interesting? When I was a small girl we saw a few of these old sailing ships but Old Ironsides is one of the very last."

As they approached he could see the hull was black with a long upward curving bow that seemed to express a need to run forward into the wind and sea, and to his increasing amazement as his gaze followed the black arc upward and forward, he saw that it ended in a magical human figure whose arms were outstretched as if reaching for the sun, and whose blacks eyes stared straight ahead from its perch high over his head.

From the middle of the figure, so it seemed to the boy, ropes ascended back and up to the top of the front mast, appearing to encircle it, expanding into eight or ten more that descended down and out to the curve of the deck railing on each side. Behind this first mast were three more with their spars, their maze of ropes and winches and furled canvas sails.

The boy and his mother stood under the bowsprit in silence as the boy let his eyes rove over the ship, along the side rails, up the masts, towards the huge cast iron anchor and chain and the thick ropes that tied the ship to the dock. He stared in awe at what it seemed to express. He could easily imagine this ship heeled over under its white sails, the sun shining on a blue and green sea, its colorful pennants fluttering and white froth formed by the wind and the waves flying upward as the bow split into the water.

It was so exciting! His delight grew as he let his mind roam. Finally, he looked up at his mother and asked, "Mama, where did 'Old Ironsides' come from?" She thought for some time and then answered, "Oh, probably from China or maybe the South Seas. It came in from the big, blue Pacific Ocean, way beyond the Golden Gate."

At that moment the boy's imagination welled up and the old sailing ship became for him the awakening of the Dream of Adventure, to set out and see the world, to become free like the wind and the sea and the sky, to have experiences, and he sensed then that these adventures would happen farther west, out past the Golden Gate and onto the shining sea.

Once again he lifted his eyes to the bowsprit figure over him, which reached forward forever grasping for the wind and with its gaze fixed outward and ahead in anticipation of what was to come. As the boy stared it seemed to speak directly to him, "Come with me where I go.... across the seven seas."

"Mama", he said, pulling on her arm to be assured he had her attention, "Someday I'm going to go on a sailing ship to China!" he promised. "I'm sure you will," she said, smiling down at him.

Later, as a man, he never forgot that afternoon with his mother on the docks of San Francisco, nor those first feelings of wanderlust that arose in him as a small boy gazing at the old sailing ship, its sails now furled, but his imagination running like the tide, unstoppable.

0 to 13 in only 4747 days

*Wherein our young hero is awed by nature, finds love,
takes a wrong path, pays a penalty, finds adventure in books,
learns to hunt and fish, and accelerates toward teenhood*

When I was very small, my eyes just able to see the top edge of the sink, I used to watch Dad shave with his straight razor. He would lather up his face with his shaving brush and then carefully draw the razor down his cheek gathering a large glob of shaving soap on the razor and then he would shake this onto a piece of toilet paper placed on the flat rim of the bowl. I would look at this blob and recognize some form in it, usually an animal, and gleefully point this out to Father. Each time he shook off a pile of lather and whiskers he added a little flip that created a new form for me. This was great fun and he seemed to have a lot of patience with me even though it slowed down the shaving process.

Later on I became particularly interested in his razor strop and how he whipped his straight razor back and forth, turning it over with every stroke to sharpen both sides. This strop was also an instrument of some latent fear when I heard of it being used on the backsides of some children, by their fathers, as a mode of punishment. I had a healthy respect for this weapon but Dad never even threatened us with it. I'm certain he knew his hand would be sufficient.

We lived in the Bay Area from 1930 to 1935, where the cast of characters remaining of the Kergan, VanGorden, Street and Bruck families I grew up knowing, all lived. My Great Grandmother, Wilhelmina Street (Grandma Bill) lived in the Piedmont area of Oakland, my other Great Grandparents, Monnie and Poppy VanGorden, in Danville, east of Oakland, and my Grandmother Anna Kergan near Lake Merritt in Oakland. Mother's older sister, Marian, married to Dr. Edwin Bruck, and their children, Ann, Kergan and Meredith, my first cousins, lived on Lake Street in San Francisco. There were others, great aunts and uncles, and some second cousins, but my early world, with few exceptions, revolved around these few.

George Van Gorden, "Poppy", my adventurous great grandfather.

Family gathering on Poppy's 89th birthday. Front row: Georgann,
Poppy, me, Jack, Ann Bruck, middle row: grandmother Anna, Monnie,
Kergan Bruck, Morris Edward, back row: My Aunt Marion Bruck, mother.

Some of the highlights of these very early years are still with me in vivid memory. We made occasional trips out to Danville where Monnie and Poppy Van-Gorden had their small 75 acre ranch. I loved to go there but it could not have been many times. The road through Walnut Creek to Danville, long before the post WWII building boom, was lined with big trees on both sides forming an arbor of shade, the hot sun sparkling through the leaves for a long ways before one arrived at the gate that led up to the old wooden house. The drive inside the gate was through a small orchard of fruit and nut trees that served for the front yard of the house. In the back were the stable, barnyard and miscellaneous sheds.

Behind the stable was a fenced pasture wherein resided the last of the racehorses that Poppy had raised and raced. I suppose after his 65 years in the saddle, before the automobile was invented, many years managing the cattle ranch at San Simeon, and breeding race horses, he needed to keep at least one horse around even after he could no longer ride, as a reminder of his long connection with horses and the joy and satisfaction they had brought into his long life. The last horse's name was "Sir William" which I thought very appropriate and from my two-foot tall perspective, "Sir William" had the longest legs I could imagine.

The ranch house was turn of the century Victorian. One climbed up six or seven rather steep steps to an old wooden front door with lace curtains showing through an etched ornamented window. Once in the hallway, a set of stairs on the right went to the second floor and on the left was the opening into the living room. Monnie and Poppy had a wonderful collection of old Indian baskets that were on the walls or on top of several armoires, relics from early California. An icebox in the kitchen used a block of ice as the coolant, and a cooler for food storage hung on the pantry wall in an opening separated from the outside by a fine screen so that the air could move around the food without the numerous bugs being able to beat the humans to it. Outside was a small icehouse with large blocks of ice bedded in sawdust, hopefully enough to last through the hot summer.

On one trip to the ranch when I was about two years old, I wandered into the back barnyard area where there were all sorts of interesting things to investigate. Pieces of farm machinery, chickens running around picking up bugs, early 'free range' I suppose, a few bantams and one very big, bigger than me, tom turkey. I loved to chase the chickens around but of course could never actually catch one. I then thought it would be great to chase the turkey. As I began walking over toward Mr. Tom, he did not budge from his position, but slowly raised his big vulturous head, his red wattles hanging like bloody strips of raw liver. As I got closer he continued to grow higher and his feathers filled out, and by the time I was within two feet I stopped because of the look in his demonic eyes, which were right at the height of my eyes and somehow seemed to signal that I would be the one chased. My courage evaporated at the evenness of his stare, and at that moment I turned and ran screaming as fast as I could with him in hot pursuit, flapping his wings and aiming his long beak at the top of my head. Luckily, Mother was a witness to the atrocity about to be perpetrated on one of her offspring and ran over to grab me and chase the turkey away.

Mother and Dad rented a house on Lake Street near my aunt and uncle and cousins and not far from the Presidio, a military facility that included a short airstrip. I was fascinated every time I saw the beauty and gracefulness of an airplane in flight, but had no understanding of what held it up, and unlike the awe I felt in watching a meteor race across the night sky, I knew there was an engine of some sort that propelled it upward. When I was three or four, I often begged Mother to take me along the road above the Presidio where we could park and watch the old WWI biplanes take off and land. I could never get enough of this activity, and consequently the idea of my getting to fly someday became a mini obsession, but one not to be satisfied for many more years.

Some years later, after moving to Milwaukee, we occasionally visited our cousins back on the West Coast. I learned to roller skate on one of these visits, leaving a little hide here and there on the sidewalk in front of the house on Lake Street in the process. The land dropped from Lake Street towards the bay and we could see the Golden Gate bridge which was then under construction. Uncle Ed had set up a telescope in the big view window overlooking the bay, so whenever we wished we could look at the construction project with the workers like little ants crawling up on the suspension cables and the jutting orange colored towers, like giant Lego pieces, rising out of the blue white capped water. On calm days, the long swirls of tidal action undulating slowly back and forth along with the wakes from boats of all sorts coming and going, excited my imagination every time I looked through the glass.

When we visited our cousins at their home, Jack and I slept upstairs in a room from where we had a perfect view of the bridge, and there were always ships coming in from, or leaving, for some far off exotic land. At night as we lay in our beds we could hear the fog horns of the buoys with their slow deep "whooooo..uump". It was a little scary in the dark, to think of the fog and black waters swirling through the channel and around Alcatraz Island, but in the daylight, in the sunshine, the blue water with myriad white foam lines, the soaring gulls and fluttering colored pennants of the ships coming and going, seemed to speak to me about the world across the sea. When I hear a similar foghorn now, I am still overtaken by a strong feeling of déjà vu, back to that time.

During these early years living in San Francisco, I met my Grandfather, Harry Kergan, a general practitioner and surgeon. In May of 1933, Mother and Aunt Marion each took their children to visit him in his offices one afternoon. He weighed and measured and jollied us and I remember him reaching out to tousle my hair and this is the only time I can recall being with him. He was a lovely, kindly man but he died several days later and unfortunately, except through the stories Mother told me, I had no time to come to know him. Mother and her father had a very special relationship and I remember asking her some years later to tell me about how Harry died, and as she did so tears welled up in her eyes and slowly began sliding softly down her cheeks. Her sense of loss still palpable.

I met my other grandfather, William Schwerdt Street, a purser for a steamship line that ran from San Francisco to the Orient, only one time that I can remember when I was quite young. My father's mother, an Irish Catholic girl whose family disowned her when she married out of the faith and would have nothing further to do with her, died when he was a baby and father was put into a foundling home for several years. As a consequence, Dad never saw a picture of his mother until he was in his late 40's, Mother having secured one from a distant relative.

Right after the San Francisco earthquake, Dad was picked up by his grandfather, Johnson Ford Street, and raised by his paternal grandmother, Grandma Bill, but he always called her "Mother." She lived to be 94 but when I knew her she was already in an old folks home and almost blind.

We moved to Milwaukee in 1935. We went by train, following Father who had already gone on ahead to begin his new job as General Merchandise Manager of the Boston Store, so named even though not in Boston. His boss and the major owner of the store was Stanley Stone, a man my siblings and I came to like very much. He lived within a block of us, which in hindsight my father felt was way too close since we children were always up to something at his house.

From the time I started my education in Milwaukee at the Country Day School, until I graduated from high school in 1947, my life seemed crammed full of interesting experiences and was overwhelmingly happy. This is not to say that I did not suffer all the various pangs and pains associated with growing up, I did, but on balance I always felt loved and cared for by my parents and even, in a different way, by my siblings, Jack and Georgann. I found that I could make friends, could do the schoolwork when motivated and took great pleasure in the variety of things that life had to offer a youngster in those interesting times, such as music, color and art, sports, animals, reading, and of course girls, as I added a few years.

Whatever setbacks I encountered, such as getting hurt, losing a girlfriend or not making the first team, never kept me long from regaining a feeling that life was a wonderful big adventure and my cup, as they say, was almost always way more than half full. I have been an incurable optimist about life and this trait in my personality has led me to make some big and costly mistakes at times. But by being able to believe in the brightness of the future, this same optimism has helped me to deal with whatever pain my misadventures brought down on me.

Our three years in Milwaukee was a time when I began a lifelong interest in the natural world. In a wooded area behind our house and several vacant lots nearby, Jack and I could find all sorts of interesting insects and animals. Some of these we periodically deposited down the mail drop into Mr. Stone's front hall, until finally in exasperation their nice house boy provided us with a special box in which he asked us to put our specimens, "so as to have them in better shape for Mr. Stone."

We encountered for the first time, fireflies, Cecropia moths that flew and sounded like humming birds and had large colored circles on their wings; large green caterpillars I think were from the Cecropia moths; garter snakes; "walking sticks"; "jack-in-the-pulpits", a very interesting plant found right behind the house; "yellow jackets" and long skinny "paper" wasps; and some bright colored birds like Cardinals and Baltimore Orioles, not seen in California.

Country Day was a private school that made learning interesting. I started there at age 5 in first grade and stayed through half of third grade. A terrarium in our classroom fit perfectly into Jack's and my field collecting. During one weekend we accumulated thirteen snakes, twelve common garter snakes, whose odor I hated on my hands, and one grass snake that was a solid beautiful emerald green. We took them home and put them into our bathtub to watch them swim, and tiring of that, left them there while we went outside to play. When the maid went in to clean the bathroom, Mother heard her scream, and of course we had to gather them all up again. Not wanting to lose them outside, because we were intent on taking them to school for the terrarium, we put them into a box in the small greenhouse between the side entrance of the house and the garage and went out again to play.

When Dad came home the snakes were all over the greenhouse and we were told in no certain terms that we had to gather them up and secure the box or "out they would go!" Monday morning we carried the box of snakes with us as we got on the school bus and later proudly offered them to our teacher who, at the sight of so many snakes together, was somewhat disconcerted to say the least. She induced us to let some of them go, but the rest ended up in the terrarium, with the turtles and salamanders.

Our introduction to the ways of yellow jackets was not so friendly. Jack and I were playing cops and robbers one day, each of us carrying a short stick for a gun. At one point in our fantasy game, probably hot on the trail of Pretty Boy Floyd or John Dillinger, much in the news then, we jumped for protection down into a hollow moat encircling a large oak tree. This moat, three feet deep and lined on the outside with rocks, provided a space of about eighteen inches from the tree to the rock wall. After being in one of these hollows for a few minutes we noticed some yellow jackets coming in and out between two rocks. This was pretty interesting. I saw that the entrance to whatever was behind was guarded by one yellow jacket, so I suggested to Jack that he push his stick slowly at the bee to see what would happen. Always following big brother's advice, he did this and the bee beat a hasty retreat.

As it turned out, it had just gone for reinforcements and suddenly with a huge buzzing sound a large squadron swept out from under the rock and attacked us. By the time we could climb out we were stung all over our faces, arms and hands.

You could have heard us screaming from a mile away as we both had about sixteen stings. For the next few years we each blamed the other for this fiasco. Jack's argument was "I told him to do it" and mine was "how could he have been so stupid as to poke a stick into the mouth of a yellow jacket nest, when I was only kidding?" I don't know whether or not this experience had anything to do with it, but Jack became quite allergic to bee stings later in life and a sting on his arm could make his face swell up oddly.

Around this time I became fascinated with colors. I don't know where this came from, possibly from doing art works at school, but I asked for crayons and colored pencils and spent many happy hours working on coloring books. At one time I got my hands on some squared paper and spent hours, after picking two colors that I felt went well together, coloring the alternating squares. When finished I showed these art works proudly to Mother, who dutifully clucked her approval.

One day while walking in the woods I found a buttercup. I think it was the first one I had really noticed and I bent close to look at it. I was amazed by the yellowness of this tiny bloom. It was shiny, almost iridescent in its brightness and the purest yellow I had ever seen. I rushed it to mother as a gift, making sure she looked carefully at it, so as to see in it what I saw and be properly impressed with the magnitude of my offering. She was touched and gave me a hug and kiss and I felt wonderful after that. With such a reward I was motivated to bring Mother more flower offerings over the years and always got the same result and continued to feel the glow of her love for me each time.

Later, in Seattle when I was eleven years old, we lived in Broadmoor whose homes and golf course were surrounded by a high woven wire fence. Along the fence wild climbing roses had been planted as an extra protection and these plants created a barrier in places up to fifteen feet wide. Part of the value of my flower gifts lay in overcoming the difficulties of collecting the flowers, and I recall the most prized blooms seemed to always be found deep inside the widest part of this thorny, almost impregnable wall of roses. The blooms were a beautiful pink and I would work my way carefully inside this protective thorny bower of green and pink, suffering plenty of scratches in my effort to find Mother the perfect blooms. In my imagination I was like a Knight Errant on a quest (having recently read about King Arthur) the Holy Grail being the flowers, and My Lady was Mother. She was always delighted with these small gifts, but her pleasure was nothing compared to the feelings of accomplishment I had in overcoming the imaginary dragons in order successfully to pluck the flowers for her.

In Milwaukee, we also came into contact with poison ivy, a very nasty plant. Georgann had a friend who thought it a great joke to rub her face with poison ivy and poor Georgann's face swelled up like a balloon, her eyes disappearing into the puffiness and she spent a few agonizing days in bed recovering. As it turned out, the friend also had a bad case which the family decided was her just reward, proving also that sometimes justice will prevail.

One of our projects as a class at Country Day was to study early American history and to build a log cabin in the classroom. I could not for the life of me figure out how we were to do that, but the teacher helped us make logs by rolling butcher paper around cotton batting or crunched up newspapers. We worked on the logs for quite a few days and then stacked them up forming two walls coming together at a corner, with a doorway and window. It was pretty innovative and contrary to most dull history courses, the cabin represented Abe Lincoln's cabin and helped build our interest in this most illustrious President and the calamitous Civil War period he lived through.

From this first introduction to history, and with only a mild defection in high school where I hated U.S. History mainly for the way it was taught, I minored in History at the university, and my interest in the broad panorama of human history is more intense now than ever before. I feel there are so many things to learn and answers that might be found for today's complicated life questions from studying history, and am amazed that many adults have so little interest in the subject. Especially since there is no novel written any more exciting than the real occurrences in the twisting trail of human events, but of course, it is usually from real life that fiction writers find their stories.

It was during this early part of my life that books began to make an impression on me. Before I could read, Mother mostly, but sometimes Father, read to us at bedtime or when we were sick in bed. I remember many of those old books such as Mother Goose, Uncle Remus, The Wizard of OZ, Winnie The Pooh, Aesop's Fables and Little Black Sambo, to name a few that were read to us. Later on as we learned to read ourselves, we still loved to be read to. I did not fully appreciate this effort on our parents' part until much later when I had children of my own.

I think mother read all of the Oz books to us when we were back in Seattle and nine to eleven years old. What a labor of love, or perhaps it was easier than listening to Jack and me roughhouse every night at bedtime? We had many animal books. Black Beauty came along and we devoured it, and then I got into stories of heroes, such as The Story of Siegfried, The Story of Lancelot, and King Arthur and The Knights of the Round Table. I ate those up as they depicted the kind of hero I fantasized someday to grow into.

There were many books and stories that were magical and fantastic. These really got my imagination into overdrive. There were flying carpets from the deserts of Arabia; genies trapped in bottles that might be found on any beach, and only needed some lucky person to rub them in order to release the genies from their glassy prisons, ready to grant any wish the lucky finder might desire; magic wands wielded by fairy godmothers; flying horses; and of course the trolls, gnomes, sirens and cyclopses that could wreak havoc on anyone's life. It seemed that my whole world of imagination and daydreams was filled with endless possibilities for exotic adventure. The world seemed truly a fascinating and exciting place, and though I knew these stories could not be real, my imagination made them seem so to me.

Some of the books I remember more for their pictures than for the story. Or is it that I retain images better than words? This is possibly true of most people and may be the reason TV is so compelling to many. When I am in a bookstore, especially if it sells used books, I get a real rush of *deja vu* when I sometimes come on a book that I remember from childhood. A good example for me is a certain edition of Peter Pan with wonderful pictures of Peter and Tinkerbell flying through the air, the scary pirates and the terrible Captain Hook finally falling into the jaws of the crocodile. And Wendy, the beautiful black haired girl who was in fact, the first girl, after my mother, that I fell in love with, and just from her picture! Her image has stayed with me to this day and still exemplifies the soulmate I was searching for over half my life. To come upon this old book with the very pictures I had years ago stored so firmly into my memory was a huge treat, like once again finding a long lost and dear friend.

The old fables and stories, many of them from the times of my grandparents or even great grandparents, were irresistible to me as they were to most children of my generation. The myths, legends and stories carried down from generation to generation gave a common denominator of knowledge to us about our history, who we were, where we came from, and in their own way established a moral code for Life, quite as relevant it seems to me, as that learned in Sunday school.

In the days of my childhood there was a certainty about right and wrong, good and bad, much of which came from old stories and tales that always seemed to establish a moral issue, resulting in either redemption or a terrible fate, depending on the hero's actions.

Before entering my early teen years I became an avid reader of adventure stories. I particularly liked the tales of sailing ships, like Two Years Before The Mast, Mutiny On The Bounty, Moby Dick, and the stories of the North such as Jack London's Call Of The Wild, and the poems of Robert Service about the Yukon, the northern lights, the gold fields, and dog teams, and of course, Mark Twain's Tom Sawyer and Huckleberry Finn, adventures from another boyhood time.

Me, Georgann, Dad and Jack in Milwaukee 1935

My interest in reading continued on into high school where books that depicted more of the American tradition and history especially of the West, like The Virginian by Owen Wister, Willa Cather's My Antonia, Roelvaag's Giants In The Earth, and James Fenimore Cooper's Last Of The Mohicans hit my best books list. These were exciting and robust and told tales of exotic places, very strong willed people and amazing adventures. When I was thirteen, I read Wind, Sand and Stars by Antoine de St. Exupery, who became my favorite author for his insights into the human condition, flying, especially in the early days, his unique adventures, and of course his beautiful prose style. I was therefore shocked to hear he had been shot down in the war flying a P 38 on a reconnaissance mission by a German fighter pilot who was a great admirer of his books. A true irony of the war.

My days in Wisconsin played out with school, which I loved, our activities in the neighborhood or in the woods, that I also loved, and our at-home time with Mother and Father. Father was the breadwinner, working six long days a week for Mr. Stone, and mother was the helpmate, raising us children and keeping the home. This included maintaining certain standards of behavior from their children. We always waited for Father to get home from work before we ate dinner. We kids were expected to show good manners at the table: no chewing with your mouth open, no burping, no interrupting when someone else was speaking. We were exhorted to "Sit up straight," "Lay the fork down between bites," "Use the fork right side up, we are Americans not English," "Elbows off the table," "Eat everything if you want dessert," "Remember the starving Armenians" and "Be thankful for what you have."

When we questioned Mother about the author of all these repressive blandishments it turned out to be Emily Post's book on manners, and in answer to the constant question, "Why?" the final exasperated answer would be, "Because Emily Post says so!" We were made to understand that this set of behaviors was what separated us from the "lower classes." Since Mother and Dad had been raised by Victorians, this concept was accepted, and it was only later that I came to believe that many, if not most, of the morals, manners and rules laid on us were really for us middle class folks, with pretensions to join the upper class. Or more importantly, to be assured that we would never be taken for commoners. We were taught early on that hard work, clean living and abstinence, were the paths to rising in our society. It all seems to me now that this was a very Protestant upbringing, and I secretly suspected that my Catholic friends were being raised with a much more relaxed philosophy.

Our dinners together as a family were fairly tightly controlled. While Mother and Dad held forth on some subject calculated to be educational to us children, we strove mightily to remember everything Emily Post demanded of us. If we forgot a major one it was possible to be banished to the kitchen, or worse sent to our rooms. This almost always meant no dessert, which was deemed by us to be cruel and unfair. What could it possible matter if we did not want to eat Brussels sprouts or cauliflower? And how could not eating them affect the Armenians, who after all, lived a long way away and my particular plate of Brussels sprouts and cauliflower could certainly not be successfully sent to save them? These arguments failed to move Dad, although at times we felt Mother weakening as she always hated to see us unhappy. Weekends seemed more relaxed in the meal department and were happy days for us, since mother, a wonderful cook, always made something special for breakfast like pancakes or french toast, with real maple syrup.

One of our favorite Sunday events was getting Dad to read the comics to us. We loved the Katzenjammer Kids the best as they were always in trouble, and Jack and I could identify with them in that regard. But also Tom Mix; Flash Gordon, the first to rocket to other worlds; Popeye, who got his strength from eating spinach; Terry and The Pirates, always a step ahead of the Dragon Lady; and Andy Gump, the totally chinless character. We loved Blondie and Dagwood, especially in how he dealt with his boss Mr. Dithers, and the gigantic sandwiches he made from raiding the icebox, a trait I put into practice as a teenager.

Sunday mornings in Milwaukee, while we sat around the table, Dad would tell us wonderful stories of his heroic exploits. Attacks by tigers with eyes the size of headlights and mouths so large he could jam a rifle in so they could not bite him, elephants charging which he always escaped with amazing agility, or about his actual trip to China as an 18 year old, working on a freighter, or playing football at the University of California. We always begged him for stories until maybe our growing skepticism about the tigers moved us to his real life tales. In our eyes, father definitely was our family hero, tall and strong, handsome and athletic, truthful and honorable, and of course, he knew everything, and this feeling we had about him never changed.

Jack and I learned to ride two wheel bikes in Milwaukee starting with wheels a mere 15 inches in diameter. Georgann, of course, had a much larger bike than Jack or I, since she had learned bike riding while still in California. I clearly remember father holding the bike upright for me and running along with me to try to make sure I didn't fall and at the same time encouraging me to go faster because "it would help me maintain my balance." At first this seemed like an oxy-moron idea, but as I became more secure I found it was true.

Once when our parents were away over a weekend Jack and I got out a couple of Father's golf clubs, found some old golf balls in his bag, and proceeded to the front yard to see if we could hit them. We missed a lot or dubbed them and were not making great progress at all. I was determined to knock one out of the yard so I again set the ball on the tee, carefully arranged myself, took a couple of practice half swings like I had seen Father do, then wound up and started a tremendous swing, my eye locked on the ball, and did not see Jack stepping in front of me. The ball stayed firmly attached to the tee but the five iron hit him right at the side of his nose and nearly tore the left side of his nose off. Talk about a bloody nose. There was blood everywhere, all over his face, down his shirt, and it seemed impossible to stop. The baby sitter took control and Jack went to emergency where he had the whole thing stitched back tight. I was plenty scared and was sure that Mother and Dad would figure I did it on purpose, which this time at least was not true.

In 1937 we moved ten miles out to Fox Point into a remodeled farmhouse that was on a point overlooking Lake Michigan, with a deep wooded ravine fall-ing away from the edge of the yard. It was at the end of a road properly named Lilac Lane, with the most beautiful lilacs planted along both sides the entire length, which in the spring gave off a wonderful scent along the lane. There was a large grassy yard to play in and a separate garage housing an old style washing machine with a hand-powered wringer. Jack and I were watching a thunder and lightening storm from inside the garage once when electricity somehow came down off the roof, into the washing machine, and with a loud "Bang", exited from the tip of the wringer handle about eight feet from where I was standing. I almost jumped out of my skin and was very excited to tell everyone about my "near miss."

Jack was fourteen months younger, and Georgann two years older than I. These two years' difference in age, along with her being a girl, always put Geor-gann in a category by herself. We were too young to give her much pleasure as playmates and since Jack and I were so close, we were constantly together. I was always an inch taller and ten pounds heavier than Jack, giving me the advantage in roughhousing and other games and I tried diligently to be the boss of Jack. He would take my efforts at control for a while and then refuse to continue with this blatantly unfair family organization, demanding some parity or leaving me to myself, which was much less fun for me than trying to dominate a younger brother. This went on until high school when he became two inches taller and fifteen pounds heavier than me. Luckily, by then, he and I were fast friends.

In a general way the arrangement of Jack and me together, and Georgann alone, and seemingly aloof, continued until we were adults. Jack and I were often in trouble and found our share of corporal punishment and we tended to think Georgann got away with things we would be killed for. But we were having fun!

But we were also cruel to Georgann. When she was nine or ten and had put on a little excess weight, (the only period in her life when this was the case) we were merciless in our teasing, and must have hurt her very much. We just never thought about the pain we were causing her and only much later could we begin to understand the importance of empathizing with other human beings, even including siblings.

During our time in Milwaukee, mother took us several times back to San Francisco by train, to see our grandmother Anna, and Aunt Marion and Uncle Ed Bruck and our cousins. I loved these train trips and the most exciting was on the streamliner, City of San Francisco. We traveled west through North Platte, Nebraska; Cheyenne, Wyoming; Ogden, Utah; then to Reno, Sacramento and into San Francisco. We could jump off the train at many stops and in Nebraska and Utah there were always Cheyenne or Souix Indians on the platform, dressed in their deerskin shirts and leggings with pretty beadwork or with colorful blankets around their shoulders. This was still in the middle of the Great Depression, with little opportunity for employment on the reservations, and they were begging or trying to sell small bead trinkets to the passengers. They were real, not any longer in a book or in my imagination, and I found them wonderfully interesting and exciting to behold.

As the train clicked and clacked along, the country we were travelling through kept my attention and my face glued to the window. I especially was moved by the grandeur of the arching blue sky over the open prairie, the brushy and tree lined rivers and creeks, and the unending flat, or sometimes tilted, geometric slabs of high plain that finally connected into the distant hazy purple mountains. It was a continuously changing canvas and every so often, as if an artist felt the need to give this vastness a human face, I would see a horse and rider moving across the empty grassland, or a small group of cows grazing, or a windmill atop a tower pumping water into a trough for livestock, or a small ranch house with a barn nearby nestled into a patch of green cottonwood trees shading the buildings from the dazzling sunlight and heat of summer.

Although I was happy living in Milwaukee, it was interesting how even as a little boy the place where you are born will carry some unconscious reaction, some awareness that you are back home to your roots. This feeling came to me every time I returned to California, even as an adult, until California changed so much as to be a completely different place with a different set of people who had little connection to California's early history. We enjoyed seeing our cousins, Ann, Kergan and years later, Meredith, an after-thought. I loved Aunt Marion, a pretty, friendly, but blunt speaking woman with a great sense of wry humor, but Uncle Ed Bruck, a successful physician and hospital Chief of Staff, was a totally different kettle of fish. He seemed gruff and humorless, and when he got after Kergan I tried to keep a low profile because he scared me. I suspect his bark was worse than his bite, but at that time I was not going to test this theory.

My grandmother, Anna VanGorden Kergan was a slim, lively woman, living as a widow twenty seven years after my grandfather Harry Kergan died. She lived to be ninety and I got to know her very well. We loved visiting her in the Woman's Athletic Club near Lake Merritt in Oakland. She was a little bundle of energy and always doing something productive. She crocheted and did needle-point work and never sat down without her hands busily creating something. She also hated to see us kids sitting down doing nothing but "lollygagging around" as she called it. When she visited us later when I was eleven or twelve, I could not sit down in front of her to rest from whatever I had been doing without her saying, "Billy! You lazy lout! Your mother and father are working themselves to the bone, and here you are lollygagging. You'll never amount to a hill of beans!" I probably heard this a thousand times which doesn't say much for my late-to-arrive personal drive, but I loved her dearly just the same.

Notwithstanding her critique of my leviathan laziness, she had the most marvelous stories to tell about her childhood in early California. She loved to tell these stories and I loved to hear them told, and as she talked I had some respite from her eagle-eyed attention to my personal shortcomings.

She told me about being raised on the Hearst Ranch at San Simeon where her father, my great-grandfather 'Poppy', the ranch manager, was fluent in Spanish because they employed Mexican vaqueros to run the cattle. She spoke to me about the old days when there was whaling still going on along the coast south of San Francisco, of holding in her hand the first nugget of gold found by John Wimmer that started the California gold rush; the trips by horse drawn buggy to her schools in San Jose and Oakland, several days' travel away; the gold mining ventures of Mr. Hearst that Poppy was involved in; and Poppy's later adventure to the Klondike gold rush in 1898.

She also described to me her relationship with Pheobe Apperson Hearst, George Hearst's wife, and how much Mrs. Hearst liked her and the many things they did together. It's interesting that Granny talked to me more about Mrs. Hearst than of her relationship to her own mother "Monnie", and I sensed that Monnie might have been a rather severe taskmaster. The stories of her early life in California that she shared with me, fleshed out our family's special heritage in California, and became the sustaining family tale I grew up listening to, instilling in me a tremendous pride in our family.

I was somehow greatly attracted to the exploits of Poppy. It was only later that I learned that his father Ira had joined Fremont's effort to wrest California from Mexico soon after the family's arrival in California. His relationship with Mr. Hearst that lasted many years, involved cattle ranching, horse breeding, and gold and silver mines in Mexico, California and Nevada was a great adventure story. And the description of Poppy getting ready to go to the Klondike gold rush, buying the supplies and the dogs to pull the sled, and finally sailing to Seattle and then to Skagway, simply turned me on to hoping that I could have a life of adventure like his.

Back in Milwaukee, Father had been making friends in the retail merchandising business across the country through attending meetings and conferences. He impressed people and through these contacts he was offered a job with Marshall Field & Co, one of the largest and most influential retail businesses in the country at that time. Since the Boston Store was privately owned, and much as Mr. Stone wanted Father to stay, there was no real future for someone who aspired to run the store if they were not in the Stone family. I was eight years old when Father and Mother told us we were headed back west, but this time to the Pacific Northwest and a city named Seattle.

We made this family journey during the Christmas season of 1938 in the middle of my third grade, and moved into a house at 601 36th Avenue East, at the top of a long hill leading down to Madison Avenue, opposite the entrance to Broadmoor, a swank gated community built around a golf course. It was a long, wide street, lined on both sides with large chestnut trees, but since it was mid winter, we could not at the time imagine the beauty of 36th Avenue during the rest of the year when the leafy branches, sweeping up and out to meet in the middle, formed a shady canopy the entire length of the street.

I soon found out that there were lots of children near our age living on or within a few blocks of 36th Ave. Many of these children went to J.J. McGilvra, the closest public grade school; others to Lakeside School, a private boys school in north Seattle; Helen Bush School, a private girls' school just a few blocks below us on the other side of the hill; and St. Nicholas, another girls' school on Capitol Hill, which is where Mother and Dad decided to send Georgann.

Jack and I went to McGilvra, he into the second grade and I into the third. This was a big change for us from Country Day School and I was scared and embarrassed to walk into a classroom with twice as many students as were in third grade at Country Day, none of whom I knew, and the other big change was that half of these students were girls! This was my first experience associating with girls my own age and this change was destined to be the cause of much pain and pleasure for me over the next five years of grade school.

When I arrived at McGilvra the classes had already started after the Christmas break. I went into the 3B class, but there was some talk about moving me up to fourth grade as I was a bit ahead of the class due to my years at Country Day. On my first day in class the teacher asked me to give the answers to some multiplication problems in front of the other kids. I was terribly embarrassed but did okay until she asked me what nine times twelve was and I was stumped. This evidently convinced her I should stay in 3B, probably a good decision as I was almost the youngest in the class as it was.

The class was quite a polyglot group, some of the kids being from upper and middle class families whose fathers were lawyers or doctors or had their own businesses, but others were from rather poor families whose parents had come west to find work, off farms or businesses that had failed because of the depression. We had kids from Arkansas, Oklahoma, the Dakotas, and Montana, whose families had loaded up an old Ford or Chevrolet with their worldly possessions and headed west. Some of these boys were tough, but generally we all got along. It was an interesting mixture and we became friends through our shared experiences at McGilvra, and of course, we found ample ways to get into trouble as well. In those days most people thought that corporal punishment was a good remedy for bad behavior, and more than once I was marched up to the office of the Principal, Mr. Roble, to get whacked across the hand with a ruler.

When we arrived, Jack and I wore knickers and long sox. We looked just like the turn of the century photos of Irish kids in New York City. Of course, our sox never stayed up and were constantly fallen down around our shoe tops. These sox were ugly, multi colored designs, so maybe it was a good thing they were always down. And our shoes were high up to the ankle. Our sweaters were drab, plaids of greens and browns with highlights of red and orange, worn over white shirts. We had small caps that we wore on wet days. It is hard to describe how very depressing this get-up was, but around 1940 some boys began to appear in long pants. These were almost always corduroy, and in a variety of colors, from light yellow to tan to black. I begged for a pair as soon as I had seen some, telling mother that I would be the only boy at McGilvra left in knickers and soon after I was presented with a pair.

About this time the first jeans started showing up as well. Some were bell-bottoms, like the sailors wore. They soon became the weekend outdoor pants, saving the cords for school. It was a year or so before the Levi brand of jeans came out. These were the ones that shrank six inches in the leg, and two inches in the waist at the first washing, so we had to calculate how large to buy them so they would fit after washing. In those days it did not matter too much about length of the leg as we all rolled them up, one side higher than the other.

Father's new job was with Frederick & Nelson, one of Seattle's best retail department stores, owned by Marshall Field & Co. in Chicago. He was Vice President and General Merchandise Manager, the second highest position in the store. He very soon became a well known man in Seattle due to his varied and extensive involvement in the community. As I grew older his stature in the city grew and I found much of this to be an embarrassment, especially when his name or picture appeared in the newspaper. I hated the idea of having to live up to some expectation others had for me. In fact, I never thought I could or would measure up to my father and this grew to be a heavy burden for me, as I'm certain it does for any son of a noteworthy father. I just wanted badly to be well liked for myself by the kids in my class, and almost as important, never to be the last person chosen for a team.

When we lived at 601 36th Avenue, there was always something going on with the many children also living along 36th. I think I counted at one time 26 kids in about a four or five year age span. In the summertime, with the long evenings after dinner before dark settled in, we gathered in the street and played "kick the can", soccer, "500", or marbles to name a few games, or just played catch.

There was no TV, but radio was a big thing. We tried to never miss Jack Armstrong (the "All American Boy"), The Lone Ranger, or Little Orphan Annie, that were on in the hour before supper, the last two also found in the comic sections of the Seattle Times or Seattle Post Intelligencer. One reason we did not want to miss listening to these programs was that they gave out a coded message at the end of each day's broadcast. If you had purchased a box of Wheaties, or whatever brand was being advertised on the program, and had sent in the box top, they sent you the code book to enable you to decipher these secret messages. What a hook! There must have been boatloads of breakfast cereals sold so that American kids could keep up with the secret messages coming from their radios.

As part of our new life in Seattle in 1939, our parents decided we could be improved by attending Sunday school. We lived about a mile from Denny

Blaine, a neighborhood that included an Episcopal church overseen by the Reverend Mr. Christie. On Sunday mornings, Mother would see that we were dressed and fed, and Jack, Jan and I would walk on over to Denny Blaine and go to Sunday school on all but the most rainy days, when Mother would relent and drive us over. The goal of this instruction was to be "confirmed" as Episcopalians.

Sunday school was a perfect place to goof off. The teachers were very lenient with us for our transgressions and misdemeanors in class and never kicked us out even when it probably would have been a good idea. I suppose this laxity of discipline was not because they didn't want to brain us sometimes, but they wanted to make sure, even more, that we all made it though confirmation and became good Episcopal Christians. We sometimes went to the regular adult church service that started a few minutes after Sunday School, perhaps to give us a taste of what lay ahead after confirmation.

As I was learning all about the Christian moral code, I simultaneously could be a terrible transgressor. One Sunday I hit a new low for me on the moral charts, with a strong rubber band and a few hairpins that I loved to shoot at things. On this day there was a kid who was huge compared to me who unfortunately was sitting about six rows ahead in Sunday school. Presenting a large target, I very foolishly let fly with a double hairpin missile that hit him so hard at the base of his right ear it actually stuck in the skin and quivered for a second as he yelped and jumped from his seat. By then, as he scanned the room for the culprit, I was dutifully reading my Christian story for the day. In a few seconds he looked at Joe Holmes, and sort of nodded with some satisfaction, thinking how he would deal with Joe after Sunday school was let out.

When we emerged into the sunlight, the wounded kid was looking around to make sure he had the right person to mete out terrible physical punishment. He began to ask some of us if we had done it, and when he got to me I said, with as earnest and honest a look on my face that I could muster "Absolutely not! I don't even know what you're talking about," all the time my knees knocking with fear. Then he saw Joe and started walking toward him. Joe earnestly pled he didn't do it, but was not believed, and the big kid grabbed Joe by the head and swung him around till he was horizontal to the ground and then let him go crashing to the grass. I had stood by and let Joe take the punishment I should have had, while I said nothing. I was so terribly ashamed by my cowardice that years later it still haunted me whenever I thought about it.

The Reverend Mr. Christie was a kindly man well liked by everyone associated with the church. He had two sons, the younger Tom, was about my age, and was as wild as could be. He had freckled face and red hair and was always in some sort of trouble. Our parents gave us money for the offering plate, maybe a dime or even a quarter, but Tom taught Jack and me how to get more money out of the offering plate than we put in, or pretended to put in. We worked at giving a dime and getting a quarter out surreptitiously, and when successful Tom, Jack and I would go to the Denny Blaine drugstore a block away and buy candy.

This minor pilfering from the collection plate grew more sinister as we saw all the interesting items in the drugstore that we might like to have. Thus started our careers as thieves. We became more adroit at stealing as we went along, success building confidence, and confidence building greater risk taking. The few things we did not eat were accumulating in our rooms and never ever used. Mostly it was candy and bubble gum, but the thrill of pulling it off was what drove us to do it again.

In the summer of 1939, the San Francisco World's Fair opened. When we learned that Mother and Father planned to fly the family to San Francisco to attend the fair, we were tremendously excited. I was particularly anticipating the first airplane flight of my life, an experience I had longed for ever since seeing the airplanes flying up from the Presidio aerodrome by San Francisco Bay many years before. We were told of this trip early in the year and were looking forward with super enthusiasm for the time to arrive. The thought of flying to San Francisco was the focal point of my life for many months.

Somewhere along the line when my parents got wind of Jack's and my light-fingered habits, they called a family meeting to discuss it. We were not aware of the extent of their knowledge, but they made it very clear immediately, that they knew of our stealing and that they were determined to have us stop such unsavory pursuits. We were to pay a heavy price for our transgressions. The penalties laid down on us were much worse than a good tanning by Father, who I'm sure thought that would also be appropriate under the circumstances. First, we were to go to the Denny Blaine drugstore we had stolen from and admit our guilt to the store manager, promise never to do it again, and repay the value of the stuff taken. Second, in order to underline the gravity of what we had done, Father announced that Jack and I would not be making the trip to San Francisco.

I was really stunned. I had been looking forward to this trip more than anything in my life. The thought that my first chance to fly in an airplane had disappeared to be replaced by the anguish of walking into the store we had stolen from and admitting this to the manager was a terrible double blow. But Father was firm. There was no recourse. He would not have a couple of crooks for sons if he had any chance to remediate such behavior. He was a man who believed that sometimes strong punishment actually could rectify such anti-social tendencies.

When the time came, Jack and I were left in the hands of a babysitter who looked like she could manhandle a sumi wrestler, while our sister Jan, sedately, maybe even primly, in her now greatly elevated position, went off with Mother and Dad and flew to San Francisco. I think we hated her for her absolute superiority to us and in general, what we considered she got away with that we never could. About those two weeks I can only remember having to eat a terrible rice pudding every night for dessert. All other negative thoughts were subsumed into the fact that I did not get my chance to fly. The satisfaction of this dream of mine would have to wait for a very long time.

Jack and I continued Sunday school and finally were confirmed in 1942. This meant that I could take communion with the adults, but try as I might, I just could not get blood from wine or body from bread wafers. However, I did answer the call to sing in the choir, which Jack, Joe Holmes, and I did for several years, and for some unknown reason I really enjoyed singing the wonderful Christian songs. This meant that I was singing most Sundays at the morning service. We in the choir wore white robes and entered the church following Reverend Christie, two abreast, walking towards the altar where a more senior boy lit the candles on the altar as we took our places in the choir loft behind the altar.

The most difficult thing for me during the service and between hymns was to not start laughing when I looked at Jack or Joe or Tom Christie. Sometimes it was just impossible to stop and I would try to cover up an outburst with a cough. A few times I provoked a stern look from Reverend Christie who could not imagine what I thought was so funny. By the time I retired from the choir in 1942, I'm sure none of the serious minded church folks were too sorry to see me off. Of course, my voice had begun to change as well, going from not very good, to really bad, due to this impediment.

Going to church was to be a family exercise, but somehow both Mother and Father seemed to avoid it while we went dutifully off each Sunday morning. Since father worked six days each week, I'm sure they enjoyed their freedom from three kids those few hours each Sunday morning. Perhaps they got more from that than going to church, which, when I grew older I could well understand. As for me, I loved the story of Jesus and the lessons it taught, but I could not understand why the Episcopal way was the only true way. By age eleven I was having trouble with dogma and the formal structures of the services and the prayers, like we were actually talking to someone way up there. One Sunday after I was confirmed I was listening to a sermon when I had my own personal epiphany. It was not the kind that Reverend Christie might have preferred me to have, but nevertheless, it has had a lifetime impact on me.

My revelation was understanding in a flash that what I was listening to was almost entirely nonsense. The descriptions of God's power and goodness were not only counter-intuitive, but contradictory. None of it matched the world I was living in, and all of the arguments put forth to prove these notions were really self-serving for the Church. The words that had a fatal attraction for me and defined formal religious dogma as I saw it were "hypocritical" and "nonsensical". I came to this personal truth at age twelve and feel the same way today as I did then, the day of my personal "revelation."

At family dinners during 1939 and into 1941, our parents discussed the crazy events happening in the world at large. The beginning of WWII in Europe, with the invasion of Poland by Hitler's Germany, and the on-going war in China where the Japanese army had invaded, headed the list of topics by a wide margin. The newspapers were full of this war news and our parents made sure we were aware of what was happening, as they said it could very well affect our lives, even here in America. The Chinese, adept in proselytizing support in America for their need of military equipment, went so far as to sell small sheets of bubblegum supported on a card with a picture of Japanese atrocities being perpetrated on the innocent Chinese citizens, usually women and children, and the worst of all was a picture of a Japanese soldier bayoneting a baby.

But our American life was far different than the war and chaos elsewhere. Until the attack on Pearl Harbor, early in the morning of Sunday, December 7, 1941, we children had little to divert us from the normal childhood life of school, friends, and play. Without TV, the larger world and its magnificent problems was held at bay, out of our living rooms, and we children, although knowing terrible struggles were taking place elsewhere, remained largely isolated from these events.

Without hand-held electronic games it was the newspaper comics section that grabbed our attention. There also were entire comic strip stories put together in what were called "Big Little Books," sized about four by four inches and two inches thick. One page had a picture and opposite was the printed story. These books, about 400 pages, cost five or ten cents and were great fun to read. Some of the drawings were wonderful such as Flash Gordon, a space traveler, handsome and daring and always getting out of terrible and unbelievable situations and thus saving his girlfriend from the awful clutches of Ming, the evil master of some wretched planet. Also detective Dick Tracy, Lil' Abner, the handsome and strong hillbilly, and his girlfriend, Daisy May (dressed in the first mini skirt I had seen), Tom Mix, and Terry and The Pirates, which took place in China, pitting Terry against the evil but beautiful Dragon Lady.

The Lone Ranger was also featured in a 'Big Little Book' and these western tales of good triumphing over evil were a great complement to the Tom Mix and Gene Autrey western movies of that time. The always-masked Lone Ranger was mysterious and left his calling card, a silver bullet, so all would know he had been there with his wonderful white horse, Silver, and faithful Indian sidekick, Tonto.

Around 1942 the comic book as we know it today replaced the Big Little Books. It was wartime and I think the economics of bookbinding and printing these small cut pages of the Big Little Books became too costly, compared to just stapling the sheets together as was done with comic books. Comic books also brought in a plethora of new characters, such as Batman, Superman, Spiderman, The Phantom, and Wonder Woman. Female characters had perfect bodies and over time, wore fewer and more revealing clothes or uniforms, and struck sexier and sexier poses, none of this lost on a twelve year old boy growing into adolescence and already secretly in love for the fourth time.

Soon after our arrival in Seattle, we children were presented with new bikes. For Jack and me, they were much bigger than the ones we had learned on in Milwaukee. The reason behind the gifts of new bikes was that there were no school busses in those days. Students either walked or rode bikes to school. These bikes did not have gearshifts or hand brakes. They were balloon tired and one speed, which meant that on many hills we were pushing the bike up rather than riding. The brake mechanism depended somehow on the chain and was activated by putting pressure backward on the foot pedal. We rode everywhere from our perch atop 36th Avenue; along Lake Washington Boulevard to Leschi, Madrona Park and Denny Blaine from Madison Park; through the Arboretum to the University of Washington, and back through Broadmoor, but we usually kept a wide separation from where most of the black folks lived, except for those times we made a fast incursion into the area followed by a hasty retreat when our courage ran out.

One rainy day while Jack and I were riding our bikes to school, we were speeding down the 37th Ave. hill, where at the bottom there was a choice of going straight to Madison or making a sharp right hand turn at the bottom towards 39th Ave. The intersection itself was a section of the old, smooth and slick red brick that had not been black topped and was slippery when wet. When Jack reached the bottom he tried to make the right turn. Instantly his wheels slid out and down he went face first, leaving behind one front tooth, some hide, and maybe some brains as well, since not too long after this fiasco, he made another that cost him plenty of skin.

He was knocked out cold and was just lying there, face up in the drizzle with the water forming little rivulets of blood running down from his mouth. I jumped off my bike and ran to his aid thinking what an idiot he was but worried he might be hurt really badly. He woke up a minute later, not knowing what had happened, but beginning to feel the pain. I got him up and helped him walk the four blocks back home. He was a mess, bleeding from his cut lips, and now toothless mouth, plus all the road scraped parts that had slid across the pavement. However, when I saw him after school later that day, he had been to the doctor and been made to look reasonably well, except for the now big gap in his smile. After several weeks this was filled by a partial plate and false tooth that he wore the rest of his life, and which he enjoyed pushing part way out with his tongue when he made faces at me.

One of my close friends, Joe Holmes, pushed his bike up to where I was fooling around one Saturday and asked if I wanted to get on the bar and go for a ride down 36th Ave. Our house on 36th Ave. was at the top of the hill. It was three blocks downhill to Madison Avenue where it intersected 36th, and a right turn at the first intersection led one down Madison another two gently sloping blocks toward Lake Washington, and finally two long very steep blocks down into Madison Park. He pointed out that he did not have a chain on his bike and therefore had no brakes, but he thought it would be a novel and challenging idea to ride the bike that way down the hills towards Madison Avenue and the lake. I must have been brain dead or possibly in a trance of some sort because looking down the three blocks to the car traffic on Madison sailing past the intersection at 36th, I was sure this had to be a pretty dumb thing to do. But for some inexplicable reason, maybe Joe had made a reference to my being "chicken," I said, "OK."

Joe was to steer the bike. I had to sit sidesaddle on the bar between him and the handlebars and could rest my hands on the handlebars in order to stay on. I sat on the bar facing left, but looking straight ahead and we started to roll as Joe pushed off. Within about ten feet, as we began to roll, I suddenly had an overwhelming realization that I had made a terrible mistake, and worse, it could not be undone. I was an innocent passanger, and a mightily stupid one at that, on a vehicle I had absolutely no control over and that could not be stopped. In 100 feet and about 20 mph the full force of fear hit me, growing as we accelerated and at the end of the first block doing 40 mph, I was certain that I was going to get killed when we hit Madison Avenue and the traffic.

Down we flew, gaining speed all the time and as Madison Avenue grew rapidly larger in my eyes I could envision the spot where we would hit a car, or vice versa, and be broken to bits. Or maybe worse, fall in the turn and leave our unprotected hides in a long and bloody swath across the avenue. Either way I was rigid with fright at our impending and certain disaster. I think I felt exactly as I would have, had I jumped off the top of the Empire State Building, which at that time was the highest building in the world, knowing that there was no stopping the eventual impact.

But, praise be! when we shot out onto Madison, at somewhere close to the speed of sound, making a long arc into the oncoming lane due to our speed out of the turn, there were no cars in the way. This was the first moment I felt we might actually live through this World's Most Stupid Idea Of All Time. But ahead was another challenge: we had two blocks before Madison took another long steep pitch down into Madison Park proper. If we could not make the turn at the top of the hill we would have to scream down Madison and if not killed by a car before we got there, shoot off the end of the Madison-Kirkland ferry dock, for a landing far out into Lake Washington.

Perhaps we had somehow pleased St. Christopher, or he was riding with us in gay abandon knowing the impending catastrophe could not hurt him, but again there were no cars coming toward us as Joe made a high speed left turn off Madison before the top of the hill onto a two-block long level road that dead-ended in some woods. We shot down to the end of the road, and luckily, because we were still going fast, there was a fairly straight walking trail we could navigate through the trees as we slowed down and finally came to a stop almost at the playground of J. J. McGilvra school. I'm sure I was glassy eyed and completely drained from the fear and certain knowledge I would not get out of this stupidity without a great deal of pain, but there we were, still whole, and we began to giggle and then laugh and finally it all seemed hysterically funny.

I had learned a few good lessons: don't let someone talk you into doing something as creatively insane as this; never go down a hill on any rolling vehicle without brakes; and say your prayers every night because they might actually be answered when you most need help.

Later that summer a similar episode took place when a few of us were playing near our house and Joe asked if anyone wanted to take a ride with him down E. Mercer street from 34th Ave. in a simple red wagon, the kind steered with a long handle to the front wheels. This was a short half block but very steep and you had to make a 90 degree right turn at the bottom because straight ahead the road ended in a concrete staircase leading down to Lake Washington Boulevard. I told Joe he had shit for brains (remembering my ride with him down 36th Avenue), and would never make it in one piece. He persisted, and finally Jack said he would go. I pointed out to Jack, for whom I felt an older brother's responsibility, that there was no way a red wagon without brakes was going to make the turn at the bottom without rolling over and spreading them both all over the concrete.

Jack still insisted on going, probably because big brother had warned him against it, this perhaps a budding step at independence from me and away they went.

Of course, what everyone watching this spectacle knew would happen, did happen. At the bottom they tried to make the turn going like hell and rolled over and left about a pound of hide on the road. Jack was crying as he came back up and I could see that his knees and hands and elbows all looked like hamburger. I was both sorry for him and angry that he had done such an obviously brainless thing and felt he was very lucky not to have broken a bone or lose another tooth. But I tried to console him as I walked him the block home to get cleaned and bandaged up, but also secretly thinking that stinging of iodine on his wounds might smarten him up.

When the family had first arrived in Seattle, Father was intent on finding outdoor activities that the Northwest had to offer, so one weekend he and mother went to Mt. Rainier to try skiing. It did not go at all well. Mother broke her ankle and had a cast on for quite a few weeks. Father being the rational man he was, decided that skiing was not for them, so he looked elsewhere, determined to find an activity both of them could enjoy.

It was this search for an outdoor activity that brought Frank Gilbert into our family's life. He was instantly loved by us kids for his great smile and a personality that always had time for us. We figured he knew more about hunting and fishing than anyone else and it was his great love in life. He easily qualified as one of my most unforgettable characters. He was a fun loving man but he also worked at the store as a Divisional Merchandise Manager. He and his wife Cassie were accomplished bird hunters and fishermen and there were countless opportunities in Washington State to enjoy both. There was great salmon fishing then and both summer and winter steelhead runs in the countless rivers that flowed to the Pacific or Puget Sound. The ready availability of duck, geese, pheasant and quail, as well as deer, elk and bear were possible if hunting was one's inclination.

Frank became Father's mentor and he and Cassie went often with Mother and Dad on day or weekend fishing and hunting trips all over the state. This was an activity that both of them came to love and they passed it on to us children as well. Soon the whole family was going on fishing trips on Sundays. We started with salmon. We would go to bed Saturday night only to be gotten up around two a.m. for a long drive up old Highway 99 to La Conner or Anacortes to meet the guide and boat, fish all day long, usually without much success, and then take the long drive back to town in the Sunday night traffic.

The best part of the day was listening to the radio in the car on the way home to all the good programs on Sunday night. I remember Amos and Andy, a "blackface" type comedy; One Man's Family, about a family working through all the problems that came along; and Fibber McGee and Molly, another funny comedy in which Fibber at some time in each program opened a closet he had failed to clean out forever and the stuff came out on top of him in an almost endless clatter and banging much to our delight. Jack Benny was also a funny program, and his black servant Rochester with the raspy voice always tried to keep Jack out of trouble, but usually to no avail.

Frank and Cassie built a small cabin on the north fork of the Stillaguamish River, at Oso, fifteen miles east of Arlington. The "Stilly" was a very good steelhead river limited to fly fishing only, where our family was often invited to fish with the Gilberts. This is where I learned to fly cast. It was a perfect place to practice due to the wide flat gravel bar on the Gilberts' side of the river and one could learn fly casting without getting the fly tangled in trees on the backcast. Of course, I did snap the tip off many a fly by hitting the rocks behind and Dad was always admonishing me with, "Don't let your rod tip go too far back on the backcast." I'm certain I must have fished many hours without a barb on the fly so the fish were fairly safe with me on their trail.

Steelhead fishing became Dad's obsession, and Mother, accompanying him on all these trips, became an excellent fisherwoman herself. I can remember on many a winter Friday or Saturday night in the kitchen, preparing bait lures from salmon eggs for bait casting the following day. We would cut a small gob of eggs loose from a skein of salmon eggs and tie them up in red cheesecloth so they would hold together when cast. I learned to passionately hate the smell of salmon eggs and many years later was appalled when I was offered salmon eggs at a fancy restaurant as "red caviar."

Much as Jack and I wanted a BB gun to play around with, Mother and Dad refused to grant this oft-stated wish. However, as they began upland bird and duck hunting they decided when I was eleven or twelve to begin to teach us how to properly use a real gun. They bought a single shot 22 caliber rifle that had a 410 gauge barrel and used a 22 cal. long rifle shell with birdshot. They also purchased a clay bird thrower and we began to get lessons in a field up at the Stilly. This was a giant step above a BB gun and satisfied the latent hunter residing inside me. The first thing taught was gun safety, which was drilled into us in an ongoing manner. When we learned to shoot the 22, they moved us up to a 20 gauge shotgun, the real thing, and we learned to shoot skeet at the Redmond Gun Club.

From then on we had quite a few hunts as a family when I was in seventh and eighth grade. We fished both summer and winter for steelhead, sometimes it was so cold the fishing rod eyes would freeze shut. Mother always packed a big picnic for these outings, often eaten by a campfire in winter, or in the shade of trees along the riverbank in the summer. Mother was a master maker of sandwiches, often rivaling Dagwood's.

Over the fourth of July in 1942 we went on a camping trip with a pack string up to Mirror Lake near Glacier Peak, in the North Cascades. We were blessed with weather that was hot and clear and the scenery beautiful. The stars at night were brilliant and the fishing for small trout was great. I did receive a beautiful black eye from a horse abruptly raising his head from grazing as I was leaning over him. It swelled right shut, but was good as new in a couple of days. On the fourth day we returned to the Gilberts' place on the Stilly and that night it rained hard for the first time in over a week. What perfect timing.

Early the next morning we all went out to fish Sally's Riffle, a famous stretch of water formed by the confluence of Deer Creek and the Stillaguamish. A new run of aggressive steelhead had started moving up during the rain, after having been brought to a stop by the hot weather. We landed many fish, but not as many as we hooked because they were so wild. The one I remember best, hooked by Cassie, took off jumping down river, with her chasing it along so as to not run out of line, and shrieking with each of its jumps. When she got it stopped it turned back up river until directly in front of her and then went on another crazy run right up onto the opposite bank of the river, flopped vigorously a few times and fell back into the water to continue its fight. Afterward, Ken McCloud, the outdoor writer for the Post Intelligencer, also fishing Sally's Riffle that day, lined us up along the river bar holding our steelhead catch and took our family picture.

About a week after this 4th of July trip, an article appeared in the Seattle P.I. sporting section, headlined, "All American Outdoor Family" and included the photograph of Mother, Dad, Jack and me, each holding the steelhead caught on the Stilly that morning after our pack trip. It was a great picture, but I was troubled by the somewhat mixed feelings I had. On the one hand, I felt proud to see our family thus depicted and also secretly thought I looked pretty good in the photo, but on the other hand I felt personally undeserving of this appellation and was dreading going to school the next day when I was sure to hear about it from my friends. And I did hear from them, however it was actually soon forgotten and other things began to occupy my mind.

Seattle Post Intelligencer photo.
Jack, Dad, Me and Mother

One of the special treats for us children with the trips to the Stilly was meeting Sally Pemberton, who with her husband Harold, had a small but interesting cabin a hundred yards downstream from the Gilberts'. Sally was Swedish and a great fisherwoman, for whom "Sally's Riffle" was named. She was also an outrageously good cook and introduced our family to, among other things, Swedish pancakes, which she made for all of us on Sunday mornings. She kept two frying pans producing pancakes and we ate them as fast as she could cook them. She gave us her recipe and we transferred this dish to our family's special Sunday breakfast tradition.

We had moved into a house at 1236 Lexington, in Broadmoor. I don't remember why, because I thought 36th Avenue was just perfect, but maybe it had something to do with moving up in the world for my parents. This was in 1941 and we had a live-in maid by the name of Nessa, who also was a cook, baby sitter and resident Sergeant Major over us kids. She was a small, wiry and tough Canadian woman in her early forties. She had a 22 year old son named "Sonny" in the Canadian army tank corps and of course we were fascinated to hear how he was doing whenever a letter appeared from North Africa. We knew she was worried and we all hoped that no military telegram would find its way to our house, addressed for her. During the war, any family that lost a member in the armed forces, displayed a small flag rimmed in blue with a gold star in a white field. As the war went on, one saw more and more of these small flags displayed in windows of homes in the neighborhood. We did not want Nessa to receive such a flag and so far as we know, she never did.

On one memorable day Georgann and I were at odds over some insignificant thing and I provoked her to the point of retaliation. I took off running with her close on my heels, intent on killing me. I ran into the house slamming a glass paneled door behind me to slow her down, but she put her hand up to stop it from closing completely and ran her hand through a window pane. I heard her scream and turned around to see what had happened and saw blood squirting from her wrist. Nessa came running and took total control in an instant, getting a tourniquet on her upper arm and calling mother. Georgann was taken to emergency where they did over 100 stitches to sow back the blood vessels, tendons, and ligaments that had been severed and placed her wrist in a plaster cast. It was many years before she regained most of the feeling back in the area. It was a case of kid stuff going very bad and could have had a much worse outcome

We kids liked Nessa very much and were always kidding with her until she threatened to break our bones, an act we were certain she could have easily carried out. One day in late 1942, Nessa quit to go to work in one of the many factories producing war material, like airplanes or ships. We hated to see her go, but the war effort was 'all out' by then and we understood the necessity of everyone, including women, taking jobs to replace the men who had gone off to fight. This was the beginning of the change, continuing to this day, of women in America getting out of the house to take on jobs that had previously been considered for men only.

During seventh grade, unbeknownst to me, my close friend, Les Snapp, had started to take boxing lessons at a downtown gym run by Lonnie Austin, a professional fighter of several decades before. I could never figure out where Les was off to on certain afternoons and he deftly deflected my questioning until finally, one day, he confided to me that he was disappearing down to 2nd Avenue, a rather tough part of town in those days, to learn how to box. When I immediately said I would like to learn this manly art as well, he allowed me to join him in this new adventure.

We went to Lonnie once or twice a week and I began to learn the fundamentals of the sport. Lonnie, a lightweight, was probably in his 50's by then and seemed to relish teaching youngsters to box. He had a kindly face that showed, by a flattened nose and scars around the eyes, that he had been a boxer in his younger days. With twelve year-old kids like Les and me, he tried mainly to teach us how to defend ourselves from the ubiquitous bullies found on most school playgrounds. We learned, in addition to the fundamentals of left jab, right hook, and uppercut, his time-tested, first law of defending oneself against a person who was determined to fight, his famous "school boy punch." It was very simple: if you knew you were going to get into it with another kid, you unleashed a single up-from-your-waist punch to the jaw, hopefully devastating enough to end the recipient's enthusiasm for continuing the brawl. It really worked perfectly as I was to find out later. He taught us how to put some power into that blow and we loved practicing it on the heavy punching bags in the gym.

Les, finally let his closest friend, Bartow Fite, in on our boxing lessons secret and he joined us for a time in the gym. Lonnie would pit us against each other, which in a way was hard because we were very close friends, and friends don't usually like to break other friends' noses. So we really sparred against each other with our different styles. Les fought standing straight up in a classic stance and had learned all of the punches pretty well. Bartow held his gloves in front of his face to protect his nose, and then would charge in a flurry of jabs that was quite unnerving. The only way to defend against this was to try to hit his nose as he came in, which tended to slow down his frontal attacks. I tried hard to look like Joe Louis and not get myself killed. We went at sparring like fencers using finesse and trying to score hits without bodily injury. It was interesting and fun, and I gained some confidence from the experience, developing an interest in the sport that I took along with me to college.

This was a time of some great prizefights, and our family, like many others, gathered around the radio to listen to the sportscaster giving the blow-by-blow report. The great figures were in the Heavyweight Division, with Joe Louis being by far the biggest name from the mid 1930's until after WWII. On June 22, 1938, I heard his second fight with Max Schmelling the German fighter and only man who had ever defeated Joe, done in their first fight. Our American hero, Joe, vindicated himself by taking Schmelling out in the first round. Listening to these important fights on the radio was as exciting for me then as being able to see them later on TV.

In the fall of 1941 Mother and Dad began annual hunting trips to the Canadian Rockies with the Gilberts. They were after elk, grizzly bear, moose, deer and Rocky Mountain sheep. These trips were for two weeks and while they were away, we lived under the heavy thumb of Nessa, or later, after Nessa took a job 'riveting,' some other 'appropriate' babysitter, usually built like Ilse Braun, the person who liked to skin folks to make lamp shades from their hides, and who brooked no misbehavior. And worse, they were not nearly as good cooks as Mother. Those two weeks seemed to go at a snail's pace, but as the day got closer to when we expected to see them return, we became more and more excited, speculating what great trophies they would have on top of the car as they turned into our driveway.

Invariably, we were playing outside on the afternoon they were expected, waiting for the first sight of them and when the great event came, would follow the car with much shouting and finger pointing at the animals tied on top, until it stopped and we would get a great hug from both Mother and Dad, questioning them the rest of the day for the details of their adventure. The final delights would be viewing Dad's 16mm movies of the trip and then several months later the animal heads would arrive from Jonas Bros., the great taxidermy shop in Seattle. This collection of trophy heads slowly grew until their final Alaskan hunt for the Field Museum's Brown Bear diorama in 1958.

Sports were a big thing in grade school and with no TV or video games, we boys were always playing at one game or another, with poor equipment and poorer training, but with great enthusiasm. We essentially had only softball and soccer as school sports, but we all skied during the winter. Our baseball mitts were treasures that we oiled or saddle-soaped religiously, until the pocket was perfect and the glove flexible. We usually had a special bat we kept at home, the one we knew held the power to hit a home run.

Each spring with the advent of baseball season many of us boys liked to arrive at school an hour early to play softball on J. J. McGilvra's baseball diamond. Kids would walk or ride their bikes from home, choose sides and get into a great game before classes began. I was most interested in becoming a pitcher and my skill got better in 7th and 8th grades. Les became a really fine first baseman and later played for Garfield High.

An event occurred one day while playing softball at school during our lunch break, which in retrospect is rather instructive of human nature, or perhaps semi-human nature would be a more apt description. For some reason we were not playing on the primary ball diamond but on one in the southwest corner of the school grounds made somewhat smaller by the encroachment of an unused portable classroom located in right field. I was playing centerfield near the building when someone hit a long fly ball that crashed through a window of the portable, even though the windows were covered by chickenwire to stop just such projectiles.

Seeing that the window was not completely broken, one of the other outfielders, I guess an inveterate rock-thrower like me, picked a rock from the playing field and threw it at the remaining glass in the broken window. When his rock missed, another boy tried his luck and soon we were all chucking rocks and laughing in competition to see who could throw through the chicken wire to take out the rest of the glass. Soon another window was hit and after that the game stopped and a real frenzy ensued and when it was over every window along the side of the portable was broken out. It was over as quickly as it had begun and a great silence descended as we all gaped at what we had done.

We had no sooner gotten back to our desks than a few of us were called up to the Principal's office for a serious discussion about the high probability of the Seattle Superintendent of Schools expelling us from school. I knew when Father received the notice about why I had been thrown out I would be due for a good thrashing so was mightily relieved when I heard a few days later that we would not be kicked out. It may have been that the portable we attacked was headed for the bone yard in any event, but whatever the reason I was greatly relived to survive this youthful excess.

In thinking about this episode it is easy to see that small things can set off very destructive antisocial behavior and there is not much distance between a bunch of youngsters in a frenzy of breaking windows in an unused building, to the awful spectacle of real mob violence now seen often on TV, that has been a part of human history forever.

During the fall season we played soccer in grade school. This was before any shin guards and our big worries were getting kicked in the shins, or worse, in the balls, which happened more often than one might imagine. One day I missed the ball on defense and laid Johnny Hubbard out with an errant kick to the groin. I really felt awful but there is not much to do when the victim is writhing around on the ground in agony. Words do little to help in that situation.

We used to take the ski train from the King St. Station on Saturday mornings to ski at the Milwaukee Bowl, near what is now part of the Snoqualmie Summit ski area. This was a train full of kids from all over the city that were heading for the mountains for a day of skiing and was usually pure bedlam with the noise. The gear in 1941 was a far cry from what it is today, baggy wool pants and jackets, and with the often rainy Saturdays we encountered, we all came home smelling of wet wool.

We used to walk to the University of Washington stadium to watch the Huskies play football on sunny Saturdays and always formed a pickup game of touch football on the grass behind the east end bleachers during the game. We could usually find a way to get into the bleachers, as security was lax, but I found it more fun to play football ourselves, than watch the big guys play.

Often on summer nights some friends and I went down to Sick's Stadium on Rainier Avenue, home to the Seattle Rainiers of the Pacific Coast League, to watch real baseball. As none of us had any money, we would always try to sneak in, and if this proved impossible, we went around the back of the stadium and sat on a hill behind center field where we could watch. There were some great players, including the DiMaggio brothers who played in the league. I was especially taken with the pitchers, like "Kewpie" Dick Barrett, or Hal Turpin, or Fred Hutchinson. Baseball was a big thing in 1940's. Of course, the World Series was the big baseball happening each fall and once or twice, maybe in gym class, our teacher, Miss De Gaulle, allowed us to listened to the game on the radio, sitting at our desks.

The Post Intelligencer newspaper sponsored a boys' pitching competition, that I entered when I was 11 or 12 years old. It was a competition to see what boy could pitch the most consecutive strikeouts by throwing at a wooden frame with a cutout the exact size of a strike zone. In other words one had to throw at least half the pitches through the strike zone. It was a big deal for the winner with lots of publicity. I thought that this would be easy but found much to my surprise and embarrassment that from the pitcher's mound the strike zone looked tiny and I was not coordinated well enough to get far in the competition.

All of the boys in my class loved Miss De Gaulle. She was pretty, athletic, a good teacher, and a stickler for us students to pay attention, not cut up in class and doing what we were told to do the first time. Somehow, Johnny Hubbard and I managed to get ourselves in trouble with her and she told us to come to the classroom after school to see her. We could tell she was not in a good mood when we came in. She sat in one of the front row student chairs and asked us to stand right in front of her. She told us how badly we had made her feel, saying our actions were like a slap in the face to her. And then she made the startling statement that if we wanted to act the way we had, it would be simpler to just slap her face directly, which she ordered us to do right then and there. Slap a teacher in the face! Especially one we truly liked! It was impossible, but she insisted until both of us tapped her cheek. "Harder," she said to us with a stern look. We slapped a little harder. Again she said, "Harder!" and then the tears came to both of us and we just stood there blubbering and could not do it. She had stuck a knife in our conscience and then twisted it, and we never forgot her lesson.

Also during those grade school years at J. J. McGilvra I became enamored of a few of the girls in my class. Starting in 4th grade, the first was Barbara Berg, who lived in Broadmoor. I was pitifully prepared for a girl friend, being terribly shy and embarrassed by the whole thing and I worried that her ardor for me, was less than mine for her. The big, and for me, feared event, was Valentine's Day, when one was supposed to declare affection via a Valentine card which appropriately was to say, "To My Valentine" or even more horrendous, "You Are My Valentine." This was a real declaration of love and really too much for me to deal with in my awful anxiety. It was also appropriate, if one was in a world-class love affair, to give a heart shaped box of candy and I was determined to do this for Barbara Berg.

Resolved as I was to carry out this declaration of love, I bought the candy with my allowance and got Mother to drive me over to Barbara's house while I stewed in anxiety about walking up and ringing the doorbell. Jack went along on this adventure, in his mind a silly, beyond belief exercise, but then he was a year younger and how could he possibly imagine what being in love was like? But when we approached Barbara's house I chickened out and after all kinds of agonizing arguments with Mother, who couldn't help laughing at me one moment and trying to get me into action the next, I talked Jack into taking the candy to the door while I hid on the floor of the car. The hideous mortification of the whole scene was just too much. How I could feel such exposure and embarrassment was beyond me, but that I did was painfully apparent. Love would continue as a truly heavy load for me to bear, but I continued to pursue it with even greater urgency as the years went by.

By the time I was twelve, I became very conscious of how I looked to my classmates. I was quite proud of my pompadour hairstyle, a precursor to Elvis Presley's when he burst onto the scene in the 1950's, and I was careful to dress in ways that I thought showed me off to my best advantage. Sort of a combination of rugged but tasteful, at least until it became important to never, never, have your jeans or yellow cords washed until they were greasy with grime and dirt. I think this may be the true predecessor to the very poisonous looking "Seattle Grunge" fashion style of the 90's, perhaps a nostalgic backward look into the 1940's.

Looking in the mirror I always felt I was fairly good looking, but one day a real tragedy entered my life. I was admiring myself in the mirror when I thought I might add to my narcissistic pleasure by checking out my profile. I positioned myself in front of the mirror while holding another hand mirror that allowed a spectacularly accurate side view of my face. The initial shock in my seeing, for the first time, a face overpowered by a huge nose and a receding "Andy Gump" chin, was truly devastating. This was a much more profound blow to me than suffering from a large pimple. At least the zit would go away in a few days, but that nose would be there forever! I could only imagine how ludicrous I must have been perceived by my friends and classmates. I was in a deep blue funk for a long time whenever I remembered how ugly I saw myself and I made a conscious effort to never expose myself to a side view.

If my face gave few options for improvement, I determined to work on other parts of my body, having been influenced in this regard by the many ads from Charles Atlas, the great body builder of the time we grade-schoolers saw in our comic books. The ads always pictured some skinny young man on a beach while his beautiful girlfriend watched sand being kicked in his face by a tough looking dude, and read: "I was once a 97 lb. weakling, but through Dynamic Tension I became the world's strongest man." We were admonished to send for his book on how to overcome the 97 lb. weakling curse. I found out that the concept of Dynamic Tension was to pit one muscle against another and I began to secretly work out on my biceps and latisimus dorsii. After several months of this endeavor I looked in the mirror with my shirt off and after tightening my muscles to the max, saw to my amazement some real lats showing up, and even possibly a small improvement in my almost impossible-to-detect biceps. This improvement helped defray some of my anguish over my big teenage beak and I thenceforth walked around trying valiantly to keep my lats tightened up to show as much of this new male attribute as possible.

I became enamored of Nancy Gray in sixth grade, during my long period of impossible infatuations. Nancy lived in Broadmoor, was a classic tomboy and part of a large group of kids that played together. She was a real friend in addition to being the new love object, so the pressure was off and I found I could actually talk with her, of course not about love, but most anything else. During the summer of 1941, Nancy and my sister went to Camp Tamarack near Sisters, Oregon, while Mother, Jack and I stayed at Lake Quinault, with Father joining us for the weekends. When it became time to pick Jan up from camp, Mother offered to bring Nancy home as well and I jumped at the chance to go along. It was a great trip until we started back and I lacked the courage to try to organize that Nancy and I would sit together in the back seat for the drive home. I burned with humiliation sitting next to Mother and I don't remember a single word passing between Nancy and me the whole trip. Although I lacked the courage to try to develop even an innocent boy/girl relationship back then, we were always friends and remain dear friends to this day.

Some time early in my 12th year I made the wonderful discovery of how the male body was equipped to work, and I quickly became an artist of subterfuge and deviousness in catering to this new treasure trove of sensation, and it put all my future attractions to pretty young girls on a wholly new level. All that I had previously thought I knew about love and relationships with the fair sex was suddenly pronounced obsolete and almost infantile in comparison to what I now understood was the big picture. It was like looking into infinity, at the same time profoundly interesting, profoundly scary, but also profoundly enticing, pulling me like an irresistible magnet inexorably forward towards a future entwining with another human being in a way, I felt then, would be somehow life defining.

My real big-time passion came in seventh grade when I slowly discovered that Susie Pratt began to fill my imagination and daydreams with my first really animal sexual attraction. I thought she had the deepest, largest, liquid, 'bedroom' brown eyes I ever expected to see and she became my constant center of attention. She could not wiggle in her seat across the classroom without my being aware of it and I found fascination in her every movement. A new appreciation, a new art form, a new galaxy of sexual consciousness developed as I drew in her mouth and lips, her devastating smile, her hair, the curve of her neck, the femaleness of her waist, her wrists and ankles. I was drowning in an ocean of love in no uncertain terms, and almost beyond belief, she seemed to care for me in return. She completely took over my thoughts, as well as both day and night dreams, and my school work was headed into the tank. I just could hardly get her out of my mind even for a minute.

Now doing something about all this passion was a totally different issue. I knew what made the world go round and had a major interest in testing those waters, but I was just too backward and scared to do anything. We were usually with friends and I was not "cool" enough to figure out ways to get her alone, so we had a dearth of opportunity along with my basic ineptitude with girls. Once we played spin-the-bottle at a party, a game where you got to kiss the girl the bottle pointed to on your spin. Having never dared to kiss Susie, I prayed the bottle to point to her so I could do it in the safety of the game and I did get to kiss her once, but was so up tight I just gave her a little peck on the mouth and realized immediately I had missed a big opportunity to impress her.

I had a lot of boy friends and none of them seemed to share the same agonies I went through in dealing with girls. I found it very difficult to build a regular friendship with a girl that I was "in love" with. At age thirteen, I had no idea how I was expected to act or what a girl might want from a relationship, but it seemed I always elevated my girlfriends onto some new plane where she became an object and I seemed to lose the ability to just enjoy the friendship in my worry and jealousy about how she felt about me and related to other boys. Plus I had a huge anxiety over asserting myself for fear of being rejected. It is probably safe to say that my phobias towards rejection, ridicule and embarrassment always overshadowed the attraction I felt for girls and my behavior towards them until I was a lot more grown up.

During eighth grade Mother and Dad bought a bigger house in Broadmoor. It seemed a large and pretentious home and they began to re-decorate it from top to bottom. We children were appalled by this whole scene. We had not even been asked our opinion of this new house, and had we been, there would have been three resounding "No way's!" A palatial looking French Provincial design, it was much too fancy for our tastes. It even had a ballroom on the third floor. We were horrified that Mother and Dad were so unaware of how much they had inculcated into us a hatred of showing off, especially outward signs of wealth. The project kept moving along, despite our objections, towards the dreaded day when we would have to move into what seemed to us a palace. And then everything changed.

One evening in October of 1942, Father gathered my siblings and me for a family meeting after dinner, saying that he and Mother had something important to tell us and wanted a family discussion. I could hardly imagine what the subject might be, perhaps something about the new house and dances they thought we would need to put on so as to use the ballroom, or the worst thing possible: me being sent to Lakeside school and having to wear a tie and jacket every day, an image that totally turned me off. I was determined not to become a sissy which was how I felt about the Lakeside boys, but I was not working hard at J. J. McGilvra, and my grades, thanks to Susie, were slowly sinking into the C's, so moving me to a different school seemed a real possibility.

When we had gathered in the living room after dinner, we knew this was not going to be the usual family meeting, so we settled down with us children holding a mixed bag of feelings ranging from curiosity to interest, and finally, to a certain foreboding as to what we were about to have imparted to us.

Father began by reminding us of how we came to Seattle because of his new job with Marshall Field & Co., who owned Frederick & Nelson. He told us that he always wanted to have an opportunity to run Frederick's as President, and it appeared that this could now be assured. The only proviso was that he would have to take an interim job in Chicago for three years and this meant the family would be moving from Seattle to Chicago during Christmas vacation!

I was totally stunned. Lakeside School suddenly sounded wonderful! I could not believe this terrible news; leave all my friends in the middle of my last year in grade school? Not play baseball in the spring? Leave Susie? This last thought was It, and I started to cry. My siblings were horrified at my behavior, and Mother and Dad exchanged rolling eyeball looks, like "what next!" or "why is it always Bill who makes things more difficult than need be?"

Father tried to tell us all the positive reasons why this move was good for us. We would be living on the North shore near Winnetka, which was twenty miles outside of Chicago and would be going to a great school, New Trier Township High School and we would make all sorts of new friends. At this I wailed, "I don't want any new friends. I want the friends I already have!"

Father explained that he was to be Vice President and General Merchandise Manager for Marshall Field, which was a big job and that he had been promised he would return to Seattle in three years, after the current President retired, when he would become President of Frederick & Nelson. He said he could not say "no" to Jim Palmer, the CEO, who needed him in Chicago, and as long as the store had agreed to his conditions, he felt there was no option. He and Mother explained that they had grown to love the Northwest, and Seattle, and Fredericks, and both wanted to return as much as we children did. This last statement I believed not at all at the time. No one could possibly want to be here as much as I did, nor feel such pain with the idea of leaving.

The more they told us the worse I felt. And the worse I felt, the more I began to think up reasons that might argue for my being left in Seattle to finish eighth grade. I wiped my eyes and then said, "Please let me stay until June and finish grade school with my class. I know I can find a place to stay and I'll come in June." "We'll talk about it," Father said, "but I can't promise you a thing. We'll just have to see what is possible." I'm sure that neither of my parents, or for that matter my siblings either, felt too badly about getting away from me for a good long rest from my histrionics.

The next day I started on my quest to find a place to stay after the family left for the Midwest. I'm not too sure how it all came about, but I was finally accepted by the parents of one of my best friends, Les Snapp. Within several weeks the arrangement was agreed to by Mother and Dad and the Snapps. I was happy as a lark, a huge burden lifted from my heart. I think Jan and Jack were willing to go to Chicago, if for no other reason than to not have to move into the new home being readied for us in Broadmoor. None of us children liked feeling like pawns in Mother's and Dad's plans for enlarging and improving our social lives commensurate with *their* station in life. At least we had escaped that fate!

In December 1942, we all pitched into the moving job. I sorted out the clothes I needed to get through until summer, including my baseball mitt, several baseballs and a bat. When all was done and the movers arrived to load the household goods, I was driven over to the Snapps' home with my stuff and moved into one of their spare bedrooms. It was a brilliant conclusion to the horrible thought of leaving all my friends and I guess the safety of my existing relationships. I was euphoric with my new situation. I was on my own and only had to make myself useful around the Snapp household to make it till graduation without untoward problems.

Thus, in January, when I turned 13, I entered my teen years away from my family and would not be reunited with them all until eight months later.

Those Teenage Years

Wherein our hero, separated from his family, found true love,
discovered joy in work, became a hunter, and entered
high school near the Windy City

In mid January, 1943, I turned 13, and was living away from my family for the first time, boarding at the home of my good friend, Les Snapp, on 40th Avenue East, one block off Madison Avenue in Seattle. I thought my arrangement was about as perfect as it could get. My family was in Kenilworth, Illinois, and I felt this provided a special opportunity for me to show that I was capable of taking care of myself away from them, but I'm not so sure my parents had the same optimism I did about my situation. The plan was for me to stay with the Snapps until June graduation from eighth grade when I would head east.

Les and I shared a major interest in sports and airplanes, and Les and his brother, Lin, had made some wonderful flying models. Les also had a great music library of 78's and 45's. He was into blues and boogie and of course the big bands which were popular during the WWII. Les always had work and chores especially on the weekends at Hansville, where his family had a summer place. I tried to participate, but Les's parents were not enthusiastic about my sharing his load.

For about three months, all seemed to work well, but tension was building between Les and me, because the family dynamics were very different with an outsider living in the home. It is one thing to have a good friend, and a totally other thing to have that good friend living in your home, cramping your space and freedom, and burdening you with the need to always accommodate him. Also Les's parents were pretty tough on him about chores and pretty lenient with me, even though I wanted to do my share to feel less a freeloader.

Ultimately, I realized that I would either have to leave, or risk putting Les's and my friendship under a big strain and I let my parents know about the problem. I'm sure this was a real pain for them, but they called on Joan and Hector Escabosa, the Vice President at Frederick and Nelson, to take me in, which they kindly did. They also lived on Madison Avenue at 38th, a few blocks from the Snapps, in a small but interesting house and they had only one child at that time, a baby boy. Again, I tried to make my invasion of their home not too difficult for them by trying to be helpful around the house. I offered to do the dishes, baby sit, work in the yard and always tried to be in a good humor. That is my perception thinking back from the disadvantage of an intervening 60 years. They no doubt saw me as a typical 13 year old needing improvement in many areas.

But they were very nice to me, including me in some of their cultural activities, like going to the symphony, which was a learning adventure for me. I stayed with them until I graduated in early June, and when spring arrived I was even more on my own, as the Escobosas gave me a long leash and I could usually get out after dinner and was mostly free on the weekends. None of this helped my grades the last semester of my eighth grade, as I was coasting, concentrating hard on having as much fun as possible my last few months in Seattle, away from the watchful eyes of my parents. So much for my thirteen-year-old sense of responsibility!

Dad had arranged, for Jack and me, our first jobs working for wages on a farm in British Columbia. I was to leave Seattle as soon as school was out, go by train to Vancouver, B.C., and then catch the eastbound Canadian Pacific to Golden, B.C. I would be met there by Joe Danikan who owned the small farm located near Briscoe, about fifty miles south of Golden, in the Columbia River valley. Joe, a native of Switzerland was brought to Canada with a group of mountaineers by the Canadian Pacific Railway during the twenties to act as guides to climbers in the Canadian Rockies. Jack was to work with me on Joe's farm and later in mid August, we would be joining Mother, Dad, and Jan, for a pack trip and hunt up the Kootenay River. I was really excited about this whole adventure, anticipating this would be a wonderful summer and it turned out that way.

The Escobosas were to take me to the King Street Station in the morning to catch the 8:00 AM train for Vancouver, but I begged them to let me go out after dinner to say goodbye to my friends, meaning mostly, goodbye to Susie. I had been dreading the day when I had to leave my friends, but Susie provided far and away my biggest feeling of potential loss, since unlike my boy friends, I could not count on her being there a year later. I had such strong and mixed emotions about her and worries as to whether or not she would continue to care for me, that I was a bundle of anxiety when I walked down in the twilight to her home near the Seattle Tennis Club on Lake Washington. I knew she really liked me and I wanted desperately to tell her I loved her and always would and that I would write her from Kenilworth all the time next year, and would be out to see her next summer, and I hoped she would write to me as well, and I was going to miss her, and, and, and …

Susie was all smiles when she came to the door, and Oh! those eyes just melted my heart. We went into her living room and talked but I did not have much time as it was already dark. When I got up to leave she asked her mother if she could walk me to the gate, and we stepped outside. I took Susie's hand and we walked over to the large tree in their front yard. We stood quietly under the branches for a moment, the shadows from the moonlight filtering through the leaves protecting us from observation. It was a perfect warm summer night as I finally struggled to say all the things I had planned to say. They came out awkwardly but she just stood very close to me, looking directly up into my eyes and I finally uttered the most major phrase in the English language, "I love you," and with that she stood on tiptoe and I kissed her. If I wasn't hooked before, I was really hooked then. This was my first real grownup kiss and I was walking on air all the way home.

Of course, when I thought about it later, as I often did, I realized that I had not performed the best kiss in the world and really wished I could have a chance to do it over again much better, and much longer, than the quick peck I had bestowed on her. But it was destined never to happen. Unfortunately, some of life's chances only come to us once and we had better not be faint of heart at that moment. I was learning that a life full of regrets for things not done was not the way I wanted my life to turn out.

Now I was off to a new adventure. The immediacy of my coming job in Canada and then moving on to Chicago pushed Susie from the constant forefront of my mind. But she continued to creep into both my day and night dreams for the next three years. My personal self-inflicted unrequited love story.

However, my leaving Seattle was not very auspicious. I had my new work boots which Frank Gilbert had helped me choose and he had also provided me with one huge duffel bag to hold all of my stuff. When I had filled it with all my worldly possessions the night before my departure, try as I might, I could not lift it off the ground.

The next morning I was up and ready, but the Escobosas were late rising and in a mad scramble Hector drove me to the depot and just dropped me off. I had only five minutes to catch the train when I started dragging my duffel bag towards the doors to the tracks, looking for a Red Cap porter to help me. There were none to be seen and when I got to the door and asked a uniformed person where the train to Vancouver was, he informed me that it had just left.

What a fiasco! What to do? I was almost in tears trying to pull my bag, get to a telephone to call for help and try to figure out what to do about catching the train in Vancouver for the next leg of the trip. I finally got Hector on the phone at the store, told him what had happened and he ordered one of the store's divisional managers to pick me up at the station and drive me to Vancouver in time to catch my next train. This was all very embarrassing, but not really a problem of my making. The rest of the trip went as planned and Joe was there to meet me when I stepped down from the train in Golden, B.C.

After the depression began in 1929, pack trips and climbing in the Rockies came to a standstill and Joe had made the smart move to become a Canadian citizen rather than return to Switzerland. Joe, and his wife Ida, had moved from Golden to a small farm several miles from the tiny town of Brisco, which itself was scarcely more than a gas station, post office and single store, surrounded by a few homes of retired farmers and loggers.

The farm was in the 200 yard-wide bottom of a steep valley formed by Vermillian Creek, which flowed west toward the Columbia River several miles away. The property was cut through the middle by Highway 93, a two lane asphalt road descending into the little valley from hairpin turns at the tops of each side. West of the highway the valley widened out into the cultivated fields that Joe had planted to oats and hay. They had a beautiful flower garden, a large vegetable plot, fruit trees and berry bushes, from which they canned and preserved fruits and vegetables for wintertime use, there being little fresh produce available in the winter. Joe hunted for their meat as deer were thick around the forested bench land and undulating breaks leading down to the Columbia River. There were trout in the creek, Ida kept chickens for eggs and meat, a cow for milk, cream and butter, and a few horses. We picked all kinds of berries, even gooseberries that she had planted years before. To supplement their income, Joe had become a licensed hunting guide, an occupation that he worked at for two months each Fall.

Dad had met Joe in 1941 on his first big game hunting trip to Canada. After this trip an idea evidently began to form in Father's mind that perhaps his eldest son might be improved by some hard healthy outdoor summer work during his high school years. Following another trip in the fall of 1942, Dad talked to Joe about his hiring Jack and me the following summer and teaching us about farm life and work. Joe had agreed and he and his wife, Ida, proved to be very good and kindly first bosses to Jack and me. We learned a great deal in the nine weeks we labored with Joe and we must have eaten much more than we were worth, as Ida was a superb cook and we had boundless appetites.

The first tractor I learned to drive 1943

Our work consisted of an eight-hour day, usually with no chores before break-fast and we were free to roam after supper. We were to be paid a dollar a day, which unbeknownst to us was supplied by Father. We thought this pay was absurdly low for what we did, but neither of us would have left Joe's even if he said we were to get no pay. Each day was an adventure and we were constantly learning new things. Joe taught us to drive his small Ford tractor which pulled the hay rake and made windrows of sweet smelling hay that cured in the sunshine. We learned how to handle a pitch fork to construct a proper "schock" of hay, a small rounded stack that if done correctly would shed a light rain, and how to load the shocks, when cured, onto the hay wagons so that the load would not fall off getting it to the barn. We learned to milk the cow, separate the milk and churn butter with a hand churn. We repaired fences, dug our share of post holes, cleaned the manure from the barn, fed the livestock and filled the barn with the tractor working the hay forks to lift the hay up from the wagon and into the loft.

Almost every evening after supper, Jack and I would hike out into the nearby woods to look for Whitetail deer always foraging at that time. We would pretend we were Indians and sneak along in single file, me in the lead of course, as I was the elder, to see how close we could get to the deer before they saw or smelled us and took off with their white tails straight up flashing from side to side.

These deer also came into the hay fields each evening an hour before dark to forage, and one afternoon while we were working, Joe said they needed some fresh meat and asked if we would like to go with him on a deer hunt. I had dreamed of hunting large animals ever since Mother and Dad had made their first trip to Canada and now it was going to happen. I was truly pumped up in anticipation of this adventure, my first big game hunting experience.

After supper, Joe took down his rifle from the wall, a 30.06 caliber Winchester, loaded it with shells, slung it over his shoulder, picked up his hunting knife and said, "Let's go." Jack and I followed behind him, crossed the highway and started down toward his hay field. As we stepped through the gate Joe stopped, and turning to us said, "Let's be real quiet and move slowly. There should be some deer in the field by now, or we may see them come out of the woods as we move ahead. If we see one and get in position I'll give you the gun and you can take it." There was no "Maybe you can take it," or "You can try to hit it," but just the simple expectation of success.

We followed Joe as quietly as we could and after several hundred yards he stopped, motioning me to come forward to where he was. He pointed to a deer whose head was down grazing and handed me the gun. He showed me where to sit down with my legs in front and my knees bent and how to brace the gun with my elbows resting on my knees. He said, "Take your time, and when you think you are ready, take in a deep breath and let it out and then gently pull the trigger." I did everything I had heard him tell me and after letting out my breath I squeezed off a shot. It was such a jolt and loud bang that I blinked my eyes and then I could not see the deer at all, but Joe said, "You hit him, and he won't go far." We moved forward and a short way from where the deer had been grazing, there to my great relief, and pride, he lay stone dead.

Jack and I then had our first lesson in gutting a wild animal. Joe handed me the knife and directed our work. I made the major cut up the belly line and Jack waded in with both hands, helping to spill the innards or move things to make my job easier. It seemed to me there was an awful lot of blood and guts to deal with, which gave off a warm special odor that rose up into our faces with the diminishing heat in the deer's body. Joe kept up a constant stream of directions. He pointed out all the internal body parts, showing us where the bullet had entered and left the deer. He was determined that Jack and I would do the complete butchering job as an educational project. We were soon bloody to the elbows, but when the job was finally done, we had learned our first lesson in what meat hunting was about. I was elated, to say the least. My first deer at 13 years old was pretty good I figured. Not too many city boys had such a chance and I wallowed in a feeling of self-satisfaction that I had not flubbed my opportunity. I learned later that not all hunts went as easily or turned out as well as this one had.

I had not ridden a horse since I was 10 years old after having a very frightening runaway when learning to ride English saddle in north Seattle at Gay's Academy. This had taken the starch right out of me in regards to riding, but Joe encouraged Jack and me to ride the horses he had around the barnyard. He gave us several tasks to do with the horses and soon we were riding most Sundays, our day off. I felt much more the cowboy riding western style, using saddles with horns and plenty of leather thongs to tie stuff on with. Riding was finally turning out to be the great experience I had always thought it would be for me and my confidence returned and grew over the summer, so that by the time we left to go on the pack trip in mid-August, I was ready, at least in my own mind, to ride the most difficult horse they might have.

The day came when we were to leave to meet our folks for the hunting trip. After loading up Joe's pickup we said our goodbyes to Ida and set off for Kootenay Crossing about fifty miles away in Kootenay National Park where we were to meet Bill Harrison and his pack train, our cook Ernie, several more guides and of course, Mom and Dad and Jan (nickname for Georgann). The drive took us to Radium Hot Springs where we entered the park, continuing up through a short canyon and then down to the Kootenay River flats where the road followed the river north about 25 miles to Kootenay Crossing. At this point the highway crossed over the Kootenay River continuing on its way to Banff,

Lake Louise, and Calgary, but we left the road before the bridge, where there were a ranger station and corrals and where the trail started upriver towards the high country of the Canadian Rockies.

We were very excited to see our family all back together and we started our new adventure in joyous anticipation of the next several weeks. The pack train consisted of 24 horses, including ten riding horses for our family, the guides, cook and wrangler and the rest were packhorses carrying the camp tents, stoves, food and personal clothing. Although we children tried to help all we could, mostly we were in the way, but we immediately liked all the guides and especially the cook Ernie.

That very first day following the trail along the Kootenay River was exciting for me, as everything was a new experience and in the summer sunshine with the backdrop of the mountains always in view, I felt a real joy in my life and an unfettered feeling of pure happiness. I had picked a good horse, the best of the bunch I thought. He was jet black, built a bit like a Morgan, and showed lots of spirit. Then there was Mother, obviously overjoyed at having us all together for our first real family adventure, who could not stop singing the words that expressed exactly how she was feeling, "Oh, what a beautiful morning, oh, what a beautiful day. The corn is as high as an elephant's eye….," the song from the musical, "Oklahoma," which Mother and Dad had seen in New York a month earlier. And finally, at our first night's camp along the Kootenay River, we were told by Bill Harrison, the outfitter who owned the horses, that we might expect a visit from a moose that evening.

Later, sitting around the campfire after dinner, we heard water splashing that sounded like some large animals chasing each other in and out of the river. Bill explained to us that rutting season had begun and suddenly a cow moose trotted up off the river bar right into camp. She stopped 25 feet from where we sat, took a long look at us, the glow from the fire outlining her against the trees between us and the river and then moved slowly out of camp on the trail we had come in on. Thus ended our first day of the trip with our family around the campfire and us kids having our first sight of a real live moose in the wild.

In subsequent days we moved up river and finally set up a permanent camp on the bank of a tributary of the Kootenay named Moose Creek, whose source was up a long valley high into the shale slides and cliffs of the Rockies. Father was mostly interested in Grizzly and Big Horn sheep hunting and on most days we accompanied him and Mother into the high open slide areas where the bears might be seen searching for marmots and other small rodents or eating berries. A typical hunt would begin with a long hike ever upwards, until we could top out on a ridge where we could see for miles and use the binoculars to search the various slide areas for game. We managed to see only one small bear, far below and moving rapidly away from us, no sheep, but lots of Mule deer.

After a few days camping on Moose Creek we were out of fresh meat and then early one morning, a yearling moose began crossing the creek about fifty yards downstream. When halfway across Moose Creek he became aware of us, stopped dead still in his tracks looking intently in our direction. With the guide's encouragement, over the protests of Georgann, Dad grabbed his gun and shot the moose then and there. Georgann was incensed at this slaughter, practically in front of the cook tent and felt it was not at all sporting. She was correct on that score, but we had fresh meat in camp and everyone but Jan was wearing broad smiles in anticipation of the steaks to come that night. As it turned out, Jan had no problem whatsoever in devouring her fair share of meat from that poor, hapless animal.

About a week later, Jan herself was asking about having a chance to hunt, so it was agreed to have Joe take us three children Mule Deer hunting and see if Jan could get a shot at a deer. We climbed high up into a basin just below the rocky cliffs and in the early afternoon saw a small herd of deer about 100 yards away. It was agreed that Jan would have the first shot and I was to back her up. We found a spot where we could both lie down and steady our rifles. The deer had started moving straight down a little shale gully when Jan pulled the trigger.

The herd began to move a bit faster, and since I had not seen the deer she was supposed to have been shooting at fall, I let fly with a round, and then she shot again, and then I, and soon it sounded like World War III as we emptied our magazines. What a hullabaloo! The deer were out of sight and probably half way out of the country when we walked over to the gully to see if after ten shots, we had gotten anything. We searched around and found one deer dead, which Jan immediately claimed. We started to gut that animal and then Jack, who was checking the draw below us said, pointing his finger down hill, "There's another one down below." We had murdered two deer instead of one and only God knew how many we might have wounded with such a fusillade. It was more meat than we could possibly use and I felt very guilty about that

I felt like an idiot, but secretly held Jan responsible since I assumed she missed her first shot, the reason I started shooting. The truth was, I was really excited and quit thinking beyond shoving another shell into the chamber and pulling the trigger. We never did sort out who killed what.

This trip was our first long-lasting outdoor experience with Mother and Dad and we really had a wonderful, exciting adventure with them. It was our first glimpse into the world of big game hunting that had so captivated our parents, but more than that, it was our first extended camping trip into the mountains and our first time being around hunting guides and mountain climbers who seemed to know an infinite amount about getting along in the mountains, hunting and animal lore, climbing, horses and the countless small things that make some men appear very much at home in the wilderness. We had learned a great deal, much about ourselves, and hated the approaching day when we had to leave the mountains in time for the beginning of school.

But that day did come and we left the horses and guides, among them Joe Danikan, my first boss, at Kootenay Crossing and headed for the Canadian Pacific Railroad station in Golden, to catch a train going East. We arrived at my new home in Kenilworth, Illinois, the night before classes started at New Trier Township High, a four-year high school of over 2000 students. The next morning, I was to enter this school as a freshman, knowing not a single soul except my sister Jan, a junior, and who would not travel in the same company as I and would be of little help in introducing me around.

I was up early, my stomach churning with anxiety and after breakfast I set out walking with Jan the four or five blocks to the school. The first day I, along with thirty other boys, was assigned a homeroom advisor. This man would remain our advisor until we graduated from New Trier. His name was Mr. Coburn, a likeable, big, thick-set man, who would know more about me in a few years as my advisor, than my parents did. It was a good thing I liked him, because I found out later it would probably take a special act of Congress to change an advisor. That almost never happened and this gave the Advisor some extra leverage in dealing with troublesome kids, of whom there seemed few.

The very first day all freshmen were sent to the auditorium for the introductory information we would need in order to get on at New Trier. I immediately learned that by virtue of being a male student, I was automatically in the Boys Club. This small thing helped me feel accepted without having to go through an invitational process. The girls were in the Girls Club the same way, and each class sent class representatives to the Boys and Girls Club meetings. There was also a student council, again with representatives from each class and there were class officers as well. With the myriad of hobby clubs and a full blown sports program, one would have to be a real social misanthrope to not find something of interest to participate in at New Trier.

New Trier was a special school and was consistently cited as one of the best public high schools in the country. The student body was large and almost entirely white and by and large the parents were interested in high educational standards and participated in the many school activities. The faculty was first class and enjoyed respect from the students. One of the more interesting things to me was that at New Trier there was an honor code. If any students had been caught cheating with homework or on tests, they would have been simply ostracized. The system worked and the students did not cheat. It was a school with very high expectations for both students and parents.

There were full boys' and girls' sports program, with beautiful grass fields and a fabulous swimming facility complete with warming rooms for contestants and grandstand seats above, all done in blue tile. There were both indoor and outdoor tracks, and since it was wartime, the indoor track also held an obstacle course. Students were required to attend a gym class every day, as fitness was one of the wartime themes we heard constantly and very few overweight kids were seen. The result of all this attention to create a quality educational experience was that almost all graduates of New Trier went on to higher education, with a large proportion going to prestigious private colleges around the country.

All this was very positive and I became determined to try to find a place for myself at this school. My first plan was to turn out for football. I had never played, but having heard my father's tales of playing both American football and Rugby, I was intent on following his footsteps down this path. I was two weeks late, since turnout had started in mid August. I was amazed to find out that over 250 boys had turned out for football.

I was allowed to register late and picked up my sweatshirt, pads, helmet and clothes locker key and carried them into the locker room full of boys putting on their uniforms before practice. I was very nervous and shy as I walked between two rows of lockers looking for my number. Feeling greatly exposed as a new kid, I was sure all eyes were on me and each boy was making his own personal judgment of me. I saw my locker ahead, between two that were being used. The nearest boy was big and as I got close he saw I was to use the locker between him and the other boy. He greeted me with, "Well, hello shitface. You're a little late for turning out aren't you?" On the other side of my locker, a kid named Marc, just laughed. I said nothing to either, tending to my business of undressing and getting into the pads, but I wanted mightily to lay the famous Lonnie Austin school boy punch, right into their smirking faces.

I felt devastated and embarrassed and hurt. His words were like a knife in my heart. I had many friends in Seattle who liked me and now the first words I heard at New Trier, directed to me from another student, were maximum unfriendly. I didn't understand why someone would do such a thing, or could do such a thing, for that matter. But I never forgot it or forgave the two boys that did it. I hated them for taking advantage of me and hoped I could even the score someday. And I did, but in doing so, I learned that anger and revenge extract their own toll on the person who carries these two vices around with him.

I settled into the routine of school: classes, football and studying, and as time went by became more determined to make friends and build a reputation as a student leader. I'm not sure where this determination came from, because my first impression, even aside from the locker room incident, was that these kids were not very friendly. They seemed totally ignorant of the West Coast and were mainly oriented to the Northeast, probably where many of their parents had gone to Ivy League colleges. They had not experienced skiing, being in the mountains, hunting, or fishing for anything larger than Blue Gill and Crappie.

Living in the Midwest, they were much farther removed from the war activities, compared to the Seattle area and seemed to lack an interest in the war similar to what I had experienced in the northwest. That is, until Jan headed up a drive in 1944 to sell enough war bonds to buy a B17 bomber. This effort really turned the kids on and sent them out into the neighborhoods selling "Bonds to buy a Bomber." By the time it was over, she had also conscripted help, through Dad, in downtown Chicago, and the bond drive, like most things Georgann turned her hand to, was hugely successful. This one contribution to the war effort helped greatly to instill a sense of participation in the student body, as well as a real sense of pride in their accomplishment.

Early on during the war years, Dad and many other Americans purchased E-Series War Bonds that would mature in ten years and pay interest at 4%. Their purpose was to help fund the tremendous cost of the war. Dad proposed to us kids that he would match any bonds that we purchased ourselves, either with our weekly allowance, which was not much, or with money we earned. I think he started the three of us out with a $1000 war bond to help us get the idea of trying to build a little nest egg for ourselves. Each summer I put my meager earnings into these war bonds and Dad matched my input, thus doubling the size of my holdings. This continued throughout the war and by the mid fifties, after I had graduated from college, the first of these bonds were coming to maturity.

After goofing off for most of my eighth grade year, I settled into some serious schoolwork. I decided that I was going to get onto the academic Honor Roll and stay on it, believing if I was trying to show people I could become a leader at the school, I had to have good grades. I also became a politician. I smiled at everyone. I caused no problems. I was friendly to all, as they might vote for me if I ran for an office sometime in the future. I was in a mechanical drawing class that was open to any grade and there were two seniors in it who were big 200 lb. guys, both starters at End on the varsity football team. I made friends with these two popular boys and I think my ability to do that and be able to chat with them in the halls impressed others. After all, they were seniors with enough letters on their sweaters to make alphabet soup and I was a lowly skinny freshman.

One day at football practice, where I played right end on the freshman team, a pass play was called and I was to be the receiver. When the ball was snapped I ran up the field, faked outside, then cut in and the ball sailed right into my arms and it was all green grass to the goal line. Except for a defensive back, the hated Marc, who had slipped trying to cut and was now on his knees, facing me and helpless. All I had to do was give him a little jig and go right past him to glory, but when I saw him there, all the pent up anger lying inside me flooded into my consciousness. I forgot the touchdown right ahead and ran right at him with my knees high and tried to knock his head off. I went into him with all the force I had. I knew I hurt him, which had become my object, but I also went down and in doing this, I lost the chance to make the touchdown, and even worse, lost the opportunity to make him look silly as well. Instead, I had made myself look stupid. I settled a score, but you might say, I had lost the game.

After football season, in January, I turned out for the swimming team. I swam more laps than I care to think about, but it was great being around another group of boys, somewhat different from the footballers, although there were a few who had played football as well. Like the varsity football team, which won the league title the year I arrived as a freshman, the swimming team was one of the best in the country, as judged by the times in the separate events. The team would have competed well with most colleges.

As the year went on, I slowly made more friends, stayed on the Honor Roll and kept busy all the time. I did not find a girl friend, however, as I still was carrying the torch for Susie and though our correspondence was haphazard, it was enough to keep my feelings for her intact. Also, I was getting into good shape with all the physical exercise and my times on the obstacle course kept coming down. I turned out for track in the Spring, but possessing no talent for running or jumping, I decided to put my 165 pound body into throwing the shot. The Frosh/Soph shot weighed eight pounds and I could heave it about 45 feet, usually good enough for a third or fourth place in the meets. The bigger guys could chuck it about fifty feet.

As the end of my first year at school approached, my thoughts began to bend towards Seattle and my friends there and what to do with my approaching summer. Getting a job became my paramount concern and I wanted to work on a ranch out west, if at all possible. A friend in my homeroom, Alfie Davis, was the son of a successful lawyer in Chicago. The family owned the Y Cross Ranch near the tiny town of Horsecreek, Wyoming, forty miles northwest of Cheyenne. I don't think Alfie had an oversupply of friends at that time, as he was smaller than most of the boys and not athletically inclined, but I always tried to be friendly with him and I really did like him. So when I asked him about the possibility of getting a job on his family's ranch, he seemed to think it might be all right to have his own friend with him for the summer.

Alfie's father, Courtney Davis, agreed to take me on at $30 a month, plus room and board. I was excited about the prospect of working on a real cattle ranch in Wyoming since it sounded so much a part of old time western history. In my mind I could picture the cowboys and horses, the livestock they tended, and maybe above all, the grandeur of the open country way out West. This scene seemed to fit perfectly with my forebear's trek west in the 1840's and the subsequent ranch upbringing of my Grandmother in California. I was eager, as well, to get back to riding horses and could see myself bringing up the dusty drag while we moved a herd of cattle across some vast prairie expanse.

The school year ended in early June and within a few days I was on the train headed for Cheyenne. I was met by Mr. Davis at the station and after picking up a few things he needed for the ranch, we headed northwest from the city to Horsecreek and the Y Cross. The country we passed through on our way to the ranch was generally flat, but in the distance in most directions long flat buttes could be seen rising a few hundred feet above the sloping floor of the plain. The mostly dun colored land was lightly brushed by the light green of spring grass, which by July, turned dry and yellow in the summer sun, but remained always speckled with the silver green clumps of sage brush. Wherever there were little draws or coolies, they were outlined in green from the vegetation, mostly willow, supported by the moisture found there.

This dry landscape was cut by irregular blocks of bright green irrigated fields of alfalfa and grass, to be used as hay for winter feeding of livestock and these fields were dotted with residual hay stacks from the prior winter.

We turned south on a gravel road out of Horsecreek and in several miles I could see a typical ranch entrance marked with tall posts topped with a cross pole, from which hung a sign saying, "Y Cross Ranch" and their brand burned into the wood. Passing under the sign, following a road that curved to the left into a complex of buildings and corrals, we pulled up in front of the Davises private residence, an odd two story house surrounded by gardens on all sides and a green lawn, enclosed by vegetation, formed a spacious back yard.

I was not put in the bunkhouse with the other men working on the ranch, but would instead remain in the family home where Alfie, his sister, Amy, and their parents were. The Davises were nice people and treated me very well and I tried hard to show them that they had not made a mistake in hiring me. Mr. Davis was all business concerning the ranch. Although he lived most of the time in Chicago, he was still the Boss on the ranch and he appeared to know exactly what he was doing. He was patient with me and also helpful in teaching me more about riding and working cattle on horseback.

He assigned a nice bay gelding to me, explaining however, that it had one bad habit. If you did not take care in how you cinched the saddle down in the morning, he sometimes reared up enough to actually go over backwards. I did not want this to happen when I was on him, so I was very careful to not make the cinch too tight before walking him around. I saddled him in the barn on mornings I was to ride and as I would lead him out with the lines, he invariably had a big hump in his back and walked stiff legged. Until that hump settled down I stayed off him. Even with these precautions, one morning when he stepped out of the barn, he reared up and over he went, landing on the saddle in a cloud of dust. Luckily nothing broke, but it did increase my awareness of the depth of his idiosyncrasy.

But my dream of riding drag was shattered when Alfie and I were assigned our jobs. We started in the large vegetable garden hoeing weeds, work which I truly detested. I kept asking for other more useful things to do besides hoeing and was soon put to repairing fences with some of the men in the crew. I dug postholes, re-strung and tightened barbed wire, making sure the fence was cow proof. We did chores around the barnyard, greased the farm machinery and caught and killed chickens for the kitchen. On occasion I operated on the chickens showing a condition named "bumble foot," where the pads swelled up on the bottom of their feet. Using a sharp knife, I cut out these growths and swabbed the wounds with Lysol. A gruesome job and all the while I was working on a chicken it inexplicably never squawked, only stared ahead blinking now and then.

Just before haying was to start we had to brand, castrate and dehorn 350 calves. This project was planned for a Saturday in late June and many neighbors came over to the Y Cross to help. I labored on one of the holding teams that threw the calves down and held them still while the work was done on them. As the bull calves were castrated, the testicles were thrown on top of the steel barrel holding the fire to heat the branding irons, and from time to time a cowboy would reach out and grab one or two mountain oysters and pop them in his mouth, chew them up and swallow them down. After much kidding and teasing I decided to try them as well and learned, with a little salt, they were just fine.

The two mounted ropers were old time cowmen and although both were in their 80's, they almost never missed catching the hind legs with each throw of their lariats, then dragging the bawling calf over to one of the two-man holding crews. Their horses were never out of a slow walk as they worked around the cattle in the large corral. Dressed like old time cowboys with the high peaked hats and a bandana, red or blue, tied around their necks and long sleeved shirts from which protruded their tanned, work-worn, but still strong hands, they were a marvel to watch and being there with them, I felt like I was back into the time of the Old West.

In the evenings, Alfie and I often rode out onto the upper benches looking for Antelope and rattlesnakes. We tried several times to run down baby antelopes but there never was a horse fast enough to catch even the young ones. As for rattlers, there were lots of them. These snakes were Diamondbacks that could grow well over four feet in length with a thickness of three to four inches. That summer I saw two horses that had been bitten by snakes. One was a yearling that suffered a bite on his inquisitive nose and his whole head became badly swollen up to his ears. Most horses were well acclimated to living around rattlers and would jump straight up or sideways when they heard, close by, that unmistakable buzz. They knew better than to lower their nose to investigate the sound. The startling rattle of one of these snakes pumped a big shot of adrenaline into my system as well, but they usually paid with their lives for scaring me and I had a dozen rattles in a box by summer's end.

Mr. Davis used Sundays for any necessary riding and one such Sunday, a week after branding, he decided to move the cows and calves from a large pasture near the branding corrals to another section of grazing land about five miles away and at a higher elevation. All of the hands were to be used to do this, including Alfie and me, making eight to ten riders in all. We started early in the morning, as the job had to be finished by 10 a.m. before the day became too warm for herding cattle. We rode into the pasture where the cows and their calves were held and very slowly began to move them out through a gate and into a large open field through which we would take them to our destination. One of the difficulties in moving cows and young calves, this being my first experience with it, is that when calves become separated from their mothers, they want to go back to the place they last nursed, instead of moving forward with the herd.

Everything went smoothly for a couple of hours, but the calves were getting tired and hungry and beginning to bawl for their mothers as they slowly drifted towards the back end of the herd, unable to keep up. A cow without its calf beside her would stop and bawl and look back to see if she could see her calf and it became hard to keep the drag end moving forward. Finally, one calf turned to run back but we headed it off and back to the herd. Then another turned, and another, and soon we riders bringing up the drag were at a full gallop trying to hold them in the bunch.

It was like trying to herd cats in an open field. We began to lose some we couldn't round up and then the mothers, seeing their babies running away, began to turn. Within five or six minutes of hard riding, we had to give up and just watch as all 350 cows turned and went running back down hill, their udders flopping side to side, heading to where we had started. Every animal was bawling for either its mother or its calf, all headed exactly to the place where they had last been together. Mr. Davis was really disgusted but there was nothing we could do. It had gotten too hot and that meant an hour earlier start on the following Sunday when we would try again.

Directly outside the corral and barnyard area was an inner fenced pasture with a small lake about a hundred yards across, separating the barnyard from the hay meadows beyond. The horses being ridden were kept there, along with any sick or infirm animals brought in for further observation. There was one old "lump jaw" cow that had been in the pasture for about six weeks, thin as a rake, with both sides of her head swollen grotesquely from a piece of cheat grass that worked its way into the lining of her jaw and became infected with actinomycosis. She was slowly getting worse so one day Mr. Davis gave me a rifle and told me to get a horse and move her out of the pasture, up a small hill nearby and shoot her.

I saddled up, put the gun in a scabbard slung on the right side of the saddle and proceeded to slowly haze the poor cow out through a gate and up the hill towards her personal Calvary. She was very docile and lethargic and I knew what I was about to do was going to end her suffering. When I got her almost to the top of the rise I stopped and she turned to look at me. Dismounting 40 feet from her, I shot her between her two big brown eyes that had been looking, rather expectantly, directly at me. She dropped straight down instantly, like her legs just went into the earth and didn't move or even twitch. I left her there and went back and reported the job done to Mr. Davis.

The next morning I went out to catch a horse by the lake and saw a cow drinking at the far end. I didn't know there were any other cows in the pasture, so I went for a closer look and saw that it was the cow I had killed the day before. I just could not believe what I was seeing and I was a greatly embarrassed to tell Mr. Davis what I had found. He simply handed me the gun again and said to go finish the job I had started. So I killed her a second time, and unlike a cat, that was all the lives she had.

I spent most of July and August stacking hay, having talked Mr. Davis into letting me try. Alfie was driving a team of horses pushing a buckrake which I had no experience with, but to my mind, building the haystacks was the most important job in putting up hay. I did this work with a man who showed me the important features of making a good, rainproof stack. The loose hay was delivered to the haystack, by an overshot stacker which was loaded by the buckrakes sweeping up the windrows of hay and depositing the pile onto the tines of the stacker. Once it was loaded, a team of horses pulled on a cable attached to a pulley and the loaded end of the stacker was raised past vertical, the hay falling onto the stack we were building. This wad, weighing about 300 hundred pounds, would land in a heap and the stacker's job was to pull that apart and distribute it evenly, building up the outside edges and tromping the hay down to tighten the stack until we might be fifteen feet off the ground.

In building a haystack, the name of the game was to end up with four straight vertical sides and a rounded cap that would shed water from rain and snow. This was hard, steady work and I became useful enough at it that Mr. Davis let me do it throughout the haying period. It was the kind of job that had a visual result. A straight-sided stack, looking just like a huge loaf of bread, was something one could be proud of.

One day when I was on top of a high stack watching a load of hay coming off the overshot stacker, I saw the black ominous line of a four-foot long snake coming with the hay. At the same time I saw the snake, my partner on the stack, hollered, "Watch out! Snake!" and jumped off. I took one look, figuring the daddy of one of the diamondbacks I had killed was coming for me and headed for the side and jumped, thinking the hard landing would be better than getting bitten by a big rattler. As it turned out, it was a large, but harmless, Black Snake, but everyone had a great laugh at our expense.

Once, when cleaning loose hay sticking out from the sides of the stack from the ground, I was bringing the pitchfork vertically down the side as I worked my way around the stack. At one point the pitchfork stuck on something and I gave it a big pull down to get it free. When all of my body weight was on the pitchfork, it suddenly popped loose and the thrust drove three tines into the ground but one tine entered my boot between my big toe and the toe next door, penetrating the ball of my foot for an inch and a half before exiting. In shock, I let go of the handle, which just stood there quivering, held tightly lodged by my foot around the steel tine. One of the crew who saw it happen ran over to me, put an arm around my waist and with his other hand down low on the pitchfork handle, swiftly jerked it out in one quick motion. I hobbled around for a few days with a very sore foot and was much more careful after that about how I handled a pitchfork.

Saturday night became the big event each week and was looked forward to with anticipation by the whole crew. The work days were long and the weather was hot, although cooling down at night because of the elevation. We were tired, hot and sweaty all week, but after a shower on Saturday we were all ready to hit the metropolis of Horsecreek, Wyoming, population about two, if you did not count the Y Cross and other neighboring ranch hands, that congregated there on Saturday nights. Horsecreek consisted of a one building complex that included the post office, a single counter and display case selling sundries, soft drinks, cigarettes and chewing tobacco and at the far back was a small bar and dance floor with a Wurlitzer juke box loaded with western songs, with a few tables scattered about.

One beautiful Saturday night Alfie and I crowded into the back of a pickup truck with the crew heading to Horsecreek. I had a powerful thirst that I soon slaked with orange and grape soda pops. Watching the cowboys come in from other ranches I saw that many of them were chewing tobacco or smoking. One of our crew asked if I had ever tried chewing tobacco and when I told him no, he said I ought to try it some day and assured me that I would like it lots, suggesting that if I wanted to be a real cowboy I had better learn how to chew. The more I thought about it the more I was inclined to take him up on his idea and try some. Finally, acting very casual, I sauntered over to the counter, hoping in proper cowboy style, and bought a plug of Horseshoe brand chewing tobacco. I took no note of the raised eyebrows of the proprietor when he heard my request, but he said nothing to dissuade me from fulfilling my destiny of becoming a spitting, rather than a smoking, Marlborough Man.

I opened the cellophane covering and bit off one corner from the plug and headed towards the far end of the dance hall where the Wurlitzer was located to see what Western music it offered. About halfway there, the small bite I had taken had expanded exponentially into a mouthful and with no easy way to spit, I swallowed a big gulp. By the time I covered the next twenty feet to the music machine, I realized something was terribly wrong and knowing I was going to be sick or faint, I turned and started for the door that I could see at the far end of the building.

All of a sudden I was in a room that was moving around something awful. The floor would tilt up hard to the right and just as I was about to crash into the floor becoming a wall, it would swing back to the left and I would almost crash again into that wall, which a moment before had been a floor, and then back again to the right. I tried to keep my eyes focused the whole time on the door at the far end, which seemed to stay vertical as I reeled my way towards it, but the floor continued to swing from side to side in a ghastly fashion. I was certain I was on the verge of being violently sick or of passing out cold, but finally I was at the door, pushed it open and stumbled down the steps. I ended my journey, and my long awaited Saturday night, spread-eagled out flat on the ground sick as a dog. I have never been a big fan of chewing tobacco since.

Most of the men I worked with were veterans from the army, a few of whom had been wounded and mustered out. One evening, Alfie and I and his sister Amy, walked over to where the crew was gathered around the bunkhouse. Several of the men were wrestling, friendly like and when they were done, one of the vererans challenged anyone to wrestle with him. There were no takers, so I finally said, "I will," not wanting the others who were watching, especially Amy, to see me scared. When we came together I was promptly thrown to the ground very unceremoniously to my awful embarrassment, notwithstanding the fact that he was bigger, stronger and nine years older. Getting slammed into the ground did not hurt near as much as feeling so much a kid and unable to stand up to an older male, but there was little to be done about that except hope to someday grow up.

Because this was a time before hay baling machines and tractors, men with pitchforks and horses still did most of the work. Large draft horses were used for pulling most equipment and every ranch had quite a few teams. It was a time when people came together to help each other in the major work that needed doing to survive in such a country. I never saw the like again, of the old generation of ranchers and cowboys that peopled much of the West. Of course, things had been changing in many rural areas and new machines and methods were being introduced to farms and ranches everywhere, but tradition never leaves without a struggle and it would take a new generation to complete the change. I am grateful for the privilege to have had a small glimpse of it, before it was gone forever.

When I parted from the Davises at the end of summer, perhaps my biggest surprise and pleasure came from receiving a bonus from Mr. Davis of $20 a month, above my $30 salary, for the effort I had put in. To have my hard work recognized by a man I admired meant a great deal to me, and fortified my efforts to always try to earn whatever I was paid.

It is hard to summarize all of the events and meanings for me of that summer of 1944. I know it was a fabulous adventure and I am forever grateful to Mr.

Davis for taking me on. I have many memories of experiences and things I learned, both in the practical, how-to-do world, and about myself, that summer. The antelope we saw and chased when riding in the evening after work; meeting the Merritts, an old time ranch family who were early breeders of quarter horses when they were still referred to as "Steeldust" horses; the pride these men took in their horses and their ranches, and their abilities as both working and rodeo cowboys; going Sunday to the Cheyenne Frontier Days Rodeo and seeing "steer busting" the way it was done out on the open prairie in the old days, which a few years later, was banned as too hard on the livestock; the rattlesnakes; and my first meeting with veterans from the war still raging in Europe and the Pacific.

My sophomore year at New Trier was a building year for me. I stayed on the Honor Roll with my average grades hovering around 3.7. My brother, Jack, entered as a freshman and my sister, Jan, was now a senior. Jack had become an Eagle Scout the year before, attending a very good public grade school. He had his own friends, and even though he and I were only a year apart in age, we now were traveling in different social circles.

Jan, a gifted athlete like Father, was into basketball and field hockey, but in those days there were no formal inter-school leagues for women's sports and therefore the opportunity to letter in a sport did not exist for girls. This was to be the final year of WWII, and Jan, fascinated about the idea of flying dreamed of joining the WAAF, the Woman's Army Air Force and have a chance to ferry military aircraft from factories to air bases, as many women were doing. Jan wanted to take flying lessons when she was fifteen and Father said she could, but she would have to pay for the lessons from money she earned herself, Father no doubt thinking that would inhibit her desire somewhat. He had not reckoned with her innate determination when her mind was made up about something. She soon reported that she had found a job for the Christmas break, and this led to her being asked to work through the summer as well. She found a flying school near Glenview and began her lessons, soloing at seventeen.

Jan's talent and drive and popularity also led her to the Student Council where she was Secretary of the Council in her senior year and upon graduation won that year's coveted Tri-Ship Award, for being the outstanding graduate based on a combination of success in athletics, academics and student government.

In the late Spring I decided to run for a Junior class Student Council position and so took all my limited political skills into the race. I was elected, and really felt I had achieved a big portion of my goal of making something of my student life at New Trier. I was now a student leader of sorts and I found that many wanted to be my friends who had ignored me when I had first arrived. One of these was Sam Bass, the freshman football player who had called me "shitface" when I entered the locker room two years before and I am ashamed to say that I still did not have it in my heart to forgive and forget, in order to build a meaningful friendship with him. I had not yet learned the value of unloading anger and actually practicing forgiveness in order to make my own life more rewarding.

While all three of us kids were busy with school, our home life was that of a well-off, middle class family. Dad had a big job at Marshall Field and mother was busy doing her war oriented volunteer work. Since the family had only one car, a two-door 1941 Cadillac and a C gasoline ration card, it was hard to drive anywhere. Therefore, Dad went to work on the "El", the commuter train that took him and many other suburbanites into Chicago, twenty miles away.

There was also rationing of other items than gasoline, such as sugar, butter, meat, shoes, and many items available before the war, such as rubber, certain spices and silk, were not available at all. And of course, many things had not been invented during the 1940's. Back then there were no TV, cell phones, fresh fruits in winter, jet airliners, computers, Barbie dolls, electric typewriters, air conditioning, panty hose, polyester, polar fleece, diet coke, Nikes, skateboards or snowboards, rock and roll music, hang gliders and possibly most important, "the pill."

But if things don't exist, you don't think about their lack. As for the shortages and rationing during the war, people accepted that this was the civilians' contribution, in a small way, to the huge war effort. This was especially so, since we encountered a daily barrage of war news with pictures of the death and devastation in Europe and the Pacific, which made us all feel very fortunate that the actual fighting was not taking place in our own neighborhood.

Our family life went on very much as usual, but we were growing up and our parents' expectations grew with us. Jack and I put in a fairly large "victory garden" to grow vegetables in an empty lot across the street from our home in Kenilworth, which we both tended during the Spring of 1944 until I went to my summer work in Wyoming, after which he tended it alone. We saved up gas coupons and every so often on a weekend in the Fall we went to a farm for pigeon hunting, or found some woods near an open field where we could hunt crows. This made for a full day family outing with a picnic and some hunting excitement.

Our interesting neighbor next door was Chuck Anderson, a traveling salesman for a pharmaceutical company, a weight lifter with huge biceps, a model airplane builder and a hunting fool. He owned a large stuffed owl whose hinged wings could be made to flap by pulling a string and since an owl is a crow's mortal enemy it was a sure fire way to attract crows. Several times, with Chuck and his owl in tow, the family would head for the countryside and find a likely spot to place the stuffed owl on a fence post, with the end of the long string in Chuck's hand, while we all hid in the woods away from the fence. Soon a single crow would fly over. "This is an observer," we were told by Chuck, and we would stay very still while Chuck flapped the wings of the owl. The "observer" would disappear for a few minutes and then return with a whole flock of his brothers and sisters and start a really amazing attack, with tremendous cawing and swooping down at the totally unconcerned owl. When they were engrossed in this harassment process, we would jump up and shoot. Then all would be quiet for about half an hour, until another observer would fly over and the process repeated.

During part of that period, we had a Negro maid, named Cora. She was tall and thin and not only a very nice person, but a famously good cook. We kids loved her and it is from her that we have the recipe for chocolate bread pudding and French Puffs, which have remained two of our family's favorite treats. We ate every dinner as a family of the whole, which usually meant that we kids ate a sandwich about 5 p.m., because Dad did not arrive home much before 6:30 or 7 p.m. and we would have expired by then if not for a snack in the afternoon. Dinner was not formal, but good manners were a requirement and Mother and Dad strove mightily to keep the conversation on a fairly high plane. They told us about many things and looked for comments and questions. They did not much like clichés or inane answers, or put-downs of any sort, especially of folks who were not as fortunate as we. And often they steered the talk in certain directions that carried a moral, or Right-Thing-To-Do thought

We were being taught that work was an important aspect of life. Dad especially, talked to us of the value of work, for both one's pocketbook and one's sense of self worth and we grew up expecting and actually enjoying, our opportunities to work. We were never held back because of any fear our parents might have had for our safety. This included traveling and working far from home as teenagers. We had the opportunity to meet many friends of our parents who came to our house, usually brought about by Father's position in his industry and as a Director of the U. S. Chamber Of Commerce. We did this often, becoming comfortable with adults and since many of their friends really were important or interesting people, we enjoyed such occasions.

During Christmas vacation in 1944, the family took its last long trip together. Dad arranged a visit to the Fieldcrest mills in North Carolina, supplier of cotton goods to Marshall Field & Co, where we would have a day of hunting quail behind well trained pointers, as a special treat. From there we would make our first visit to Washington D.C. and New York.

This trip was my first time in the South and I found it both interesting and mightily disturbing. For the first time my sister and brother and I actually came into contact with the discrimination of African Americans, referred to then as Negroes and often worse. We could not believe our eyes at the signs saying "whites only," at restaurants and other public facilities. It was terribly uncomfortable for me to even walk around being white, feeling that the Negroes saw me as the same as any other white person walking Southern streets. More unbelievable, if that is possible, was to find the very same discrimination in our nation's capital of Washington, D.C. It outraged us to think that this seat of government, that had fought a terrible Civil War to free the Negroes from generations of bondage, still allowed such practices right outside the doors of Congress and the White House. It was a tremendous eye opener for us kids and very disturbing to see this terrible flaw in our country's moral strength.

While in New York, Dad arranged for a limousine and driver to take us through Harlem and Queens, so that we would have a better understanding of the differences in living conditions between ourselves and the many poor people living in large cities of America. We three were horribly embarrassed to be driving anywhere in a limo and it was even worse to be gawking from the windows of a posh limousine, at the tenements, the mess, and people idly standing around or sitting on doorsteps. I felt practically naked as the people we passed looked at us going by. When their eyes would meet mine, the huge differences between us lay a heavy hand on my conscience. It was not a pretty sight but valuable to see and a strong lesson for us, backing up the many times this subject had come up at family meals.

The trip was unique in many ways. Its purpose had been mainly educational. To visit the huge Fieldcrest mills with their monsterous machines weaving towels, sheets, bedspreads and many other cotton items; seeing America's Bill of Rights and Constitution, as well as the shrines for Washington, Jefferson and Lincoln and the Supreme Court in action; the big city of New York with its theater and after theater Delis; the Statue of Liberty; and of course, the less fortunate citizens that showed a different side of American life. I came home from this trip with a new respect for what my parents were trying to teach us and the trouble they took to plan this experience so that we would not only see a lot of important things relating to our country's origins, but perhaps have a renewed sense of how very fortunate we were as a family, to live in such a great country, and to be relatively well off economically. It also was graphic evidence of how much still needed to be done to help those less fortunate. These feelings are still, 60 years later, foundational in how I think about my good fortune and in my reverence for America.

I turned fifteen in January, 1945, and was eligible for a driver's license which I went after and acquired forthwith. As gasoline became more available I was to be allowed occasional use of the family car, which like most teenage boys, I looked forward to with relish. I also began to figure out my next summer's job. I wanted very badly to get to the West Coast to see my friends in Seattle, and thought it would be great to work somewhere in Eastern Washington. I called my friend Bartow Fite a month before school ended for the summer to see if he had any ideas where we could get a job, knowing his family had a small farm south of Ellensburg, a cow town 105 miles from Seattle. It turned out that his Uncle, Bill Patterson, was a partner in a cattle and wheat operation in the hills north of Ellensburg and Bartow told me we both might get a job on his uncle's ranch.

Bartow put it together and after school was out in June, I boarded a train for Seattle with a duffle bag of clothes and work boots, where two days later I was met by Bartow. We went to Ellensburg to meet with Mr. Kern, Uncle Bill's partner in the operation 20 miles north of town, to discuss the job and especially our pay, which I think was settled at $50 a month plus room and board.

This was very different country from Wyoming. We were in the pine forests west of the Columbia River and the operation had grazing land in the broken hills west of the river, with grain fields on the flatter country extending almost up to the canyon rim overlooking the river. From the rim, one could look east across the Columbia for miles and see the town of Quincy, shimmering in the heat, surrounded by cultivated fields and dotted with grain elevators and smaller silos. The terrain along the river was broken by countless draws cut by small streams making their way down to the Columbia. Grazing in most of these watersheds was good because of the ample water, but it was tough trying to move cattle around on this range due not only to the brush in the coulee bottoms, but also the steep slopes that rose up from the bottoms to the timber range on top. It was also mighty hot, but in the evening, because we were up several thousand feet in elevation, it cooled down and was wonderfully pleasant.

Bartow and I started working under the direction of a big, tough man directing the field work for Uncle Bill. His wife, who astounded Bartow and me with her foul mouth, could, and did, swear just like a man. This was the first woman Bartow and I had ever come up against who cursed long strings of profanities, without showing the slightest embarrassment at all.

We worked primarily as 'spike pitchers', that is, lifting and stacking straw bundles with a pitchfork from the ground onto a wagon, head side in, butt side out, forming a solid load seven or eight feet high when finished. Once the wagon was stacked full, Bartow and I would clamber up and sit on top while the woman drove the team pulling the wagon down to an old barn, where we unloaded the bundles the same way, forking them up into the barn and then climbing into the barn and placing the bundles neatly until the barn was full, each bundle having been pitched three times to its final resting place. This was hard steady work and by the end of the day we were ready to relax.

Our most excitement each day came when we rode the wagon down the last steep pitch to the barn where the horses practically had to sit down on their haunches to hold back the wagon. We were certain that inevitably, on one of the trips down that pitch, the team would lose their footing and either jump to the side or try to run to keep the wagon from overtaking them and we would get creamed as it all went ass over teakettle. But luckily the woman was not only strong mouthed, exhorting the horses with "Easy does it you sons-of-bitches," but strong armed as well, and she made it every time, although I elected to walk down quite a few times after having talked myself into thinking this would be the time to not be on that wagon.

Bartow and I slept in a small tent set up with two low cots. By dark we were really tired and would hit the hay. One night I had a dream that one of the horses had walked over me and his two front feet were on either side of my head and I was in imminent danger of getting my head crushed. I grabbed one of the horse's ankles in each hand and hollered, "It's a horse! It's a horse! get it off of me!" My shouting out woke me up, and Bartow as well, who found himself standing over me, with me clutching his ankles thinking he was a horse. He had been sleep-walking and where he was headed he didn't have a clue.

In the evenings, we would take it easy as it cooled down and maybe walk around an area within a mile of the ranch house or go looking for rattlesnakes, of which there were quite a few. We were close to the Columbia River canyon, and I liked to walk alone over to a ledge perched right on the rim where I could sit and look east across the river to the rolling farm land and orchards. As the sun began to go down those fields of grain and hay would be bathed in a golden glow and all the lengthening shadows would become purple accents on the yellow, brown and red of the canyon walls. It was quiet, almost still, the day's work done. I loved the peacefulness of that time of day, just sitting there watching night descend to force rest on a restless land, while giving me an intense feeling of belonging and oneness with our beautiful planet.

When our work at Uncle Bill's ranch ended in the fall, I spent a few days in Seattle before heading back to Chicago. I knew by then that we would be returning to Seattle in January, so leaving to go East was not such a big deal, and I actually looked forward to starting my junior year at New Trier. I did find out that summer of 1945 that carrying the torch for Susie was really a one sided affair and I slowly began to lose some of my magnificent obsession for her, but the old flame died out slowly.

Once back at school I turned out for football and played end on the Junior Varsity team, not being good enough to make the varsity. I was involved in Student Council activities and working hard to stay on the Honor Roll. The fall season was usually beautiful. The weather was mild until mid November when it began to freeze at night and the football practice field became unforgivingly hard. The leaves on the many oak trees colored, turned rusty, then brown and began to fall and the fragrance of burning oak leaf piles was almost constant until Autumn was over and winter set in.

As the time approached to leave New Trier in December when my family would retrace its steps to Seattle, my thoughts became oriented to the joy of getting back to the West. And although I had had a wonderful experience and made lots of friends during this time at New Trier, I looked forward to leaving. In retrospect this was very short sighted of me that I did not take the time to nurture those friendships into the future. Perhaps the main difficulty had been my being there only for the school year and off somewhere else far away each summer and having no chance to build a strong base of non-school experiences with any of those boys. I don't know the answer, but I now wish I had tried harder to keep the fires of friendship alive after I left.

The day before Christmas vacation was to begin would be my last day at New Trier. In my home room, Mr. Coburn announced that there was a little surprise for me and after some nice things being said, I was presented with a new pair of beautiful leather Bass ski boots, everyone having heard of the skiing I was looking forward to out West. This was a going away gift from the 25 boys in my home room. I was really overcome with emotion as I had not expected anything of the sort to take place and found it difficult to express my sentiments without choking up. All the memories of the hard times when I had first arrived were washed away with expressions of friendship and acclamation I received from this group of boys.

I had desperately wanted not only to be accepted by the students at New Trier, but also to achieve some recognition as a student leader. I found out from this two-and-a-half year experience that if one is determined enough about achieving a goal, if one is willing to stay the course no matter what, one's goal may have a chance of realization. I also learned that you get out of an experience about what you are willing to put into it. I had worked hard and was goal oriented and because of that, had been rewarded beyond my expectations.

The experiences instilled in me a confidence in my abilities to achieve my goals, but for some reason did not provide me with a burning desire, once I had returned to Seattle, to continue to set short and long term life goals. Falling back into the easy life of many friends and activities, a growing interest in the opposite sex, the lack of even a glimmer of interest in a future vocation, and a sense that I had already proven something to myself that did not have to be re-proved, led me to put enjoying my last year and a half of high school at the top of my "to do" list. I continued to crave experiences away from the mundane that helped maintain my interest in seeking summer working experiences, but during the school year, I went with the general flow of somewhat self-absorbed teenage life.

Return To Seattle

Wherein our teenage hero changes schools, wrecks a car, breaks his first knee, meets a tough judge, joins a haying crew and plans on following footsteps

I turned sixteen in January 1946, soon after arriving in Seattle and entering Garfield High School. Georgann, away at the University of California in Berkeley, became an Alpha Phi in the same sorority that Mother had belonged in the early 1920's. Although my parents had purchased a beautiful home on Lake Washington in Medina, across the lake from Seattle, Jack and I were allowed to go to Garfield, in the city, instead of nearby Bellevue High. This meant we had to travel, most often by hitch hiking, across Lake Washington into Seattle, to attend school. It was easier than one might imagine, as there were businessmen driving into town for their jobs each morning, and sometimes Dad would take us, although his schedule was far too erratic to count on.

Garfield was a very different sort of school from New Trier. For one thing, it was smaller by about 600 students and it had the most diverse student body of any of the eight high schools in Seattle with large groups of African Americans, Asians, especially Japanese and Chinese and about one third middle class whites, including a large contingent from the Jewish community. It occasionally made for some rather difficult situations between students, especially between Blacks and Whites, but it was a great cultural learning experience. There was little actual interracial social mixing in those days, no dating among blacks and whites and Asians and an interracial relationship or marriage was a very rare and somewhat scandalous occurrence, generally frowned on by all communities. Society was still very rigid in its cultural attitude up through the 1950's and it would be our children's generation that would begin the effort to truly break down the racial walls that have been the cause of so much strife, unhappiness and despair.

Except for team sports and other school functions where all interested kids were welcome and could participate, these different ethnic groups, as one might expect, were doing their own things amongst themselves. Garfield was located in the heart of the African American community on 23rd Avenue and Cherry Street and I have to admit that I did not want to go walking around that area alone, where I might meet up with the wrong person with a chip on his shoulder. There was a certain level of fear amongst the whites concerning that, and I am certain the black kids had similar fears. I could not understand why these attitudes persisted after WWII, but my understanding of the depth of prejudice of some people about these issues was sadly lacking at that time. I had been brought up in a family that believed, taught, and practiced the idea that all people deserved to be treated with deference and should be given the same opportunities, and I tended to believe that this was how most people felt.

Once I remember my Father stating, during a time when a race riot somewhere had erupted after the war, that had he been a young black man he would be out there throwing Molotov cocktails as well. He could understand the frustration at the lack of fairness and opportunity most blacks suffered. But my experience was different. All the boys turning out for team sports as I was, no matter which race they were a part of, shared the same goals of working together to win, the same locker rooms, showers, nudity, jokes and banter back and forth and friendships developed as we got to know each other better. The sight of even a minor conflict between a black and a white seemed utterly stupid and unnecessary to me, when in so many ways it was being proven every day that it was possible to share our school experiences with good feelings for one another.

Unlike my first days at New Trier, I was very fortunate attending Garfield to have had a group of old friends from grade school who also were going to Garfield, and I was instantly adopted into a much larger circle of their friends they had met after coming to Garfield. So I felt I belonged right from the start. It turned out that Susie was not there, but at a boarding school in Canada. This made it easier for me to begin to date other girls who were not attached, or pinned to a guy, which was the way a couple publicly stated that they were going steady. This meant hands off, (no pun intended) unless they broke up of their own accord.

I was also interested in making a name for myself if I could and by the time summer came I had been asked by my friend Les, who was a member of the Student Advisory Board, Garfield's equivalent of the Student Council at New Trier, to attend a meeting where I could describe some of the ways things were done at New Trier that I felt could improve student life at Garfield. The Board seemed interested in my comments and sometime later I was invited to join the Board for my senior year.

Because of all my extra curricular social activities outside of school, the first casualty was my grades, which began a slow but accelerating downward spiral. I had been on the honor role at New Trier the whole way, but going into the last half of my Junior year at Garfield, the slippage started almost immediately. In Seattle there were a proliferation of high school fraternities and sororities for boys and girls. I was asked to join The Revelers, a high school fraternity, in which we members tried hard to live up to its name. These outside activities included dates on Friday or Saturday nights, "all-city" dances in various places in and around the city where kids from many schools congregated and doing things with my growing circle of friends.

With Jan away at school, home life settled down to a routine of Dad working long hours, getting home around 7 p.m. and then dinner for the four of us. We did not have live-in household help after WWII. One of the great social changes to come out of the war was that women like Nessa and Cora had taken jobs in factories alongside men and never again would they do the kind of work they had done as domestics for middle class families, as had been necessary for them in the past.

Jack and Me, back in Seattle, 1946

The Medina property was six acres, with large formal gardens, a four car garage, three bays open for cars and the other turned into a utility room for laundry and garden tools. Apple, Italian plum, and pear trees lined the winding driveway between the entry gate and the house, situated on a fairly high bluff above the lake. A switchback path led down to the lake and a long dock stretching out into the water. However, Dad would never buy a boat for the family, I suspect because he did not want his children to get the feeling that they could have any toys they wanted and he probably saw clearly that we had as many distractions from school and other good works, as we needed. This attitude included not only boats, but cars as well, which, he told us, if we wanted, we could work and earn the money to buy our own. (He was very smart about things like that.)

Above the garage was a two bedroom apartment occupied by Fred Ishibashi, a 50 year old Japanese gardener, his wife, Ida, and a teenage daughter. They had been working for the previous owners when Dad bought the place and he had asked Fred to stay on with his family, to take care of the premises. Fred was an American of Japanese birth, from Hiroshima, which had been the first Japanese city hit by an atomic bomb. He had many relatives there and some that were lost in the war. Over time, when I had gotten to know Fred well, I tried to get him to talk about the war a bit, but I always felt he was reticent to share with me what was really in his mind. Jack and I grew to be very close to Fred and sometimes we worked together on projects around the property.

During our first year in the house we had occasionally smelled a skunk and Dad determined it had used the crawl space beneath the house, so he asked Fred to seal up any openings where a skunk could get in. This was done and that seemed to be the end of it, until some weeks later when we began to smell the skunk again. Dad told Fred to check it out and if it was there, it should be killed to make sure it did not build a nest under the house and start raising a skunk family, as one was more than enough. I got my shotgun and a large flashlight and went with Fred to the opening he had made in the boarded up entrance to the crawl space. He flashed the light and scanned under the house, and sure enough, we could see the skunk lying against the far wall. I went to full choke on the gun and put a duck load in the chamber, lay down and drew a bead on the skunk and pulled the trigger. The shot hit the skunk which literally exploded into pieces and the smell was ten times worse than we had been experiencing. It turned out the skunk was already long dead when I shot it, having evidently died of starvation by being trapped inside when Fred boarded up the openings. The house smelled terrible for two weeks after this successful hunting trip, but it was poor Fred who had to go in and retrieve the pieces of the animal scattered throughout the crawl space, which he did with a large white handkerchief tied tightly over his nose and mouth.

Dad always had homework after supper and Jack and I worked at our own. TV was still far in the future so it was not a deterrent to our study time and when I think about it now, I feel incredibly lucky that the intrusiveness and addictive power of TV was not present in my growing up years. What is so strikingly different from today is that we read many more books than most kids do now and these books fulfilled our needs for excitement and human drama, and stimulated our imaginations as TV has never done.

Mother became involved in many social obligations brought about by Father's position at Frederick and Nelson. And Dad began to get involved in community work, first with the Chamber of Commerce, then for the retail store association that dealt with the multitudinous unions all retailers had in common, and he became a trustee for various nonprofit organizations and a Director of four or five large corporations.

Mother and Dad always hosted Thanksgiving dinner at home and for quite a few years invited two childless couples that we children really enjoyed seeing. These were Cassie and Frank Gilbert, our hunting and fishing friends and Connie and Kay Burn, Connie being the Vice President of Frederick & Nelson, who reported to Dad until 1961, when Dad retired and then became President himself. These two couples seemed to genuinely like us young people and we were very much at ease with them. I was especially interested in Frank Gilbert because he had a great twinkle in his eye, had been a cowboy in Wyoming sometime in his past and became one of the Divisional managers at Fredericks. Connie Burn was a short, somewhat rotund man with a wonderful smile who was just fun to be around. We dressed up for these dinners and were allowed to have a cocktail with the adults, no doubt part of our training in how to handle alcohol.

These were wonderful dinner parties. Mother was a great chef and made everything look so beautiful, the table decorations, the serving platters with the food and the plates heaped for each of us. I loved Thanksgiving. It was my favorite holiday in those years and still is today. And it was never lost on us how many things we had to be thankful for, which Father emphasized to us all in his dinner toast, our family's alternative to saying grace. This was a goodly list of things, but he always ended saying something about our opportunity to live in America, where the greatest experiment in democracy and freedom in all of history was unfolding. He believed this with his whole being and was certain that only in America could he have had the opportunity to build his own life as successfully as he had. This was pretty close to a religious belief with him and became, at least for me, one of the important legacies from Father that I have carried with me to this day.

I occasionally was able to drive our one family auto, the same old 1941 two-door Cadillac Dad had bought in Chicago. In the early Spring of 1946, when Mother and Dad went back East for two weeks, the last words from Father were, "Don't use the car unless you have to!" The day after they left I just had to use it to drive my friend Les to his family's summer home near Hansville for the weekend. After driving to Edmonds we caught the ferry to Winslow and covered the eleven miles from there to Hansville in eleven minutes on a two-lane blacktop road. On Sunday morning as we prepared to leave I was in no hurry, figuring I would be out the gate eleven minutes before the ferry departure time.

About twenty minutes before the departure time, Les's parents started agitating that we had better get going or we would miss the ferry. I was confident that this was not the case and dawdled around until we had exactly eleven minutes to get there. We then jumped in the car and started out into a light Northwest drizzle, hitting 75 mph on all the semi straight stretches. I was feeling very Parnelli Jonesy as we came to the last long curve a quarter mile from the ferry landing. As we started into the curve, much to my horror, the end of the long line of cars waiting for the ferry suddenly appeared dead ahead.

I stomped on the brakes and on the rain-slick blacktop we hardly slowed at all. We were in a long silent skid. I knew I could miss the last car in line, but when I got nearer I saw another car turned sideways trying to get out of the line and at the last split second I tried to shoot between these two cars and I almost made it. But not quite. My right front fender hit the left rear end of the last car in line as we went shooting past and the few people out of their cars walking around were jumping in all directions trying not to get hit by the maniac who had just blasted into their midst.

In my post accident mortification and embarrassment I was angry at everyone but myself and the embarrassment increased since we missed the ferry and were sitting in line for the next ferry when Les's and Bartow's parents drove up to catch it also. When they saw my Father's car with the fender torn almost in half and bent up and over itself in a very ugly way, they wanted to know what had happened. I tried to explain the unexplainable with all sorts of what-might-have-beens had only the other car not been doing what it was doing, etcetera, etcetera, but admitted nothing about my own stupidity in driving like a teenage jerk. I could see in their eyes, as I talked, the reflection of the adolescent nonsense I was blathering.

When we finally got back to Seattle I called Hector Escaboza at Frederick & Nelson for advice and he told me in no uncertain terms I should get the car into a body shop and have it fixed before Dad got home. I took it the next day into All

Body Shop on Broadway Avenue and asked them to try to have it repaired in ten days. Then I started getting calls from the man whose car I had damaged, who was now threatening to sue me if I didn't get his car fixed and soon I was in so far over my head I didn't know what to do and figured I would probably be in jail when Mother and Dad got home. I called Hector again to please talk to the man and assure him we would look after everything. For some reason the car was not fixed when Mother and Dad got home and he went up to see it, in all its glory, after which we had quite a talk about the incident, starting with what he had told me about using the car while he was away.

Actually, I had been extremely fortunate to not have hurt someone seriously with my macho driving. And I have to say that Dad must have known how awful I felt about the whole episode for he did not punish me nearly as severely as I had expected, although later on I'm sure he wished he had. That fall, driving in the car up the Stillaguamish River from Oso, the car engine caught on fire and before we could put it out, the fire had burned a big black 16 inch circle in the paint on the hood. Dad turned to me and exploded, "This car has never been the same since you wrecked it and now look at this!" There was nothing I could say to that observation. I just hung my head in silence and hoped his disgust with me would soon be over. I have to confess that I did not think this blanket indictment exactly fair, but not long after that Dad sold the car which was a big relief from having the residue of my escapade constantly coming back to haunt me.

Many years later when I was out for an evening, my then 16 year old son, David, "borrowed" my Mercedes 280SL that I loved and which was off limits to all my kids and rear ended another car with it. Scared to death, he called his grandmother for advice as he was sure I would murder him with a certain amount of pleasure for this awful transgression. She, remembering my past malfeasance, told him, "David, you be right at the door when your father comes home and before he can say anything, just tell him you feel terrible about taking the car and what happened to it and I'm certain he will not be too hard on you." When I returned home and drove into the garage, I saw the smashed front end of the Mercedes parked sedately in its place. With my anger building up towards a rage, I opened the door to start raising hell and there was Dave, standing right there to tell his story and as I listened to his story I had a rerun of my own experience going on in my head and what could I say? I could not help but see the humor, if not the justice, in the whole episode that had truly come full circle.

In the spring of 1946 some of my friends asked me to find jobs for them and I made a trip to Ellensburg, knocking on doors at the various farms in the valley I had seen the prior year, asking for summer work. It was in this manner that I secured a job for myself and three other friends at the Bar 14, owned by Mr. S. L. Savidge, a car dealer in Seattle. As soon as school was out, Warren Haight, Tinker Hawks, Harry Dohm and I, were driven over the Cascade mountains to the Bar 14 and joined a somewhat motley crew of around ten, including several Yakima Indians, in the bunkhouse. The Bar-14 ran some cattle in the high country north of town, but down in the valley they had extensive irrigated hay fields. I had wanted a riding job but they had none and the four of us worked in the haying crew all summer. I was made to feel that the friends I had brought with me were my responsibility and I hoped that they would work hard, which they all did.

The Ellensburg farm was modern compared to the Y Cross Ranch in Wyoming. Hay was put up in bales, with the baler pulled by a large tractor. No teams of horses were used at the Bar-14. We four worked on a wire-tie baler, a machine that traveled down a windrow of hay gulping it up into a forming chamber where a large square piston with a cutting blade on one side cut and punched the hay into the forming and tying chamber. This is where my friends, sitting opposite each other along the side of the long chamber, pushed the wires through the blocks separating the bales that would automatically be tied by a wire knotter. Weighing about 90 pounds, the bales fell to the ground behind the baler, and later, using bale hooks, would be bucked by hand onto wagons for delivery to the stackyard.

The hay had to make a 90 degree left turn to reach the cutting piston in the baling chamber. My job was to help keep the hay moving evenly so that the volume going into the chamber was always the same. I spent all day standing on a platform with a pitchfork, pulling the hay around the corner from right to left as hard as I could, to keep it from jamming up in the corner. At times there was a lot of Sweet Clover in the hay, some of it with stems almost half an inch thick. These large plants were extremely difficult to pull around the corner and onto the side conveyor after being rolled up into the windrow like huge ropes. As long as the baler was moving forward I was working very hard and steady, with a stream of sweat running down my face and upper body.

On a few occasions the pitchfork would get stuck into a rolled up ball of clover and as I was trying to pull it out, the pitchfork would be jerked out of my hands and sent into the bale chamber to be cut into chunks by the knife and shoved into the bale tying section without even a hiccup from the machine. This scene would always make me think what would happen to me if I fell onto the side conveyor. No one would even know until they saw an arm or leg sticking out of a bale! I would holler to the boys to be careful that a pitchfork was coming through, as sometimes a tine would be sticking out the side of the partly open bale chamber and could do egregious bodily harm to the unaware.

We worked hard all summer and since Sunday was usually a day off, we often hitched a ride into Ellensburg on Saturday night to see what action this cowtown provided. There was a large dance hall we went to, always filled with farmers and cowboys, with western music and everyone dancing with their hats on, cowboy style. We were a little young to participate but it was great to watch. One Saturday night we decided to visit Bartow instead of going back to the Bar 14. Around midnight we started hiking the eight miles to their farm south of Ellensburg. We jogged half of the way, since no one would stop to pick up four guys hitch hiking at night, not being able to see our honest faces. It was pitch black and we couldn't find the place, so around 2 a.m. we saw a haystack in a field, crawled through the fence, and buried ourselves into it for some sleep.

When daylight finally arrived, I could see the farm was not far away from us so we walked the last mile and knocked on the door. We were greeted by Bartow and his parents with some surprise, having landing on their doorstep about 7 A.M. on a Sunday morning, but we were fed a hearty breakfast and then Bartow showed us around their farm. They had a manager who lived on the place year round and did the farming, which consisted of a goodly proportion of potatoes. We had a great Sunday with the Fite family, a welcome change to spending Sunday mostly in the bunkhouse at the Bar 14. When it came time for us to leave Mr. Fite took pity on us and gave us a ride back.

Marvin Guptill, the livestock manager of Bar 14, was in charge of the cattle operation. His mother did the cooking for the farm and ranch hands and was a wonderful cook! One Sunday, Marvin, who knew I was anxious to ride one of their Quarter horses, offered me a chance to ride to take care of some little riding chore. It was my first time on a purebred Quarter horse. This one was two axe handles across the rump, muscled all over and weighed about twelve hundred pounds. He could move quickly, accelerate fast and was a joy to ride. I would have given about anything to switch from the farm crew to the cowboy crew, but it was not to be.

Late in the summer, I was missing Mother's picnic skills so I called home to see if she and Dad would like to come over on a Sunday and I would figure out where to go if they would bring the picnic, which I hoped would include a blackberry pie. Mother and Dad agreed, and when they arrived the next Sunday around noon, we drove up into the hills and the open pine forest above the Kittitas Valley where we found a beautiful panorama viewpoint back over the valley. Mother laid out a blanket and on it placed her famous fried chicken, potato salad, sliced tomatoes and cucumbers doused with her special French dressing, stuffed eggs, and a huge blackberry pie. We three had a very pleasant and lovely afternoon.

It is interesting to me now, when I think back on the times I was away from home working for two or three months at a time, that even though I was busy with work and having interesting adventures, I occasionally experienced periods of intense homesickness mostly centered around Mother and the wonderful food we all enjoyed at home. The pain of waiting for Father to get home from work in the evenings so we could all eat together faded away and only the memory of the food and loving atmosphere remained. Anyway, that picnic shared with my parents in the hills above Ellensburg on a perfect summer day, has been indelible in my mind ever since. It became for me, the image of what the word "picnic" still conjures up in my mind to this day.

When the haying ended in late August, we collected our pay and headed back to Seattle a week before starting our senior year. This year was to be an eventful one for me. I was turning out for football, I had to choose where I wanted to attend university, I was to go through fraternity rushing in the spring at the University of Washington and I was destined to meet my future wife.

I was also a bundle of conflicted emotions and having a difficult time settling into my proper time and place. I had real pride in the fact that I had been working on farms and ranches for the last four summers, encountering many things most city kids could never experience, but I still felt a long way from being a man, in all the connotations that meant. I was confident in my academic abilities, but I was not motivated to work hard at this chore as I had not the least clue of what I wanted to do in Life. I only knew, for certain, some of the things I did not want to do.

I was yearning to somehow fill my life with adventures and travel, but I was yet to picture how I might make that happen, much less how to make a living doing it. In an abstract way I pictured my future as a series of experiences doing exotic and manly things like sailing around the world, deep sea diving, visiting other lands and places I had read about years before in travel books by Richard Haliburton, where each experience would be a chapter in the novel of my life. I thought I had a small start on this future book with the summer adventures I had already catalogued and stored, ready to sort some day in my mind's library. A book yet to be written and all I had then was the cover and a few paragraphs stored away in my consciousness. I wanted badly to fill these pages with exciting and interesting tales.

As I think back on this period now, I see how adolescent my thinking was, but perhaps it was not as unique or abnormal as I sometimes felt then. At that time my future was more of a nebulous dream than a practical plan, but I was still an optimist that it would turn out as I hoped. I can see now my dreams were not so heroic, but much more like those of a dilettante Don Quixote, dashing off simultaneously in all directions to vanquish imaginary windmills, and, of course, maybe to win my Dulcinea after all. The adage, "If you don't have a goal any road will get you where you are going" seems to be fitting for the way I was handling life as I started my final year in high school.

My senior year would be the last playing high school football when my hopes for a good season ended on the very first defensive play when I tackled the running back and in the ensuing pile up someone landed on my outstretched leg and broke the cartilage in my right knee. I was in knee cast for six weeks, arthroscopy not yet invented and was out for the season.

I was still using crutches on Halloween when a bunch of us boys were out doing some incredibly dumb things, like having fun at someone else's expense. We fashioned a straw body stuffed into a shirt and pants and tied a long rope to both legs. We thought it would be great fun to scare drivers on the highway near Bellevue, so we laid the straw body out on the highway as if it had been hit by a car. Coming upon it the cars screeched to a stop. When the driver jumped out to go back to look, we would have pulled the body out of sight into the brush beside the road and after a minute we would start laughing at our great joke which seemed to only beget curses from the road aimed at our stupidity. After repeating this several times it did not seem quite so humorous and the light dawned on us that someone could actually get hurt so we began to look for less foolish things to do.

A few minutes later as we were stood around planning our next move, a couple of guys drove up and got out of their car. There were eight of us so we expected no trouble, but after asking what we were doing and without waiting for an answer, one of them stepped forward and punched one of my friends in the face for no reason at all. I was in the leg cast, but I raised one crutch to use as a club and started for the kid who threw the punch, intending to wrap it around his neck. When he saw me coming he pulled a pistol out of his pocket and warned us to stay put as they got back in the car, the gun never wavering until the door shut and they drove away. We were all stunned and amazed at this sobering turn of events. I thought we were lucky no one was hurt with crazy people like that running around, and I guess, like us as well, and this incident ended our night of fun and games with all of us feeling somewhat down and embarrassed by our own poor judgement.

I turned 17 in January 1947. Although maintaining a C+ average in my senior year academic work and having lots of fun, inside I knew something was not right. I was bouncing around with no purpose except fun, in which girls were playing a part, but deep down I was not happy with my performance. I was popular, had friends, was on the Student Advisory Board and my days were absolutely full, but I had no sense of purpose past the next weekend.

I was starting to drink too much on some weekends when out with Reveler friends, with the main purpose of getting a buzz on. Luckily there were no drugs around that we were aware of. Marijuana we had heard about, but it was only used by some musicians, like Gene Krupa, a great drummer of the era, and I doubt anyone I knew had a foggy notion of how to acquire any had we wanted to try it. Drug users were in a class which none of my friends and I wished anything to do, or be identified with. Drugs simply were not a factor in middle class America in 1947, partly, I think, because of the class distinctions. From what little we heard about drugs, they were not used by white, middle class, bound for college, kids. And to be smoking dope would have meant instant ostracization by the group to which we belonged. I would have felt as out of place as I did on the rare occasions I found myself downtown at night on 1st avenue or Pioneer Square in Seattle, walking past the girly shows, pimps, bums and social outcasts who frequent such streets in all big cities.

I finally decided I would like to go to Stanford for my university years and hoped that my grades from New Trier would carry the day. In the end they did, but I had to take "bonehead" English in my first quarter at Stanford. I could live with this ignominy but I hated the thought of having to take a grammar course with a passion. While I was waiting to hear from Stanford, I went through rush at the U of W. On one occasion I was invited to the Phi Gamma Delta house for lunch and one of the members introduced me as Bill Street, such and so, and a Reveler. With that more than half the guys around the table jumped up and cheered as they had all been Revelers as well. I figured I had that one in the bag. But I went in a different direction and at Stanford there was no fraternity rushing until the end of the freshman year and being a Reveler would count for nothing.

My skills with the girls were still non-existent. I got along with them as friends but did not understand what my behavior ought to be when I became really interested in a particular one. In other words, my attraction to their female sexuality was a difficulty I found hard to circumnavigate. I knew I would never consider myself a man until I had had sex with a woman and how to go about this with some girl I knew as a friend, was a major hurdle for me. I was not going steady with any one, but there were a few girls that for a short time I was somewhat serious about. But none had affected me anything like Susie had.

It was during this time I began to notice a sophomore girl, a good looking blond whose name was Karen Mattson. After a time I invited her out, a bit to the horror of my senior friends. We had a good time and started to be a fairly steady couple going to dances and getting more familiar with each other as time went by. Her father, John Mattson, an architect, a short, heavily muscled man, though born in Finland, was pure Swedish. Her mother Jessie's heritage was English and she was a school teacher. I think they were a little concerned that their daughter was dating a boy two years older and they had reason to be, but they were very nice to me and I was always deferential to them.

Our family finally had two cars so it was possible for me to get one to use on most weekends. I had not learned much from my accident of the year before and was still driving way too fast whenever I could. I was over confident of my skill and under-appreciative of others using the same roads. One day in late April, returning from having driven my parents to Boeing Field to catch a plane, I was pulled over by a policeman and given my first speeding ticket for going 50 mph in a 35 mph speed zone. I was ticked off at this and figured it would be a cold day in hell before I got another one, but by the time I got to Madison Avenue fifteen minutes later, I was pulled over and given my second speeding ticket of the day. On the very next day I was handed a third speeding ticket. Three in two days must be some sort of record and a few days later I received a summons in the mail ordering me, along with one parent, to report for a hearing in juvenile traffic court a week later.

When Mother and Dad returned from their trip and read the summons, they were totally disgusted with me. They decided Mother would accompany me to Traffic Court. We went, and after reading out the facts of my three traffic transgressions, I was given a proper dressing down by the lady judge who had a bad reputation amongst the high school kids for her toughness. When she had said all she wanted, she asked me if I had anything to say, I suppose hoping for some sign of contrition on my part, but instead, I blurted out, "I suppose you have never gone over the speed limit yourself?"

Mother practically leaped from her seat, exclaiming loudly, "Bill! What are you thinking! What's wrong with your head?" trying to show the judge that at least someone in the family had some sense about the situation. The fact that Mother was siding with her was not enough to move the lady judge to compassion for me and she answered me with, "Young man, with that remark, I am suspending your license for thirty days and perhaps without your license for this period you will have some time to reflect on improving your driving habits a bit!"

THIRTY DAYS! I could not believe it. My last month of high school and I would not be able to drive at all! It was a very big blow, but one I totally deserved. Thinking back, 30 days in jail might have been more appropriate. I could see society becoming increasingly determined to bend me to more rational actions and it was none too soon.

With graduation and summer fast approaching I began to think about summer work. I was intent to work somewhere, but preferred not to go back to the Bar 14 where I had been offered a job. Earning more money was a factor, as I wanted to buy a car at the end of summer to take to Stanford. As it turned out, Lou Anderton, an outfitter that Mother and Dad had met on a hunting trip in the White River area of Alaska, was coming to Seattle in early June to buy some horses to take back to Alaska. When he called to say hello to my parents, they mentioned my interest in talking to him about the possibility of a job. I made an appointment to meet him a few days later. When that time arrived, I took the bus downtown to a third class hotel on 2nd Avenue, found his room and knocked on the door.

Lou turned out to be a hawk-nosed man with the brightest, sun crinkled sky blue eyes I had ever seen, set into a rugged outdoorsman's tanned face. He had a hard time looking me in the eye and was a chain smoker, two traits I came to know very well over the next few years. He was a real country boy from Camas County Idaho and probably had no more than eight grades of formal education, if that. I could see that he had done physical work all his life, most of it on farms or ranches and in the out-of-doors. He said that this was his first time "outside" since he had gone to Alaska in 1919 after being mustered out of the cavalry at Ft. Lewis at the end of WWI. As we talked, he was sitting on the bed smoking, the sweat collecting on his mostly bald head and I could see that for Lou, "outside" had changed very much indeed since he had last seen it as a youngster and he was feeling out of place in the frantic, noisy city scene.

He planned to buy 16 horses to add to his pack train and would be taking them up on an Alaska Steamship Line boat. We talked for a time while I tried to convince him I knew how to ride and would work hard for him. He said he didn't really need anyone and there were lots of men he could hire in Alaska. Finally, after much talk, he said he would try me, but only because he liked my mother so much was he willing to do it. He would pay me $300 a month and board. I was elated! This was easily twice what I had been earning in my last farm job. I just knew this was going to be my greatest adventure yet and I was eager for the time to come when we would leave.

I graduated in the second week of June, survived a wild all-night party at Beaver Lake near Lake Sammamish, followed by a drive in the light of early morning to Hansville, where the party continued into the next afternoon. Recovering enough the next day at home, I began gathering the things I would need in Alaska. My parents gave me a pair of binoculars as a graduation gift, and loaned me Mother's Mannlicher-Schoenauer 6.5 mm rifle and a hunting knife to take with me. I had purchased a rain slicker, a wool jacket and shirt and long wool underwear, the kind with a trap door flap over the bum and new work boots. I took my down sleeping bag and a duffel bag to put everything in and was ready to go. I was to meet Lou the next day at the dock and follow in the footsteps of my Great Grandfather Poppy, to Alaska, and I hoped, a new chapter in the novel of my life.

Summer 1947

*Wherein our hero joins Lou and has a voyage, takes a long horseback ride,
becomes a wrangler, and meets several grizzly bears and Bush pilots*

(Note: The excerpts from the journal I kept during my trips to Alaska have been
used without change or editing, in an effort to give some insight into how experiences were described by me at the time they took place)

From my Alaskan Journal 1947 Friday June 13th

*Loaded horses in forenoon and pulled out at dark. It was very beautiful with all
the lights of the city in the distance. The horses are all bedded down for the night
now—They were a little nervous when we hoisted them into the hold but they are settled down now. Lou says we get up at 7 A.M. so seeing as I haven't recovered from
commencement (party) yet I will hit the sack—9:30 P.M.*

Lou Anderton had organized with the Alaska Steamship Line to build 16
wooden stalls into the cargo hold, with storage space for a week's hay and grain
and straw for bedding. We had several big buckets with which to water the horses
and feed sacks that fit over their heads for feeding them oats. Another small loading stall was built with chains securing a steel ring attached to the top planks, just
wide enough for one horse to fit into snuggly, to be used to hoist each one in
turn, up off the pier and into the hold, and again to offload them from the ship
when we reached Valdez.

On the day of departure, Lou had the horses trucked to the dock from a pasture where he was holding them and one by one, they were loaded into the small
stall that a crane picked from the dock and lowered them into the dark hold. The
horses were terrified at this process and we could see the whites of their eyes as
they rolled them around and whinnied loudly in fear as they were raised high up
into the sky. I worked down in the hold of the ship where I backed the trembling
animals out of the little stall and led them to their permanent stalls, which
though not big, allowed plenty of room for them to lie down. When all were

loaded, Lou and I got our stuff stowed and then I went below to water the horses. This was done by filling a bucket from a nearby tap and putting it inside each stall. When all had been watered I went topside to watch disembarkation from the dock and the beginning of our trip north.

The six-day voyage settled down into a routine, with me doing the work and Lou under the weather from the rolling around. The Inside Passage, a somewhat protected stretch of water, was quite smooth, but when we hit the Gulf of Alaska we got into big swells as we headed towards Valdez and I had a few hours with a rollicky stomach as well. The ship stopped in Ketchikan to unload freight and take on a few passengers. One of them was a red haired woman who took a cabin several doors from Lou and me. Later that night we heard a small hubbub of talking outside our stateroom and saw a lineup of men there from the ship's crew. I asked Lou what the big attraction was and he told me that the lady was a hooker and seemed to have a pretty good business going. By morning the Captain had heard about the crew taking time off for a little sport and when we docked in Juneau, our next port, we saw the woman escorted to the gangway and put off the ship. After that, there was little excitement other than the whales and porpoise we often saw.

From my Alaskan Journal Thursday June 19th

Got up at 6:30 and fed horses. Got to Valdez around noon and unloaded horses under eyes of all kids in town. With much difficulty we took them through town to pasture and then hit a tavern for a beer. Ate dinner and went back to hobble horses. They broke hobbles and went in all directions. Took us until 10:00 P:M: to get organized again and we just let them go. Got a room in the Golden North Hotel and had another beer. Hit sack 11 P.M.

We landed in Valdez which was a very small town in 1947, but with a good harbor and dock facilities. (It would later become the end of the Alaska oil pipeline with greatly expanded facilities for loading oil tankers and a much larger population.) We unloaded the horses by reversing the loading procedure, saddled two horses and ran the bunch through town and into a large pasture nearby, much to the enjoyment of most of the kids in town who came to watch. We planned to give the horses several days to rest and graze before starting up the Thompson Highway towards the Wrangell Mountains and Chisana, three hundred miles away.

We found out that most of the younger children in Valdez had never seen a real live horse, so we had fun giving rides to many using the horses that were broken to ride. There were three mares in the bunch and the rest geldings, except that one strawberry roan turned out to be proud cut (improperly castrated) and was certain he was still a stallion. When we put the herd into the pasture, it took him about five minutes to cut the mares out for himself and run the geldings off. Lou had not noticed this problem when he had purchased the horse, but he figured that I could ride "Roan" as we called him, otherwise we would have a lot of trouble managing the horses with him loose. Lou was right. I grew to hate that horse after about 200 miles of "jigging" as he was always frantic if he could not stay close to the mares.

From my Alaskan Journal 1947—Wednesday June 25th

Up around 6:45 A.M.. It is a swell day (finally) with lots of sunshine. Did all the last minute errands, etc. and then brought in some horses to pack. This done we left around 12:30 (after having some lunch. The horses were wilder than h___ and a pack fell off one horse after ¼ mile. I had to chase the horses for the first 2 miles anyway. We got about 16 miles up the road to the entrance to a tunnel. They started through but spooked and ran out and back down the road. I chased them for over a mile (running) and overtook 8; the other four kept right on going. Lou came back so we went to 13 mile camp and tied up our horses. Burnard Wagland came along and we put our saddles in his car and went back to town. Had a beer and then dinner and went to bed around 9:30 P.M.

With a few townsfolk watching, we left Valdez to start our journey to the White River. I had saddled Roan and Lou chose a big footed, rangy white horse he named Bill, and leading two pack horses, went to the front and started out. I rounded up the other horses and pushed them after Lou. The horses were wild, maybe sensing this was the start of something different. In a while they settled down into a long line and all went well until entering the quarter-mile long tunnel at 16 Mile, where the loose horses I was herding from the rear of the string, panicked half way through, turning and running back at full speed past me. My job was to head them off, so I put Roan into a run back down the highway, to get past them. Roan and I overtook half of them, but when I tried to pass a mare, Roan, no matter how hard I kicked or smacked him with the end of the reins, flatly refused to leave her and turn the rest of the running horses. To Lou's disgust and my embarrassment, after our grand departure from Valdez, we were back in town again that night, with horses scattered all the way to 13 Mile.

The next day we caught three horses that had come all the way back to town, saddled up and rode out to 13 Mile collecting all 16 head along the way. This time Lou caught and tailed the three mares to his horse, Bill, and we started again. Lou had organized several people to drive up from Valdez to help us get through the tunnel. This time, once the horses had entered the tunnel, with car horns blaring and me yelling, we made enough racket behind them that they continued going forward towards the daylight at the other end.

The tunnel was the last obstacle in our path except for a few rivers we would have to cross, many miles farther on. We camped wherever we found water and good grazing for the horses. They were long days. In early June, the mosquitoes could be a problem at times, but a little breeze kept them mostly at bay and it was daylight enough to see pretty well all night.

We settled into a routine of me taking care of the horses, Lou cooking, me cleaning up after dinner, and depending on the weather, organizing tarps for cover over, or under us, for sleeping. After dinner each night as we sat around the campfire, I kept prying stories out of Lou about the early days in Alaska. He seemed reticent at first, maybe because he wasn't used to having me around and still wanted me to prove myself before he was comfortable in a closer relationship. I sensed he was not used to reminiscing much, perhaps due to his many years living alone in a bachelor existence. But slowly he began to open up and finally, every time we were not fully occupied with work, he would tell me of his life in Alaska from his arrival in 1919.

I was captivated by his stories, as they seemed to match the descriptions in Robert Service's poems of the north country, especially wintertime and in the books of Jack London. Almost all of the characters Lou spoke of had nicknames, like "Pink Whiskers," the man who never washed his beard, and N.P. "Northpole" Nelson, one of the prospectors who discovered gold in the Chisana country. Lou told stories about these men, the dancehall girls, the hookers with hearts of gold who would stake a man in need, and traveling around the country by dog team, horse, or on foot, common through the 1920's and 1930's. There were many stories of the cold and the storms, of some unfortunate individuals freezing to death and about the Tanana Indians who sparsely populated the broad area north of the Wrangell Mountains.

I was able to meet a few of these people myself, including Earl Hurst, a man who had been scalped by a grizzly that attacked him while travelling with a pack string. Earl was knocked down by the bear that took a swipe at him and ripped a large piece of his scalp off before being run off by the other men. In their effort to help Earl, his companions who had found the scalp lying on the ground, washed it off and slapped it back on, bandaging it down the best they could. When a doctor finally saw him some days later, he laughed and pointed out they had put the scalp on backwards and it was too late to change since it was already firmly attached. And so it was the day I met Earl later that summer.

To me, Lou was a perfect example of one of the characters from his stories. He had done a lot of things, from mining gold to running a dog team taxi in Kennicott and McCarthy in the winters; smuggling booze by dog team or pack string from Canada, up the White River or Beaver Creek during the Prohibition years; trapping during winter and spring; and guiding hunters. A true outdoorsman and a real man. Over time we became very fond of each other. He was the first adult male I was able to talk to easily about anything and I became for him the son he had never had. In fact, he'd had a rather lonely life as far as women went. His one big love, as far as I knew, was a hooker in McCarthy that he fell for and wanted to marry. I think he was beaten out by Harry Boyden, an Englishman, who was tall and handsome and much more sophisticated than Lou and I think Lou found it hard, after that, to harbor any warm feelings for Harry. I was to see, first hand, how their relationship actually was, since Harry would be a guide on the hunting party in the fall and would be bringing his pack string along as well.

Lou was not the only storyteller. When I spent time with any of the older men who had been there in the early days, I found they all had tales to tell. Many were about encounters with animals, some comical but others scary, especially about bears, as well as a few about wolves. One night later in the fall, we were camped on Notch Creek for the night when Lou told me that he had once been camping by himself on the exact site where we were. In the dark he had been holding a frying pan over a fire cooking when he realized he was not alone. A grizzly, smelling the cooking, had come into camp and right up behind Lou, without his hearing it. All of a sudden Lou said he felt and smelled the hot breath of a bear and realized it was right behind him in the dark and he let out a tremendous YAAaHooo! simultaneously throwing the frying pan back over his head and jumping for his gun. Luckily, the shout frightened the bear so much that it wheeled and ran.

As I heard these adventure stories, Alaska became in my mind the most exciting and spectacular place I could imagine and I could feel in my 17 year old bones that I was destined to be tied somehow to this great and wild country for life.

At night, when Lou turned the horses loose, he put bells on them and hobbled several of the mares, so they would not wander too far. But this meant that I, and occasionally the two of us, had to track them for several miles in the morning. It often turned into a fair hike before we found them, got a bridle on one or two, jumped on and hazed the others back to camp.

One morning after a week on the trail, Lou and I were riding down an old logging road with a four foot high cut bank on the right side, tracking the other horses. About fifty yards ahead I saw an old reddish colored stump, but suddenly the stump moved backwards and it turned out to be a 2 or 3 year old grizzly that had heard us approaching. The horses stopped in their tracks, nervous, ears straight forward, and Lou let out a big yell. Frightened on hearing Lou's loud holler, the bear took off full tilt, but not seeing where we were, headed straight for us on a flat out run. The horses were instantly going crazy, trying to turn and get away, when Lou let out another big yell and waved his arms. The bear saw us then, skidded to a stop about fifty feet away, instantly whirled and jumped up the cut bank, crashing through the underbrush up the hillside and disappeared into the forest. This was my first look at a grizzly up fairly close in the wild, but it was not to be my last.

By June 30th, we were at Tonsina Lodge, 80 miles from Valdez, and we rode into Copper Center, 103 miles out on July 1st.

From my Alaskan Journal 1947—Wednesday July 2nd

Woke with the sun in my eyes again around 7 A.M. Ate at the lodge and then Lou left for Chitina. I watered the stud and cooked some meat at the RH (roadhouse) Came back and went for a swim in the pool by the Copper River and then went back to the RH for a beer. Ate dinner and then Lou came back with the shoeing outfit. I went to get the horses and found they had pulled out. I saddled up and caught them 6 miles out—drove them back 2 miles and then met Lou in a car with our stuff and then went on out to 112 mile and made camp. Two cars stopped and gave me a beer—(we found a semi (truck) full of beer tipped over) so had another bottle and went to bed (11:45)

From my Alaskan Journal 1947—Friday July 4th

Up around 7:30 A.M. to another hot day! Ate and got a fairly late start. My stuff hadn't gotten to S.C. (Santa Claus Lodge) I discovered too. We started up the hill accompanied by three eagles and didn't stop once until we had gone 22 miles to some sort of camp on a little stream. When we got here it was 90° by the thermometer but it was cool compared to what it had been. We didn't have any lunch today—nor any *water till we got here so the first thing I did was to go swimming and take a bath in a swell hole (I also put two beers in to get cold) We ate our 4th of July dinner with the mosquitoes and are resting now. We are almost to 19 mile on this Nabesna road, making over half way there (to Chisana) with 150 miles. We ought to get to Chistochina tomorrow. It sure is a swell evening (except for the flies, etc.) I guess I'll have a beer. (7:30 P.M.)*

We arrived in Chistochina on the 5th and then did another 12 miles to Indian River on the 6th. I had a chance to fish a bit at this stop, while Lou was following in a truck from Chistochina with all our duffel, which had finally caught up to us there. The sockeye were running and I helped a man gaff a couple of the bright red salmon, using a long pole with a gaff pressed on one end, but secured with a leather thong. When a fish was gaffed, the gaff pulled off the pole but was held by the thong, allowing the fish to jump around without tearing loose.

From my Alaskan Journal 1947—Monday July 7th

Got up around 6:30 this morning without much sleep again. Ate and then caught our horses—I rode the buckskin again. We went 18 miles to Slana R.H. and camped on a river (underneath the bridge). We got here about 3 P.M. & made some lunch. I had to chase the horses again and now my calf's are sore as hell! Its been overcast all day and very <u>cool</u>. (Also it rained a little last night). It's very windy now. We aren't getting much sleep trying to keep the horses from leaving—you are afraid to go to sleep for fear they'll slip by without you waking up. We ought to get a big sleep when we get to Nabesna. We have now traveled 185 miles and we'll get to Chisana with 5 more days on the trail. We have come around the end of the Wrangell Mts. and now we're following parallel to them about ESE. Lou came back from the R.H. & brought me a beer—that Lou is one <u>swell</u> guy! We ate dinner and it began to rain so I put up a lean-to out along the road (to watch horses) and let Lou sleep under the bridge. Went to bed around 10 P.M.—Was up chasing horses twice in the rain last night. It hasn't stopped raining yet.

We began to have trouble holding the horses that wanted to return to where we had been several days before and that meant I was up several times each night chasing them. Perhaps the feed did not agree with them, but whatever it was they were determined to go back. Several nights I slept in my clothes, boots and all, to be instantly ready to go after them. We began to put in some very long days. We left Slana Roadhouse and after 22 miles we arrived at Twin Lakes, but as there was not enough feed for the stock, we rode all night in the midsummer twilight without a stop, arriving in Nabesna around 3 A.M. We then had to go to Lou's cabin a few more miles along the river bar where we had a terrible time trying to push the horses across a small but deep stream near the cabin, a job that should have taken one hour but took three instead. We finally rode up to the cabin, dog-tired, at 6:30 A.M.

Once we were at Lou's Nabesna cabin, we spent about ten days working with the young, green horses, sorting the food and gear, repairing rigging on some of the saddles, shoeing horses and getting loads organized for each horse. We worked back and forth from several caches a few miles apart and Lou took several truck trips to bring in aviation gasoline, kerosene, and white gas for the camp lights. In the meantime he was approached by a U.S. Geodetic Survey crew leader for a mapping project around Tok Junction, near the Alcan Highway, to see if they could hire us and our horses for a few weeks to help them haul their equipment to the tops of some mountains. Lou agreed, since he was to be paid a handsome amount that would help defray some of the costs of his trip outside to buy the horses.

From my Alaskan Journal 1947—Saturday July 19th

Got up around 7:30 and ate a leisurely breakfast and then we walked out and got 4 horses. I caught a 3 yr. old to ride him the first time and he was all right. We got up to the road around noon and were just about to eat lunch when a truck with the Geodetic boys.... and so Lou and I are going to work for them for around 15 days. We went up to the mine to see H. Boyden and Homer Holtes gave us a shot & 2 bottles of home brew which was pretty potent on an empty stomach & I was a little woozy. Afterwards we went down to the (river) bar to get 4 more horses which took about 5 hours. Got back at 10:00 and ate dinner at Boyden's, put 4 horses in the truck and then had to drive about 70 miles so I went with the first load. We got there about 4:30 A.M. to the camp but went 3 miles further to find water and feed and then went to bed around 5:30 A.M. Saw a moose—2 calves.

I packed equipment up the low mountains for the survey crew from July 19th to August 4th. It was tough work, but during that time I had several days of doing nothing because of bad weather. The mosquitoes were really something to behold. As I moved the pack horses along, there would be a mini cyclone of mosquitoes about one foot wide and three feet high, whirling in a circle over each horse. I stated in one journal entry that I wished I had some DDT to deal with them. That was in the days before many of the chemicals, like DDT, were banned.

My job for the survey work was to use the horses to pack valuable surveying equipment and several very bright lights with their large batteries to the top of a designated peak. Lou, maybe 15 to 20 miles away, was using his four horses to do the same thing with another crew, and a third crew climbed on foot to another peak. The aim of the surveyors in that summer of 1947, was to fill in the unmapped blanks still showing on maps of the area. Once the instruments were in place on a rocky peak and usually at the darkest part of the twilight night, the searchlights would be turned on and the surveyors would take their triangulation readings. The peaks would then be exactly placed on the section of map being working on.

This was my first packing experience on my own and I had responsibility for a saddle horse, three pack horses and the equipment of the survey crew. There were no trails up to the peaks and some of the terrain was steep. A few times horses fall down on steep pitches and I had a few close calls myself, but I was learning something new every day. On the days when bad weather stopped operations and I had no one to talk with, and nothing to do, I would often feel terribly homesick. I was eating canned food and not cooking much, as the weather was often rainy and I had only a campfire and damp wood and thus I couldn't help thinking about Mother's cooking and what I would be eating if I were at home. Sun-ripened fresh tomatoes and melons, stuffed eggs, ice cream and cake and Dagwood sandwiches made with everything from the refrigerator. I almost drove myself crazy thinking about all that wonderful food, as I poked at a can of beans or salmon, feeling very sorry for myself.

But everyone in the crew was friendly to me. In fact I had not come across a single person I did not like since coming to Alaska and some were the most interesting old timers you would ever want to meet.

On August 4th, when we had to quit the survey work in order to get back to Nabesna in time to pack up and go on to Chisana, I was picked up by the Geodetic truck along with my four horses and taken to Nabesna. Lou followed a day later. We finalized our preparations for the hunt over the next few days, but due to bad weather and some problems with the horses, we did not start out until August 10th.

From my Alaskan Journal 1947—Sunday, August 10th

Got up and ate around 5:30 A.M. at Boydens. Got the horses in except two that Lou went after. I got the stuff ready while Lou was out and ate a bite & he got back around

2 P.M. We started out in a cloud of dust—and that is no fooling—as soon as we let the horses go they stampeded—packs & all, it was quite a site with 23 horses all galloping & running around. The only trouble was that a lot of the packs came off. It was quite an experience getting all those horses across the Nabesna and Jacksina rivers, especially when they don't savvy water at all. The river was fairly low but the water still came up over the hind end of my horse. We finally got across and started down the bar to the Nabesna Village about 7 miles away which was to be our first camp. Saw lots of fresh bear tracks and later on saw one & watched him through the glasses. One of the horses lost a pack & they stampeded again & he smashed our grub boxes all to heck. We have pepper in everything. We slept in a cabin that night & the weather was swell.

We reached Chisana (pronounced shoo shana), which was Lou's home base, on August 11th. We had covered 300 miles, not counting the miles looking for the horses each morning or working between the caches at Nabesna, or for that matter, the miles put into the survey work for the government. Lou calls going to Chisana, "going to town", although it was hardly a town with only six or seven log cabins and four old men living there, including Lou, along with six sled dogs. Chisana is actually on Johnson Creek, a tributary of the Chisana River, about two miles from the river itself. The source of the Chisana River is Chisana glacier, about eight miles west.

Chisana was a gold rush town in 1913, when gold was discovered several miles up Bonanza Creek, a tributary flowing into Johnson Creek about 10 miles from Chisana. The rush lasted into the early 1920's. One of the old timers living in Chisana was N. P. (Northpole) Nelson, one of the two partners who found the gold and staked the original claims. They had been prospecting since the Klondike rush in 1898, and had slowly moved from the Yukon into Alaska territory. He was a very big Swede aged 80, had made and lost several fortunes to women and bad investments, but he still worked his claim in the summertime when the ground thawed. It was exciting for me to talk with him about the early days and he was interested to hear that my great grandfather had also gone to the Klondike gold rush from California.

According to Lou, some 13,000 people came through the area during the gold rush period. They came traveling on foot, by horseback, or by dog team, up the Chitina River from McCarthy, through the Wrangell Mts., or up the White River from Canada, or up the Chisana River from Northway and Fairbanks. Lou said at one time there were almost 500 cabins in Chisana, but almost all were long gone, having collapsed from old age or burned for fuel by the remaining people living there, with others swept away by the occasional flooding of Johnson Creek.

Lou's cabin was about thirty five feet long and twenty feet wide, separated into a kitchen/dining room, a small back storage room, and a large living/bedroom. The kitchen had a large wood stove and room for a table about eight feet long, a sink, counter space and open cupboards loaded with pots, pans and dishes. The living room had two single beds against the walls, a four foot square table and several chairs, and a 55 gallon converted oil drum space heater in a corner ten feet from the front door. The bathroom was an outhouse a hundred feet away and of course there was no running water except in Johnson Creek. Next door, Lou had a second larger cabin serving as a warehouse for most of his pack string and trapping gear, including three sleds and foodstuff he brought in to sell to the other inhabitants or use himself. I guessed if you looked at every nook and cranny of that warehouse you could ultimately find anything you could ever want and a few things you probably wouldn't want on a bet. Like many of the old log buildings in the Alaskan interior, it carried a slight perfume of pack rat.

The cabins, situated in a line, faced Johnson Creek 75 yards away. Behind the cabins was a flat open area, probably a gravel bar from the creek's movements over the years, covered with low weeds and clumpy grasses. It was in this area that six kennels were located for Lou's dog team. These kennels were built of wood forming three foot cubes with sloping tar paper covered flat roofs and separated by enough distance to assure that the dogs could not reach each other and fight.

These malamutes were large and when excited set up a huge commotion, barking and howling, and although they were securely fastened with light chain to their collars, could jump a full three feet straight up into the air. This same performance took place every afternoon at feeding time when I would carry to each dog a 2 gallon tin container, almost full, of barley and meat soup which they were fed in the summer when they were not working. I was a bit scared of these dogs, having heard some tales of malamutes and seeing for myself the size of their teeth, but I soon found that other than being both big and exuberant, they were good tempered and soon became friendly with me. It probably helped that I was the one feeding them. The dog dish had been converted from five-gallon aviation fuel cans left here and there around the country by bush pilots.

Two five-gallon cans of fuel had come packed in wooden boxes, which Lou used for holding food when packing the horses. Once full, each box was slipped into a canvas pannier with a flap that covered the top of the box and helped keep things dry in bad weather. When ready for loading, the pannier with its box of grub was lifted and the leather strap attached to the back of the canvas pannier, slipped over the pack saddle forks to simply hang there by the strap. It was an easy way of packing horses, but required that both boxes be close to equal weight so that the pack saddle would not rotate over to one side when the ropes loosened up, frightening the horse into trying to buck the load off completely.

When I first walked into Lou's warehouse in Chisana and saw the big freighting sled and the two smaller Yukon sleds, I knew I was going to have to experience mushing a dog team. The stories Lou had told me about dog sledding, the winter cold, the Northern Lights, coupled with my own Alaska reading, contributed to the huge desire building in me to run Lou's team sometime in the future. And this came to pass sooner than I thought it might.

Now we had to get ready for the hunt, and set up our first camp on Francis Creek, about five miles from Ptarmigan Lake where we would meet our hunters.

From my 1947 Journal: Aug. 18—Monday

Lou and I got to Francis Creek last nite & got to bed around 12:30 A.M. The spot we camped in was the site of Mom & Dad's sheep camp last Fall. It was pretty cold out in the morning around 4:30 A.M. when we got up—there was ice on the bucket. We ate a little breakfast & then Lou took two horses over to the North Fork to get two tents & stoves. I then packed two horses & took two other saddle horses down with (Harry) Boyden and Don Spalding's string (grub for the 1ˢᵗ party) to the sight for the sheep camp. We got there around 10:30–11 A.M. & Don and I went on down to Ptarmigan Lake to pick up the hunters. We got there around 2 P.M. and found Harold (Harold Curtis was the guide from Anchorage that organized the hunting trips) Mr. Smith & Mr. Mooney, & Dr. and Mrs. Hazlitt of the other party. We didn't have enough horses so I walked back up to camp. Don and I ate a little and then went back down to the lake to get another plane load. Harold who had stayed at the lake introduced me to Dr. Smith and Dr. Pearson & Jimmy Moore (cook and wife to Tom Moore, a guide)—and then we packed up and got back to camp about 11 P.M. Ate some crackers and went to bed around 12:30 A.M. Very beautiful day—not a cloud in the sky. Coming up the trail that nite we saw a beautiful display of Northern lights too.

My job for the hunting party was as wrangler and camp helper. This meant it was my responsibility to round up the horses and saddle them for the hunters each morning. If we were moving camp I had to get the pack horses ready as well. The rest of my time was spent helping the cook, cutting wood, cleaning up and wishing I was hunting. The days were uniformly long. I was usually up by 5 A.M. and hit the sack around 11 P.M. I had to go after the horses on foot, since Lou refused to keep a picket horse in camp, and often this meant a good five mile hike, one way, before finding them. I carried a bridle and small sack of grain to catch the first horse I found, and once it was eating the grain I could get the bridle on with little trouble, then jumping on and hazing the rest of the horses into camp. I got even when at last I could eat my breakfast, after the hunters had departed for the day, and the cook was amazed at how much food I could consume. But then I was a growing boy.

As the name implies, our "sheep camp" was located near some low mountains that formed natural Dall Sheep habitat and sheep moved all over this terrain with ease. These sheep are white like mountain goats, with smooth curving horns, that in the largest Rams, grew to over 44 inches in length and were prized hunting trophies in North America. Our camp, above timberline, at that latitude about 3000 feet in elevation, was located on the south side of a mile wide, gently-dished valley. Across this valley the land rose up another 2,000 or 3000 feet, cresting in shale slides and rock outcroppings that formed many basins.

To the south there was a low range of hills falling away in a succession of creeks flowing in a southeasterly direction, until they joined the White River that flowed east, parallel to the Wrangell Mountains, into the Yukon Territory of Canada, where it turned north to join the Tanana and finally the Yukon River. Lou called the area we were camped in the "flats." Walking was difficult unless on a game trail or the main trail used by people who passed through the country from time to time. Grass grew in clumps a foot or more high and about eight inches across the top. I learned to hate these clumps, as they made walking off the trail very difficult. In summer the whole area was green from this grass, with two to three foot high willow brush or berry bushes scattered about, and wherever there was running water or a spring, willows grew to a height of ten to fifteen feet.

From my 1947 Journal—Aug. 20—Wednesday

The sheep season starts today—(I can't write very well since I've had too many hot rums) … I'm writing this the next day (21ˢᵗ) when I am in better condition. Lou didn't get back today (when expected) and the Drs. went out alone. Lou got in around noon & helped me get 8 horses down to the lake. The tents he got at the White (river cabin) were all torn by bears so I had to get to the lake before the plane got there to order 2 more. I had 5 horses & was about a mile from the lake when the plane came so I tied the horses & almost killed my horse trying to get there. The plane took off but I flagged him back down & put in the order—We then packed 5-6 horses with the duffle & came back to the camp around dinner. The hunters came back later after looking the layout over; spotted some good sheep too. Went to bed around 10 P.M.

When we got back to the camp, Lou took me aside and said he appreciated the work I had been doing and was doubling my salary to $600 a month, or twenty dollars a day. I was really surprised and gratified that he had seen the effort I was putting in. That was a lot of money in those days and I knew because of this raise in pay, I would be able to afford a car when I returned home. I was also tremendously proud of this recognition and I knew Dad would be pleased that some of his efforts to instill a sense of obligation to those who paid me to work had actually rubbed off onto me.

I went to the lake again on the 20ᵗʰ and 21ˢᵗ and finally, all the duffel and people were in camp. I rose at 5 A.M. each morning to walk out to find the horses, but the hunters usually did not leave camp until after 9 A.M. I then worked around the camp. It was located in a patch of large Spruce trees along Francis Creek, our source of water, and consisted of a large surplus army cook tent, 10 by 14 feet with 4 foot side walls, and four smaller tents, 8 by 10 feet with 3 foot side walls. The people on the hunt included a cook, a wrangler, four guides, four hunters and 23 horses. The hunters slept two to a tent, Lou and I shared one tent, two guides the other and the cook and her husband used the cook tent for sleeping. We set up small tables near each tent for washing or shaving with a mirror hanging from a limb for easy use. There was no outhouse, just the great "outside."

Jimmy Moore was the wife of Tom Moore, a husky halfbreed Indian serving as one of the guides on the hunt. They lived in Anchorage and Tom was used by Harold Curtis for hunts he organized in different areas of Alaska. Jimmy was a superb cook. For breakfast, we always had bacon and eggs, hash brown potatoes, pancakes and stewed prunes, applesauce, or other dried fruit. For supper, she prepared sheep, caribou and bear steaks or roasts, fresh bread or rolls, canned vegetables and fruit, and always pies or cake for dessert. The coffee pot was always on, as was hot water for washing in the morning and evening, delivered by me to the various tents. She also prepared the lunches the hunters and guides took out each day consisting of sandwiches, dried fruit and cookies or some other goody. She was a nice lady and I tried hard to make her job easier by lugging water in five gallon buckets and making sure her woodbox was always full. She was in charge of the camp and I understood she was my boss when Lou was not around. I learned early that it is smart to keep the cook happy.

In the cook tent everyone could be seated at the table, and gas lamps were hung from the main rope holding up the tent peak. There were camp stools, a large wood burning stove with oven, and food storage along the sides of the tent in the wooden fuel boxes turned on their sides and stacked three high. A woodbox sat beside the stove. On the 22nd Dr. Smith killed a sheep for camp meat, and because that was against the law, this started some serious talk amongst the guides who were responsible to make sure things like that did not happen. As it turned out, the meat was not needed because Mel Pearson, one of the hunters, had killed a ram that day hunting with Lou in a different area. It was not a great trophy measuring 35" long and 28" wide, but he was excited.

From my 1947 Journal—Aug 23—Saturday

I got up around 5 A.M. and got the horses ready. The Drs. were out to photograph & the older men were hunting. I worked around camp until they came back to camp. They didn't get any sheep but they shot a 7' grizzly sow that charged them. Dr. Smith got pictures of it all too. Everyone was very excited. We've been eating sheep meat for breakfast.

The grizzly that charged the hunters was protecting a sheep kill. They were above her on the mountain when she realized they were near her cache, and she had to charge up the hill which slowed her charge just enough for one of the guides to kill her. She dropped within thirty or forty feet, but Vern Smith, who was taking moving pictures of the incident, said that as he looked through the camera lens, her head seemed to fill the entire screen.

From my 1947 Journal—Aug 24—Sunday

Didn't get up till 7 A.M. Everyone's tired today. I got the horses ready and it was around 10 A.M. when the hunters finally left camp. The 2 Drs. are just out for pictures. I just worked in camp today—getting wood & fooling around with the blue colt. Tim (the buckskin horse) ran away dragging a big log. It rained a little and then cleared & then around dinner time it really rained & stormed. The hunters didn't get anything but wet. We had grizzly roast & sheep ribs for dinner—also a lemon and mince pie for dessert. The bear was really good.

When we had used all the days allocated to sheep hunting, we moved the entire camp down to Solo cabin near the White River bar. The cabin was on Solo Creek, which joined the big, coffee-colored river several miles below the Russell Glacier, its source. The White River flowed southeasterly, following the Wrangell Mountain range, which rose out of the river valley to 17,000 feet, a spectacular scene. The valley, several miles across, was cut by a myriad of fast running channels of water that slowly but inexorably cut and filled, back and forth across the wide sand and gravel floor of the valley, all the time forming new islands and eating away at other islands old enough to have large patches of dark green Spruce trees growing in abundance.

We had to be extremely careful moving horses across these tributaries due to the invisible areas of quicksand below the surface that, according to Lou, had more than once engulfed a horse. Because of the silt, I could not see bottom in six inches of water and Lou never tailed horses one to another for fear of losing a whole string if one got into serious trouble. It was my job, in bringing up the rear, to try to keep each horse entering the water where the lead horse had gone in. This was next to impossible as the horses wanted to enter the water slightly downstream from where the horse ahead had entered, probably because those already in the water were slowly forced downstream by the heavy, fast running water, and those still on the bank wanted to go straight towards the ones in the water.

We came close to losing horses several times, but in the end were able to get them out each time. Of course, I also wanted to survive the crossings, but since I was responsible for the pack string I usually was crossing at a place downstream from where Lou had ridden Bill into the water and until I could "read" the water like Lou could, I was apprehensive to say the least. The water carried so much silt and sand and ran so fast, that it was very hard to for me to stand up securely in water two feet deep. I could feel the sand and gravel moving under my feet all the time when wading in the river, and if I fell, I knew it would be hard to extricate myself. I could count on my socks and boots being filled with sand if I had to walk into the water. I was always very cautious when by myself on the river bar, as I knew it was a long, bumpy and cold float to the Arctic Ocean.

Hunter Elmer Smith's photo of me at Solo 1947

Lou Anderton at Notch Creek 1947

One day riding Tim up the bar toward Solo cabin I saw a grizzly a hundred yards ahead. Having heard that a horse could not catch a bear, I decided to see if this were true. I kicked the horse into a run and as soon as the bear heard us it took off full tilt up the flat sand bar. I smacked the horse with the ends of the lines to get more speed out of him and we were in a flat out run but could not gain on the bear. I thought it might slow down to cross when it came to the first tributary of the river and I could get really close, but no, he hit the water in a full run and the spray went high up in the air in a most spectacular way. I was not about to do the same with Tim and I hauled him up at the edge of the stream to watch the bear continuing to run up the bar widening the distance between us until out of sight.

The area we were now hunting was habitat for grizzly bear, caribou, and moose, with a few wolves and wolverines thrown in, but the trophy everyone was interested in was the grizzly. The bears in this area grew to a fairly large size when mature, with the largest hides measuring up to 8 feet 6 inches. They ranged in color from the typical dark brown, to blond, almost yellow. The hunting was done with horses over the broad river bar which the bears roamed, using binoculars to search the open hills above the river on the north side, or actually hunting alongside the Russell Glacier moraine from beneath which the tumbling waters roared that formed the headwaters of the White River.

I was also about to have my first experience of adults dealing with difficult problems when the hunting resumed on the White River. We'd already had one 'incident' when Vern Smith killed a sheep for camp meat. A few days after setting up camp at Solo cabin, the two doctors were out hunting and came on a good sized bear. Since Vern had already killed a large grizzly on a prior hunt, it was to be Mel's shot on the first bear, with Vern backing him up in case he missed. Evidently Mel was slow to get arranged into a position he was comfortable with, while Vern urged him several times to shoot. As Mel took deliberate aim and slowly tightened his finger on the trigger, there was a shot and the bear was knocked down. Vern, unable to wait, had killed the bear which was to be Mel's. When the two doctors came back to camp that evening no one was talking. Mel was furious as well as being disappointed, since collecting a grizzly was the main reason he had come to Alaska to hunt.

Things went from bad to worse a few days later when Harry Boyden allowed Vern to take a caribou when he had already killed one. This was a direct violation of the game laws and all the guides were in an uproar, some going along with it and others, like Lou, not happy, but also not quite sure what to do about it. There was some ugly talk with threats back and forth and Lou had been warned by Tom, who was much younger and bigger, he would be beaten up if he said anything more. I was standing nearby when this threat was made, and I saw the look of impotence in Lou's eyes and his embarrassment that it happened in front of me. I hated Tom for this. The furor finally died down in camp, but was not forgotten by anyone. Later that Fall, several months after the hunt was over, I was told the Fish and Game Department confiscated Harry Boyden's license, the first one assigned when guides became required to have licenses, a license he must have carried for many, many years. I came to believe, from some things said, and done, that Harry had purposely tried to cause trouble for Lou, who was becoming a competitor with his expanded pack string and it backfired on Harry.

Near the end of the hunt, Lou and I had to go back to Rock Lake and set up the final camp where the planes would come to lift the hunters out. That evening the two of us were alone, sitting around the campfire frying caribou steaks, and we commented to each other how pleasant it was to be out of the camp with all its dissention and bad feelings, to be there with our work done and just enjoying the night and each other's company. I don't think I realized how much tension there had been in me until we had this one evening to ourselves. And the memory of that perfect night under the stars sitting around our fire in that huge country has been with me ever since. It is the image I see when I think back on those last wonderful days when my boyhood was coming to an end.

After the planes had carried away all the hunters and guides then going back to civilization, Lou and I and Don Spaulding a guide, and his wife, Miriam, who had been the cook for the other hunting party Harold Curtis headed, set about breaking down the camp and arranging packs for the two day trip back to Chisana, about forty miles away. We had 23 horses of which about 10 had riding saddles and the rest we packed with all the camping paraphernalia. The first day we traveled from Rock Lake back down to the White River and followed the river bar up river to Solo cabin. The next day, the trail to Chisana took us from the White River up Solo Creek into the higher country to the north, through a low pass and down Trail Creek in the watershed of the Chisana River. As the land rose we came out of the timber and into the open clump grass and low brush country everyone called the "flats".

On that last day going towards Chisana, we came across five different grizzlies. Most of them took off but one of them, on hearing the bells worn by a few of the mares, stood up on his hind legs watching us approach and then dropped down and nonchalantly crossed the small creek to the other side and walked along with the packtrain for more than a quarter mile, completely unconcerned with us. This was unusual behavior for a grizzly, noted for their shyness, but it gave me a wonderful chance to observe a bear as he moved along sniffing things and turning over rocks. After fifteen minutes he must have received a whiff of our smell, because he abruptly changed course and moved speedily away.

When we got to Chisana I spent several days working with the camp gear, storing it away in Lou's warehouse, pulling the shoes off the horses for winter, and cutting firewood. When all was done, Lou and I moved the horses across the Chisana River and eight miles up to the Chisana Glacier where we turned them loose to graze the wild peavine growing in many places on the river bar. It was a highly nutritious food source and they stayed out all winter, growing hair like a moose to enable them to survive the —60° weather that occasionally descended into the interior valleys north of the Wrangell Mountains. I said goodbye to Tim as I took off his bridle, and patted his neck. He turned away, and then took off on a run after the other horses like a kid just out of school for the summer, and Lou and I turned for the hike back to town.

While waiting for the plane to come in to pick up me and Don and Miriam Spaulding, my thoughts began to consider what going off to university would be like. I had some apprehensions, but generally felt I could handle whatever lay ahead of me. In the few days I would be at home before leaving for Stanford, I had to pack my stuff, buy a car to drive to school and I also intended to take in a good dose of Mother's cooking. I hoped maybe I could talk Mom into a leg of lamb, my all-time favorite food, especially when supported by her famous chocolate cake.

When the plane landed, we loaded our things and I then had to face Lou to say goodbye. We had become fast friends and leaving him was hard, and made harder by the obvious emotion we both felt. But I shook his hand, said I hoped to see him next summer and turned away to climb aboard the plane. I kept watching out the side window while the cluster of cabins in Chisana, a tiny spot in that great wilderness, receded into the distance. As we climbed out towards the mountain pass a myriad of memories of this first Alaskan experience cascaded through my mind. The boat trip to Alaska, our long ride into Chisana, packing for the Geodetic Survey, the hunting trip and all the people I had met, especially Lou, were memories now cached away safely in my mind's library, and then I turned my eyes away from Chisana towards the mountain tops ahead to face my onrushing future.

Transition Years

Wherein our hero tries mightily to take control of his life, is off to university, fearfully inches toward manhood, fishes in Arizona and hitchhikes home

As I look back from 59 years later, it strikes me that I was now entering a period when it was up to me to write the Story Of My Life the way I wanted it to be. Until this time my actions had been limited while undergoing parental preparation and control based on my age, experience and knowledge. I felt ready for this transition to self-rule primarily because of what I considered my unique experiences since 1943 when I started working for other folks. Looking back from today, I'm certain my parents were not as sanguine as I concerning my readiness to step out on my own and of course they were closer to the reality of my life than I was.

In the two weeks I had upon returning to Seattle before my college experience began, I had much to accomplish in preparation. First and foremost, I was intent on having a car at Stanford and set about looking for one immediately. I had come home with about $700 dollars in summer wages, more than I had ever made in a summer of work and I decided to spend half of that on a car and take the balance with me to school.

After searching around for a few days at the used car lots, I came across a beautifully redone 1929 Ford Model A convertible with a rumble seat. It had just been painted bright buttercup yellow, had red leather seats and a black soft top. I thought it was amazing and just what I wanted. I could visualize myself driving along in the California sun with the top down and a pretty girl sitting next to me. It was too perfect to resist and I bought it for $325 dollars. It also came complete with a crank in case the starter didn't work.

Over the next week, between dates with Karen whom I had not seen all summer, I gathered together my clothes, typewriter, toothbrush and razor and other items I could take in the car and packed up everything else to be shipped. I prepared to take leave of my parents, my brother Jack, who had one more year of high school before he would join me at Stanford, and Jan who had transferred to the U of W and my family living situation for the past 17 years. I felt ready for this new adventure, but realized that the comfort and security I enjoyed in my parent's home would be forever changed when I left for school in California.

The drive to Stanford was interesting in the Model A. It seemed to run fine, but in the nighttime, with a steady foot on the accelerator, I could see, through the cracks in the floorboards, the engine block glowing orangey red along the side with the heat being generated. I hoped it would not melt somewhere south of Klamath Falls and send a tie-rod flying out the side into the night sky. However, everything held together and about 20 hours later, in mid-september California sunshine, I drove up the palm lined boulevard onto the beautiful Stanford campus to Encina Hall where all freshman men were required to live.

I found I was assigned a room on the third floor and that I would have two roommates. When I opened the door I found that the other two boys had already claimed their beds, which made my choice very easy and I began to bring up my stuff and get everything put away into the closet and drawers allotted to me. The shipped boxes had arrived so I had blankets and the small desk soon had my Royal, non-electric typewriter sitting ready for use.

In the midst of my getting things organized, my two roommates walked in. I introduced myself to them and we talked for a few minutes sharing our basic backgrounds. It turned out that I had lucked in with two good guys to room with, and in the case of one, we have remained close ever since. One of them was Carl Abercrombie, from Modesto, whose father was working for a bank in some undisclosed capacity. Carl was a bit shorter than I, but broader, with straight blond hair and an easy smile. He turned out to be a diligent student who worked hard at his studies and seemed very comfortable doing his own thing in his own way, meaning that I rarely saw him around on campus. But he was easy to live with as a roommate and we shared some good times together.

My other roommate was Frank X. Gordon from Kingman, Arizona. Frank's father was a well known lawyer in Kingman, but I did not suspect then, watching him as a freshman, that Frank was headed in the same direction. Frank was taller than I at around 6' 2", with a permanently tan complexion and seemed full of life, exuberance and laughter. We soon formed a friendship that has continued all our lives. One of Frank's other great qualities was, according to my understanding, his experience with girls. A perception he did not work too hard to dispel. In this area he made me feel like a complete failure, an inept, immature, mere boy, and I soon encouraged him to be my mentor in this momentously important facet of my transition to manhood. Progress in this transition was to be measured by my skill in applying his never-fail techniques to this new chapter in my life.

A freshman at Stanford, 1948

I also had other close friends from Seattle and Chicago who were entering freshmen. Warren Haight, Bartow Fite, Jane Moffitt and Stewart Rogers had been my friends since grade school, and Charlie Donahoe, a graduate of Seattle Prep was enrolled, as was Phil Neilsen, from New Trier. Stewart had been President of the Senior class at Garfield, and Phil, Student Body President at New Trier. I was certainly not without friends and began adding new ones as well. What little homesickness I felt was mostly being away from Karen and missing Mother's cooking. I was too busy with classes and having fun using my new freedom to find excitement in the area around Stanford, to spend much time thinking about home.

Like all entering freshmen I was required to take three courses for all three quarters. These were Biology, History of Western Civilization, and English, and I could also pick an elective course that interested me. I chose one quarter each of introductory psychology, anthropology and philosophy in my first year. I confess that in the case of the English requirement, I had to take a quarter of "bonehead" English since I did not pass the English entrance exam. Other than this ignominy and my hatred of grammar throughout my prior education, which I suppose, was the main reason I ended up in the 'bonehead' class, I thoroughly enjoyed the other courses that I was taking.

Stanford graded on a curve, so I was competing against a bunch of smart students to land an A or a B. The other structure that I found important was the honor system that required the professor to leave the room during an exam. Putting the students in a non-policed atmosphere seemed to bring out the best in everyone and I never heard of a case of cheating while at the school.

The History Of Western Civilization course was taught mostly by Teaching Assistant graduate students. We used a textbook written by an historian named Burns, a book on the Catholic banned reading list which only intensified our interest in finding out what things the Church did not want people, especially those with young formative minds, to know. I think this was rather difficult for the Catholic students, who had never heard other than Church dogma, but then it was supposed to be grow-up time when the Truth, as it was understood, was the prime objective in teaching. A far cry from many of the objectives of today's professors. The tests for this course were all 'blue book' type, expecting lengthy analysis of the various parts of the course.

As for sports, Frank was a swimmer, and Carl and I were interested in boxing at the intramural level. We were all devoted to bending our elbows as we used to describe drinking and Stanford provided some great watering holes. My favorite was Rossotti's Beer Garden, a couple of miles up the road into the hills behind the campus. Another was Mora's in Palo Alto, where we liked to drink tequila and sometimes sing and where we would get ample warning if the inspectors guarding against underage drinking were apt to come in. The risk only added to my liking for Mora's.

In order to help defray expenses I managed to get a job hashing in the main dining room on campus. This was the place where faculty, staff, parental visitors and dignitaries ate while on campus. My job was to be a waiter, taking and filling orders and clearing tables. I was very nervous about mixing up orders or spilling something onto a patron, but soon got into the swing of things. This job allowed me to cover all the cost of my food while at Stanford. Of course the beer and tequila were on me. One day while serving lunch, Herbert Hoover came in to eat lunch and for the time he was seated, his presence intensified my commitment to excellent service.

But it was not all work without any fun and after working in the dining hall for some time, things began to loosen up, especially on the dinner shift after a few afternoon hours at Rossotti's when some of us returned to work a little tipsy. We waiters, as we got to know each other, began to occasionally play tricks on one another. One of the favorite ones was to lock the swinging door from the kitchen, so that a waiter carrying a huge tray of dishes, assuming the door would open easily, would smash into it in full stride and the tray of plates and cutlery would come crashing to the floor. This would infuriate the nice lady who was supervising the student staff, but to my knowledge no one was ever fired for such antics.

It is difficult to recall all of the conflicted feelings I had about my life at this time although I know it was a mixed bag of thoughts and attitudes. On one level I was confident in my ability to handle the educational curriculum at Stanford, despite the fact that during the last year and a half at Garfield, where I sustained a major lapse in motivation to excel academically, my grade point fell to 2.5. My confidence came from the experience in my early years at Country Day School in Milwaukee and two and a half years of high school at New Trier, the apogee of my scholastic efforts thus far.

I was proud of my work experiences on ranches, packing horses in Alaska, hunting and fishing, and how I thought this appeared to others. But behind this facade was a whole other layer of feelings of not measuring up, not being popular enough, not being mature like a man, and in a general way, a lack of being satisfied with who I was in relation to some others on campus. I wished mightily that I was a gifted athlete and could participate in college level sports which I was sure was one key to easy campus notoriety and acceptance. I suppose these are the mixed up feelings of most entering college freshmen, especially one who is seventeen and still immature in many ways. When I think back on my life as a freshman in Encina Hall during that first year at Stanford, I am mostly embarrassed at the things I did that were stupid and adolescent and probably worse, the things I did not do in staying focused on my education.

Even though most of the time I felt I was doing okay, I realize, looking back, that I did not take the opportunity to get from Stanford what was there to be taken. Lacking a vocational goal, I did not make the kind of commitment to learning that could have served me well in future years. However, I was terribly interested in new ideas, politics, philosophy, literature and history but without the least concept of what I might do with this knowledge in a vocational sense, especially since I knew I did not want to be a teacher. I simply did not know what I wanted to do in life and still carried my earlier dreams of not settling down in a conventional sense, but wanting instead, to fill my life with adventures, travel and freedom. I am certain had I come to life a generation later I would have been totally at home spending some years as a hippy. But it was hard to break far outside the 'norm' when raised by parents who themselves were raised by Victorians and I didn't have enough strength or independent resolve to revolt against my upbringing, which, when I was honest with myself, I felt had generally been on the right track.

My first quarter at Stanford was full with classes, working in the dining room and football games. The Stanford "Indians", political correctness having not yet forced the school to change their mascot, lost every game. But I met a few girls for dates, took a few too many afternoons at Rosotti's and studied in the library or in my room in Encina Hall. Occasionally we drove my Model A up to San Francisco, but it was a high risk trip on the steeper hills like Lombardy Street, brake pedal to the floorboards, handbrake pulled tight and dragging our feet to help slow down and get the car stopped.

Bartow arranged a date with some girl from Mills College in Berkeley, and when I found out that Susie Pratt was at Mills, I asked her out and we double dated, ending up at a fraternity house party on the Cal campus. I had not seen Susie since I was a sophomore in high school, but I had never quite got rid of my emotional feelings for her. I hoped that this would be an opportunity to reestablish the relationship, but I was tense at the thought of seeing her again. When we picked the girls up, I immediately felt in my heart, the heavy burden of her beautiful eyes, and was totally tongue-tied. The date turned out to be a disaster practically from the get-go.

I was so up-tight with her, so mixed up in my head, that I lacked the ability to just accept her as a friend. In this confused mental state I was still acting like a 14 year old and had not even the courage to hold hands. When we went inside to the party I felt completely left out as she seemed to enjoy herself in the fun and laughter going on, while I was just eaten up with jealousy at every look she took in from other boys there. That evening ended my four year unrequited addiction to Susie and turned out to be the last time I ever saw her. I found that being forced to painfully confront my total lack of maturity when with her that night worked like aversion therapy and made it possible to put her out of my mind completely. I did not need a repeat test to know I was doomed with Susie until I grew up and by then she would be long gone in another direction.

Encina Hall freshmen were kept in line by Monitors who were upper classmen living in the hall and working to reduce their room costs. They were charged with making sure the freshmen followed the rules, of which there were quite a few. Our room had several windows that opened into a three sided box formed by the building and looked down on a paved service courtyard three floors below. Most rooms had drinking water delivered in 5 gallon glass jars as Frank, Carl and I did. Every so often we would hear one of these jars exploding with an amazing sound onto the concrete below as someone tossed it from the window as a prank. After a few of these high diving bottles the word got around that if there were another one throne out, the culprits would be kicked out of school.

This challenge stimulated Carl and me to see if we could get away with it. After careful planning we arose one night around midnight, not many days after the edict had been sent around banning this particular atrocity, and sent our bottle through the open window, arcing it out into the night as far as we could toss it, to a thunderous crash on the cement below. We were back in bed before it hit. The next sound we heard, almost immediately, was the Monitors banging on each door, demanding entrance, determined to find the perpetrators. We were a bit scared but when the knock came on our door, we had on our most innocent faces as Carl let them in. When asked if we knew anything about who had done it, we answered, "How could it have been us? It was way over there under those other rooms, we've been sound asleep for hours." Frank, who refused to participate and thought we were nuts to take such a risk, just lay there pretending to still be asleep, ignoring the adolescent actions of his two roommates.

As the Christmas break came closer, I found myself thinking more about Karen and very much wanting to see her again. After listening to Frank and Carl talk, I began to feel that I was the only virgin living in Encina Hall. This feeling of so far missing an experience as profound as making love to a woman, added to my incentive to use the approaching Christmas holidays at home to try to take this required step towards manhood. I thought that were I successful in this endeavor it definitely would be the start of a new chapter in my life and I was certain I would feel a profound change in my self image. Little did I suspect just how profoundly my life story would be altered by starting down this road.

Karen and I had been going out for over a year, to a variety of functions, including movies, drive-ins, and parties at friends' houses. We also went to all-city dances, where students from quite a few high schools would gather at a large dance hall, sometimes as far out as Juanita Beach at the north end of Lake Washington. Although there were some couples who could jitterbug, Karen and I liked to dance the Avalon, a slow and sexy, cheek to cheek, body to body dance, interspersed with occasional trips to the parking lot to drink beer. It was also the custom, I guess unchanged much from each prior and succeeding generation, at least since the invention of the automobile, to end the night parked somewhere for a little necking.

A lot of the adolescent high school talk amongst the boys was concerning how far we had gotten on the previous date. Although most of us were reluctant to go into any detail concerning our physical relationships with our girlfriends, we needed to indicate some progress in the natural familiarization process with the female body which took place in the back seat classroom. For me this familiarization effort was slow going, from holding hands, to a goodnight peck, to real kissing and finally touching. The whole process, due to my lack of aggressive behavior, which in turn was due to a great fear of rejection, took all four years of high school. And now as a freshman in college, I was big-time ready to go all the way!

I was to turn 18 in mid January and like shooting my first deer at thirteen, I wanted desperately to lose my virginity as early as possible and if while still 17, all the better. In a way this major life quest was also a hunt of sorts, except that the innocent deer in my sights was Karen. I thought it was going to be a very short move to go from where Karen and I were in our relationship and familiarity to actually having sex, but in reality, this step would be a huge one for us both. I was eager and frightened and knew that any such decision was stepping into potentially very serious territory, and once done, could not be undone.

Of course, Karen knew none of what I was thinking. I had never pressed her to do anything against her will, but I was two years older than she and a college student, while she was still a junior in high school. This age spread gave me an advantage in rationalizing my point of view on what kind of relationship we were to have. My intention was to convince her that we were ready for the "'real thing" and being the eternal optimist, assure her that if we went trough with it, all would turn out just fine.

With all this in mind, I was impatient to take my final exams. As soon as they were over, I was in the car and on my way to Seattle. It was good to get back home, but I was tired from the all night drive and crashed for a few hours of sleep. When I awoke in the afternoon I called Karen and arranged to pick her up at her house near Madison Park. I knew her parents, John and Jessie, would want to see me, probably to calculate whether, now that I was a college student, their only daughter, still in high school, was safe to go out with me. She wasn't, as it turned out. I was also prepared to hear some admonitions on safe driving and be told the hour that I was to bring her home. It turned out to be 12:00 midnight, a time I strove hard to meet. They were very nice to me and I felt guilty harboring the thoughts I had for their daughter.

Karen and I had a good time picking up about where we had left off when I went down to California. We spent a lot of time together since she was on vacation also and as Christmas approached I began to press my case with her. She was a long way from feeling the way I did so I had to pull out all the pathetic male arguments to try to break her resistance. Did she "really love me?" If she did, "wasn't this the best way to show it?" "I wanted her to be my first experience." "Why wait any longer, we were in love," etc., etc. When I hinted "If not her, then maybe someone else at Stanford," knowing perfectly well there was not another girl at Stanford who was remotely interested in me, she finally said the magic word, "Yes!"

Now the fat was in the fire. It was my problem after all my talking and cajoling, to put a plan together which would allow us enough time to go somewhere and make certain all could be clouded in secrecy. I wracked my brain. Trying it in the car seemed a bit immature, a motel would probably call the cops, a hotel was out of the question, too expensive and would leave a trail. I could not think of a friend's house we could use where all of Seattle would not hear about it the next day. And I really did want it nice for Karen, where she would not be frightened or compromised in any way.

I finally devised a plan using New Year's Eve as the time. The place would be River Haven, the family cabin on the Stillaguamish, an hour and a half drive north of Seattle. I knew that Mother and Dad were invited somewhere else and they would not suspect one of their children would drive all that way and back in the same night. In order to get a little more time, I asked Karen's parents for a 1:00 o'clock curfew seeing as it was New Year's Eve and I would soon be on my way back to Stanford. They agreed to give us the extra hour. So it was set.

I began to fantasize about how it would all work out. I went over everything in my mind a hundred times. What I would say. How she would answer. How we would start. I would build a big fire for her and warm the place up. We would turn on KJR for music or put on a classical 78 rpm record. The lights would be low. It was too perfect and I was eager for the day to arrive. Then I began to think of the risks. How would I explain a driving accident far away from where our parents thought we were? What if the key didn't work to let us in after making the long trip up there? What if Karen got cold feet at the last moment and decided not to complete the mission? And even worse, MUCH worse, what if she got pregnant! It would be my duty to make sure that would not happen, since there were no easy pills or patches to use in those days. No girls in high school, or college, for that matter, were asking their parents if they could get fitted with a diaphragm so as to have safe sex with their boyfriends. Quite the contrary, in the late 40's it was socially unacceptable and almost unforgivable for an unmarried girl to become pregnant. She would automatically be knocked out of the class of "good girls," a devastating blow to her family's prestige, and at the very least would turn a happy family inside out with wrenching pain and anguish.

To buy condoms in those days, I would have to ask a clerk to get them for me as they were not on open display, but hidden away like forbidden fruit. Unlike my sense that a real man would casually and confidently walk up to a counter in any drugstore and ask for box of Trojans or Sheiks, the best known condom labels at that time, I was petrified at the very thought. What if the sales clerk turned out to be a woman, or worse, a girl my age? I scouted out several drugstores trying to determine if a man would be the clerk. It was fast turning into a horror story eating into my confidence that I was up to this task after all.

One of my biggest hangups had always been about getting into an embarrassing situation in front of other people and I was certain I would look about 12 years old to any sales clerk I asked to hand me a pack of Trojans. He might just laugh out loud, or threaten to call my parents, for all I knew. But if I were going to take this passion of mine to the ultimate act, I had to go in and say to some man or woman I did not know, "I want to buy a box of Trojans!" I could picture it perfectly, me, a kid with a beet red face, trying to act like a man. But after pacing up and down for a while outside my target drugstore, trying to build my nerve up, I finally steeled myself and went in and did it.

On New Year's Eve, I picked Karen up early, said Happy New Year to her parents and hit the highway to Arlington and River Haven. When we arrived, the cabin was pitch black and cold. I started a log fire and turned the heaters up and we sat in front of the flames immersed for a while in our own thoughts. It became obvious that this was not going to be a night of natural passion, but rather almost a hurdle to cross. It was not going to flow spontaneously from tenderness and love, because we could not get out of minds what we intended to do before we left the cabin. I'm sure for both of us we just wanted to see it through, but for me was the added concern that I desperately wanted to make it right for Karen. We began to hold hands by the fire and then kiss and the scent of her perfume, "Tabu" helped lead us on and then took us over.

Later, we changed the bed, were careful to get rid of any sign that someone had been there and headed back to town. We did not talk much on the way back. Again both of us were sunk in our own thoughts, but her head was on my shoulder and my arm was around her as we drove through the night. My thoughts were very mixed. I was elated to have finally had this experience, but my euphoria was dampened by a feeling I had pushed Karen into something she probably would have been happy to have come to her later in life. And of course, there were several other little problems, like how to get rid of the sheets, and worse, the famous Trojan had failed and we would spend the next two weeks worried sick about pregnancy. I was beginning to get a glimmer that sometimes the cost could be very high for taking certain actions, especially those of a self-serving nature.

I was also a bit troubled over my feelings for Karen. I enjoyed spending time with her, as it was easy for me to feel somewhat in charge of what we did. But I could not say that I really loved her in any mature way. I did think I loved being with her, but she was not the person I ever seriously thought I would marry. This made me feel guilty on one level, but pleased on another. She said she loved me, but again I think in a very immature way and considering her age, how could it have been otherwise? It may have been that the thought of marrying me appealed to her, since I might have looked like passable husband material coming from a well known family in Seattle, this in the days when most married women did not have careers and their lives and social position were determined by the status of the man they married. One thing I knew for sure: I was not thinking of marriage as anything but a very distant possibility to an as yet unknown person.

I continued my vacation with no thought to attempt a repeat performance of our big night. We still faced the HUGE worry as to whether Karen had become pregnant and this put a major damper on everything we were doing. One afternoon, before I left to return to school, she called to say that we had escaped this particular fate. This had been a major weight on my shoulders and to have it lifted by just the two words, "I'm OK," brought the usual sunshine back into my life.

I returned to Stanford, feeling both triumphant and chastened. I had definitely dodged a bullet, but I had finally made it with a girl. It had seemed like such an important thing to do, but now done, quickly faded from the list of important things in my life and I mentally moved on to concentrate on my studies. I had passed bonehead English, which allowed me to take a course in literature, with an emphasis on poetry, a subject I really enjoyed. The other school work was going well and I settled into the routine of classes, working, studying, with a few pleasant afternoons at Rossotti's in the fast approaching Spring weather thrown in.

I invited Frank to come to Seattle with me to spend spring vacation in the Northwest, an area he had never visited and much different from where he was raised. Frank had a car so we drove it north when school was out, much easier than making the trip again in the Model A. I fixed him up with a friend of Karen's and we double dated most of the time. Once we four went up to River Haven for the evening, but with no intent to duplicate my last visit there. Frank charmed my parents with his personality and very good manners and they were happy I had been dealt such an upstanding young man for a roommate. I allowed this perception to remain undisturbed.

When we returned to the campus, we dug back into our education. During this spring quarter, I was set up for a blind date with a girl from one of the woman's dorms. My date was Diana Gatch from Milford, Ohio, near Cincinnati. We went to the Sigma Chi Sweetheart dance in San Francisco, riding up on a large bus where we were served cocktails to get everyone in the right mood. Before the evening was over, I knew that I had found a girl I would be proud to "take home to mother". She was intelligent, tall and pretty, played the piano, knew her own mind and came from a family similar to my own. She laughed a lot during that evening and I was, for almost the first time in my life, totally comfortable being with a girl and just having a good time in her company.

Of course I regaled her with all my exploits of ranches and Alaska and I supposed I was the first boy she ever met who had actually done much outside a country club. We got on famously and I became very attached to her. I knew instinctively that this would be the type of woman I would want to marry. We went out quite often during the last quarter and I knew our feeling for one another were becoming stronger. As for sex, she was very much in control, and it would be fair to describe our relationship, at least in my mind, as almost platonic. She was so innocent she did not really know how to kiss and I set about becoming her mentor in that department. But that was it and even though I was always in there pitching, I admired her for her ability to turn me away without damaging my fragile male self image and always being in control of herself. This actually made my time with her less stressful. Of course, she was interested in just what experience with girls I had had and I only told her "more than I'm having with you," and we could both laugh about that.

I had decided to sell my Model A, as it was getting a major growl in the transmission and gearbox. After consulting with Frank on how best to deal with the noise coming from the gears, he advised putting sawdust into the gearbox and very heavy gear oil in the transmission. We spent one afternoon teaspooning sawdust in, changing the oil, and polishing the car so it looked perfect. I put an ad in the Palo Alto paper and immediately had a call from a man who wanted to buy it for his son who was going to school in Reno. I was elated as I knew a typical adult would know little about Model A's and I was starting to count my money.

But when he arrived to inspect the car he came with his son and three of the son's friends who were determined that he would not get taken in by a shyster like me. They went all over that car, including looking at the oil in the gearbox, while I was getting more nervous with each passing minute. I knew they would find me out and I was preparing my defense for what was defenseless. Finally they all piled into the car and drove it around to hear how it sounded and at the end of this two-hour inspection pronounced it OK and bought it for $300. I was back in the money again and planned to defer buying another car until my return from Alaska in the fall.

As the quarter came to a close, I had already signed on with Lou Anderton to go back to Alaska around the end of June. As we had done before, we were to work with the mapping surveyors for a month and then take another hunting party to the White River. I would again be the wrangler, packer and camp helper. But first I was going to visit Frank and his family in Kingman.

Frank Gordon's parents had visited the campus in their new 1949 Cadillac sedan, a car both Frank and I were much impressed with. This was one of the first Cadillacs with the rear fender extended back and up to house the tail lights. It was a design that over the next ten or twelve years produced an array of grotesque fender patterns looking more like weapons than practical wheel coverings. Frank and I were allowed to take this car across Arizona on highway 66 to Holbrook, where we were going to meet Dick Whitlow, an older friend from Kingman, who was a Lieutenant in the Arizona State Patrol.

Frank and I were both interested with speed and how to drive. He had more experience than I on how to handle a car in extreme conditions like skidding in a turn and how and when to accelerate to reduce centrifugal forces. Part of our plan was to ask Dick to show us how to handle this new toy and talk in general about cars.

We drove across Northern Arizona in the late spring sunshine of 1948, two boyhood friends who thought that life could not be better, driving their parent's almost new Cadillac and listening on the radio to "Get Your Kicks On Route 66," a song popular at that time. Frank kept the car at a high speed and all eyes were checking the rear view mirrors to avoid a speeding ticket, which Frank's father would no doubt be informed of as the top lawyer in Kingman. We were not alone in driving fast and every now and then someone rolling along in a Lincoln Continental would sail past us even though we were doing 80 mph. But we were not going to be suckered into a race and maybe deliver the car back to Frank's parents with a blown engine.

When we arrived at Dick's house, we settled in and after some small talk induced him to drive us, in Frank's father's car, to see how fast the car could go. We drove out of town in the early evening and then on a long straight stretch of highway he induced 105 mph out of the car. That was even faster than I had gone with Dad when I was 10 and he went 97 mph in the old Buick convertible, as I egged him on to go even faster yet.

The next day we were allowed to go with Dick in his 1948 Ford police special patrol car as he worked along the main state roads in and around Holbrook. The car could do 115 mph, he told us, and the only American car he knew that could beat it was the Lincoln. In the early afternoon as we were heading out of town, he took a call on the radio about a car recently stolen by two men in Gallup, New Mexico and believed to be heading west toward Holbrook. Dick took the description of the car and five minutes later at a cross street, a car turned left in front of us, heading the way we had just come. Dick recognized it as the stolen car. Things instantly changed to all business as he did a U-turn, hit the siren and lights and pulled the stolen car over to a stop. As he got out he unsnapped his holster and loosened his revolver and said to us, "Frank, you guys stay right where you are and don't get out!"

He stood partially behind his door and called to the two in the car to "Get out, and keep your hands in the air!" It was just like the movies and Frank and I were entranced with the whole thing. The doors to the other car opened, and one by one, two 16 year-old kids stepped out, turned and put their hands on the top of the car. What a disappointment! No gunfight. No action, other than two kids wishing to hell they had not done such a stupid thing as to cross a state line in a stolen car, a federal offence. After they were carted off, we had a long talk with Dick about what he saw every day with kids getting into trouble, running away, generally screwing up and getting involved with legal agencies at all levels. It was obvious to us that our lives were very different from that and we realized how fortunate we were to come from caring and loving parents.

I thought I was a pretty good fisherman and having talked some with Frank about fishing it followed naturally that when we got back to Kingman he organized an overnight trip to Lake Mead with an older man named "Sidewinder" Ray Thomas. We would be Bass fishing up Virgin Canyon, casting plugs from a boat. We drove to the Lake in the afternoon and settled into a motel. Ray said he was leaving to meet someone and Frank confided in me that he had gone to meet a woman for some sort of sexual encounter. I was amazed, since to me he looked like he was well over the hill in that department. That got our teenage libidos driving the conversation until we fell asleep.

We did not see Ray until we woke up in the morning to a bright sunny day and the prospect of fishing took over. We packed a lunch in the boat and set out for the 25 mile trip from Temple Bar to the fishing site. Later in the day and after catching a few fish, Ray was sitting, maybe dreaming about his past evening and Frank and I were standing and casting. I'm not sure to this day how it happened, but on a particularly long cast I put everything I had into whipping the rod around and instantly heard a "splat" and simultaneously, a gasp. The plug had gone, not to the lilypad I was aiming for, but into Frank's back! On close inspection I saw I had driven the hook in past the barb. I was totally aghast at such a mistake and knew that it hurt like hell. We had no first aid items but we did have a bottle of whiskey. So as they do in the movies, we made Frank drink half a cup and then Ray started to cut out the hook with a jack knife. Frank never peeped during the whole thing and soon the hook was out, the blood stanched, bourbon poured over the wound as our best antiseptic and we went back to fishing.

I decided to add another adventure to this trip by hitchhiking home rather than taking a bus. I had been warned how hard it was to get rides in the desert country after the war, as we often read about hitchhikers killing the benefactor that picked them up, leaving the corpse lying like a road kill, which I guess was an apt description. I was determined to do this thinking it would be sort of exciting. As an assist, and to dispel any fear that a driver might think I was a homicidal killer, I made a sign that said "SEATTLE FOR A WEDDING" as my sister Jan was being married the next week to Phil Evans at our home in Medina. I set out in the late afternoon to stand at a gas station on Highway 66, my small suitcase at my feet, holding the sign, my thumb stuck out. I was still there as it turned dark and was beginning to feel like maybe it was not such a good idea after all. I feared I might be there in the morning when Frank's father drove by to work, which would be very embarrassing.

Finally around 8 P.M. an older couple came in for gas and the driver came over to talk to me. After he heard what I was trying to do, he said "My wife and I are going to rest a while in the motel and if you are here when we start again we can take you with us to Bakersfield." I thanked him, but said I would probably have a ride by then. At 1 A.M. I was still there when they drove over to me and said I could come with them. In fact, the man asked if I would be willing to drive.

I quickly agreed and we set off in the dead of night across the desert towards California.

When Frank and I had driven to Kingman from Stanford, he had shown me a shortcut through the mountains past Needles that cut many miles from the trip. I told the man and woman who had befriended me that I knew a shortcut that would cut a half hour or more off the trip. This must have given them pause, but they agreed that we should do it. When we came to the place where I thought the cutoff had been, I turned and started across the deserted desert, accompanied by only the moon and stars. I have a congenital defect towards wanting to get somewhere as fast as I can so was driving pretty fast. Occasionally the man would ask me to slow down, but slowly, unconsciously, as I concentrated on the road ahead, my foot would press down the accelerator and soon we would be again going at a speed that was making them uncomfortable.

I was not seeing any sign that I remembered and with the fast driving I could see the water temperature creeping up, and the gas gauge dropping perilously low. By this time I was sure the old couple believed they were in the hands of a maniac who was determined to do them in somewhere along the road. I was fast getting into a panic myself, worrying that I might actually be on a road that would come to an end somewhere out in the vast night desert. Soon I began to smell oil from the overheating engine and knew I was in big trouble if we did not find some sign of life soon. There must be a god up there that has a particular affinity for looking after foolish young men, for in several more miles we came over a rise and ahead on the left side was a service station, all lights out.

I turned in and went up to the door and rang a buzzer. Soon a man emerged in a sweater over his nightshirt, knowing without asking that we had a problem. He checked the oil as we gassed up and found it was down a full 2 quarts, barely touching the dipstick. I had been lucky that the engine was not ruined. I offered to pay the gas and oil bill, which the man allowed me to do, got some directions from the attendant and started out again on the downhill side of the mountains into California. When we arrived in downtown Bakersfield in the morning, I stopped and got out at an intersection near Highway 99, thanked the couple profusely and watched them drive off, no doubt promising themselves they would never, ever, pick up another hitchiker and how lucky they were to have survived me.

Using my "Seattle for wedding" sign, I picked up several long rides, ending in Cottage Grove, Oregon, in the late afternoon. I was let out near a motel where I decided to spend the night having been without sleep for 36 hours. In the morning I was standing with my thumb out at a gas station for an hour or so when I saw a Model A with a young couple with several kids go by and I could see them looking me over. They kept going which was fine with me because I didn't see how I could possibly fit, with all their kids and boxes of stuff, in their old jalopy.

A few minutes later a man in a new Chrysler stopped at the gas station where I was hitchhiking and as his car was being filled, he walked over to talk to me. This was looking very good to me. He wanted to know my name, see my identification, asked if I was in school, etc., etc., trying to decide if I was safe to take along as he was also going to Seattle. It turned out he knew my family and was in the process of inviting me to go with him when the same old Model A with the family drove up. They had thought it over as they drove along and feeling I was in need of help, were willing to stuff one more person into their car even if it made things more uncomfortable for themselves. I was so moved by this generous gift from an obviously poor family offering to help me, that I told the man with the fancy new Chrysler, "Thanks, but I guess I've got a ride now," and walked over to wedge myself into the Model A.

Much as I wanted to be riding in that Chrysler, I just couldn't, in effect, say to these people, "His car is better than yours, so I'll go in it." They were not asking me my life history, just offering a ride to someone they thought worse off than themselves. A few miles up the highway I saw the Chrysler cruise on by us and wished I was going up the road in style and not in a rig that could only go about 35 mph and looked like it had come straight from the Oklahoma dust bowl.

However, these young parents were very nice, just poor. They were moving from California to look for work in the Northwest and had all their worldly possessions tied on, along with their three kids, one of which was a little baby that the mother kept nestled in her lap. I paid for their gas when they stopped, bought ice cream cones for all and tried to be patient as the hours went by, but could not help thinking at one point, that the Chrysler was already pulling into Seattle and we were still several hours away. When we finally got into Seattle they let me out and after thanking them for picking me up, I walked over to Frederick and Nelson and up to Dad's office, looking a little the worse for wear from the trip.

My sister Jan's wedding to Philip Evans, at the end of June, was a big family event in the garden at the Medina home, after which the newlyweds were off to Europe for two years. Phil was to work for the U.S. Government on World Trade Shows in France and Turkey and was to be a special correspondent for the Seattle Times, writing a weekly column.

Jack and I with Georgann

After the wedding I had two weeks to prepare for my return to Alaska and I
intended to use my spare time doing things with Karen and my friends who were
still around. Karen and I were becoming closer but I still was not pushing things

too far in our love play. I was not at all certain how I felt about her and whether or not we could have a real future. I had met Diana, a girl that I actually felt offered more potential as a serious life partner than Karen, but she was a long ways away and Karen was available. I was not at all ready to give up my ideas of living an adventuresome life after graduation three years away, and I did not want to do anything to make Karen think I was seriously looking ahead to marriage and a nine-to-five job. At that time, no girl was going to keep me from going off to Alaska and I set about readying for my second summer working with the horses and Lou Anderton.

Alaska 1948

*Wherein our hero returns to the far north, learns much
of horses and wild animals, and dreams of mushing dogs
under the Northern Lights*

Journal # 1—Alaska 1948—July 14th

*I've finally become a little excited about my coming trip to the Northland now that
I am to leave today; I was beginning to wonder if the thrill of last year's trip had worn
off for good, but now I am very impatient to be off on another adventure.*

*I finished packing and after making a few calls and saying goodbye to Fred (Ish-
ibashi, our gardener from Hiroshima), mother and I left for the plane.*

Dad loaned me a pair of binoculars and Mother let me take her rifle again,
which because of its smaller size, fitted well into a scabbard hung from the saddle.
I also had a new green plaid heavy wool shirt and red plaid "Mackinaw" button
up jacket, new boots and several pair of new jeans. I packed most everything into
a duffel bag and also had a knapsack, borrowed from Dad, to carry my toilet kit,
camera and film. When the day came to leave, Mother drove me to the airport
where I gave her a hug and heard her say, for the fortieth time, "Please be careful
and don't take any foolish chances." She was my special worry wort, for which I
dearly loved her.

I took off in a DC-3 from Boeing Field at 12:10 p.m. and after stops at
Annette Island and Cordova to let off fishermen and cannery workers, we landed
in Anchorage at 7:30 p.m. and I went to Harold Curtis' home, the guide who
had booked the hunters and also knew Mother and Dad from their hunt two
years earlier. I was to leave the next day for Chitina, located at the confluence of
the Copper and Chitina rivers on the Southwest side of the Wrangell Mountains.
From there a bush pilot was to fly me over the mountains into Chisana where my
job with Lou Anderton, my boss from the prior year, was to begin. It was about
40 miles from Chisana to where we would meet the hunters flying into Ptarmi-

gan Lake on August 15th. We had just a month to get everything ready for the hunt.

Journal #1—Alaska 1948—July 15th

Harold and I got up around 7 a.m. and had a big breakfast. Today I am to take the second lap of my trip to the hinterland, that being the 240 mi. Drive to Chitina where I will take a plane the next day to Chisana.

Bill Curin picked me up at 8:30 a.m. and we started immediately. The weather was still fine and the drive down the Matanuska Valley was very, very beautiful. The country is all very rugged—glaciers, rock, snowfields, swift dirty rivers and evergreens all blended to make it very picturesque—I like it. While going by Sheep Mt. we saw a sheep very far down the mountain (400–500 yds. from us), and on the cut-off to Chitina we saw a 2 yr. old bull moose which I took a picture of. We got to Chitina late in the afternoon.

I bunked in the old Commercial Hotel run now by the Steelman's (the local pilot and his wife). I met some very interesting people there, one especially I remember.

His name was Dr. Gillespie, an old timer from the boom days in McCarthy. He told us some very interesting stories about frontier days in Alaska.

The story of his operation on the eye of one of his cows, in which they killed the cow by giving her too much chloroform, and then he (knowing she was dead) made his friends give it artificial respiration for 1 1/2 hr. 18/min. and how it came out in the paper as being a successful operation but the cow had died, was very entertaining.

This Dr. was also the coroner, & he owned the jail & handled all funerals. His stories of burying the Swedes backwards & all their drunken hilarity at the funerals were interesting. He told us about Joe Murry who was a brilliant lawyer except he drank too much, and how if he gave Joe 6 drinks before a funeral he would be sure of a good funeral speech.

He told how the Marshall (in McCarthy during prohibition) ran the prohibition officer out of the bar & also how he took a couple of quarts of moonshine to some of the Swedes in his jail as a present & how they tore the place apart.

I hit the sack about 12:30 a.m. that night very tired but also satisfied knowing I had learned a little more of the old lore of this cold North country. More adventure looked forward to tomorrow.

One of the most fascinating aspects of Alaska in those days was the fact that many of the old timers that had gone there after the Klondike gold rush in 1898, or in the decade that followed, were still alive and one could find them living in most of the small towns and hamlets that dotted the interior. These were the interesting, hardy ones, the others having already moved into old folks retirement homes situated near the cities. I never tired of the stories these old men could tell about early Alaska.

Journal #1—Alaska 1948—July 16th

Out of bed at 8:30 a.m. and had a good breakfast. Today is the day 'Pappy' Steelman, a bush pilot, is to fly me into Chisana. We loaded my duffel and some grub for Chisana and took off around noon. The day was wonderful, bright sun and some billowing cumulus clouds.

The plane was a large, single engined, high wing, silver Norseman on wheels. As we had high mountains to pass over we steadily climbed for 45 min. Our top altitude was 11,700 ft. And we made 100 mph on the up grade.

I have never flown over such beautiful country. One mountain range after another as far as the eye could see. We flew down the side of the 16,000 ft. Wrangell Mts. (on our left), to the right one could see Mt. Logan that was difficult to climb some yrs. ago (19,500'). We flew to the left of McCarthy and Kennicott mines and I could trace with my eye the trail used by the dog mushers and packers in the gold rush days. This went from McCarthy through Skolai Pass and over the Russell Glacier to the White River, up past Solo cabin (on Solo creek), & down Trail Creek to Chisana. We passed over Kennicott Glacier and I could see the backside of Mt. Bona and Mt. Natazat by the White River. We came through the pass over Chisana Glacier at 11,500 ft. And immediately went into a shallow dive in which our air speed went to 160 mph, and our altitude dropped to 3000 ft. In a few minutes. I saw the horses on the river bar as we came over and then saw Chisana directly ahead. We landed 55 min. out of Chitina.

That short flight made it a red-letter day for me. I know what Col. Scott meant now, when he wrote his description of flying along the Himalayas. Everything is so vast & limitless; it's quite aweing. I sort of felt that it was all mine and I held my pilot as an intruder. It was one time I felt I wanted to be alone in my airplane. It was truly an experience I'll never forget.

We spent the next three weeks building corrals, shoeing horses and getting all the equipment ready. This work was made harder and a lot of time was wasted, since we had no fenced pasture we could hold horses in. We sometimes kept one or two horses in the corral after we rebuilt it, but had to turn the others out and they always headed for the Chisana River bars where there was good grazing on peavine. Bringing in horses for work or for shoeing meant a long hike or ride to the river bar to catch them.

Journal #1—Alaska 1948—July 17th—Saturday

Harry woke Lou and I (hard to believe I passed 'bonehead English) around 6:30 A:M: and we ate the usual breakfast of pancakes, bacon & eggs & coffee & fruit. Today Lou & I had to go over to the Chisana River to get the 6 horses left over there.

I took Lou's gun & we both took bridles. We walked without speaking through the woods for about 4 mi. in Indian fashion (single file). We have no (wading) boots so we wade all the streams we come to with no hesitation at all, knowing that at least we will have cool feet for a ways.

We came out of the woods on a bank overlooking the Chisana River bar and saw the horses a few miles away through glasses. We had to walk around the wide curve the river makes because the horses were on our side & the river was too high to cut across. We saw no bear tracks at all so the gun was unnecessary after all, but we did run into some fresh moose and caribou tracks, although we saw no game

We finally got to the horses and I was amazed to see how much they had changed since last summer. They were sleek and fat & had grown very much. I caught Tim who had not been ridden since last summer & climbed on bareback. Much to my surprise he was docile as a lamb. We rode back to town (Chisana) and were there in time for a late lunch. All told, we walked about 6-7 mi. And rode the same back.

Going after the horses each day made the miles and river crossing numbers stack up until they were impressive, but I was getting back into shape physically and did not mind these trips, other than what seemed to me, wasted time in trying to get ready for the hunt to come.

We inventoried the foodstuff for the trip, and began filling the pack boxes with food, heavy stuff on the bottom of the boxes and lighter on top. We gathered up the tents, heaters and stoves, grain for the horses, riding saddles and pack saddles. We would have about 28 horses for the 3 hunters, 3 guides, Lou, a cook and me, the wrangler. It was detailed work and Harry Sutherland, who lived in Chisana and was to go as cook, spent hours making lists of what he needed, checking everything off as we packed. Lou maintained a cabin next door that served as a warehouse where he stored foodstuff, some of which he sold to the three other men living in town. Also stored were camp gear, rigging for the horses, tools, traps, two small Yukon sleds, and one big 13' freighting sled, along with dog harnesses he used for winter and spring trapping.

As soon as I saw the dog sleds and the four new dogs Lou had acquired, all the images of winter in Alaska in books I had read by Jack London and the poems of Robert Service came crashing into my mind. I had a feeling growing in me that I needed to run a dog team sometime in the future. Harry took care of Lou's dogs, which meant feeding them once a day. I helped Harry with this chore and never tired of seeing the dogs jumping straight up into the air and barking in excitement, as Harry approached them with a half bucket of food. These dogs weighed around 90 pounds. Three of the new ones were litter mates, real malamutes, having maybe a quarter wolf blood, with nice conformation and not hard to handle after they got used to me. They were kept from getting at each other by light chains with spring clips, one side attached to the dog house and the other end to their collars.

On the 23rd of July we started a two-day, 35 or 40 mile trip to the White River to prepare some camp sites for the second half of the hunt, when we would be in grizzly, caribou and moose country. The route went up Trail Creek to Solo Mountain cabin and then down Solo Creek to Solo cabin, located on open level ground near the creek, a half mile above its junction with the White River. On the way up to camp the first night at Solo Mountain we saw 13 caribou which were very inquisitive about us, jumping up on their hind legs to get a better look. They are very curious animals and can be induced to come closer by "flagging," waving a piece of cloth, as done when antelope hunting on the prairie. As we went higher toward the pass that would eventually drop us down into the White River watershed, we moved above timberline and into the flats. The trail we used was well indented into the land as it had been the one used by the stampeders that came through McCarthy from the coast during the gold rush days after 1914.

On the trail the next day we saw a blond grizzly sow with three yearling cubs that we had come across the year before when the cubs were first born. They were easy to tell since the cubs ranged in color from a blond, to a light brown, to one almost black.

The closer we got to the White River, the more caribou sign we saw, as well as some large grizzly tracks close to Solo cabin. When we approached the cabin we could see that a bear had gotten inside and torn the place apart. The stove was tipped over, all sorts of canned goods were on the floor with cornstarch and black pepper everywhere. An aluminum bucket and many cans of food had been bitten and the 6 inch stovepipe was flattened with big tooth holes going right through as if shot by a heavy rifle. In looking around at the mess we concluded that the bear had probably bitten into the can of black pepper, gotten a snootful and gone on a rampage, taking his anger out on everything in the cabin.

Solo cabin, along with an old log barn, was located in a grassy open area. From the cabin we could see the Russell Glacier moraine, the source of the White several miles across the bar. The barn also had a platform cache built ten feet up from the dirt floor, between the poles that supported the roof. We could safely store any meat from the game killed on the hunt, for later use in the winter as dog feed. The weather would be cold enough by mid September to keep any meat frozen solid.

We unpacked the horses, had a bite to eat and then loaded up four blocks of salt on one of the packhorses and rode out onto the river bar to look over the horses Lou had left there in the spring and distributed the blocks of salt. I rode one of the colts Lou wanted me to break that we had packed, but never ridden, and other than his being a bit afraid to have someone on his back, I could handle him. The horses looked good and fat and after taking another few miles to look around that end of the bar for signs of game, we went back to the cabin and hit the hay around 9 P.M.

Journal #1—July 24th—Saturday:

Lou told me the funny story of the little Irishman who used to pack in here. It so happened that he brought a colored woman, as a passenger to Chisana & it seems that the Marshall & Commissioner were both Irish, so they decided to have some fun with him. They called him up to the court one day & asked him all sorts of questions about his trip in with Blanche. Finally they accused him & arrested him for the white slave act. To this charge he replied most indignantly that it was impossible to charge him thus, "as she was black as hell!"

Blanche was a real character, and although I did not meet her, my brother Jack did when he went up to work for Lou, in my place, the next year. She was an interesting woman from the many stories I heard of her. She was a hooker, but one of the kind-hearted ones, that often helped men down on their luck, or even to stake someone to an investment. She had had an accident in later years, with a gas stove blowing up in her face leaving her with large white blotches on her brown skin.

That night before falling to sleep, Lou told me many stories of how it was in the 1920's, when there were a lot of characters and wild women in the McCarthy—Kennicott—Chisana area, where in the old days, Lou, and others, had run sled dog taxis or had taken contracts to haul freight by pack train or dog team from McCarthy into Chisana. Nor was Lou alone in making some runs to smuggle booze during prohibition, into Alaska from the Yukon Territory where the border was only about 60 miles from Chisana as the crow flies.

Journal #1—Alaska 1948—July 25th Sunday

Got up around 6:00 A.M. and I made breakfast. Lou went out to get 3 horses for our trip to the lakes while I cleaned up and packed. When he got back we saddled up and started down the (White River) bar. I rode the colt again. We had very light showers all the way down, but it was really a beautiful day. I don't think I've ever seen the White River so pretty. We had gone about a half mile when we came up on a bear. He was dark with a lighter patch on his back & not too big. I took a picture at about 100 yds. or less & then Lou yelled and he took out.

We went to North Island & had lunch in a little glade behind the cabins & then packed up and rode down to the Holmes Creek feed patch to see if we could keep the horses there for 5 days during the hunt. It was fairly good. We then cut across the bar to the opposite bank where the trail from the lakes comes out on the river. Lou went up the trail to cut out a little & I made up camp & watched the horses. I built a lean-to and had supper going when Lou came back.

The sky cleared around 7 P.M. and it really was beautiful. It's much cooler now & will be a cold night but a clear day tomorrow. The bugs were bad for a while this evening & if it's warm tomorrow it will be a nightmare. Went to bed around dusk.

I've spoken of the beauty of the country and I will try to describe it better. The Wrangell Mountains are part of the Alaska Range that rises to 19,500′ at Mt. Logan in the Yukon, and ends with Mt McKinley over 21,000′. It is an area of many glaciers and along the White River on the north side of the mountains in the interior, one sees the land rising from the 2 mile wide river bar at 1500′, to a string of five peaks from 13,000′ to 17,000′ forming a beautiful ridgeline of enduring snow, ice and rock. The lower reaches of the mountains are covered with Alaska Spruce, which come down to meet the river bar along a low cutbank.

The three Alaska rivers I have spent time around; the Chitina, the Chisana, and the White, all have similar wide bars formed by the river's constant meandering through the silt and sand formed by the glacial activity grinding down the mountains. The headwaters of each of these rivers comes out from under a glacial moraine and carries with it, especially in the summer with the higher temperatures increasing the melt, the silt material that is light enough to be moved around by the water in a constantly changing landscape. The water is coffee colored in the summer, swift and heavy, and when it is 6" or 8" deep, the bottom cannot be seen. This makes for rather treacherous crossings due to holes and quicksand that are hard to detect from looking at the surface. When the water is mid thigh, it is all one can do to stay upright and you can feel the sand underfoot being washed away as you stand on it. What makes it possible to cross the larger channels at all is the number of small tributaries that greatly lessen the water volume in any one channel.

These three river bars can be, in places, several miles wide and over the years islands have formed on the bars being there long enough to support patches of timber and willow. North Island, in the middle of the White River bar was one of these and had been there long enough that cabins built in the twenties were still there, although in rough shape.

The White River flows ESE into Canada and then curves around northward to pick up Beaver Creek, and the Tanana, which itself is formed of the Nabesna and the Chisana rivers, all of these flowing into the Yukon River many miles from their sources. The Chitina is on the south side of the Wrangells and after flowing into the Copper River, empties into the Gulf of Alaska near Cordova. The mountains on the north side of the White River rise up little more than 3000' to 4000' feet above the river, with vegetation covering the lower half leading upwards to open gray shale slides, basins and cliffs near the top. These lower mountains were great habitat for the Dall sheep. From the White River a trail led 6 or 8 miles to Rock and Ptarmigan Lakes. Rock Lake was larger and sat in a basin surrounded by low mountains, while Ptarmigan Lake lay a few miles farther north. It was here that we would rendezvous with the hunters when they were flown in on August 15th.

My main feelings about the country could be summed up in a few words: beautiful, gigantic and sometimes threatening, perhaps because we were also alone. There were no other people living or working there except four old men in Chisana during the winter. Whenever I had to travel by myself, on foot or riding, I knew that if something happened to me I simply would not be found. That knowledge floated around in my head at times when things got a little tight. But this was a given and if you wanted to be in that country at that time, you accepted it and tried to put it out of your mind.

Journal #1—Alaska 1948—July 27th, Tuesday

I dreamt all sorts of wild dreams last night mostly about the hike today. (the horses had pulled out and gone back to Solo the day before, and I was to go get them back) *Got up at 5:30, ate a hurried breakfast and then started out alone to Solo. I took a gun & nothing else. The trip was one big obstacle course, with fallen timber, niggerheads, swamps, streams, alders, sand, mud, wind & rain, and a double crossing of the White on foot. I covered the 14 miles in 3 hr.s & 50 mins. It seemed like I'd traveled 100 though. When I finally reached Solo cabin I cooked a pot of tea with the few leaves the bear had left scattered on the shelf & opened a can of Spam.*

I washed my feet and my socks as they were full of sand & dirt from crossing the river & then started on up the bar to look for the horses. I found them up about a mile & caught Nancy. I didn't know where the bunch with Bill & Sweetheart was but finally I spotted them about half a mile back in the alders. I caught them finally & as I had forgotten a bridle I rode Bill with a halter. After I got going a ways the gun strap broke & Bill pitched me off. I used a piece of string from my parka to tie the strap on and started off again. I rode bareback for about 8 mi. to North Fork Island & then had to walk as I was so sore. Got into camp around 5 P.M.

This morning I saw a red fox out on the bar in front of camp & then again when I got up to Solo I got within 30' of a cross fox. He couldn't tell what I was so he lay down by the trail. I started to get the camera ready & he took out.

It blew like mad all the way back & the dust was bad. Hard to keep in the right direction some of the time. I ought to sleep tonight for once, I hope. Also I'll probably get rheumatism from wading in the ice cold river up to me pockets. I guess I'm lucky to have made it. 8:00 PM.

Journal #1—Alaska 1948—July 29th Thursday

Lou's watch stopped and as it was pouring down rain we didn't get up till 9 A.M. It started to clear off by breakfast time & so Lou decided to go to town. We caught 6 horses & got out of Solo by 12 o'clock. At Solo Mt. we changed horses & I rode the colt again. He tried to get me off much to my surprise but I was able to stick him out & we started off again. We had some trouble on the way & it was 11 P.M. when we got in. We only saw some caribou and ptarmigan all the way in. Ate a cold dinner & went to bed around 1 A.M.

The next 12 days were spent shoeing horses, repairing saddles, bridles and halters, making halter shanks, patching blankets and pads, and getting the food and gear stowed into boxes, ready to pack on the horses. The nights were generally getting colder so the mosquitoes were less bothersome, but they were replaced by the little black flies that arrive after the first hard frost. I also was working with a few of the horses that had not been ridden or packed the prior year to try to prepare them for work in the packtrain during the hunt. We expected the airplane to bring us not only the mail but also George Naydengast, who was to join the party as a hunting guide. I knew that having his help to move the 28 horses over to the sheep camp on Francis Creek, where we would meet the hunters, would make life a lot easier.

A week later on August 6th, the plane finally arrived with the mail and George. I was happy to see George, but more happy to get a pile of letters from Karen.

Journal #1—Alaska 1948—August 7th Saturday

Up around 6 AM for a hearty breakfast. Lou and George took the four dogs up to Joe Davis's, so he can care for them while we are on the hunt. They had quite a time with the dogs running & tangling their lines around the horses' legs & old Bill almost went to bucking.

I spent the day packing the grub in the panniers & wrapping stuff in canvas, & taking shots (of whiskey) *with Harry in between. We were pretty far gone by suppertime.*

Lou finally came down & instead of bringing George he had a female cook from the James mine who had been fired. A female in Chisana! Now the only way she can get out is to go with us to the Ptarmigan Lake & go out with the first plane (bringing the hunters in). *Never a dull moment.*

Went out to cut hay for the two horses after dinner & hit the sack at 9PM.

On August 10th, the big day we had been readying for, naturally nothing went as planned. George and I went after the horses at 5 AM, which proved to be a major effort in itself as they were scattered in several areas along the river. It was 9 AM before we had them back in town. It took until 2 PM to be packed and heading out. Our first day's destination was Porky Point, a tent camp above timberline in the flats, but we only made it to the Willows by 9 PM, where we made a camp. We unpacked the animals and hobbled enough of them to be sure they would not go too far during the night and got into our sleeping bags close to midnight.

View of Ptarmigan Lake 1948

Journal #1—Alaska 1948—August 11th Wednesday

Up around 5:30 & it was drizzling. Ate a quick breakfast and then went after the horses, which were hobbled. We found them 2 1/2 miles away down at Porky Point & so we were a couple of hours late in getting started. Lou and I packed up in about 2 hrs. & we left around 11 o'clock.

It rained lightly most of the day but it wasn't so bad. Saw a caribou on Opher Creek.

I've been packing the blue horse (blue roan named appropriately, Blue, but referred to as 'the blue bastard') *these last two days & he's coming along much better.*

The first day we both tried to pack him & he almost tore Chisana down. That boy can buck.

We went 24 mi. today & made camp in the dark at Francis Creek. Ate a little & went to bed around 11 PM.

Weather looks better.

We were camped in a small glade of Spruce, Diamond Willow, and Bear Berry, along Francis Creek which separated us from a treeless, mile wide tussock and moss tundra gently rising to the base of the mountains to the north where the sheep hunting would take place. To the west the tundra like landscape sloped uphill 20 miles to Porky Point, the high point on the trail, then downhill towards Johnson Creek and Chisana where it disappeared into the forest. To the east of camp, Francis Creek flowed downhill 8 miles towards Ptarmigan and Rock Lakes and the trails that led to the White River another 10 miles to the south.

We spent the next few days getting the camp ready. This meant putting up the tents, cutting wood for the cook stove and tent heaters, organizing the food, building a table and benches for the cook tent and setting up outside washing stands. We expected the hunters to arrive on the 15th, but the weather was very unsettled and we had to keep a vigil at Ptarmigan Lake where we were to meet them. We finally set up a camp at the lake, with some horses. The hunters did not arrive until August 19th, but that night they were all in camp and the next day, August 20th, the sheep hunting started. The hunters were Marshall Field III, Marshall's son Bobby, and George Richardson, a very close friend of Marshall's. Marshall was then about 56 years old and George Richardson was in his 60's. I don't remember Bobby well at all.

The first morning of the hunt, ten minutes after the hunters had left camp, we heard them yelling back to us, "There's a bear in camp!" Lou reached for a gun and I grabbed my camera and we walked out behind the cook tent a little way but saw nothing in the low brush. But all of a sudden a grizzly stood up on his hind legs looking at us about 25 steps away. I took some pictures while Lou protected us with the gun. This was the most unconcerned bear I ever saw in Alaska and he soon dropped down and wandered up the hill behind camp to dig for bugs.

The weather turned cold and it snowed 6" stopping the hunting for a few days. On the 26th Bobby missed a shot at a 40" ram and killed an immature one by mistake. The horn only measured 24" and was a major disappointment for him. George Richardson also had shot a ram, but had not gotten up to it as it was in a very difficult spot and it was turning dark. George Naydengast was to go after it the next day.

Journal #2—Alaska 1948—August 29, Sunday

Up around 5:30 to a fair day. Rather cold but sunny off & on. Lou and I took a load over to Wonn Lake. We packed Blue & Blaze & I rode Baldy. When we got to the summit I had been walking & when I tried to hold Blue (I was leading Blue by a halter shank) & get on Baldy, he jumped & I didn't sit right in the saddle & he "broke in two", & in about 6 or 7 jumps the world was upside down & I lit on my back with a hard jolt, just missed a big pool. Baldy kept on bucking & bucked the saddle off, and then began to feed, as if nothing had happened. I know I can ride him if he bucks & I am ready, but I was only in one stirrup & leaning over the horn. My ribs are still sore when I do any work from the horn hitting me every jump. Next time I'll be ready.

We started down the other side and then it was the "Blue's" turn. We had left his britchin up and when he felt the pack (move up) on his neck he bucked it off & ran down the mountainside at full gallop, dragging the packsaddle by his halter rope. He tripped and rolled once & then did a complete cartwheel. When he came to the more level valley he stopped.

I had tried to mount Baldy and as I swung my leg over his butt, Blue jerked back on the halter rope in my hand and pulled me back at the same time Baldy decided to start bucking. It was no contest with one foot not yet in the stirrup and I got beat up good before arcing through the air to land right in front of Baldy on a rather soft mossy patch surrounded by big rocks and small pools of water. Baldy never stopped bucking and ran right over the top of me, coming down on my right knee, but luckily, did not hurt it too much. Only later did this injury come back to haunt me.

When Blue finished his wild run down the steep mountainside he turned to look back up at me from 200 yards below and whinnied, as if to say "That was scary!" Lou, watching all this rodeoing with disgust, said, "I'm going on to the lake and you better gather all that stuff up," and set off. I spent the next three hours searching in the low brush up and down the mountainside and lugging all I found back up to the pass. I found the packsaddle still in one piece, and surprisingly, Blue had not been hurt at all with his wild flips and rolls. I never did find one case of canned Canadian bacon.

While I worked, I let the two horses graze up in the pass and on one of my trips up the hillside with a pannier on my shoulder, as my head and load came into view, the two horses spooked and set off on a run for camp leaving me without my saddle horse. When Lou returned we packed the stuff I had gathered up on one of his horses and I rode the packsaddle back to camp on Ginger.

On August 31st we struck our sheep camp and headed the eight miles down Francis Creek to Ptarmagin Lake, then four more miles to Rock Lake and then another six to the White River. We had a campsite in the woods near the river bar alongside a small clear creek. The eighteen-mile trip down was cold, snowy, wet, and miserable for everyone. We arrived at 7 PM and soon had the cook tent up and a fire going for the hunters to get warmed up. A few stiff drinks moved that process along right well.

On the occasional days when the weather was so bad hunting would have been useless, I could find time to do things alone. One such morning I caught Bill, saddled him up and struck out for Solo.

Journal #2—Alaska 1948—September 2nd, Tuesday

It was raining & snowing when I got up & continued to rain till suppertime. Nobody is going out & as I am tired of staying in camp I caught "Bill" & rode up to Solo after a little flour and tobacco.

On the way up I got right up to a wolf. He didn't get my wind & I was within 75-80 yds. of him for about a half mile. He would trot ahead & then sit and watch me & then go on. Finally he circled me & was lost from view. I was going to shoot him but I thought I better not as the hunters were hunting in the territory.

A little farther on I saw a red fox & when I was about 4 miles from Solo a cow & calf & 2 bull caribou that were coming down the bar came within a hundred yards.

The White River camp area was mainly grizzly and caribou country, but also there were moose, wolverines, and wolves. The hunters and guides used the horses every day since lots of territory was being hunted. The main characteristic of the area was the river bar itself which was several miles wide and perhaps 16 miles up to the Russell Glacier which was the river's source. There were many bears in the area but a lot of ground had to be covered to locate them and the hunters spent many hours each day in that pursuit.

Our first camp on the White was about 14 miles down river from Solo Creek cabin. After a few days of hunting, with some success, one grizzly taken, we decided to move up to Solo Creek. The day before the move Lou and I went to bring in the bear meat which was some miles down river toward the Yukon border.

Journal #2—Alaska 1948—Sept. 4th, Saturday

Woke up to the first sunny day of the hunt. Today George R. is staying in & Lou & I are taking 3 pack horses over to pick up the bear to take to Chisana for dog feed. It was very beautiful, & Lou pointed out all the spots over on the Canadian side to me.

We could see the Genere Valley & where the Alcan Highway runs. We followed the hunters trail to where the bear lay in a little berry patch. We got back around 2 PM.

I packed boxes the rest of the day since we are moving up to Solo tomorrow. No luck for the hunters today. Bed around 8:30 PM.

Started to cloud up.

Journal #2—Alaska 1948—Sept. 5th, Sunday

Got up once around 3 AM to see what the horses were doing & then slept till 5:00 AM.

I packed all morning & the hunters left around 10 AM to hunt up the bar before we went through (with the pack train).

Lou and I were left alone to pack up & we began around 12:30 PM (to load the horses) *We were done & started out around 2 PM. Had a lot of trouble slipping packs with the horses running & fighting & rolling, but pulled in around 6 o'clock. The hunters were already there & served us drinks while we worked.*

Had a large dinner & washed the dishes & hit the sack around 10 PM.

Can see all the stars tonight. No luck (hunting).

We stayed and hunted out of Solo cabin until the 12th and then packed up 4 days of food for the trip back to Rock Lake where the plane was to pick up the hunters on the 13th. The extra food was in case the weather turned sour and the plane did not get in on schedule. Lou and I packed the horses and my journal says, *only Blue and Baldy bucked off their packs*, as if this was a "good" day. Actually it was, as the sun was shining and the fall colors were bright on the hills leading up to the snow covered Wrangells. Also, George Richardson killed a nice grizzly on the way down the White River, which made the hunt a total success for him.

Journal #2—Alaska 1948—Sept. 13th, Monday

Up at 4 AM to check & see that the horses hadn't gone back to Solo. They were all here so I built a fire & made coffee & and then the rest got up. The plane came in at

7AM & we were packed up by 8 AM. Got up to the lake at 11 & said our goodby to the hunters. They took off all right & Lou and I turned back & went to Wonn Lake to pick up a sack of flour & then we went back down to the camp at the river. We packed a little & then ate dinner and hit the sack around 8 PM to get a good sleep

It was another good day today with not a cloud in the sky. We also saw 9 sheep up on a pinnicle over the lake.

The next day was one of those days, if you are working around livestock, that is created for story tellers. Lou had gone with 3 horses to pick up the bear meat left from George Richardson's bear, while George Neydengast and I broke the river camp to move everything up to Solo with the packtrain,. We had a variety of pack horses and riding horses. We saddled the riding horses, which was all they had to carry and loaded all the camp gear, including stoves and tents and food on the pack animals. As we got them done we just turned them loose onto the bar where they grazed and worked their way slowly up river.

However, Ginger, one of the saddle horses, spooked at a noise in one of the saddle bags and stampeded right through the other horses on the bar. Baldy took off as well from the ringing of one of our cowbells in a sack of hobbles he was carrying and after he raced about for a few minutes, his pack started to roll over. I caught up to him and George helped me unload and we repacked him. The last thing we put on was the large cook tent and we tied his halter shank to one of the tent ropes so he would not step in it if he was grazing or drinking. I started to make an adjustment to the tent before tying the diamond hitch which would hold the pack tight and this set him off again, only this time he went bucking to get rid of the offending pack. He managed to get rid of everything in short order, except that the cook tent rope was hooked on the pack saddle and the tent unraveled fifteen feet behind him like a big flapping wing. All you could see was the whites of his terrified eyes as he ran in circles to try to get rid of the huge thing chasing him, and naturally, he ran through the other horses and the whole bunch took off on a dead run up the bar, disappearing in a cloud of dust.

I caught Tim, jumped in the saddle, and set out to try to head them off which I finally did in a mile or so. I caught Baldy who had finally managed to lose the tent somewhere and tied him to a willow. While I was doing that the rest started out again. I saw some of the other packs had been bucked off and camp stuff was strewn about on the sand for a couple of miles. What a fiasco! I gathered Baldy up, leaving the other horses to go on toward Solo which was home to them and rode back down the bar picking up items as I went. I found the offending tent spread out on the sand, luckily with only a few holes torn in it. I met George and we repacked Baldy and set out once again for Solo, gathering things we found strewn about and placing these into the middle of the main trail.

When it appeared we had picked up everything, I put Tim into a steady trot to try to catch up with the other horses. None were in sight when I got to North Fork Creek and I just kept going 6 more miles up to Solo. The horses had gone right past Solo cabin several more miles to the area they liked to graze. I stopped at Solo and unsaddled Tim, and then walked out with a bridle to look at the other animals. I found Pet grazing unconcernedly with the saddle under her belly and another about to lose a blanket, but the rest of the gear was still intact. I righted Pet's saddle and climbed on, rounded up the rest of the string and pushed them into Solo where I took off the saddles and packs and turned them all loose.

The next day George and I went back down river with several pack horses to find everything we could and bring it up to Solo Cabin. On the 17th we rounded up the horses, packed up and started out for Chisana, about 40 miles away. The trip took two days, with the first night camped at Powell Creek where I spent most of the night chasing horses up the creek so they would not head on into town without us. They knew they were on the way back to the barn and were eager to get there. The next day we packed up and it was all we could do to keep them slowed down and in some kind of order, but they walked fast and we arrived in Chisana at 1 PM on September 18th. After unpacking, Lou and I moved the horses, that were now acting as if they were getting out of school for summer vacation, over to the Bow Creek trail which led to the Chisana River bar. We did this in a steady lope, perhaps feeling the same euphoria as the horses that the hunting season was over and our work done and had a grand time of it, finally getting back after dark. This ended the hunting trip and my summer work and I looked forward to catching up on sleep in a soft bed.

Playing In the Northern Lights

Wherein our hero has a romantic rendezvous, sets a trapline,
runs with dogs under the Northern Lights,
and plans his journey home

Over the next few days, while waiting for a bush pilot to come in to pick me up, I organized and stored the rigging in the warehouse, cut wood, made a trip to Bonanza Creek with a few horses to freight several miners out for the winter, shaved and bathed for my entry into the civilized world.

During this time I was seriously mulling over the idea of staying up and trapping with Lou for 3 months. I thought about it more and more as I worked around Lou's dogs, and began organizing the bags of traps, sleds and harnesses. I came to realize that if I did not do it right then, I would probably never again have the opportunity to mush dogs in an Alaskan winter. I talked it over with Lou and he was very happy to have me stay and we agreed to split 50/50, the costs and the proceeds from the sale of fur. The only missing ingredients were telling my folks about it and getting some additional clothing and footgear I would need to handle the winter weather. I decided to go into Anchorage and stay with Harold again while I purchased the things I would need and also call home to get the OK from Mother and Dad. The plane came in on the 24th and I arrived at Harold's that evening.

On landing in Gulkana, on the way to Anchorage, I sent the following telegram:

SEPTEMBER 25 1948

DEAR FOLKS,
BEEN DELAYED BY WEATHER AM TAKING TEMPORARY LEAVE FROM SCHOOL TO GO INTO CONSERVATION WORK HAVE REGISTERED WILL CALL FROM ANCHORAGE
LOVE TO ALL
BILL
GULKANA 212PM

I remember I thought this enigmatic letter might bring a little levity into my coming telephone conversation with Father. It was "conservation" only in that we were to trap wolves which were under a bounty to keep their numbers down. Dad would know my real reason was to have an adventure, pure and simple, and I counted on his secretly admiring his son's interest in challenging experiences.

The next day I telephoned home and got Dad on the phone. I explained that I was going to stay up and trap with Lou until Christmas and then I would return to Stanford and go straight through summer school to make up for missing Fall quarter. After I got done telling him this I asked if it was okay with him and he said, "Well you just told me what you are going to do, so there is not much more I can say to you about it, is there? You seem to have made up your mind." I answered, "Dad, I promise I will come out at Christmas, but this is my only chance to have this experience." After a long pause as his rational mind sorted the odds of this working out as planned and probably not wanting to have a major confrontation with me, he said, "All right, it's fine with me, but try not to worry your mother more than she is already worried about you." I promised I would not, thanked him profusely for letting me carry out my plan, said good-by to Mother, telling her not to worry and hung up elated with what was now set in motion.

The next week was a rather frantic exercise in shopping for my clothes and filling a list of things Lou wanted me to buy and bring back. My new clothes consisted of a wool shirt, heavy wool "long johns", a reversible white to khaki colored military surplus parka, heavy wool socks, a winter cap with ear flaps, mittens and military mukluks made with leather bottoms and calf-high canvas tops, laced all the way around the outside. I got the first haircut I had had since Jan's wedding in June and found a ride back to Chitina in the back of a 2-ton truck with all my new possessions. I put up at the only hotel in town, which was run by O. A. Nielsen, a kindly, spare, 65 year old Swede.

Chitina, a small town located at the confluence of the Chitina and Copper Rivers consisted of a few houses, a small hotel, a general store and one or two other shops, all using 19th century western architecture with high square wooden facades. The few sidewalks were wooden plank walkways mainly in front of the businesses along the main street. Across a walking bridge over a small creek, a trail wide enough to pass a wagon or a car led to an Indian village of eight or ten cabins, from where one could look back and down a shallow slope into the town center and see the intersection of the road into town with the main street.

When I drove into town, I happened to look up into an upstairs window of a two-story clapboard apartment building and as I passed, chanced to see George Neydengast with his arm around a young Indian woman, obviously enjoying themselves and both of them laughed and smiled down at me when they saw me looking up. I had not thought about sex very much while on the hunting trip as I was working very long and sometimes hard hours, but the sight of these two people at some sort of sexual play got my libido going in overdrive.

The next day when I was in Mr. Chase's general store, in walked the woman I had seen at George's place. She was a very slim and nice looking 30 year old unmarried woman, which I found strange since most of the Indian girls married very young and she appeared very marriageable to me. Of course I had been in the woods for a long time and for that reason was not the best judge of such things, but I soon realized that she could not speak and in fact, was a deaf mute. The only sounds she could make were more like squawks than any word understandable to me, but she could laugh. She flashed a pretty smile at me which I translated as, "We have a little secret together," to which I returned a smile with the best "I like your looks" expression I could muster, only slightly tinged in embarrassment at what I had seen the previous day. Mr. Chase called her "Deafy" which I found was the name everyone knew her by. She was sort of a character in a town in which half the population could be described that way.

The more I thought about her the more my head was saying, *this is an experience you have to have. Don't let this opportunity get away. Be brave, all she can do is shake her head, yes or no. You won't have to be smooth with words as there won't be any discussion since she can't hear or speak. Think of the story you can report back to Frank about making out with a deaf and dumb woman.* One might question just where Karen was in my mind at this time, and I can only answer, "a very long ways away" and ask forgiveness.

At the hotel we all ate at a communal table, with O.A. at the head and his roomers seated all around. After eating I excused myself as soon as I could from the small talk going on around the table, "to take a walk" I explained and went to my room to brush my teeth, wash my face and hands and comb my hair, before heading down the road to the path that led over the bridge to the Indian village. It was about 8 PM when I knocked on her cabin door.

She opened it, gave me a big smile and indicated that I should come in. The cabin was a one room affair, with a double bed shoved into one corner opposite the kitchen where there were the usual cupboards, a wood stove, a window above a sink that drained into a bucket, a wood box underneath and some pots and frying pans hanging on the wall. At the other end were several chairs and an old dilapidated sofa, a chest of drawers and another window. It was small but cozy and bathed in the soft light of a single oil lamp. The entire cabin, as well as Deafy, also carried the unmistakable smoky smell combination of dried salmon and moose hide tanned leather, a very Indian odor, but one I was familiar with already from my visits with other Indians while in Chisana.

I started to talk but then remembered she could not hear me, so I pointed at her and then back to myself and then made an age old gesture I knew she would understand. With that she squawked and laughed and nodded her head vigorously in the affirmative. She then mimicked drinking, pointed to me and then back to town, meaning she wanted me to go buy a few beers. I nodded affirmatively indicating I would be back in five minutes and stepped out to hurry over to the store. Mr. Chase gave me a quizzical look when I asked for the beer, doubtless suspecting I was up to no good, but took my money anyway and handed me the beer and I set off back to Deafy's full of anxieties over the outcome of this new adventure.

When I knocked on the door she promptly opened it, and when I put the beer bottles on the small table she handed me a bottle opener and I popped the caps on two bottles, handing one to her and keeping the other for myself. We sat down on the couch to drink them. A great silence settled in as there was not much use to say anything. This made it much easier for me since I was notoriously nervous around women and usually had my foot in my mouth trying to be something other than the dumb kid I was. For her part she emitted several little squawks, giggled a bit, but was very friendly. After she finished a couple of beers, she gave me a questioning look and pointed at the bed. I was not slow to show my agreement and with that she merely walked over and undressed in plain sight and jumped in. I was too embarrassed to simply disrobe until I had turned off the gas lamp and then I quickly threw off my clothes and got in beside her.

Deafy turned out to be a good teacher who very much enjoyed her subject. It was a perfect second experience for me and during the night each time we woke up she urged another lesson on me, for which I was a grateful student. The last lesson was at 5:30 in the morning and as I lay there I was rapidly beginning to think I should get out of there soon, before the village came to life and someone saw me leave her cabin. Perhaps sensing my thoughts, Deafy got out of bed and with no embarrassment at all, walked over to a bucket near the door, squatted down and peed into it. That somewhat startling event seemed to break whatever lethargic spell I was enjoying just lying there and I jumped out, hurriedly dressed, gave her a quick platonic hug and left.

I made my way to the hotel where luckily the door was open and I tiptoed upstairs to my room trying not to disturb anyone. I really did not want to be seen, but I had to pass in front of O.A.'s open door and as I did, I saw O.A. sitting up in bed reading. He looked up at me over his glasses and said, "A little late to be coming in don't you think?" I mumbled a reply about being up early and went into my room. In my new mood of post sexual remorse, I began to conjure up all sorts of bad things that could happen to me from adding this experience to my mind's library. There was a wall-mounted sink in my room and I quickly undressed and proceeded to wash myself vigorously in the hope of avoiding some dread disease I had not given a moment's thought to when I arrived at Deafy's the evening before. I was lucky again, as it turned out, but that next week, waiting for symptoms that, happily, never arrived, was somewhat nerve wracking. But even this possibly ominous outcome did not diminish my pride in having set out on another intriguing life experience and having it work out as I had hoped, rather than ignominiously failing because I was such a callow youth. All said and done, I was satisfied I had accomplished another step in the transition to becoming a man.

Journal—Trapping, Alaska 1948—October 4th, Monday

Took off from Chitina at 9 AM and flew to May Creek to unload supplies for a couple of trappers. From there we went through Scolei Pass & over the Russell Glacier to Chisana. I could see all up and down the White River bar where I will be for the next few months.

We turned left down past Solo Mt. & came along Trail Creek the rest of the way. All the populace was there on the field when we landed. We went to Lou's for a meal and a few drinks and then Pappy took off in the plane and headed back to civilization. I spent the rest of the day around the cabin getting a few odds & ends straightened out.

Hit the sack early as we have to go bring the horses in, in the morning. I have a heck of a cold and sore throat.

The next few days were spent trying to get ready for trapping. Lou planned to set a trapline from Chisana to the White River, down the White to North Fork Creek, over to Rock Lake and back up to Porky Point and Bonanza and down Johnson Creek to Chisana, a total of about 100 miles. He figured we would have to get around it no less than every 2 weeks, otherwise any animal we caught would likely be eaten by a predator before we could return. We were to use the horses to help us move our gear to the White River.

On the 5th we went to the Chisana River and brought the horses into town in preparation to leaving the next day, but on the 6th Lou was sick from some flu bug and I turned the horses back out.

Journal—Trapping, Alaska—Oct. 8th

I decided to go hunting today as Lou is under the weather. Didn't leave till 9:50 AM (I am keeping accurate count of the time it takes me to walk between certain points as it may come in handy if I get caught out).

Walked over to Boggs Bar & climbed up to a saddle on the left side of Yuka Mt. Then traversed two sides of the mt. & didn't find a sheep. Started back down at 3:30 & got in a jackpot on a cliff. Took both hands & feet & lots of hard wishing to climb to solid rock, but I made it. Never a dull moment.

Came off the mt. a little above the end of the Chisana Glacier & then had a race with darkness back through the woods to town. Damn tired. Bet I walked and climbed 20 miles.

Lou was feeling better and we prepared to leave on the 10th for the White River. But getting the horses in took several hours and the weather appeared to be building into a snow storm so we again turned the string out. I was getting frustrated and asked Lou to sit down with me and try to make a reasonable plan.

We agreed to not take the horses to the White River, but set up trap lines around Chisana; up Powell Creek 8 miles; to Bonanza and Porky point, 16 miles; over to the Chisana Glacier, 8 miles; and down the Chisana River to Cross Creek, 9 miles. This would keep us occupied until there was enough snow to use the dog team to move over to the White River. We were also planning a hunt down river at Notch Creek, where the trail from Nabesna that Lou and I had come over the prior summer with the horses, met the Chisana River.

We started working this plan, setting traps along the river and the smaller creeks. We were after fox, mink, wolverine, lynx and wolves, which carried a bounty of $30, plus a pelt worth another $12. Lou began to show me how to set a trap properly depending on the species we were trapping. For mink, we would usually look for holes in the ice along the creeks where we could see from tracks that mink were fishing. We did not have to hide these smaller traps but used a mink musk scent located near the trap to attract them. The other traps were set along the trail we used, or close to it, as most of the animals also chose to use the easiest means of travel, rather than crawl through the underbrush.

packhorses used to establish trapping camps.

A typical set was made by digging a shallow hole for the trap, a #4 Oneida with short ½" teeth on each of the two jaws. Once the jaws were set open, the trap was gently laid into the snow and a piece of toilet paper or Kleenex laid over the jaws and a dusting of snow to cover the whole site. The last things done were to use a Ptarmigan wing to brush away any visual sign of the trap in the snow and rub some scent in a place where the animal would step in the trap trying to smell the scent. This trap could hold a wolf or wolverine if it was attached to a toggle, a 4 or 5 foot long branch about 3" in diameter, allowing the animal to move dragging the toggle but unable to put enough pressure to pull their foot out. A wolf could pull his foot out of a #4 trap chained hard and fast to a tree and in doing so actually bend the steel trap. I lost a wolf I had caught in this manner once. I quickly learned that one had to be extremely cautious once the jaws were forced open. To get a finger in the way when it snapped was to have a broken finger and I once carelessly set one off with my own moccasin clad foot, but it snapped shut under my foot, only scaring me half to death.

On October 15th Lou and I, hunting 8 miles down river near Notch Creek, came on fresh grizzly tracks in three inches of new snowfall from the night before. We followed these tracks along the bar in open country for an hour or so as they wound around in an aimless sort of circling path. Finally we saw the bear about 200 yards away, walking slowly across a gravel bar dotted with small shrubs. I had always dreamed of killing a grizzly and Lou wanted me to have this one. I took his 30.06 rifle, sat down with my elbows on my knees trying to remember how to breath and slowly squeezed the trigger letting off a shot. To my amazement the bullet hit the bear and spun him right around and slammed him down. I could not believe the force of that bullet when it hit the bear. But to my surprise, as Lou and I walked closer, the bear got up and started walking slowly in the same direction and I shot him again and that was that.

Chisana in winter sunshine 1948

Lou and moose he took for meat.
Trapped three wolverines later at the site.

After years of hearing bear stories and thinking about hunting a grizzly, I can only say it was a let-down since I could easily see a bear was unable to compete with the power of a gun. I had a sense of unfairness and lack of risk in this particular hunt, as if I had just shot a big pig. Although I was glad to have had the experience and tracking the bear had been exciting, the actual killing was almost totally lacking in excitement and challenge and I determined right then that I would never kill another bear unless forced to for my own safety. But this bear would be used completely. I would get the hide to tan and the dogs would get all the meat and we set about the slow process of skinning. When completed, the bear measured only 7'2" square, an average size for the bears in that area, where the largest went to 8'6". Later in the week after getting the bear meat into town, Lou cut off all the fat and rendered it on the stove into bear grease. The smell of this process was not so good, but the product was wonderful for use on leather.

Journal—Trapping Alaska—Oct. 19th, Tuesday

Up early & worked on bear skin all day. He measures 7'2". Took out the dogs for a little workout today. Just went a little way. They were sure wild. What Fun! Bed Late.

The dogs were crazy with excitement to get hitched up to the sled. They would bark their heads off and jump straight up in the air with all four feet about two feet off the ground until brought back to earth by the chain attached to their collars. Before hitching them up we moved the sled into position and to make sure the first few dogs put in the harness would not take off with the sled before all the other dogs were hooked up, we tied the sled to a steel ring bolted through a corner log of the cabin.

We then hooked the main towline to the front ring on the sled and stretched it out in front. The individual dog harness was a miniature of a horse harness, complete with collars, traces and a single tree attached to a ring in the main towline. To hitch the dogs up, we led each dog by the collar chain, over to his harness that was already snapped onto the towline, dropped the chain off his collar and slipped the padded harness collar over his head and connected another short rope from the tow line to his collar. This assured that his head would face forward and he could not turn around to fight the dog behind. The dog chain was then attached to the side of the sled for use at the end of the day.

We always hooked up the lead dog first as it was his job to hold the tow rope stretched out full length so the other dogs would be less able to fight during the hooking up process. Until the dogs started working daily, they were very hard to hold and I often had Harry Sutherland help me by holding Duke, the lead dog, by the collar so that the tow line was held tight, while I hooked up the other dogs one by one. More than once they took off bowling poor Harry over in their excitement.

Journal—Trapping, Alaska 1948—Oct. 20th, Wednesday

Got traps ready in morning while Lou worked on bear grease. Hitched up the dogs (with great difficulty) & went through parks (grassy openings in the woods in the vicinity of the Chisana airfield) *setting traps. I ran the sled today & tipped it over twice right away. Came back in an hour or so. Getting colder. (not bad though 13°)*

Journal—Trapping Alaska 1948—Oct. 21st, Thursday 9° F

Hitched up after breakfast & went down glacier trail setting 6 traps up to Bow Cr. I did most of the mushing today & am catching on. Tried out the snow boots today. No good. I am fixing them another way next time though.

The sled we are using is very awkward to take through the woods—about 12'—13' long, & snow is not good yet either. We cut down to the rocks. Me and the dogs is tired of running tonight. Dark at 4:45 now.

Mushing dogs in country like this is much different than what is seen on the typical race courses set up for dog sled racing, although I suspect there are some rough passages even on those trails. We never rode the sled unless you were on river ice or going downhill. At those times it was important to keep the sled from running up onto the "wheel" dogs, those two closest to the sled, to avoid injuring their hind legs. The brake was a hickory slat about one inch thick and three inches wide hinged across the back of the sled. This slat had two steel 90° angle irons bolted on at the outside edges, each tapered to a point sharp enough to hold on ice and two heavy-duty springs held it in an upright position until you stepped on it and forced the steel points into the snow or ice.

Journal—Trapping Alaska—October 23rd 0°F

I took the dogs up to Bow Cr. today (with much trouble) & Lou brought up "Copper" to kill him. He's about 30 yrs. old & worn out so we will kill him (to use) for bait for a while & then bring him in for dog feed. We built a stockade around him & set 4 snares and 2 traps.

I brought the dogs back through the woods in the dark for my first taste of night mushing. We made good time, & I've got my wind pretty good now, but my legs were getting a mite tired at the end of the 6 or 7 mile trip

On the 25th it was—8° F and we went to move some of the horses over the Chisana River and put them on a bar near the glacier that had a good growth of peavine for winter feed. They are left out all winter and paw through the snow for their food. We caught up Tim and Bill, put bridles on them and jumped on bareback. With Lou in the lead and me hazing the horses from the rear, we set out to

cross the many channels of the river. These rivers can be a bit dangerous as breaking ice can form ice dams forcing water over the dam, flowing green water maybe
a foot deep until it freezes over forming a new layer of ice and so on all winter.
What one is always aware of is that somewhere underneath all the shell ice is a fast
running river.

On the very last channel before getting to terra firma, Bill broke through a
layer but lunged to shore, but the other horses following started to spook in fright
and began jumping through the widening and deepening hole to reach shore. In
their fear they broke down several more shelves of ice and then it was my turn. By
the time Tim got into it the water was boiling up and over the ice on both sides
and as he felt the ice under him giving way he began to lunge flipping me up in
the air and I landed on my back in the water next to him, with his front hooves
coming down right next to my head as he continued his struggle to get out. The
water was running fast and I thought I would go under him, but in one final
jump he was out and I turned over and struggled out myself, soaking wet to my
waist and back. We started back with all my clothes frozen solid on the outside. It
was very chilly. Unbeknownst to me then, it was also the last time I would see the
horses until three years had passed.

Journal—Trapping Alaska—October 26th Tuesday

*Took 5 dogs to the (Indian) village to pick up a few traps. Two were sprung but
whatever it was got out. I think it was foxes. The dogs got away from me on the lake
& I had a hell of a run to catch them. I made a mink set at the lake. Home early. Get
ready to go to Bonanza (via) Beaver Lake route.*

I had stopped to set a trap for mink along the lake and when I turned to walk
back old Duke decided to take off with the sled. I hollered "WHOA," but he just
kept going for a hundred yards and stopped. When I got within 20 feet he started
off again. Running as hard as I could, I was unable to grab hold of the handlebars. Duke repeated this game about four times and each time as the dogs trotted
away, keeping the sled just out of my reach, they would be looking at me,
tongues out panting and looking like they were all laughing at me. I finally
worked my way close enough that with an extreme effort I sprinted and caught a
handle and flipped the sled on its side and that was the end of it. I gave Duke a
good thrashing and then we started for town.

Lou, on North Fork Creek

The commands of the sled dog driver came from the time when multiple teams of horses were used to pull freighting wagons, before the advent of trucks and tractors. The terms "whoa", for stop, and "gee" and "haw", for right and left, were the same. To start off we either said "mush", or just made a clicking sound with our tongues. The lead dog was important, especially in following commands, because if you could not rely on the leader to obey, you could get in serious trouble. You expected him to also know the trails, even when you could not see them due to darkness or from multiple overlays of snow or ice that often obscured them totally.

The team consisted of Duke, our lead dog, a large McKenzie River Husky, snow white all over excepting two black circles around his eyes. He was smart, but was over 10 years old and had been wind broke, so when working extremely hard he wheezed loudly as he gasped for air. Lou said this was from his having been run too hard years before which had caused some kind of permanent damage in his bronchia. Then Pat, Rowdy and Jack, three year-old litter mates who were real malamutes; and the wheel dogs were Bingo, who looked like a large German shepherd, and "The Bulldog," a black and white cross bred with a flat face like a bulldog. Real ugly. These dogs all had their respective personalities. Pat was affectionate while Rowdy was mischievous and Jack was quiet. Bingo was a born malingerer and constantly and slyly tried to slack off on the pulling, while the Bulldog just got in there and pulled with all his might. We hooked Pat up next to Duke as a way to learn to be a lead dog.

Sled Trail to Beaver Creek

Journal—Trapping Alaska 1948—Oct 28th, Thursday

I took 5 dogs (Pat is lame so we left him) to Bonanza. Sort of a tough 8 miles with a heavy load & a few inches of snow. Lou set traps behind me. Worked on woodpile until it got dark. 22°F cloudy, windy

Journal—Trapping Alaska 1948—_Oct.29th, Friday

It snowed a few more inches last night but cleared up around 8 AM. It's very beautiful. I took the dogs on out to Porky Point (8 mi) & Lou followed making sets. Harder sledding than yesterday. About 6" snow to break trail through & steep climbs. Had trouble cooking dog food so fed each (dog) one of Andy's fish which we fetched out for him. Almost got a shot at a caribou.

Handling a heavy sled behind a dog team is very hard work. On all rough or uphill stretches I kept both hands on the handle bars, to help the dogs by pushing or to keep the sled from rolling onto its side if one of the runners dropped lower than the other and to help me keep my balance with all the slipping and sliding occurring while walking in the snow or on ice. We often had over 200 pounds of gear, traps, rifles and food, plus our personal clothes and sleeping bags. There is an old Alaskan saying that the musher is the hardest working dog in the team and I can attest to that in spades. In general it was plain hard work interspersed with a few moments of pure pleasure when I could get on and ride the sled, the dogs in a trot, their tongues hanging out, looking back at me with what looked like big smiles on their faces with the easy going.

In deep snow the trail had to be broken with snowshoes ahead of the sled, or the dogs could not pull it at all. In this situation I used a G pole, a six foot long round wooden pole about three inches in diameter that fit into a steel ring bolted to the right front runner of the sled. The idea of the pole was to enable me to snowshoe directly in front of the sled runners with my right hand on the G pole, moving it right and left about two or three inches in a rhythm. This slight movement helped somehow to relieve the drag and kept the sled aligned in the snowshoe track and out of the deep snow.

We had been working the country along most of the creeks around Chisana and as we slowly prepared to move everything over to the White River, we began to pick up these traps. This move required relaying multiple loads up Powell Creek, then over the summit pass to Solo Mountain cabin and from there downhill to either Solo cabin or North Fork Creek cabin on the White River. We spent November 1st to 3rd cleaning up the trap lines around Chisana, with very little success other than a few fox and on the 4th I drove the team with the first load to our camp up Powell Creek.

Lou's cabin in Chisana, Winter 1948

Journal—Trapping Alaska—November 5th, Friday

Had a very heavy load to take to Powell Creek & and so I got my first taste of working on the "G" pole. Lou made a couple of sets behind me, but I didn't beat him in by very much, it was such slow going.

I caught a red fox & had trouble keeping the dogs from tearing him to pieces. We set up camp and got a bite to eat.

On the 6th I took a heavy load up to the head of Trail Creek to cache, being too far to make it up and back from Solo Mountain cabin in a day. That day the wind on those upper treeless flats blew so hard the dogs constantly wanted to turn or just lie down and quit and the wind blown snow almost cut my face, it hit so hard. Coming back down however, was a much different matter and we covered the last six miles in an hour. On the 7th I took another load up to the cache and had a hard time working through the new drifts of snow that the wind had formed. In one spot I had to unload and backpack the load over some drifts to lighten the sled so the dogs could get across. On the 8th it snowed hard all day and we didn't move. On the 9th we moved on to Solo Mt. cabin, with me snowshoeing a trail ahead of the dog team and Lou working the G-pole. It was fairly slow going and I broke trail for 10 miles up to the summit. It was too warm for that kind of work, but the day was beautiful.

A warm Chinook wind came up in the night and blew away almost all the snow. I left camp to bring a load from the cache and when I hit the open area on top it was blowing harder than any wind I had ever seen. I could barely keep the empty sled upright even bracing against the downwind side and finally it knocked me down and the sled rolled right over me and continued cart wheeling over and over in a 90° arc, ending with the towline twisted like a rubber band on a model airplane. After this happened a second time and worried about really breaking something or hurting a dog, I gave up and turned back. I know Lou was disappointed in me and I felt bad that maybe I could have persevered harder and made it, but that was the strongest wind I had ever experienced and I was unsure of what it might portend.

Earlier that fall, after I killed my grizzly, we had brought all the meat back to Chisana to use as dogfood. We took the tenderloin, however, for ourselves, and ground it up adding onions and spices and formed 44 large bearburger patties. We had eaten a few and frozen the rest by simply putting them out in the warehouse. When we started our trek to the White River, we put them in a flour sack, frozen hard and threw them in the sled with our other food. That night I brought them into the tent with me so no animal could get them and put the sack under my head as a pillow.

The next morning I went out to hook up the dogs and could see Rowdy looking very lazy. When I unchained him and take him to the sled, he jumped up with his paws on my shoulders, his face near to mine and gave a tremendous belch of awful smelling breath. I looked at his stomach and instantly saw it was bulging out and then a terrible thought occurred to me and I ran to the tent to look for the meat sack. It was gone. Rowdy had clawed it out from under my head as I slept and eaten every one. We went meatless for almost the next three weeks, not finding any game to kill.

We made it into Solo cabin on November 12th. The next day I had to go back to Solo Mt. to bring another load.

Journal—Trapping Alaska—November 13th, cold—15° F

It cleared last night and was very cold this morning. I took the dogs back to Solo Mt. to bring in the rest of the stuff. Lou went to break trail to North Fork Cr. which will be our base & set out 5 traps.

After some delays I got started & went up the bar a mile or so before I turned into the timber to go up on the flats. I stopped to rest the dogs & and take a picture back down the bar & and was about to start again when I spotted a wolf coming up our trail.

I grabbed the gun and waited (slightly tense). He came on and then about 300 yds away he stopped & looked at us. I held my breath for fear he would cut into the woods but again he came on & stopped about 200 yds (240 paces) away. I waited as long as I dared & then I lowered the boom & down he went. He was dead when I got to him. Hit him right above the breast bone & out through his back (he was sitting).

He had a horrible skin but that left foreleg is worth $30. Anyway I am excited about it.

Trying to snow again.

I had been extremely lucky to get the wolf. He was a long way off and such a small target, sitting straight on, the bead in the rifle sight more than covered him. Mother's rifle had a set trigger system and since I knew I would get only one shot, I used this to set the trigger to fire by just be touched. I sat behind the sled with my elbows on my knees, raised the peep sight and got lined up. Just as the bead moved across the animal, I touched the trigger. The wolf was a brindle colored old male, was losing his hair and had bad teeth, and probably would not have made it through the winter. But we would have a bounty paid for him anyway.

Our plan was to use North Fork Cr. cabin as our base camp on the White River so we prepared to relay our loads down the bar from Solo cabin, setting traps along the way.

Journal—Trapping Alaska—November, 15th Monday—low overcast

We got stuff ready to take down to North Fork. I took a load down & Lou broke trail down through the woods for me to use the next day. As the trail was very fast I decided to go back to Solo for another load so I gave the pups a rest while I swept the cabin & went back. Each trip with a load took only 1½ hrs. Got back just when Lou got in. Cooked dog feed in the dark.

We have been living primarily on beans (in various forms) for the last two weeks. If not beans it's some other dried thing & they have my stomach on the blink all the time.

Trapping season starts today.

Of course, we had been trapping all along, but the official opening was November 15th. We were a long way from the closest warden though and gave it no thought at all.

Feeding the dogs was quite interesting to me. In the summer time we fed them barley soup with whatever meat and bones might be around. They did well on this gruel and stayed in good shape. In the winter it was a very different matter as the weather was cold and the dogs were working very hard and the calories had to go up exponentially. We had frozen, and thus saved, all the meat we could from the hunt the prior fall. We cooked food for the dogs every day in the bottom 1/3 of a metal barrel, either before we left in the morning or after we were back in camp and before we fed ourselves. The main ingredient was corn meal cooked into a mush, with chunks of bear or moose meat, bones, hide and all, thrown into the pot to boil while I stirred. Each dog dish was one half of a two and half gallon kerosene can, cut with the sides rolled over so as not to cut the dogs. They really dug into that meal and you could hear the bones cracking as they chewed them into small pieces that they ate as well. Every now and then you would hear them howl in pain as they passed one of these bones sideways. Rather humorous so long as it was not me in that position. On very long days we also fed each dog one dried salmon around noon when we stopped to rest.

Lou trapped the wolf I had seen during the hunting trip, which turned out to be a beautiful gray female with a lustrous, thick pelt. We had found earlier that a wolf was climbing up a log that had fallen down to the ground on one end that allowed her to climb onto the roof of the barn at Solo and then jumping down through a hole in the roof onto the cache of bear meat about five feet below. Lou made a "blind set," (no scent) with the trap right where the log touched the ground, so she would walk into it on one of her journeys to the cache. She was very much alive when he got there and so he shot her with a 22 cal. rifle we carried for just this purpose. Lou left her hanging in Solo cabin until the dog team was to come up for her and take her down to North Fork Cr. cabin. I went up once, but did not bring her down because I was worried about breaking off her frozen tail, which stuck straight out. This proved to be a mistake, because sometime before my next trip to Solo a wolverine got into the cabin and not a piece of her remained larger than a nickel. I really felt terrible about that stupid mistake of mine.

Journal—Trapping Alaska—November 18th, overcast

I went up North Fork to the first canyon & then cut up a little creek to a lake where I made some sets (all along). Lou went hunting.

The dogs took me over a 10' bluff today & nearly killed me. My face was cut and bruised & I ache all over. I lit on top of the sled. Ugh! They gave me a bad time all day.

Dogs are like horses when they are on the way home. They become excited and eager to get back. As I came down the trail beside the small creek that flowed into the larger North Fork Cr., the trail took a sharp left turn and then sloped down a 10' cut bank formed by the meandering of North Fork Creek. At the point of the turn was a very large Alaskan Spruce tree with wide branches to within about four feet of the ground. The dogs, instead of turning down the trail to the river, took the straightest path to the river and charged straight ahead under the spruce branches. I could see disaster coming and screamed, "HAW, HAW" and then "WHOA", but in the next split second I had to jump off the brake, duck under the branches running to keep my hands on the handle bars trying to stop the sled from arcing over the cut bank, but all to no avail. First the dogs and then the sled flew into space over the edge and then me, all of us landing in a great crash beside the frozen creek.

I landed astraddle one handle bar, then crashing face first into the floor boards of the almost empty sled. I was very lucky to have avoided a serious injury, but I was pretty certain I would only produce dead babies in the future. It was just such a problem that could lead to a person's untimely demise in that country. A broken leg or back and the deck would be heavily stacked against survival. When I could finally walk around a bit, I took a dog chain and worked the dogs over in an effort to let them know I was a bit unhappy they did not understand "HAW" or "WHOA".

On the 20th it cleared up and began to get very cold. Lou figured—20° F, and it kept getting colder all week. The cold weather was interesting but also challenging. I could tell when the temperature fell to—5°F because I could feel the moisture freeze if I breathed in through my nose. As it got colder other things began to show up, for example, working with the steel traps in light gloves, my fingertips felt as if they were burning when in fact they were beginning to freeze. If the temperature was colder,—30° F to—40° F, all of this happened much faster. Luckily there was not much wind when the weather turned cold otherwise it would have been very difficult to trap. Another phenomenon that always fascinated me was the formation of ice crystals in the shape of tiny ferns on any clear smooth ice. There was quite a bit of moisture in the air in the form of ice crystals over any open running water and sometimes looking out across the White River bar it was like a fog bank beyond which the white mountains rose up high into the sky.

At—40° F, if you dropped a hatchet into the water, the instant you got it out a 1/16th inch of ice froze all over it. If you took a piece of fractured shell ice and dunked it in water for a moment, the water in all the small fissures would freeze almost instantly, causing the ice to shatter when brought into the cold air. Below—50° F it was very hard on the dogs, as the snow formed ice crystals that cut their feet and the sled did not slide well in the dry snow. Also at these very low temperatures, the problem of overflow on any creeks and the main river became extreme. Once, over on the Beaver Creek, I crossed the creek on solid ice in the afternoon and by the next morning a foot of green water was running on top of that ice but under a new, one and half inch sheet of clear ice formed overnight. It is hard to imagine how running water can form solid ice, but in that extreme cold it does.

As the weather got colder, Lou and I both had fingertip, noses and ears frostbitten enough to cause scabs of peeling skin. Maybe worse than that was the fact that in the cold weather the animals we were trapping did not move around but hunkered down in an effort to keep warm. I came upon an interesting story laid out in the snow one day. A mouse had come out of a hole in the snow which I assume led to the nest, ran around in circles on the surface looking for something maybe to eat, and either got lost or just froze before it could get back to the hole. In either case it lay right on the surface frozen hard.

Journal—Trapping Alaska—November 25th clear and colder—55° F?

Thanksgiving today & lots of thoughts towards home. We decided to go down river today regardless of the cold. It must have been getting colder all day for when we got there it was really bad. Lou wanted to go back but decided to try her one night in hope that the weather might break.

I got the dogs in the overflow several times & they had foot trouble all the way. (the dogs were forming ice balls on and between their toes, which had to be taken off for them to work at all) *It is very beautiful in the valley with the effect given by the thick haze.*

I got wet feet again and frost bit both big toes. Our Thanksgiving meal consisted of strong tea, red beans, rice & raisins & left over salmon casserole dish. The Thanksgiving thought prevailed with myself though & it was a very substantial if not an overladen table.

We found it was impossible to heat up our 9'x 11'tent and ice crystals prevailed all over the inside of the tent except in a 4'circle over the stove. I stayed up until 10 PM huddled over the stove & still shivering & decided to try & sleep. I slept in all my clothes except my moccasins, which were wet, & crawled inside my double sack. As it was, my feet got numb in two heavy wool socks & I had to rub them together all the time.

Lou stayed up until 12 PM for fear he would freeze if he went to bed. He fared all right though. Lou thinks it is almost—50° F & we should have turned back in the morning.

After arriving at the campsite and trying to work fast, we unpacked the sled and I built a fire outside over which to cook the dog's meal, while Lou built one in the Yukon stove inside the tent. It was bitter cold and all the dogs were busy chewing at ice balls on their feet and constantly licking the small ice cuts they sustained during the day's run. I prepared the water and cornmeal mixture, threw in some meat chopped from a frozen bear haunch and then went inside to warm up. I could stay out only a few minutes at a time without some part of my anatomical extremities beginning to burn with frostbite. Lou said that this was the coldest weather he had seen since he had come to Alaska in 1919.

In the morning it was really cold and we decided to go back to Solo and then on into town for more grub. At the first open water I came to I dipped my moccasins quickly in and out of the water, forming a thin coating of ice to keep any other water from penetrating into my socks and feet if I was forced to go through overflow on the way to Solo cabin. On the six-mile trip back up the bar, a tiny airflow was hitting my right cheekbone and I had a good frostbite by the time we arrived. It thawed and then swelled a little that evening and began oozing liquid and a day later I had a scab the size of a silver dollar on that spot.

On the 29th we went up the 16 miles to Solo Mt. cabin on the way to town. The next day I took the team to Chisana via a digression up to our Powell Creek camp where Lou was going to spend the night and hunt the following day. There was no trail over the summit but Pat seemed to know exactly where he was, even if I did not. When I reached the camp, an hour's work was needed to get the tent back up from under the snow, build a fire to warm the place and leave hot water for Lou. When finished, I turned the dogs around and headed for town down Powell Creek in the dark.

It was pitch black as the dogs and I mushed down the creek on the ice, with me on the sled and hitting the brake occasionally to keep the sled going straight and not running into the dogs. I could not see where the trail left the creek and went into the woods and I figured we would just follow the creek down to the Chisana River and then follow the river trail to town. But all of a sudden, Pat, in the lead, cut to the right, went up a bank and I realized we were on the main horse trail through the woods. I was elated since finding the trail would cut at least an hour off the trip and thus I didn't mind that through the woods I had to trot behind the sled with my hands on the handlebars helping guide the sled through the trees. An hour later we came out of the woods into the opening where the trail crossed over the Johnson Creek bar near the edge of town. Looking to my right towards the low-lying Nazotin Mountains, I could see the green and cream colored Northern Lights shimmering along the ridgeline, and directly ahead, tiny flickers of light from cabin windows 300 yards away.

It always felt good to get back to town, even if there were only three old men wintering there and on this night Harry came out to help me with the dogs and after that to get a fire going in Lou's cabin. He invited me to have supper with him and we talked while I ate. He told me that Chisana had hit—56ºF, which meant it was probably—60º to—65º over on the White River.

Journal—trapping Alaska—December 1st—25ºF

I went on up to 'Copper Lake' to bring in the last mortal remains of the no-good horse. (shot after the hunting trip) *I found one fox still alive in a trap & 2 others in snares. One was a cross fox.*

Me at —55°F Chisana, AK 1948

The ravens had worked on three of them & two were almost completely ruined except for (use as) trimmings.

I picked up all the traps and tried to chop old 'Copper' into several good sized chuncks but found it impossible & came on home after dark.

Lou had gotten in at noon and hadn't hunted as he didn't feel too well.

It started to get colder on the 2nd with—35ºF on the thermometer hanging on outside by one of the windows in the cabin, and by dark it was—45ºF. The next morning it was—52ºF. It was very interesting to note how dense the air was at those temperatures. I used to liken it to water, in that it seemed to flow down into the valleys, pushing the warmer air higher and usually was not accompanied by any wind to speak of.

Animals, such as moose, moved higher up the creeks where the temperature was warmer. On one occasion a bush pilot landed in Chisana when it was around—20ºF and, after having lunch, could not start his airplane engine due to the cold. He said it had been +10ºF at 10,000 feet, so he had not worried too much about getting out again. He ended up staying the night.

Journal—Trapping Alaska—December 3rd—52ºF

I was going up Powell Cr. To fetch in the camp but it is too cold to use the dogs. I worked on the wood pile & cooked dog feed. Sewed on my pants & took a whore's bath.

On these clear cold days with darkness falling around 3:30 P.M. we were often treated to beautiful Northern Lights, usually the green or crème colored variety, but sometimes with reds and blues thrown in for added impact. At those times when mushing alone with the dogs in the dark, the sky seemed to almost crackle with an intense feeling of energy. This was especially true when above timberline where the reflected light from the snow outlined the low mountains lying to the north but leaving me out in the open, fully exposed to the dancing Aurora pirou-etting in long drapes of shimmering light across the heavens. It was then, though separated from other humans, I did not really feel totally alone and I never tired of seeing this phenomena as it always filled me with a certain feeling of awe and a sense that the night sky was filled with life of a different sort.

Journal—Trapping Alaska—December 5th—50ºF clear

Cut wood after Harry got the saw sharpened & worked on my snowshoes for a while & on the sled. Lou washed some of our clothes. Cooked dog feed.
Just as it was getting dark the sky turned pure violet over the tops of the hills behind town. It was dark purple at the crest of the hills & shaded to light violet and then on to the regular blue gray sky. The whole town met at Harry's for the news. (on the short wave radio)

Journal—Trapping Alaska—December 6th—55ºF+ clear northern lights

Loafed primarily. Cut some wood & read in my spare time.

Life in Chisana in the winter was fairly uniform day to day. We had used the horses in the fall to haul in logs from trees we felled across Johnson creek and these were piled up in a large opening between Lou's and Harry's cabins. I used a crosscut saw to buck up the logs, since gas powered chainsaws had not yet been invented as far as any of us knew and then split the rounds into firewood sized for either the kitchen stove or the heater in the main room

The heater was a converted 55 gallon oil drum, set on its side with a swinging door built into one end and a hole for a stovepipe chimney cut into the top at the opposite end. Each night we filled the heater with round three foot long logs, some up to five or six inches in diameter and shut the damper. Usually there were smoldering remains in the morning making it easy to start a new fire, but in cold weather the increased draft created by the difference between the indoor and outdoor temperatures usually had consumed all the wood long before morning. Sometimes when it was really cold one of us would get up in the middle of the night and refill the heater. Even then, the windows (long before double pane glass) would be frosted half way up on the inside, with a beautiful lattice of fern-like frost and the water pails in the kitchen would sport a half inch of ice by morning.

All of the water we used was from melted snow, or if we were lucky, from ice, several hundred yards away along the edges of Johnson Creek. I made many trips, with two five gallon pails swinging from the end of a yoke I carried across my shoulders, to the creek and back, filled with ice or snow. These I poured into a large metal tub we kept on the stove as our water supply. On days when we took a bath or washed clothes, we had to melt large quantities of snow to produce enough water to do the job and all of this took time. It was easy to work most of the day with these chores and not accomplish very much else.

Me, determined to stay warm

Time was running out for me, as I had to return to school. I had notified the flying service in Chitina to try to send an airplane to pick me up in Chisana on December 17th and we still had to make a trip back over to the White River to check traps, but the cold snap the first week of December delayed us. However, on the 8th it began to cloud up and the temperature climbed up to—20ºF by nightfall and on the morning of the 9th it was—12ºF, and we started out.

Journal—Trapping Alaska—December 9th—12°F

Up around 5:30 AM & had breakfast. We were all ready to go just as it got light enough to see. I went on ahead with the dogs to Bonanza while Lou fixed up the traps behind me.

When I got there I tied the dogs & went on to Porky Point by way of Beaver Lake to look at the traps out that way. Lou brought the dogs the rest of the way.

I got in about an hour after dark but there was a moon & it was very beautiful. We heard wolves howling over towards Flat Cr.

The next day was a very long run from Porky Point to North Fork cabin on the White River. We started in the dark up in the flats and ended the day four hours after dark having worked our way through the canyon of North Fork Creek.

Journal—Trapping Alaska—December 10th—20°F?

Up at 5:30 after a horrible night & had our bacon & spud breakfast. Lou went on ahead to break trail on snowshoes (there was a foot of new snow). I packed up the sled in the dark & went on after Lou.

Got one red fox in a trap on Beaver Cr. & then cut across the clumpgrass flats for 5-10 mi. We saw where the wolves had been fooling around the night before. They walked all over two more traps on a little lake but they were frozen down and did not go off.

It was really tough going & hard to keep the sled right side up over the hummocks. I traded Lou after a while & snowshoed about 3 miles more until we dropped into a tiny creek about 10 feet wide which drains into North Fork (creek) & then we followed it down to the ice of North Fork & and thence 12 miles more down to the cabin.

If the first 17-18 miles were hard the last 12 were worse. The creek was all overflow—sometimes over a foot deep & with the heavy load I got stuck a lot & had to wade around in the water until both moccasins weighed about 5#.

I got in around 8 PM & Lou about 15 min. later. He also had ice an inch & a half thick on his snow boots. I frosted my big toes before I could get mine off.

Cooked dog food & got to bed around 10:30 PM. Killed a porcupine & two ptarmigan & saw 7 caribou.

We had made North Fork Creek at dark, near the entrance to a canyon several miles in length. Somewhere below where we entered the creek, ice had formed a dam that forced the water up over the top layer of ice and into the snow cover, where it was flowing slush up to a foot deep in places. The surface of this overflow was already thickening the slush about one inch thick when we arrived, but it would be a hard two-inch thick sheet of ice by morning. Trying to get the sled through this mess was very difficult, partly because the footing for the dogs was slippery and the sled was becoming very heavy with the freezing slush accumulating all over the frame and runners, like a crab boat in the Bering Sea just before capsizing.

By the time I got to the cabin I had an inch of ice frozen on my mukluks, up almost to my knees. My feet were warm enough while I was working hard, but as I built a fire in the stove I began to feel my toes start to freeze. I used an axe to hurriedly chop some of the ice away since I could not unlace the straps or bend the mukluks enough to pull them off. In fact, on the inside, my socks and felt insoles were frozen together, as well as frozen hard to the inside of the mukluks, so everything had to come off together. I hacked away at the ice sitting in front of the stove and as I worked on one mukluk I kept the other in the open oven to soften. It was a race against time. Working as fast as I could, I still was not fast enough and frostbit both big toes right on the tips before I could extricate my feet from the mukluks.

It turned cold again on the 12th, down to about—40ºF. I spent a day looking at traps and resetting some. A wolf had come down the creek the night before and we also had lost a wolverine in a snare. I walked up a small tributary creek following a trail of another wolverine we had caught in a trap attached to a four foot long heavy wooden branch serving as a toggle he was dragging with him. The sign was easy to read since there had been no snow after he was caught. When I found the trap I saw that he had been eaten by several other wolverines and all that was left were tiny pieces of fur and bone chips and the trap.

On the 14th we left for the two-day trip back to Chisana, arriving on the 15th. Harry had a fire in the cabin and the dog food already cooked, and he even invited me to dine with him at his cabin since Lou, hunting up Powell Creek, was not expected until the next day. Typical Alaska good neighborliness! I was always impressed with this aspect of Alaska. People were usually friendly and helpful to each other and in the wilderness, where we were, one could always count on there being dry firewood left at every campsite or cabin by the last inhabitant and the game Lou and I killed was always shared around to the others in Chisana who could not hunt.

Journal—Trapping Alaska—December 17th

Got up rather late & since it is very overcast & was improbable that the plane would come in I went up to 'Copper Lake'. There hadn't been a thing up there since I was there except a magpie I caught in a trap. Saw a fresh wolf track & several fox tracks but that is all. Came back early.

The town had a regular carnival time when we had two new arrivals—Andy and the Indian. We spent most of the rest of the day telling all our woes of trapping (which were not few).

Husty (the Indian) *brought up a hunk of moose meat so we dug into that most ferociously. Lou baked a cake & biscuits too, so we really had a feast.*

Tonight our cabin was the local gathering place & there was hiyu talk until 10:30 PM. We hit the sack afterwards.

That was the last entry in the journal about my first experience trapping in Alaska. I was still expecting the plane to come for me, but in case it was unable to make it, I talked with Lou about my walking out to the Alcan Highway, about 75 miles away and hitchhiking 300 miles to Fairbanks to catch a commercial plane, as an alternative. We discussed the prospects for such a trip and all the alternative routes available, which were not many. I found out that Husty Sanford, a Tanana Indian was wintering in the cabin at King City, 25 miles down the Chisana River from town. Husty told me that if I came down there he would take me the rest of the way, or at least to another cabin where some Indian friends of his were trapping perhaps 25 miles farther. From there, he stated, there would be good trails to the Indian village and the Alcan Highway beyond.

I was very excited about the prospect of having this new adventure and finally made up my mind to go for it if the plane had not arrived by the 19th. I packed up all my stuff for Lou to send out with the airplane if I had left before it arrived and planned what I would take with me if I walked out. It was not much: warm clothes; moccasins and shoepacks and socks; matches and paper to start fires with; toilet paper and a knife. A gun was not necessary since no respectable grizzly would be out of hibernation. With this planning done it remained to wait another day for the plane.

The 18th came and went without the airplane, so the die was cast, and in the morning I would set out down the river on the adventure that would very much change my life.

Stretching the Limits

Wherein our young hero bites off a bit more than he can chew
but perseveres and learns much about himself
that had been heretofore hidden

The following story of my winter hike in Alaska from Chisana to the Alcan Highway, which almost cost me my life, was originally written at age nineteen while I was recovering in Seattle General Hospital in late January 1949. The writing ended in March 1949, and for many years I consciously tried not to start thinking about the event because every time a thought about the trip came to me, like a movie on a reel impossible to stop, my mind instantly was caught up in the memory and could not let it go until the entire trip was replayed, in all its anguished detail, right to the final scene of being carried in the arms of Alaska State Patrolman, Sgt. Brand, into St. Joseph hospital in Fairbanks the evening of December 26, 1948.

Thus it was a surprise when I picked it up again many years later to share with Bobby, that I realized it had not been completed. I will try to do that now. Most of this story consists of pages excerpted from my 1949 journal. These parts have been put into italics.

I had not touched the journal for such a long period that when I read it as a grown man, I was struck by some of the language used and should point out that many of the descriptions of feelings may remind you of some other writings of that period. I remember being particularly influenced by the poetry of Khalil Gibran and the writing of Antoine de St. Exupery among others and I fear a bit of their style entered into the narrative. I beg your indulgence and ask you to remember that I was a teenage boy, much into poetry, who had just experienced a very traumatic struggle and was going through another ordeal of multiple surgeries and hospitalization at the time of the writing.

I planned to hike from Chisana, down the Chisana River about 50 miles, then overland to the Scotty Creek Indian village and from there to the Scotty Creek Roadhouse on the Alcan Highway about five miles from the boundary with the Yukon Territory. I intended to hitchhike from there to either Fairbanks, Alaska,

183

or Whitehorse, Yukon Territory, whichever seemed the easier to get to in that manner, each being about 300 miles from Scotty Creek.

I did not have to make this trip. I could have waited for the plane to come in as originally planned the prior October, but the more I thought about having this experience, the more I wanted to do it. It was very easy then to rationalize that by hiking out I would be sure to get home by Christmas, whereas with the unsettled weather in mid December, perhaps the plane would not get in to pick me up and I would miss Christmas with my family whom I had not seen since July. More than that I wanted the experience to be the capstone to my other Alaskan adventures and I relished the thought of telling my friends about it.

◆   ◆   ◆

Around noon on the 18th, Husty Sanford, an Indian living and trapping at King City, came to town for some supplies. I talked with him about the trip to Scotty Creek, and he assured me that it would be quite easy. He even offered to take me from King City to the village, some thirty miles distant. He said that I could follow his trail back down to King City and that he would put me up for the night. I asked him what the snow conditions were and he replied that there was very little snow below him and that we would hit the trap line of the Scotty Creek Indians about seven miles below his camp. He also said that with the dogs we could get to the road by nightfall. This all sounded too good to pass up, so I told him that he would probably see me the night of the 19th.

Husty Sanford, in 1948, was a 28 year old Tanana Indian from the interior Tanana River basin. He had occasionally passed through Chisana on his travels and I had met him once in the summer of 1947. He was not too tall but husky and strong and from what I heard from Lou, who had known him for some time, had a reputation as a tough man, and it was alleged he had killed another Indian in a fight. Lou did not entirely trust Husty's word about things, but he seemed straight-up to me as we talked over the trip I was to make the next day.

The weather looked very depressing—cloudy but warmer (-20). I was certain that the plane would not get in the next day so I set about gathering together what little I was to carry with me. The fact that I would have warm places in which to stay each night made it possible for me to leave behind my sleeping bag. I intended to take a parka, heavy Indian overmitts and as I was to wear my shoepacks, I would take my moccasins and extra socks in the little gunny sack I was to carry. I packed about a quarter of a pound of raisins, a large piece of salami, several candy bars, and two large sandwiches. I didn't have to take snowshoes, as Husty was to provide them. I went to bed with the tight feeling of expectation in my stomach. I was sure that I would now have something really novel to tell my future grandchildren.

December 19, 1948—The Beginning

The morning of December 19th dawned overcast and gray. For me it only meant that the weather would not be too cold for the three-day hike to the Alcan Highway, 65 or 70 miles away. In my quest to have experiences to add to the story of my life, I was confident and eager to take on this new adventure and I could picture myself, in understated tones, telling my friends about my 70 mile walk out of the wilderness, as if it were just another common experience of those hardy souls who chose a life of action away from the ease and security of civilization.

Confident as I was, I still had a small knot of trepidation in the pit of my stomach from three little thoughts: hiking in the winter alone in country I had never seen, except for the first eight miles down the Chisana to Notch Creek; concern that a weather change in a few hours, could bring—50° temperatures that would add considerable challenge to my enterprise; and overhanging everything, the finality of the risk should I get into a serious problem, knowing for certain that I would never be found. But once my mind had set on the hike out, I'm sure nothing could have changed my determination to go, other than a precipitous drop in temperature, which seemed unlikely, and then Lou would not have let me go alone anyway.

My parting with Lou the morning of the 19th was difficult, as we had become very close, and there were tears in his eyes when I pulled on my rucksack. I tried to thank him and say my goodby without embarrassing myself with tears so finally just said, "So long Lou, thanks for everything," shook his hand hard and turned away to open the cabin door, stepping out to start down the trail to the river and face the adventure ahead.

I did not know at the beginning of my journey that the coming ordeal was to be the start of my transition from boyhood to manhood. The struggle that I underwent was not just the battle for existence; it was that, but was also the struggle of youth to attain maturity. My experience was one that began with youthful exuberance and ended in an earnest struggle to maintain life.

All I can do to convey what happened is to give a chronological history of the trip, trying to show what I thought at the time I was undergoing the hardships, how certain problems of a basic nature accumulated and presented themselves to me as they do to all men in similar predicaments and also how it affected my physical being over the period of seven days and seven nights.

Husty and his 3-dog team

It might be worth noting a few more details of the clothing I was using in the winter of 1948 and would wear on the hike. The first layer was a pair of woolen "longjohns", over which I wore a pair of heavy wool pants and a wool Pendleton shirt. I most often used a pair of thick felt insoles and two pair of long wool socks inside either moosehide moccasins or rubber-bottomed, leather topped, calf-high shoepaks. Over the shirt went a red wool mackinaw button jacket and over that, an army surplus unlined hooded parka that came well below my waist. I used an army cap with earflaps lined inside with fake fur. For my hands I had knitted woolen gloves under Indian moosehide overmitts

The trip the first day was just a long walk. I found the trail along the river bar very difficult to follow, as the wind had blown it in with drifting snow. I lost it completely after the first four or five miles, but I was in home territory. The thought of ever getting lost while traveling in known country never had occurred to me. But to get off the trail had always aggravated me. I would be disgusted at my lack of observation in the first place and would not like at all the prospect of a harder trip which would be inevitable. Thus I was mildly put out at having to break trail in eight to ten inches of snow. It was just more work. I also was thinking about the open water and overflow that I might run into by losing Husty's trail. Again, the thought of freezing my feet did not bother me, but what did trouble me was the prospect of carrying a few pounds of ice on each shoepack. I got into the overflow, too. It had crept in under a few inches of snow and I was in it before I realized it. I had some difficulty in finding my way out of it, for it was invisible. But I didn't get wet feet. If this had been just another day of trapping, I would have been put out no end by these inconveniences, but as it was, they were the necessary obstacles that made my challenge mean something.

The overflow had been the result of an ice blockage farther downstream, forcing the water to back up and ultimately find its way to the surface of the ice to spread out under the snow, which was why I had not seen it. But I was wearing shoepacks and not moccasins for that very reason and as it was not too cold I had little to worry about unless the water became deep.

The first day was a long hike down a frozen river that had no open water to be seen. The river bar was almost a mile wide except for the canyon I went through, where it narrowed to 100 yards. Husty's trail kept generally straight rather than following the frozen channels, which meant that I was mostly walking over a frozen, uneven snow-covered sandbar and climbing up or descending the low banks formed by the water the prior summer. The sides of these smaller channels were generally steep banks two to four feet high, which in the winter the windblown snow formed small cornices along the top edges and often removed enough snow to reveal the sandy dirt beneath.

Looking down river in the overcast weather on the 19th, there was a roughness to the landscape due to these undulations, except where the water channel actually was. These channels looked like a few smooth white ribbons running through the roughly corrugated river bar, with the forest growing to the edge of the river bank on each side, the trees black in the winter light. Rising behind the trees, the low snow-mantled hills spread in all directions away from the river. One could see in this landscape, here and there, driftwood of all sizes, occasionally forming huge log jam piles and along the banks trees tilting outward at various angles depending on how long the relentless water had been eating away at the soil underneath them, making sure they also would someday fall to join the forest debris lying along the frozen river.

I can remember that I was conscious of a great feeling of kinship with nature. I felt that the mountains were like big giants who were watching over me. They would surely snatch me from the muddy waters if I fell through the ice. But, fickle nature! She can change her face very fast!

I covered the eight miles to the Indian camp at the forks of the Chisana River and Notch Creek. Here stood a little white tent and out of it, dressed in ragged clothes, came Polly, old Chisana Joe, and their youngest daughter Susie. I stopped to get information on the coming trip through the canyon to King City. "Hello! How far Husty's camp?" I asked. Polly pointed the direction. "Sixteen mile," she answered, and added, "He on that side," indicating the left side of the bank.

It was strange, though. I felt very strongly the sensation of love. I loved everything that came in contact with me. These poor peasants of the hills, the mountains, the frost crystals seemingly growing out of the ice, even the little blades of grass that cast their dauntless shadows on the overpowering whiteness as if they were saying, "I'll never give in, for I too count for something." I think this love was brought on by a feeling of comradeship. We were all comrades in the play I found myself in. It was the play of Life, but, more specifically, it was the companionship of actors all contributing to the fulfillment of the drama of my trip. I loved them because they brought satisfaction and fullness to the play. And the play satisfied my pride. I was answering a challenge and in answering it I was on the road to self-fulfillment. It is hard to explain why I felt that in some way I was on the track of maturity and it was important to me.

I had to go through a canyon in which the ice had been forced into little green "Indian mounds," due to air pressure underneath. Although the day was calm, some wind had cleared away the snow, exposing glare ice. It is quite a relief to get out of snow and onto ice, for the walking is much simpler. I found myself acting as if it were the last day of my free, lighthearted youth. I would run and then slide, run and slide and laugh all the time. I had left the knowledge of the coming difficulties as a bear or sled dog forgets his eternal struggle for existence or tomorrow's hard work and becomes engrossed completely in having fun.

In my gaiety I had forgotten how long it had been since I had last eaten and was again brought down to earth by the gnaw of a hunger pain. I went over to a small bank and leaned against it and ate some raisins, two slices of salami, a sandwich and a candy bar. I felt the overtaking darkness on my heels, so I wasted no time in setting out again. I didn't like the prospect of trying to find a cabin in the woods after dark, and as I was not prepared to spend a comfortable night out, I strained to put the last miles behind me as quickly as possible. All I had to follow were two very light, sometimes indistinguishable, scratch marks left by Husty's sled runners. I wanted to be sure to see where they cut out of the river and headed for the woods. I became rather uneasy when it really began to get dark, as I had not come off the river yet and I thought that I had walked more than 16 miles.

It was not until the last few miles that fatigue began to catch up with me. It overtakes one in stages. First, you find that you are breathing a little hard. Then it hits the legs and they become heavy and it finally wells up throughout your whole body like a dull ache. Tiredness is also something that aggravates rather than perturbs. The spirit is willing but the body just doesn't respond. It is only when tiredness begins to dull one's ability to think coherently and soundly that it begins to frighten one. It is the loss of will power that is so terrible about fatigue.

Night descended at 3 PM just as the trail climbed up onto a shallow bank and crossed a bar towards the woods. It would be pitch dark in another fifteen minutes and I still hadn't come to the cabin. I gave out with a long "hellooo" and received no answer. I was finding it hard to walk in the darkness and so once again I called as I rounded a point of trees. This time I was answered by a malamute chorus and in a few minutes Husty emerged from a lighted doorway to see what was causing all the ruckus. I greeted him and we went into the ill-lighted cabin.

This particular cabin was large and had a dirt floor. Two bunks were built against the far end of the room and a small Yukon stove was on the right of the door. The table was on the left. There were four little children living in this ill-lighted cabin who constantly grubbed around on the floor. The children would never utter a sound and the squaw talked only when she reprimanded the children. Husty made the traditional frying pan bread, or bannock, and fried moose steaks. It tasted good to me after the strenuous day. I felt good after that.

I received the first misfortune of the trip that night. Husty had broken one snowshoe completely in half. We worked on it for the next few hours and finally succeeded in bracing it together so that they could be at least used. On top of that, I found that he had only the one pair of snowshoes, but that didn't worry me for the snow was not deep around King City and Husty assured me that we would not find it deep farther down. I was quite tired by 9:00, so Husty gave me his small mummy bag and I went immediately to sleep. As I look back on it now, I remember that I was trying awfully hard to be a perfect guest of these Indians. It was my first stay alone with any of them *and I wanted to be sure that I didn't offend them in any way. But as I got into bed I remembered to quietly slip my wallet out of my pocket and take it into bed with me. I slept well that night.*

December 20th 1948

Husty had told Lou and me that there were Indians trapping about six to eight miles below King City and I would be able to use their trail into Maggie's cabin. He also said there would not be any deep snow down river from his cabin and that I ought to be able to get to the Indian Village six miles past Maggie's by the second night. From there it was only about six more miles to the highway. Assuming this all to be true and I had no reason to believe otherwise, I thought I could reasonably limit the amount of food and camping gear I would carry.

Husty and I ate a hurried breakfast. He informed me that he was not going to take his dogs but would walk out with me himself. I am quite sure now that he did not intend to go all the way. We had only the one pair of snowshoes between us, but I was still optimistic. I felt that it was going to be damn hard, but I would get there. He told me to start on alone, as he had some work to do before he came and that he would catch up with me. I set out in the dark of morning. I had decided to wear my mocassins, as they were much lighter and I didn't think that there would be any over-flow down the river that far.

The first thing that I noticed on starting to walk was that both my hip joints hurt a little. I reasoned that walking on the ice and slipping an extra few inches with each step had made me strain these muscles and they had stiffened up during the night. The sky was again overcast and a fresh breeze was at my back. The going was fair as I had walked over to the ice where the snow was only an inch deep, but the price I paid for this was wet mocassins in the first two miles. I was really disgusted with my careless-ness. I sat down on a rock and changed into my shoepacks in the dark. I started off again and right away began to get into deep snow. I found that the snow on top of the ice was only about six inches deep, while it was a good foot on the ground. But the river wound around so much that I hated to follow it and decided it was better in the long run to cut the corners.

It had been daylight for at least an hour before Husty came into sight. I slowed down so that he could catch up to me.

"Snow's a little deep, huh Husty?" I noticed that the sweat was standing out on his forehead from the exertion of trying to maintain a near running pace in order to catch up to me.

"Hiyu deep, this snow," he exclaimed, as he leaned over to catch his breath, resting his hands on his knees.

After a few minutes we started out again with him in the lead breaking (a snowshoe) trail for me. From the rear he looked very powerful and each stride seemed the essence of determination. He was crushing the snow down, I thought, not going through it. I was straining with all I had in me to keep up with him. It was hard for I sank in a good six inches deeper than he did with the snowshoes. I know that I never would have been able to keep up that pace, but at the time I was sure that I could go on the rest of the day without tiring. I have found that when going to a destination that is a few hours or a day's walk distant, the difficulties in the way are just something to be endured, something necessary in order to reach that goal. And as traveling around in the wintertime in Alaska is not too pleasant, the camp or goal is of much more importance to one on the trail. When you know that you have to get there or risk a night "Siwashing" it in the woods, you rise above the hindrances of the trip. They cease to impress themselves so sharply on your mind at the time. The thoughts of arriving at the destination act rather as an opiate on the physical hardships in the way. It is only when you feel that you may not reach the destination that these difficulties become so real to you. Then, and only then, do they become your only concern. It is then not a matter of enduring them, but fighting them.

The snow that we were not going to encounter seemed to get deeper by the mile. It was dry and light and even the snowshoes were sinking in over a foot. Finally Husty stopped. He was breathing hard, as I also was, and he wanted me to take the snowshoes and break the trail. I had not had time to dry out my wet moccasins, now frozen, so he gave me a pair of mukluks with leather bottoms. I put them on and threw my shoepacks into the sack on my back, strapped on the snowshoes and started out. I began with a very fast pace. Husty was having a hard time keeping up and it was only a half mile or so farther on that he called to me to stop.

"We not make it this way", he said. "Snow too deep; we tire." In my eagerness to get there, I felt a slight twinge of contempt at his readiness to quit. I know now that he was quite right for the snow was still getting deeper. We had come about seven miles and were now on a little bar leading up to a point of trees that was formed by a bend in the river. I knew that I had to go on or walk all the way back to Chisana and miss getting home by Christmas.

"You take snowshoes. Leave him at village with Frank. He my brother. You find him," he said.

"Can I find the way alone, Husty?" I asked.

"I show you." He picked up a stick and began to draw a crude map in the snow. "River, he make big bend. You go straight. Leave river here."

"Where's Maggie's cabin on here?" I asked. He pointed to a spot near where I would begin to cut overland to the Indian village. "How far is it from the river to the cabin?"

"He about mile," Husty answered. "You see clear stream here." He drew a curving line, and added, "You see white mountain here. Cabin at foot of him."

"But Husty, there are all sorts of white hills. How can I tell this one?"

"Oh, no. He got no trees."

"OK. Now let me go over it with you. I follow the river until I come to a clear stream. From there I can see the white hill. And the cabin is on the left hand side of the hill. How far is it from here to the cabin, then?"

"He about twelve mile," Husty replied. "You cut straight across flats from cabin to village. You see lights when it gets dark. Only 6 mile to village. You get there tonight."

I looked down the river and could see that every bend the river took made the forest stand out in alternating points of land. If I went in a straight line I would have to cut from one point to the next.

"How many points until I leave the river, Husty?" He looked down river for a minute and I could feel him trying to visualize the trip, counting each point that he passed.

"About seven," he ventured. I took his word for it.

It was around ten o'clock by this time and I was feeling very confident, even happy that I was about to go alone. The story would sound much better to say that I had found my way through unknown country. It also meant that the walk I had undertaken was really going to mean more. I was to get a chance to practice what, if anything, I had learned about taking care of myself while in the woods alone. I was eager to be off. I offered Husty the last six inches of my piece of salami, and also my raisins. He gave me in return his two sandwiches. I thanked him for his help and we parted.

It began to clear up around 11:00. It was really quite beautiful. The river bar is perhaps a mile wide, so that when I was in the middle of it I was not conscious of a great deal of winding about. I could look straight ahead for at least five to six miles down a narrow corridor formed by the alternating points of spruce-covered land. I tried to maintain a fairly fast pace, but in a matter of an hour or so I found that I just couldn't keep it up. The snow was too deep. I found myself stopping more often to look back and also to take a breather. It was fast becoming very hard work. Much harder in fact, than I had anticipated. I began to find it easier to follow along the river itself, for the snow was not too deep above the ice. I would head for the ice and start winding along on it, almost feeling the strength coming back from the easier going, but then the ice would tack way off of the course that I wanted to follow and I would struggle up a low bank into the deep snow.

As time went by, I could feel my legs losing their strength very rapidly. I guess the pace I had maintained the day before was just now catching up to me. The rests came oftener. I was not thinking about anything in particular. I found myself concentrating on my objective. I counted and recounted the points of woods that I passed. I felt that I was losing track of the number by counting them so often. I became automatic. I didn't miss the beat if I could possibly help it. Any deviation seemed to require more than the usual exertion. I guarded my strength almost fanatically. Each overexertion meant that that much strength was gone. It would be very difficult to reproduce the lost strength later in the day. I was very tight with my reservoir of energy.

I came to be almost directly in the middle of the bar around 11:30, and in the distance I could see the low rolling hills that bordered the Alcan Highway. I headed for a point on one of the main hills so that I could keep in a straight line as much as possible. Way down the bar I saw two trees that seemed to be joined at the base and leaning out at the top, forming a V. I lined them up with my peak and headed for them. I decided to eat lunch when I got there. I was getting very hungry but with each step I took they seemed to move just that far away from me, so it was not until an hour had passed that I finally came up to them. I noticed that they were much bigger than I had first thought. At least thirty feet long. I didn't get right up to them as they were in the middle of a large logjam covered with snow and the chances would have been great that I would have broken my snowshoes. I ate a hurried sandwich while sitting on a log and then started off.

I kept remembering Husty's words about Indians trapping along the river between King City and Maggy's cabin but there was no sign at all of trapping activity, a fact I made certain to check out as I went along. Also, he had said the snowpack was not deep which would have made travel rather easy, but again his information was not accurate.

In the afternoon I found that my feet were becoming very sore. The Indian snowshoe is made with moose hide bindings that go across the toe and around the heel. These straps are only a half inch in width and have a tendency to cut in at both places. I knew that I would have raw spots and probably blisters on both feet. The weather was turning colder by the hour. I felt that it was about—30 degrees as darkness approached.

As dusk fell, I could feel that I was almost played out. I had to stop very often to rest a minute and my feet were hurting very much where I knew the skin was being rubbed off. When I came to a spot where I could follow the ice a little way, I would take off the snowshoes and try to rest my feet, but as soon as I put them back on they would start rubbing again. I began to worry that I would pass the spot and not be aware of the fact. I felt that I had come at least 12 miles by about 3:00, and I knew that I had to find the cabin soon or stay out all night.

I finally came to a spot where the river turned to the right and made a bend in against a cut bank in a semicircle. On top of the bank, which was about 12 feet high, there was a wide opening in the trees that spread out into a clumpgrass flat. About a mile out on the flat was a white hill with no trees on it. It stuck out like a sore thumb just as I had pictured it, but it was in the wrong setting. There was no clear stream. I decided to walk another half mile. It was fast becoming dark, and I was very tired, so I turned around and headed for a spruce thicket on top of the bank where I intended to wait until the moon came up. I would look for the cabin by moonlight. I needed the rest, so I didn't mind the delay very much. It would also add to the experience and test my skill in woodcraft.

I know Husty did his best to direct me to the cabin, but his words did not project the true image to me, of what the "White mountain" looked like. I did miss the small clear creek that he said I should come to and to this day I do not know if I did not go far enough or passed it without notice. It is easy to over estimate the miles one has traveled, especially when the going is hard and I think now the odds are that I did not travel as far as I thought I had down river from King City.

I was playing a game. The stakes were rather high, but I didn't give that a thought. There were certain rules that had to be followed for this game and as I walked toward the patch of trees, I was racking my brain trying to remember all I had been taught. I found a clump of five or six small spruce trees well back from the bank so as to be sure that I would be out of any wind that might come up. I took off my snowshoes and proceeded to scoop out snow from the center of the clump, stacking it high around a little circle. I then collected wood enough to start a fire. Once it was going I began to look for dead branches and small downed timber that I could get without an axe. I made a large pile beside where I was to lie down. I was very hungry. I reached into the sack and took out my extra socks and my shoepacks. I saw that I had only one sandwich. I propped up a stick and hung my socks on it. I then took off my mukluks and socks. I saw to my surprise that my two socks were frozen together from sweat, but my feet were warm. I inspected where the bindings had rubbed and saw that I was quite raw on both feet. I then put on my warm dry socks and shoepacks.

I sat by the fire feeling the pleasure of rest seeping through my body. I didn't have too much on my mind at that time. I was only interested in capturing all this pleasing sensation that I could. I was happy, of that I am quite sure. I know that I was conscious of feeling that I was not undergoing any great hardship. If I did think that a night out in—30 degrees was a hardship, I also felt that it was going to benefit me in the long run. I let my mind go on and the thoughts seemed to come in a stream. I thought about all the experiences that I had had. I was pleased with myself. I didn't feel too much that I had "been around," in the popular sense of the phrase, but I knew that I had done many things that most other men had never done in their lives. And I was only eighteen. How many other eighteen year olds spend a night out alone in the Alaska wilderness in 30 degrees below zero?

Had I gone farther looking for the cabin I might have found it, but if I had not, I suspect I would not have been able to write this story. There is no way to know. But I was starting to stretch the limits of my capacity to cope and I was beginning to feel insecure.

I felt the tiredness creep over me, and I lay down in the snow and went immediately to sleep. I had been asleep several hours when I awoke with a start. I was shivering. The fire was just a bunch of embers. How long have I been asleep, I asked myself. The moon's up ... must be at least 10:00. I got up and threw some wood on the coals and a tiny flame grew up and branched and soon I had another roaring fire. I saw that the woodpile was getting low so I went out into the woods and by moonlight I gathered more branches. I felt stiff all over, and still tired. I decided to sleep the night through and start out again in the morning. I built up a large pile, stoked the fire, and lay down again and went right to sleep. I had felt quite cold, so I curled up a little nearer to the fire and tried to get some snow piled up against my back which felt icy.

I was trying to wake up, but sleep held me down. I struggled. I had to wake up. I knew I must wake up. I sat up with a start. Flames were leaping out of my parka. I struck with my hands and pulled off pieces of charred cloth. The fire was quickly out. I had been careless and I was lucky. There was a hole eight inches around through the front of my parka, but my wool jacket had not been burned. I cursed myself for the mistake which could have cost me my life. Damn the luck! You cheechako! It was not quite light yet, so I went back to sleep.

A compounding of mistakes was taking place, starting with going into country I was unfamiliar with, not being prepared for every eventuality, such as the trip taking longer than planned, a change in the weather, not enough food for an unplanned problem, not enough of the proper gear, to name just a few. I started the hike making certain assumptions of how it would go and left myself exposed with little fallback capacity to any change from the original plan. No doubt one of the great faults of a natural born optimist, always in a hurry and willing to take shortcuts, but unwilling to take the added time and effort to properly plan for the success of the venture.

December 21, 1948

I woke up as it was beginning to get light. I started to get up but my right leg refused to work. I limbered it up for a minute and got up. I tried to take a few steps but my knee hurt very much. It felt like it was out of oil and it was all I could do to walk. I certainly did not like the prospect of snowshoeing very far with my leg like that. In fact, I didn't know whether I would be able to snowshoe. I hobbled around in a circle trying to limber it up. Each step sent a stab of pain into my knee. I knew that I could be in serious trouble if I did not find the cabin, for I was almost twenty miles from King City, a long walk back. I decided to go father down river in case I had not gone far enough. I ate my sandwich and then put on my mukluks and after much difficulty got down the cut bank and onto the river bar. As soon as I got the snowshoes on I could feel the rubbing begin. I went very slowly. At first my knee hurt so much that I didn't think I could walk at all. I knew that was silly, though. I had to go regardless of the pain. It would have been the same if I had broken my leg. In short, I had no choice.

I must have walked about a mile downstream without seeing anything that even resembled a white hill. While I was walking along I heard a distant humming of a motor coming to me through the still, cold air. At first I had trouble determining the source of the noise but then the pitch changed and suddenly I knew I was hearing trucks on the Alcan Highway. I could hear each one shift gears quite distinctly. It gave me a very strange sensation. Here I was, moving slowly along this ribbon of white, much as an ant follows a line in the pavement. I was trying to get to the highway. I could hear the highway, even visualize it just over the low hill ahead of me, but I could not get there. It was preposterous that I had to struggle so hard and spend so much time getting to something within hearing distance. Man is so helpless alone!

I decided to go back and investigate the only white hill in sight: the one near which I had camped. The sun was well up by this time and it began to get colder. I felt no fear of not finding the cabin. I knew where the highway was, and I knew where King City was. I knew that I didn't want to go back at any cost. If I went back I would have walked forty miles out of my way. I also would have been beaten. I walked back up the bar two miles, to make sure that I had not gone by the place in the dark. I found nothing. I stopped and tried to figure where it should be. I could look down-

stream and see all the country, but no white hill stood out from the rest except the one near where I had spent the night. I turned back and started down the bar again. This time I went about a mile past where I had gone earlier in the morning. Again I found nothing.

Now I was beginning to feel a little desperate. I had to do something. I went back to the cut bank and climbed up on it. I decided that I would start across the flats in the direction of the highway. I would have no fear of getting lost and would be sure to make it by nightfall, or at the very most the morning after. I started out. The snow was deep and drifted across grass clumps and buck brush. I stumbled as the brush grabbed at the webbing of the snowshoes. It was much harder going than through the deep snow of the bar. It hurt my knee terrifically. I had only to go a hundred yards before I knew that I could never make it in my present condition.

I tried to think out my situation. "I have no food, I thought. It's getting damn cold. It hurts like hell to break trail any more and it'd be dangerous to risk staying out tonight if it gets any colder. I'm not certain I will find the cabin if I go on or even the trail to the village. If I go back I'll have lost and will have walked forty miles extra." As I was standing there trying to make up my mind, a phrase came into my head that I had heard my father use. I had never had occasion to carry out its advice before, nor had I given it much thought, but now it made a quick reaction on my mind. "Discretion is the better part of valor," he had said. It came as out of nowhere, but as soon as it entered my head I knew what I was going to do.

I can't describe how hard it was to swallow my youthful pride. It had meant everything to me to make this trip successfully. I had been defeated. But as I turned back, other thoughts were also coming to me which seemed to take the sting out of being defeated. These were practical thoughts that dealt with the reality of the situation: It's getting colder, about—30°, I guess. I've got to cover twenty miles before it gets too dark, and it's already past 10:00. My knee was making walking very slow, and my feet hurt more than ever. Yes, I thought, it'll be a hard day.

I had walked only three or four miles when I noticed that my feet were hurting very much. Whenever coming to some ice, I would take off the snowshoes and run as best I could to make them feel better. It would seem to help a little, but as soon as the snowshoes were back on, the pain would begin again. It finally became difficult to move my toes, and I knew they were getting too cold. I was in a spot where the nearest woods were at least a half to three quarters of a mile away. If I was to go to them I would have to break trail that far. Looking up the river, I could see the two leaning trees where I had eaten lunch the day before. They were no more than a mile away, so I headed for them. I took off the snowshoes again to try to get the cold out of my toes. It didn't seem to work. I realized that I had been walking all day with my feet slowly freezing and was not able to tell that it was happening because of the pain caused by the rubbing of the bindings. Still I didn't think they were too badly frozen. I would have liked to sit down and change shoes, but without a fire it would have been most difficult and if I put on my shoepacks I wouldn't have been able to wear the snowshoes. No, I had to get to that driftwood pile.

It must have been noon when I got there. The temperature had dropped until now it probably was forty below. I took off the snowshoes, working very fast, for every second counted, and scooped out a place for the fire. I began to gather wood. It hurt terrifically to walk over that pile of wood which was covered with a foot of snow. I kept falling through in between the logs. I knew that I had better gather all the wood that I could in a relatively short time since once I started to work on my feet it would be impossible to walk around in the snow without my shoes.

I got the fire going and began to take off my mukluks. I worked as fast as I could for the fire would only burn a short while and I had to have everything done by then. Again, the sweat had frozen my socks together and it was with much tugging that I could separate the socks from the mukluk itself. I was not prepared for what I saw. Both my big toes and toes next to them were frozen, as were both little toes and both heels. The rest of my feet were badly frostbitten.

You may wonder what one's reaction would be on seeing that he is about to lose most of his feet. I had always imagined that it would be quite a shock, and so my lack of any sharp feeling really surprised me. I was completely unconscious of any fright or shock or despair. I felt my feet. "Hard as hell," I said out loud. I then flicked my big toe with my finger. "Uh! All same wood," I again said aloud.

That was all there was to it. I accepted the fact that I would lose most of both feet as soon as I saw that they were badly frozen. Once I had accepted it, I put the thought out of my mind. I became concerned with the phenomenon of freezing. It was interesting. I noticed the yellow-white color of the skin. It was like the color of a callous. I felt its texture, but received no sensation of touch. It was like touching something apart from myself. It was a deadness, hard and cold and rather smooth. I wasted no time, though, for I was much worse off than I had imagined. I would have spent a great deal of time trying to work on my feet, but time was one thing I didn't have.

I remembered that you should thaw out slowly; probably rub snow on the frozen parts. I did none of these things. I pushed my feet into the flame for as long as I could stand it. I rubbed a little and then back close to the fire. I began to get results. The frozen parts began to turn red and then purple. The pain was excruciating. I know that if something had hurt so much at any other place or in different circumstances I should have screamed. Not so here. I was really up against it and I knew it. The thought of what had to be done seemed to dull my mind, or fill it to the point where I had no room to spare for the sensation of pain. The fire was fast dying, so I finished working on my feet and put on the shoepacks.

I probably could not have snowshoed anyway, but with shoepacks it was impossible. At first it was all I could do to stand. I made myself hobble forward. Finally I got used to the pain and it became a little easier. It is hard to describe what it felt like to walk. As I started up the trail, dragging my snowshoes by one end, I recall saying to myself, "It's just like walking on top of a stove." The sensation was like you might expect if someone was holding a flatiron against your feet, and no matter what you did, kept it there. I remember when it hurt so much that I didn't think I could stand it any longer, I would kick out sharply as if to loosen the pain that had fastened itself to the bottoms of my feet. It was strange that the burning sensation felt like it was coming from the soles of my feet rather than from the toes, and every step seemed to force my skin down all the harder onto whatever was burning me.

I can vividly remember walking along after thawing my feet, tears streaming from my eyes from pain that felt like my feet were on fire and nothing I did could shake the burning off. The description of walking on top of a stove was exactly what it felt like, but finally fatigue and the need to keep going made it bearable.

I know now that the pain after thawing out was largely due to actually burning my feet in the fire. Did this method of thawing, as opposed to using snow or cold water, actually increase the damage? I don't know, but I doubt it. I thought at the time I would lose a lot more of my feet than I actually did and the main loss of my big toe and the one next to it on my left foot, matches the observation I made on getting to King City, that those two toes were still frozen. So perhaps the quick thawing actually reduced the extent of the freezing somewhat. Again, I don't know the answer to this question.

You try to take your mind off of pain when it is with you for very long. It seems that nature helps too and finally makes you rather senseless to it. But it comes back in a wave when you think about it. I tried not to think about it.

The combination of a bad knee and frozen feet seemed to be keeping me from making any headway. I knew that I would not get to King City before dark, and I also knew that I couldn't stay out another night in the condition I was in. I did notice, however, that it was beginning to cloud up after 2:00 P.M. and began to get warmer. A breeze was coming up behind me. The walking was very difficult. When going over a snowshoe trail, only once traveled, and without snowshoes, you find that when you put a foot down you don't know where it is going to come to rest. It may stay up on top, or go through eight inches. It may stay in the middle, or go sliding off to the right or to the left, causing you to stumble and shift your weight quickly. It is work that will soon tire you out. I tried to walk off the trail to see if that would be easier. It would seem so for a time, but then I would get tired and get back on the trail. I never could make up my mind which was easier. I just kept going from one to the other, continuing to get more and more tired.

It finally got dark and I lost the trail altogether. Once in a while I could tell by the feel that I was on it or had crossed it, but I never could stay on it for any length of time. The breeze continued to get stronger, and every time I stopped it would chill me through. I finally got so tired that I decided to lie down to rest. I found a place where the wind had blown a sort of snow cornice over a gully and I scooped underneath with my snowshoes and got in under the overhanging snow. At first I shivered so that I couldn't get much rest and would get up after much effort and start out again. Finally I got so fatigued that when I lay down I would fall asleep for some time. I was so tired that I didn't care if I woke up or not, but I always did, and shivering.

In the darkness I could make out very dimly the edge of the woods and could see the points I had been counting the day before. I knew that the cabin was in between two points, but as each one looked the same in the dark, I never knew which was which. I tried to estimate how far it was from the cabin to the mountains, but it was only a guess as I had walked that part just as it had gotten dark the first day. I found that I could do only a short distance before I was completely worn out. I could not see any rises or dips in the snow and consequently fell down often and many times I would just lay there and go to sleep. When I woke up I never had the slightest idea how long I had been asleep. Finally I became fearful that I was becoming so tired I would go to sleep and even the cold would not wake me. I knew the consequences of that. I thought that I was fairly near to the cabin, so I was determined to stay on my feet until I got there.

I saw a point about half a mile away and after what seemed an age I would round it and expect to see a light sparkling through the trees. No light. I was then sure that it would be the next one a mile farther on. Again no light. Then the next. Still no light. I began to cry from the tiredness more than the pain. Why couldn't I get to the cabin? I rounded one point and called out. No answer … just darkness and wind. I staggered on to the next point and again let out a call. This time I heard the dogs but could see no light. I must have walked five miles past where I originally thought the cabin was. The dogs began to howl and I made my way towards the sound. Finally I saw the door open and Husty came out with a gun in his hands. I called out to him for fear he might take a shot at me thinking I was a moose. I continued to struggle towards him.

I remember as I came up to Husty that I was rather embarassed about being back. I saw that he was surprised to see me.

"I'm frozen, Husty."

"Bad?" He asked.

"I think it's pretty bad," I said. We went into the cabin.

"What time is it," I asked.

"One-thirty," he answered.

"Jesus'Christ," I said. "I've had a hard day. I'm sorry to cause you all this trouble, Husty."

I had a very difficult time getting my shoes off. The socks were stuck to my feet. I gingerly pulled them off and was surprised at what my feet looked like. They had all blistered in huge water blisters. Some of these had broken and the skin was all rubbed apart. They looked like raw meat in several places. All Husty could say was, "Jesus, worst I see." I looked at my toes and found that the big toe and the one next to it on the left foot were not quite thawed out.

"Have you got any cold water, Husty?" He got a bowl, filled it with melted snow and brought it over to where I was sitting. I put my left foot in and tried to rub some circulation back into it.

"Have you got any tea handy? I guess I could use some."

He made me tea and we worked on my foot about a half hour, but with little if any results. I then asked to get some sleep and Husty again gave me a robe to sleep in, and I lay down on the bunk. I fell asleep so fast that I didn't have time to think over what had happened.

It is hard to add anything to the description from the Journal. I think the writing accurately recaps all the events and my thoughts during this terribly difficult day. Memories of that day are still riveted in my mind and when I read this journal, almost sixty years later, I am practically overcome recalling how physically difficult and painful it was. In addition, the knowledge of failing to make it on my own, seriously freezing my feet, creating a problem for everyone, from Husty to my family, was a heavy mental load to cope with as well. But as I alluded to in the journal, you can't carry it all at the same time and your mind simply sorts things out and focuses only on the most critical, in this case making it back to Husty's cabin and safety.

What I do know is that had I not been in really great physical shape and built up reserves of endurance during the fall while running the dog team, I could not have survived through the 21st. It was a close call, but more was ahead.

December 22, 1948

I had a very restless night. My feet were running very much and they stuck to the sleeping bag. They hurt, but my tiredness seemed to dull the pain. I kept waking and having to turn over. I awoke for the last time as Husty got up to build a fire. He cut off some moose meat and fried some bannock in lard, and brought the food over to the bed for me. The rest of the family got up and had breakfast, and then Husty and I decided that it would be better for him to take me out with his dogs, rather than go to Chisana and get Lou and his team. That meant he would have to go up to a moose kill that day so as to leave some meat for his family while he was away and we would start the next day. I didn't want him to go up and get Lou, mainly because I knew how badly Lou would feel about my freezing, and I didn't want to trouble him with such a long trip. I also felt rather ashamed at my predicament.

The 22nd was much like lying in a hospital bed the day after surgery, with pain that would not subside coupled with inattention from the nurse, no matter how many times I pushed the call button. My feet burned all the time and were driving me crazy and it was almost impossible to stand since the blood rushing down into them increased the fire significantly.

Husty left immediately after breakfast and was gone all day. I lay in bed, dozing off and on the rest of the day. I had to get up and go outside in the morning. I found that I could just barely stand and that as the blood rushed into my feet it brought with it a throbbing pain. It took me several minutes to make it to the other side of the cabin, open the door, and take a few steps in the direction of the woods. That was all the further I went, so I swallowed my modesty and relieved myself right there. I was glad to get back and lie down once more. The Indian children scurried around the cabin all day but I could get no word out of them at all. I would ask for a drink of water and they would just stand and stare at me, not knowing what to do, but too shy to do what I asked of them. Even Mary would not do anything for me. I found out later that she is very hard of hearing and that was very likely the reason. If I wanted anything, I had to get it as best I could myself.

I found after the first trip that it was not hard to control my desires. With time to consider what had happened to me, I still felt no remorse at the thought of losing part of my feet. I was rather in a hurry to get out and to a doctor for fear that they might become gangrenous. I fully expected to be on the road the next night, with the help of the dog team, for Husty assured me that it would be only a day's trip. I know that I was much more afraid of the reaction of my parents than I ever was about losing my feet.

I thought that it would be a very simple operation to cure frozen feet. The doctors would look at them, shake their heads and simply cut them off. I hated the idea of throwing a large doctor bill onto my folks. I would have felt much better about the whole thing if I had had enough money to cover the expense. All I had succeeded in doing in making this trip was to show that I was still not able to take care of myself, and because of this I had to fall back on my parents to bail me out. This thought hurt more at the time than the loss of my feet.

My blistered toes had turned a deep red color and water blisters the size of silver dollars decorated both heels where I had burned them trying to thaw out. After getting up one or two times in desperation to get myself some water or tea, I found that the pain this caused made it much easier to just stay put in the sleeping bag and sleep as much as I could while waiting for Husty to return.

By mid afternoon when I realized that I was not going to be able to walk out under my own power, even with Husty helping me the whole way. The only possibility to get out was in the dog sled, and Husty, who understood this before I did, planned to use his sled and three-dog team to transport me down to the Scotty Creek village the next day.

I dozed all day and woke late in the afternoon when I heard the dogs come up outside the cabin. I heard Husty unhook them one by one and then the door opened and he came in. He brought in a piece of meat and began to fix dinner. After a while he went out to give his three dogs a hunk of dried salmon. After we ate, he began to gather together some of the stuff that we were to take with us on the trip. For food, he packed a small cardboard box with a little tea, some sugar and a moose heart. To this he added a few pieces of bannock. That could be ample food for a day on the trail.

December 23, 1948

The next morning we ate an early breakfast. I found that it was almost impossible to stand up at all. My feet were much more tender. I finally struggled into two heavy wool socks on my right foot, but could only get one sock onto my left since it was so swollen. I put on shoepacks over the socks. Husty got the sled ready and helped me out to it and into a sleeping bag. I wore my parka over my jacket as I would be apt to get cold from not being able to move around. Husty then hooked up the three dogs and we were off. The first two or three miles were over some fresh overflow with interspersed rocks. *The dogs pulled fairly well on the ice but the first rock we hit I saw that they were anything but strong.*

In an hour we were into the snow and they could barely pull the sled. Husty was on snowshoes and working the G-pole behind the dogs, breaking trail for the sled. Finally the snow got so deep that even that was no good. He then began to snowshoe a few hundred yards ahead breaking trail, to once again return and get on the G-pole and also pull on a dog chain fastened to the front of the sled. This went on for about an hour. We had only made about four miles since we'd started. I could see that Husty was very tired and that we could get nowhere at this rate. I didn't know exactly what to do for I was not sure that I could even stand up. We went on a little further and then it was late in the morning, so we stopped and Husty made a pot of tea and we had a few slices of the heart with some biscuits. It was then that he said what I already knew; that we weren't going to get anywhere in this kind of going. I offered to try to get out of the sled and mush the dogs myself while Husty went ahead and broke trail. We packed the food box and started out.

It hurt very much when I first got up, mainly from the blood rushing down into my feet. It made them throb. When we first started out I tried my best to hold most of my weight off my feet by holding onto the handle bars as one would a set of parallel bars in a gymnasium. It was hard to do and when I would slip and have to throw all my weight onto my feet to get back on the handle bars, it would send a shocking pain through my feet. On top of that, by having all the weight on the very back of the runners, it made too hard pulling for the dogs. In the deep snow the ends of the runners would dig into the snow and the front of the sled would go up into the air like an aquaplane. When that happened the sled would stop. I began to let my weight come more and more onto my feet. It was very difficult, but the more I did the easier the dogs could pull. Finally I was walking completely by myself with little or no help from the handle bars, save to direct the sled with my arms. Husty was way ahead of me in a short time so I could not depend upon him for any help.

I know that it was the hardest thing I had ever done to walk behind that sled, but I never thought of it in that light. I concentrated on where I wanted to be and how soon I was going to be there. Today was the 23rd of December. I was going to be to the highway that night, get a ride to Fairbanks or Whitehorse and be home on the day before Christmas. I must have figured out this trip home for Christmas every mile. I had to make sure when I would get there. It is strange that the fact of getting home was more important than getting to a doctor and more important than losing my feet. I never did think about the loss of my feet. It was not important next to getting home.

I could never, no matter how hard I concentrated on various things, get away from the pain in my feet. I often cried out with the pain that seemed to come out involun-

tarily, for I never took my mind off whatever I was thinking about at the time. I remember going short stretches with tears streaming down my face, due only to the pain but never from the circumstances. Finally I would get control of myself and stop, but it would only be a short time until I would get into some very hard going and all the difficulties would seem to be magnified and I would not be able to hold the tears back any longer. Again I would be crying.

We were not making good time at all. By the time it got dark we had gone only ten miles and it seemed that the trail was getting harder all the time. It was fairly warm out which made things easier for us, but later in the afternoon it looked like it was try-ing to clear up. If it did, I knew that it would be much colder the next day. In the afternoon I began to feel the effects of lack of a good sleep and the hardships of the day before. It took a great amount of exertion to keep going. I kept hoping that it would be better going in the miles to come but I felt that no matter how hard it became I would get through. I had to be home for Christmas. It was my responsibility to my family to get home. The thought of dying, although often entering my mind, never presented itself as a possibility. I had heard countless stories of men freezing in the hills, but it always seemed to me that if they had really tried, they would have gotten out. If it had been me I would have made it, I often thought. Now it <u>was</u> me and I was going to make it and be home for Christmas.

When it got dark I caught up to Husty at a huge pile of driftwood. He had started a fire and was cooking a pot of tea. There were a few pieces of heart for us but the bis-cuits were all gone. After eating, we tried to get the large pieces of wood on fire and finally succeeded in having a ring of fire around us which made it quite warm. There were very large trees, some a foot thick piled up in almost a circle and they sent the flames nearly twenty feet into the air. As I watched it I thought about the fire that was burned at the rally before the Big Game down at Stanford. That too was a huge fire, but what a different kind of fire from my fire here. My fire was a meaningful one. I had great sentiment for my fire that night. It was an element well used. Used as a man should use it. I loved it for its rightness.

We had only one sleeping bag with us. I saw that Husty was very tired, so I offered it to him and told him to get some sleep. I said that I'd watch the fire for as long as he wanted to sleep and then I would try to sleep myself. As I remember he was going to sleep until midnight and then I was to have the bag until morning. I know that he slept until four in the morning (when he got up to tend the fire) and then I was really tired from walking around the fire or resting against a log, so I got into the bag.

Even without frozen feet the walking was difficult due to sliding this way and that, in the deep snow only partly packed by the snowshoes. The trip was inexorably becoming just a messy struggle of slipping, sliding and falling, rather than a hike.

December 24, 1948

Husty woke me as it began to get light. I had a hard time getting to my feet after lying down, but finally managed it. We had a small piece of heart and started out with Husty going ahead and me mushing the dogs. The fire had burned well all night and was still burning when we left it the next morning, its smoke rising straight up in the still air.

It was very evident in a short time that it was going to be a difficult day. The dogs were very weak and the snow was getting deeper the farther along we went. It cleared off very soon and began to get cold. Husty was quite a distance ahead of me all morning. I knew if I got into any trouble that I would get no help from him, and as it got colder I began having trouble keeping my toes warm. Husty was cutting towards the left bank of the bar for some reason. It was a different way than I had gone three days before. I supposed he was trying to find a trail made by other Indians that he said were trapping down below his place. But if he was looking for a trail, he never found it.

I began to have great difficulty in driving his three scrubby dogs. I felt genuine pity for them as they were half starved but I had to make them pull the load. I was helping with all I had to push the sled however every time we would hit a little deep snow or a runner would slide off the trail, they would quit. They were simply played out and that was before 9:00 in the morning. I began to get rather desperate, for it was much too hard on me having to push the sled whenever they quit pulling. I finally had to resort to giving them a kick whenever they stopped.

Finally this had no effect, so I undid a chain that was used to tie them up and worked them over with it. I hate to beat a dog, but I couldn't help feeling it was their hide or my life. In my desperation I found that I was becoming furious at them rather than feeling pity for the way they had been fed. I must admit that I became quite ruthless with the chain and in more than one place I left blood on the trail. The more they howled when I struck, the angrier I would become. Finally they didn't even respond to the chain and I knew then that the sled was not going farther.

I was stopped near the forest edge when Husty returned. "We're going to have to leave the sled, Husty," I said. "The dogs can't even pull it empty ... How far are we from Maggie's cabin?"

"Six miles," he answered. He then began to unhook the dogs and roll up the sleeping bag, which he cached in a tree.

"I don't know whether I can walk without the sled for support," I said. "But maybe I can try to go ahead on snowshoes and break trail. I'll meet you at the cabin or go on to the village from there."

I thought that the next six miles were going to be very easy to get over. Why I thought this, it is difficult to tell, for it was almost 10:00 and we had only come about five miles since daybreak. I put on the snowshoes and started out beside the low bank. I had to wear the shoepacks and I had only gone about two hundred yards when I knew that it was going to be impossible for me to use the snowshoes. It was just too difficult for me. I then turned around and went back to where Husty was finishing hanging up the stuff that had to be left.

"I just can't do it, Husty. I guess I will have to follow you in."

He grunted an assent to this and took the snowshoes from me, and started through the woods. His dogs took up the trail behind him and I was soon all by myself, floundering along in his trail.

It was infinitely hard going and it was getting colder all the time. It must have been 30 below by that time. When I came back out of the woods and went out on the bar, I could see Husty, with his three dogs walking directly behind him, way down the bar. It was not long before they were an indistinguishable dot a mile ahead of me. It was then that the thought hit me that I might not get out alive. If I froze again or fainted from overexertion I was sure that Husty would not come back and look for me. I knew that he was too tired out himself and that at heart he really didn't care what happened to me at that point.

One of the clearest memories of that day that still haunts me is of Husty and his dogs leaving me to go on ahead to Maggie's cabin. As I struggled to make headway I kept my eyes staring at him, my only possible human contact, receding from me trailed by his dogs as they became smaller in the distance. Soon they were tiny specs in that vast wild landscape, maybe almost a mile ahead and I began to feel increasingly apprehensive that the sightlines that tethered us together were stretching to the breaking point. And then quite suddenly they disappeared and all my human connections were cut completely and a great feeling of being absolutely alone with no one to help me at all should I fall unable to rise, settled into the core of my being.

This afternoon, the 24th, seemed to be the turning point in the trip as far as my physical ability and mental outlook were concerned. It was at this time that I began to have serious trouble making any headway at all. I was very weak and I was standing up and walking mainly through will power and the knowledge that I had to or I would never get out. I began to fall down very often. At first I got right up for fear that

I would go to sleep and not wake up in time. Finally I got so tired that I could not get to my feet and I would go immediately to sleep. I never knew how long I would be down, but I am sure that it was not for very long.

It was always the shivering that made me wake up or come to, and I would struggle to my feet and go on sometimes for a half a mile, sometimes for only a few yards before I was down again. I also began to have great difficulty keeping the toes on my left foot warm. I kept moving them to make sure they were not freezing.

I began to take on a new outlook of Nature. It was a beautiful sunny day and the scenery must have been wonderful, but I saw no beauty. I saw rather the cruelty of nature. I felt as if every hill that rose over the treetops was against me. They were watching me and laughing inwardly. I cursed these hills freely. I hated everything around me. No, there was no beauty here.

I was also becoming apprehensive. I began to consider my chances of getting out. It was then that I began to see clearly that I was in serious trouble, but I don't think it occurred to me that I might not get out. My thoughts began to be a little illogical, but I was unaware of this at the time. Here it was, past noon on the 24th and I still thought I would be home for Christmas.

"I'll get to Maggie's cabin in two hours (I thought). There will be a trail into the village so I should be there around 7:00. I can probably get someone to take me to the road in a sled. Maybe I can eat there and get a rest. I ought to be to the highway by 9:00. Even 10:00 is o.k. Take an hour to get a ride at the most. Get to Whitehorse by early morning. I'll get home early Christmas. What a surprise. Sneak up by the front door and walk in without being seen." I smiled at the thought.

It is strange that such a trivial desire as getting home a few days sooner should have seemed so important to me in the face of the immensely more important problem of continuing existence. I remember that on Christmas day when I finally knew that I was not going to get home for Christmas at all, the thought did not bother me much. I rather immediately became concerned with getting out alive, a thought that had not given me much concern up to that time.

If I was illogical about the future, I was trying to be practical about the immediate problems. My feet began to get cold, despite how much I tried to move them inside my shoe. I was finally faced with the reality that my feet were freezing again. I had less than half a box of matches and a big wad of paper with which to start a fire. I was only about a hundred yards from the woods, but the job of breaking trail through the deep snow to get there where it would be simple to build a fire seemed insurmountable at the time. I walked until I came to a spot where there was a little brush within reach and I began to collect twigs as fast as I could. After I had a good amount I crumpled up the paper and laid the twigs on top. I struck a match. The wind blew it out. I *struck another and it also was out before I could touch it to the paper. I then took out two matches and succeeded in starting the paper, which burned a while but didn't get hot enough to start the twigs. I crumpled more paper and tried several more times and again finally got the paper going. The twigs began to burn but they acted as if they were green and finally just smoke came up and then nothing. By this time I had only one match left.*

I knew that time was of the essence, for every minute of delay increased the chance that I would lose more of my feet. I started for the timber as fast as I could manage and after climbing up the cutbank to the forest began to snap off twigs from the spruce trees. I noticed that each branch I broke off sent up a tiny cloud of dust that had settled on it since the last time it was ever damp. I still had some paper so once more I began to build a fire. I became an architect. I was constructing an important edifice. It had to be perfect or I was to suffer the consequences. I took great care to how the twigs were laid on and the direction of the wind. My small building was constructed for its sole occupant—fire. It had to suit fire perfectly. This construction was to be foolproof. Soon it was done. I took out the match and studied it. It was pregnant with fire but still had to bear it successfully.

I had to strike it right the first time. I kneeled down close to the twigs and shielding it with my hands, I struck the match gently but firmly. It flashed brightly. I waited one second to make sure that it was going well and then I placed it to the paper. It started. I had extra twigs on hand. I nursed that fire like I would my own sick child. It gathered force very slowly, but I saw to it that its appetite was satiated until I had a big bonfire.

I then began the tedious job of taking off my shoepacks. When I saw my feet I remember thinking to myself that I was sure to lose them all. The two toes on my left foot were a sickly green color and I knew that it was the first stages of infection setting in. I had really expected this to happen, for I had been told that the worst thing one can do to frozen feet is to walk on them, mainly because it brings on gangrene. I had walked forty or fifty miles on mine and now it was to begin its work on me. I tried to thaw out my toes again and also my heels. Earlier in the afternoon I had felt the huge blisters break from the constant rubbing. It had felt as if someone had poured a pitcher of ice water down the back of my boots. This blister water had frozen inside my boots and in so doing it had frozen my heels again.

Both heels were completely raw in sections larger than silver dollars, but unlike the toes they had not started to turn black. I tried to dry out my socks as best I could in the time afforded and when I was done working on my feet I put my footgear back on and set out once more. I was now apprehensive that I should not cover the next four miles to the cabin before dark. I knew that if I diidn't find the cabin I would die and I wasn't at all sure that I could get there. The rest of the afternoon seemed to pass in time. I was down almost as much as I was up, but now when I went down I could not get up. My fatigue was so great that the instant I hit the snow I would be immediately asleep. It was exactly the same as if I had fainted. I always woke up shivering from the cold.

It may be hard to understand why, when my feet began to freeze in the afternoon, I did not struggle the 100 yards to the woods to be certain I could get a fire going, but I believed I could easily start a fire out on the river bar with the small twigs I could gather from a few stumps in a tiny log jam. The exertion it would take to beat a new trail even those few yards, brought about by the pain in my feet and the fatigue and falling down I was experiencing, was more than I could bring myself to do until I was down to my last match. It was only then, with the alarm bells clanging in my head, that I pushed the difficulty of this extra 100 yards of trail breaking from my head and struggled towards the forest. It was vital to get my feet thawed out right away as every minute increased the degree of frostbite and successfully starting a fire was imperative. I did not want to risk using my one last match without the dry spruce twigs I knew awaited me in the woods.

Later on, after building the fire and thawing my feet for the second time and seeing the green color of my toes I believed this was the start of gangrene infection setting in. I then realized if I lost Husty's trail or did not make the cabin that night and being out of matches to make a fire, I was going to die. The impact of this knowledge slowly expanded the tiny knot of apprehension in my stomach into a really vivid screaming fear and a growing desperation in me to exert the maximum physical effort to make the cabin before dark.

I could hear the trucks on the highway clearly. It was almost sickening to be able to hear them. I wanted desperately for an airplane to fly over. I began to taunt myself with dreaming up visions in my minds eye of helicopters coming over and landing near me.

"Where the hell are you going," the man called.. I walked over.

"Can you help me, I've frozen my feet."

"Hell, yes. Here, I'll give you a hand."

"I want to get to the highway. I'm going home for Christmas. To Seattle."

We took off. "Do you think you could stop and pick up my friend? He's been helping me and he's awful tired."

"Sure, point the way."

"I'm a hell of a bother, but have you got room for his three dogs too?"

"I guess we can make it."

"Oh, that's wonderful"

We landed and I told Husty to get in with dogs and we flew to the roadhouse on the highway.

In the late afternoon it began to get warmer and cloud up again. I remember that I was extremely thirsty. I knew that I shouldn't eat snow but I had to. This immediately made me all the thirstier. I became obsessed with the desire for a glass of orange juice. I was constantly picturing a large clear glass pitcher of fresh orange juice. This would make me thirsty so I would scoop a mittened hand into the clean snow and suck that, and so on.

My conversation with a non-existent helicopter pilot and my fixation on wanting a glass of orange juice, were only two examples of how my mind was beginning to work. There were other "conversations" with my parents as I arrived home for Christmas, what the food would be, and visualizing in detail how the house would look all decorated for Christmas. These were like waking dreams, as real as the cold and snow surrounding me. It was as though the real live scene were these conversations and the snow laden landscape a shadow barely in my consciousness.

It was also during this same afternoon that I had an interesting experience. The going had become unbearably tough. I was slipping off the trail and falling down constantly. I remember one time in particular when sobs of desperation escaped me as I slipped and stumbled from the trail. Finally I said out loud, "Please God, help me." No sooner had I closed my mouth than I had the feeling that I had been astoundingly absurd. I stopped crying immediately and said, "You dumb bastard. No one's going to help you out of this but you." That was all there was to this at the time. I felt that all the people who would tell you to lay down and pray were fooling themselves. Man must help himself and if anything is going to be changed, it will be through Man's own efforts, not God's will.

My pleading with God to help me came out of a moment of real desperation. I can remember vividly exactly what the scene looked like. It was hazy sunshine and looking to my right towards the forest above the river bar and to the hills beyond, was a beautiful landscape. But I was constantly falling down, and if not down, was staggering barely forward. It was as if I were drowning in that snowy landscape and being slowly sucked down into the earth and in desperation, the words just popped out of my mouth without any thought what I was saying, just a crying plea for help. These words sounded so ridiculous spoken out loud in that gigantic wilderness with the impossibility that anything other than the mountains and the wind to hear me, instantly seemed so outrageously absurd that I was shamed to have uttered them and cursed myself out loud. I had at that time a very low but strongly fixed opinion on the power of prayer and the role of God in bailing human beings out of their own predicaments and even yet the plea burst forth from my lips unbidden.

Darkness was coming on me very fast and I didn't know how far I had come. I could look back to my right and see the white hill where I had spent the night of the 20th, but I could see no white hill where the trail was leading. It happened to be heading back to the right side of the bar and it was not long until it cut up off the bar entirely and began weaving through the woods. It seemed like I had been walking an eternity. I had the absurd thought that Husty was deliberately leading me off the real trail where I would be sure to lose my way after dark. The trail was so crooked that I was sure he was lost himself. It began to get dark so I pressed myself to the utmost. I had to get there before I lost the trail.

It began to get windy and the trail was very difficult to follow. I came out of the creek bed and was going across a small opening in the woods where the trees were very sparse. The wind came over the ground about a foot high, drifting the snow so that the trail was mostly obliterated. It was dusk by this time. I lost the trail! I weaved back and forth and felt it under my feet. I lost it again and then found it in the halflight. I once or twice crossed it and knew it, but I could not see it well enough to follow it and often it had been so filled with snow that I couldn't have seen it if it was light. I was exerting myself to the maximum and I was desperate to the nth degree. I found the trail once more as it turned to the left and went over a small rounded bank. I could feel the blood pounding in my ears with each beat of my heart. But something strange happened, I didn't know quite what for a second and then I realized my heart had stopped!

There was no more throbbing. Just an awful silence. "Jesus Christ … this is it!" That was all I thought. I began to pass out just as the trail went over the bank. Instead of falling, I slid down and let my head fall between my legs. I went completely blind in those few seconds, but not unconscious. My mind was frightfully active. I was listening to my heart. It seemed an age before it began to beat. The first sensation was feeling and hearing a noise like a suction pump out of liquid. Like there were bubbles in my blood that were being squeezed through my heart itself. Finally the beat started, but this time it was ever so slow. It continued to pick up momentum and I became com-

pletely conscious. I sat and waited to see what was going to happen. The beat picked up speed and in a few minutes it was once more beating as strongly as it had been before it stopped. After I could feel it in my ears with each beat, I started out again. But this time I was going slower. I didn't want that to happen again. From that time on, I was in fear that I could easily kill myself from overexertion.

If you can picture the night falling as Husty's trail led up the cutbank off the river bar and into the woods and my not being able to see the trail after a few yards and my desperation and terror at the thought of losing it altogether, perhaps you can understand the maximum exertion I was putting out and the powerful strokes my heart was making. I was panting open mouthed, like a distance runner, my chest almost bursting with every beat. And then it just stopped! The pulse in my ears replaced by dead silence and I felt myself fainting. At the time it seemed like my heart quit for half a minute but of course this cannot be true because I never lost consciousness completely. But it seemed a very long time to me then and in those first few moments I thought I was surely going to die right then and there.

I sat at the bottom of the cutbank on the edge of the river bar alone in the dark, fearful if I made the slightest movement my heart might stop forever. I did not move a muscle for eight to ten minutes and at the end of that rest time, my heart was back beating full tilt as if I had never stopped my exertions at all. I once asked a cardiologist about this experience and he gave me the medical term for the phenomenon, but that is lost to me now. He said that at that point, only one of two things could have happen; the heart begins again, or its drift into ventricular fibrillation continues and it's all over for you. I evidently had won the big coin toss in the sky for that day.

After the episode with my heart it was dark so I stayed down on the river bar where reflected light from the snow helped me to see and although it was possible to see the black forest line along the river on top of the cutbank, I could not see any details at all. Interestingly, while in the woods I had been able to feel Husty's snowshoe trail just by the difference in the compaction, but try as I might, I could not follow it by feel through the trees in the dark with snow blowing across the ground with no visual support.

I followed the edge of the trees on the river bar for about half a mile then in desperation I called out to Husty. I got no answer. I went on a little farther and this time I whistled with my fingers a long, loud, shrill whistle. I heard Husty call out an answer from about 400 yards away and I went in that direction. He had been in the cabin since 2:00 and it was now 5:00 o'clock. He had a fire going in a little Yukon stove that was there. I stumbled in the door.

"I've had an awful hard day." I saw that there was only a dirt floor in the cabin and I don't remember it having any windows. I sat down on the floor. "Is there any food left, Husty?"

"A little," he answered and reached behind him to produce a small piece of meat.

I cut this in two and we ate it in silence. Husty was about to lie down again when I said, "We better get some wood in here."

He grunted an answer and went outside. I had a guilty conscience so I went out after him and helped probe for stocks of wood under the snow. We got several armfuls and brought them inside and threw them behind the stove. I lay down on the floor next to the stove and immediately went to sleep.

December 25, 1948—Christmas

In a little while I awoke shivering and put in some more wood and went back into a fitful sleep. This went on all night, and we got up for the last time as soon as it got light enough to travel.

I felt very weak and my feet were worse than ever. Husty started out through the trees and was out of sight immediately. I went only a few yards before I was in tears. I felt for the first time that I was not going to make it. I hollered for Husty. I got no answer. I hollered again. I felt completely helpless. I screamed once more and ended in sobs. This time Husty answered and came back. I could see that he was angry at being called.

"I'm sorry to be a cry baby, Husty, but I don't think I can make it. I need more food." I tried to wipe my eyes. "How far is it to the village?"

"Six mile," he answered.

"From the village can you look back across the flats and see a person for several miles?"

"Yes," he answered. But I don't think he understood the question.

"I don't think I'm going to make it today, so if you don't see me coming across the flats an hour after you get there, come with some food. Or better still, get a toboggan to come and get me."

"I try, but this trip hard on me, too. I tired out."

"Well, I'll try, Husty, but I don't know if I can make it without something to eat. Have you got any matches? I may have to build a fire if I get too tired." He handed me a box.

"Thanks. Don't wait over an hour, Husty."

The most important thing by far on that Christmas Day was when I staggered out the cabin door to follow after Husty, I understood instantly that I was not going to make it. I had no strength left, the reserves were all used up and unless I got some food or a dog team to come for me, it was all over. This realization just shattered into my brain and I knew I had to stop Husty, now out of sight in the woods, and make him come back so that I could tell him. I let out what I now call my primordial scream.

I would have been embarrassed beyond belief if called upon to do this in public, but here, in this place and circumstance, it was the only way I knew to be certain to get Husty to come back so I could impress upon him my truly desperate situation.

He started out once more and was soon out of sight. I felt much better after that. I came out of the woods beside a line of hills. I saw the hill that Husty had said was white. It was not white at all except for a patch on the side where the timber had been cut off. I was sure that I would never have found the cabin from the directions he had given me. The snow was deeper than it had ever been, and on top of that it began to snow lightly and continued snowing for several hours. I was making hardly any headway at all, for I was completely without strength. When I fell I could not get up. I wanted badly to lie down and go to sleep. I finally came to a spot that was rather secluded from the snow and breeze and began to methodically gather wood for a fire. I don't think I had gone more than two miles. I built a large fire and lay down beside it, basking in the pleasure that the heat gave me. I was in no hurry any more. There would be a sled along in a little while and I would soon be on my way to Seattle and home. Yes, I was sure to be home late that night. What a surprise the family would get to see me walk in the front door. I got great satisfaction from the thought.

I must have lain there for some time, but I don't think that I went to sleep. My mind seemed to be working frantically. I thought about everything, but nothing for any length of time. Nothing seemed to jell at all. The pictures would flash through my mind at a rate almost too fast to be able to distinguish. I finally got up and started out again. I went very slowly. Every few steps I would have to stop and rest. Soon I was out in the sparsely timbered section that resembled a golf course under the blanket of snow. But it turned out to be anything but a golf course. The snow was almost 16 inches deep on top of the clump grass, but if I stepped in between the clumps, it was almost half way up my thigh. These clumps are the curse of Alaska travel. They vary in height and thickness. Down here on the Tanana Flats they are huge. I couldn't see them under the snow and each step was a challenge, a challenge that I usually lost. If I didn't hit directly in the center of the top of one, I would slide off in between two of them and find myself in snow up to my hips. It was just a stagger that I was doing going across those flats. If I wasn't so desperate I think I should have laughed at my efforts to stand up. It was like trying to walk with one leg a foot shorter than the other. The snow was also covered with a windblown crust that sometimes was over four inches thick. I could make out Husty's snowshoe tracks that went over this crust without breaking through, leaving just a fine imprint of the webbing on the surface.

Sometimes one foot would step on top of the crust and then as I put my weight on it to take another step it would break and I would fall down. I found that the crust was so solid that when I took a step I had to literally punch a hole in it. The hole would remain just the size of my foot and I would have to lean far forward in order to extricate my leg from the hole to place it ahead. I fell constantly and often I would not be able to get up. I became so tired that I had to stop several times and dig out a hole in the snow and get in to lie down.

My struggle that day was just a dead man walking. I was down much more than I was up. With each fall I went to sleep instantly until waking up shivering from the cold. By 1:00 in the afternoon I had only made two miles and I built my fire. After warming up and resting I started out again and came to the more open area. I began looking ahead hoping desperately to see someone coming for me. And I did see them coming, even a dog team once, but each time, the feeling of elation disintegrated into despair as what I thought I saw, reformed itself as I got closer, into the scrubby spruce trees that dotted the landscape.

I was not making any headway and I knew it only too well. About all I was doing was struggling when, if I was sensible, I should have lain down and closed my eyes in peace. The tiredness was trying to seduce me into quitting, and the more tired I got, the harder it was for me to fight this idea. I was fast coming not to care. I would fall and lie there trying to determine whether or not to get up right at that moment. I never got up for fear of dying. There was no fear involved at all. One never fears what is known and I knew what death from freezing would be like. It would be so simple. Just rest … and sleep … and death.

I just knew that I wanted to live. Suddenly this thought would hit me with all its impact and I would begin to struggle to my feet. I was like a fighter who has been knocked down too many times and begins to think that it all is not so important that he should be beaten to a pulp, but as the referee begins to count him out, his instincts force him once more from the floor. This goes on until he is counted out without his consent. I was not going to be finished until I had no more to say about it. As I made my way towards the village, I was certain that I would not get there unless I got some food, but had no food come I often think that I might have made it anyhow. I'll never know whether or not I could have made it, but I do know that I was fast approaching the end of my rope. There were too many indications that I could not go on too much farther.

I finally realized that I was not going to be home for Christmas late in the afternoon of Christmas Day. This realization did not disturb me at this time as much as it would have the day before. Now I just wanted to get home any time. I just wanted to live. I could see a few miles ahead of me and I would pick out a small bush that suddenly appeared to look like a person coming towards me. I would feel the relief come to me as I would see the object move. As I would get closer I would see that it was only a small scrubby tree. I finally saw a toboggan coming. I knew it was a toboggan for I could easily make out the dogs and the driver. I saw it moving toward me. I kept my eyes on it until they watered. The toboggan was still a half mile away when it turned into a bunch of trees. I was too tired to cry when I found that I was still alone; that no one was coming back to help me. I just fell in a heap and tried to rest, but something kept goading me to get up and move on. Husty appeared very suddenly. He was much closer than I thought he would be when I saw him. He came up to me and I saw that he was carrying a paper bag.

It was around 2:30 when Husty appeared. I did not see him coming until he was about 30 feet from me, even though all the time he was approaching I had been constantly staring across the flat open area he had been moving through, fervently hoping to see the movement of someone coming back to save me.

When he was close he said, "I find no one at village. They all move to road. Here's food I fix for you." He handed me the bag inside of which was my Christmas dinner. I opened it and found two pieces of bannock with butter and sugar, two small boiled potatoes, a half can of cold cream of mushroom soup, and a half can of condensed milk. He even had a spoon in the bag. I gulped down the soup and the milk. I had always hated condensed milk, but this was good. I then ate the bannock and struggled with one potato.

"I go to camp and send toboggan. You wait in cabin. I not able to come back myself. This trip, he hard on me, too!"

Husty, you didn't know it, but you gave me my best Christmas. You gave me my life. After gulping down the food, I went a little way and then I got cramps in my stomach. I dug out a hole in the snow and lay down for about a half hour. After that

I felt much better. I could actually feel the strength return to my body as the food began to be utilized. I got up and started out.

It was still hard going but I was a new man. I knew that I would make it. I was going to live. It could have gotten harder for all I cared. I still would have made it. I felt very lighthearted. It was dark and I still had not made over three miles since seven that morning, but I finally felt a hard trail under my feet as I got into another patch of timber and then I knew that I was not far from the village.

I came out in a clearing that went up a small hill and in the dark saw the outlines of five or six log cabins built in a line. I saw a small light in a window of one to the left and made my way towards it. I went in. It was a large cabin and the fire was still going. There was no bed in it but there was a pile of dirty clothes in the far corner. I tried to arrange them into some sort of a mattress. I then got some hot water that Husty had boiled the potatoes in and found some old tea bags. I put water into a cup and then put in a tea bag. It didn't even change the color of the water. I put in another. Again no results. I then got a handful and soaked them all, milking what little tea was left in them. I had to laugh at these poor tea bags. They must have been used a dozen times apiece. I finally got some color into the water and put in a gob of sugar and drank it down. I then lay down and tried to sleep.

I gathered up some of the clothes and put them over me and shut my eyes. I saw terrible things. Everything was red. Arms and legs bathed in blood. I couldn't get the image out of my head. Every time I closed my eyes I saw horrible sights. Even now that the struggle was over and I knew I was safe I was reacting to the ordeal. After four days of only a fraction of the sleep I needed, I found that I could not go to sleep at all.

About 9:30 I heard a dog team pull up outside the cabin. The door opened and in stepped an Indian. I spoke to him from the shadows and asked him if he had come for me. He had a toboggan which he went back to turn around and then he came in again. I got up but it was very hard to stand. I asked him for a little help and he let me hang onto his shoulder. Now that I was comparatively safe, I could not summon the strength to make myself do what hurt so much. I got out and he put me on the toboggan and threw a robe over me and we started out. I never heard one word from this Indian except when he occasionally cursed at one of his dogs. I did notice that he had four big dogs. In the dim half-light I watched the country roll by. I felt good, even if uncomfortable, and in an hour and a half we came into the Indian camp. It was a series of teepees, but all seemed deserted except the one in front of which he stopped.

Several Indians came out of the tent. I could see that they had been drinking. One was a huge man who looked more Spanish than Indian. He had a large bushy mustache and kindly dark eyes. He was all smiles and helped me into the tent. Inside were mainly old people, squaws and men. Husty was there too. There was a case of beer on the tent floor and it was evident that they had all been celebrating the Christmas holiday. The first thing that happened was that a can of beer was thrust into my hand amid much laughing and chattering.

I was asked how I felt. I said "fine."

"How are the feet?"

"Oh, they hurt quite a bit," I answered and an old squaw grimaced in sympathy.

"How you like this place?"

"Oh, I like it fine."

"Merry Christmas to you," one of the faces ventured. "You like Christmas?"

"Yes, I like Christmas very much, and Merry Christmas to all of you! You are very kind to help me."

"Oh, we like help. We no care you white man. We always help you in trouble."

"Old John Titus, he walk all way to roadhouse. Tell man he come with frozen feet. They get help for you." All of them looked at Old John and then at me as if to make sure that I knew who they were talking about.

"Thank you very much," I said to the big man.

"Oh, that all right. I like help, but he hard walk for old man like me. Took me long time to make trip."

The squaws were giggling among themselves. One of the men talked to them in native tongue and then told me that they hadn't realized that I was so young. I smiled and they blushed and giggled.

"You like more beer?" Old John asked.

"I think one is enough for now. I maybe get drunk. I not eat for some time."

"By-m-bye we take you to road. Now we have fun!" This was followed by much laughter.

"Husty tell us you have hard trip." I nodded an assent. This continued until past midnight. Then I heard another team pull up outside the tent.

"This time you go," said Old John. Everyone said goodbye and I thanked them in turn.

Old John had a small lantern made out of a tin can with a candle stuck up through the bottom so that it reflected light ahead and to the sides. Much to my surprise there were two young Indian girls who were to drive the dogs. We started up the trail.

This is one of my fondest memories. I can still see Old John silhouetted in the glimmer of the candle light as he walked ahead of the dogs, and the woods seemed alive with elfin shadows that scattered softly here and there, and then vanished behind us.

Everything seemed to twinkle kindly as the flickering candle light set sparks dancing on the leaden boughs. The girls were singing softly behind me as the woods went by close to me on both sides. It made me feel good. These were good people. I was very glad to be alive then.

We had to go up over a low mountain and I got out once on a particularly steep place. In about an hour and a half we were at the highway and started the last two miles to the roadhouse.

My 18th Christmas was very different from any I had previously known. But standing there in the snow with Husty Sanford handing me each item of the meal when I was ready to receive it, eating cold mushroom soup and drinking condensed milk from a can, I thought it was by far the most important Christmas dinner I had ever enjoyed, or ever would and I was eternally grateful to have it.

December 26th, 1948

It was a little past 2 A.M. the morning of the 26th when we arrived (at Scotty Creek Lodge). I was in high spirits when I was helped in and sat down.

I told the kind people who ran the place that Husty would be up and that if it was convenient I would like them to fix him a good meal. I bought the Indians a case of beer as Husty had asked me to and they were quite pleased and soon had put it on the sled and were on their way back. I was informed that the Alaska Highway Patrol had been notified, and that it would get here with a car to take me up to Tok Junction where another man would take me to Big Delta, and still another would drive me from there to Fairbanks. I lay down on a couch and tried to get some sleep waiting for the patrolman to arrive. I took off my shoes for the first time since I had last frozen them and found that the frozen parts had turned black. I didn't care. I knew I would lose part or most of both feet but I was safe and alive which was infinitely more important at the time. Yes, I was happy.

All that happened seemed a ...

So ended the journal, written in 1949 when I was nineteen.

It is hard to overestimate the positive effect that my fixation on getting home for Christmas had on my ability to keep going. But there was more to this than just sharing Christmas with my family. I had told my mother and dad that I would come out by Christmas and maybe more than that, I somehow felt a real sense of responsibility to survive and do what I said I would do and not let them down. I also knew the terrible pain they would feel if I failed and was lost to them.

Every ten minutes I went over how it would all work out as the hours slogged by and as my thinking became more and more illogical, I managed to always come to the conclusion that I could get home for Christmas, way past the time when it would have been obvious to anyone that this was impossible. But I believed it and thus kept moving forward.

Epilogue

By the time I was helped into the Scotty Creek Roadhouse around 2:30 A.M. on December 26th, things were already in motion that from then on put other people in control of my destiny until I was out of the hospital three months later. The Alaska State Patrol had organized a rescue mission on my behalf and a trooper was driving from Tok Junction to pick me up early in the morning to start the 300 mile relay to Fairbanks. St. Joseph's Hospital had been notified and was preparing for my arrival that evening. Even in Alaska where such things happen every so often, I was fast becoming a "cause celebre," as the news stations pumped out the story over the radio to even the smallest hamlets, most of which had short wave radios at that time.

One thing was certain, I had had my unique experience and I had something to talk about, but the strange thing was, I found doing so very difficult and therefore avoided recounting the story in any detail to anyone. For a long time I could not put the experience behind me. It was always just beneath the surface in my mind and each time a part of it popped into my consciousness, I could not stop the chain of memory from carrying me through the entire ordeal. It became a chapter in my life that I finally was able to shove deep down in order to escape reliving it over and over and over. This problem relaxed a bit in a year or two with the press of returning to university, getting married and starting a family, but I could not bring myself to read the journal until I began to think about writing this memoir almost fifty years later.

The Journal of 1949 stopped in mid sentence. I suppose I was going to wax poetic, or at least as eloquently as I could, in an effort to bring some larger metaphysical meaning to the trek. I cannot remember today where those 19 year old's thoughts were going, when he wrote, "All that happened seemed a...."

And when I finally did read the manuscript, written in 1949 by that 19 year old youth and as I reread it now, trying to do justice to what he had started with his journal, I find myself filled with anguish for that boy as I watch him, in my mind's eye, as he struggled forward alone in that giant winter landscape, believing that he would be without his feet for life and still choosing to live with every half step, for himself to be sure, but also because of a deep feeling of responsibility to the family he knew loved him.

This boy, who had started out on a journey that he thought would somehow bring him closer to manhood, a quixotic idea of youth at best, ended up in a personal, long and arduous struggle just to hang onto his young life. The experience imprinted in him forever that life was tenuous at best and could end at any time, but so long as he was alive he resolved to try to deal with life as a precious gift.

Afterthoughts;

Telegram from Harold Curtis—Licensed Guide and Outfitter—Dec 29 1948
BILL STREET
ST. JOESEPHS HOSPITAL FAIRBANKS ALAA
SORRY TO HEAR ABOUT FROZEN TOES YOU JUST MISSED THE PLANE AT
CHISANA WISH YOU A SPEEDY RECOVERY REGARDS
    HAROLD

Telegram from Bill Street to his parents—December 26, 1948
WM S STREET
MEDINA WASH
    DEAR FOLKS MET WITH A LITTLE BAD LUCK IN GETTING HOME FOR CHRISTMAS AM IN FAIRBANKS HOSPITAL NOTHING TO WORRY ABOUT CANT MAKE SCHOOL LETTER FOLLOWING
    GOD BLESS YOU ALL
    BILL

Letter from Harold Curtis—January 17, 1949

Dear Bill,
    Sorry to hear of your tough luck on the hike out to the hiway. I hope you will not be laid up long. The plane went in for you on the 20th, according to Smith. (Merle Smith, "Smitty," a bush pilot)
    I haven't had a line from Lou since you went into Chisana in October. Was hoping you would come through Anchorage as I have been anxious to know how Harry, Lou and the horses were making out. We heard in the weather reports that it was 65 below over there several times. I hope the horses make out all right. Marshall Field intends to return next Fall with the same group for another hunt. We will have to put

in some time next summer looking for another sheep spot. I finally got a 16mm camera. Maybe can get some good sheep pictures while scouting around. What are your plans? I hope you can come back with us again.

This has surely been a devil of a winter. We've had 52 inches of snow here so far though only about 30 inches on the ground at present. At Talkeetna the snow is 90 inches on the level. Between the snow and the moose the railroad is having a tough time trying to operate. The deep snow is driving the moose to using the tracks for a game trail. Most trains are considerably delayed trying to get the moose to yield them the right of way.

How did you do with the wolves? I expect it was too cold to do much in that line. Would like to hear about your experiences.

Well Bill, wish you a speedy recovery and hope you come back with us again next year. Should be a lot of fun ramming around looking for new sheep country. Best regards, Harold

Turning Point

*Wherein our still youthful hero makes a big mistake,
attempts to recover his lost honor, returns to replay
his last defeat, and changes his mind*

When the patrol car drove up to the entrance to St. Joseph Hospital in Fairbanks I was terribly worn out. Sergeant Brand, who was a big friendly man, helped me out of the car and then, deflecting any argument from me, picked me up in his arms and carried me into the hospital where the nurses were ready to help me to bed. I thanked the Sergeant profusely and asked him to be sure to tell the other men who helped in the drive that I was really appreciative of what they had done for me.

I was soon deposited in a room with another patient, an IV stuck in my arm and a metal hoop installed at the foot of the bed to keep the blankets from touching my feet. To the underside of the hoop the nurses affixed a light bulb, a low-level heat source to improve blood flow to the degree possible. The doctor came an hour later, took a look and ordered some sulfa drug for me. He asked who the family doctor was in Seattle so that he could consult with him before doing anything heroic. He wanted to know how the family wished to handle my recovery and obvious need for surgery.

The next morning I was not doing too well and they moved me into a room by myself. I always felt they didn't want me dying in front of another patient. I had a fever and developed a large hen's-egg-sized swelling in the lymph gland in my groin. The doctor explained that I had an infection from freezing my feet and having to walk on them for such an extended time and he assured me that the lymph glands were just doing what they were supposed to do. He also told me that the hospital in Seattle was sending a new blood thinning drug developed for frostbite and used extensively with troops fighting in Alaska. That there was none of this drug in Alaska was strange, but it arrived late the same night from Seattle and I was put on it immediately.

About the third day I was feeling much better physically, but continued having a very hard time keeping the recent ordeal from taking over my mind. When

I shut my eyes I still saw bloody pictures of body parts, almost like my eyelids were a screen upon which these scenes were projected, but the light sedation being administered to me helped blunt the impact and soon the images began to arrive with less frequency.

During the week or ten days I was there, one of my biggest surprises was the number of calls, cards and visits I had from people I had never met. The story of my trek had reached the radio and news media and seemed to ring a bell with folks who insisted on bringing me all sorts of goodies, fruits and small treats with cards wishing me well. They all seemed motivated to comfort a young boy who had endured a harrowing experience and had no family about. My close friend, Waffy (Warren Haight), had an Aunt, Mary Earling, who lived in Fairbanks. She made numerous visits to see me, as well as making contact with my parents directly, giving them almost daily updates on my progress.

Father arrived in Fairbanks at the end of the first week of January. There had been no use coming earlier since the doctor in Fairbanks did not think I should be moved to Seattle until I was stronger and fully prepared physically to make the trip. Dad was kind and gentle to me and very encouraging that things would work out all right and did not once mention what a stupid kid I was, perverse in doing dumb things, not to mention worrying my mother practically to death.

When the day to leave Fairbanks arrived, Sergeant Brand came to the hospital and took Dad and me to the airport for the long flight to Seattle. He insisted on carrying me up the steep steps into the DC-4 and placing me in a seat that had somehow been converted into a partial bed. I said my final goodbye to him and off we went into the night. After about two hours of flying I began to really feel terrible and soon a stewardess, looking at the color of my lips and finger nails understood that I was in need of oxygen. She set this up for me and I continued the flight in an oxygen mask, finally dropping off to a restless sleep. We landed in the middle of the night and I had made Dad promise to let me go home this one night before I went into the hospital. I just had to see my home and Mother before I could face what I knew was coming. So we arrived home in the wee hours of dawn to my Mother's open arms. The next day in the early afternoon my father delivered me up to the medical profession.

Once I was ensconced in Seattle General Hospital all efforts were made to save as much of my feet as possible and in this work things went well. The recovery process from severe frostbite is simply avoiding infection and waiting to see how much of the affected area would recover. At this point the severely affected parts of my feet had gone from green to purple and finally to black, with a clear separation naturally occurring between the flesh still served with a blood supply and that which was truly dead. The latter exuded the sickening odor of decomposing flesh. On my left foot the big toe and the one next to it were black to the halfway point, and my right heel had a dollar-sized black circle of skin. My right little toe was freeze-blackened along the outside of my foot, but it was thought this toe could be saved from amputation.

In late January the line of demarcation was apparent on the toes of my left foot and they were amputated by Dr. Berge along that line. I had asked Dr. Berge to have the toes saved for me. He was very reluctant to do this, but I begged him for this one favor and he finally relented, indulging the boy he had doctored for ten years. When I woke up from the operation my two toes were in a jar of form-aldehyde on the table next to my bed. I could deal with the smaller of the two, but the sight of my big toe in the jar brought on a wave of nausea that almost made me upchuck. I quickly fished out the smaller one wrapping it in a Kleenex, all the time trying to avoid looking at the other one, and asked the nurses to take the big toe away, a task they were very relieved to do. In the meantime I had Mother bring me a small padded jewelry box where I gently put the blackened and somewhat shriveled amputated toe, closed the box and sent it to my brother Jack, who was living in the Sigma Chi house at Stanford, as a special gift. It arrived during lunch where everyone in the house sat around eating at a long table and when Jack opened it up, he started to laugh and then passed it around the table amid tremendous laughter, squawks and gagging.

From then on, Dr. Paul Schiebel, a plastic surgeon, was put on my case, since it was certain that some reconstructive work needed to be done. He came in every day to see how things were progressing, carrying his little assortment of snippers, scissors and tweezers with which he proceeded to separate the dead flesh from the living using his instruments of torture. After a few weeks of this probing and snipping where often something very much alive would get cut, I dreaded to see him walk in the door.

One day when he was working on the side of my little toe on the right foot, he gingerly lifted with his tweezers, a little piece of black skin about 3/4 inch long by 1/8 inch wide exposing shiny white bone. This meant that the toe would have to be cut off along with this short piece of bone.

In those days large skin grafts were made by the "flap" method, a procedure done by cutting a flap of skin loose on three sides leaving one side intact for the blood flow to continue, and sewing this to the area where the graft was needed. In my case a large graft had to be put on my right heel, so when Dr. Schiebel took me up to the operating room to amputate my little toe, he started the first of three operations that would ready a big flap on the inside of my left thigh to be later sewed onto my right heel.

This he did by making a 4-1/2 inch cut lengthwise and then separating the soon to be flap, from the muscle below, a four inch by four inch piece of skin, along with its fat layer. This cut was forced to stay open so that blood flow could be reestablished to the flap from the remaining uncut upper end.

A week later I went up to the O.R. again and he made another incision about four inches to the right of the first cut and parallel to it, lifting the flap again to make sure it did not grow back. By this the blood was forced in from the top end and out the lower end. This made for a very sore leg, but all looked well when upstairs for a third time I went ten days later. This time they cut the flap loose on the lower end closest to my knee and pulling my right heel up to the flap, trimmed the flap to fit the crater that had been excavated in my heel and sewed it on. The other end of the flap was still attached to my leg to assure sufficient blood supply to allow the skin graft to not be rejected. To hold all of this connection stable I was put in a plaster cast from my mid-chest down to my calves where I remained for the next three weeks.

About two weeks later, as I lay immobilized in plaster, the big Seattle earthquake of 1949 occurred. When the shaking started, patients were out of bed running around with nurses chasing after them, patients shouting and everyone in a general panic to get out. The violent tremors just kept on and on and soon, over my head, a crack showed in the ceiling, then another, and another and then plaster started falling from the ceiling onto me, the bed and the floor.

Being still somewhat traumatized by my recent ordeal and all the operations, I became truly terrified that after all I had been through I was now going to be crushed to death in this collapsing old building. I was certain of it when a brick fell past my window from somewhere above and I turned my head to watch in horrified fascination as more bricks tumbled by. Then I glued my eyes on the Rainier Club, across the street, believing if it stayed up the hospital would also. With this idea firmly in my head, I watched intently, hoping fervently to survive until the shaking subsided, which it finally did, enveloping everything in a profound silence.

Not long after the earthquake ended, mother, who had been several blocks away at Frederick & Nelson, arrived in my room quite out of breath. She came as soon as she could safely move out of the building, rushing to the hospital to see if I was all right. She related her experience at Frederick's where there was quite a bit of damage, but she could not believe what she saw in my room with cracks and plaster everywhere. For months after that, the least movement that felt anything like an earthquake pumped a big shot of adrenaline into my system from the lingering fright.

On several occasions I was let out of the hospital to go home for a weekend, always on crutches. It was wonderful to be in my own room and enjoy Mother's home-cooked meals as she spoiled me with my favorite food. I found that I could easily wear the moosehide moccasins I had brought down from Alaska as they were very comfortable on my feet and getting around on crutches was easy for me.

While in the hospital I received good care and was treated well by everyone. I had many visitors, but the one I looked forward to the most was Karen, who soon was sitting within arms reach but it was seldom we were embarrassed in our touching by the unannounced entrance of a nurse carrying out her duties. In early February, Mother, sensing that I had too much time on my hands, urged me to try and write down the whole story of my adventure. To this end she brought down my Remington typewriter and I spent many hours typing up the details of my experience, expecting to edit it at a future time, but I found it so difficult to revisit the experience that I put it away and did not return to it until preparing to write this story.

One of the big changes I noticed in my psyche that I attribute to my misadventure and its aftermath, was the overpowering feeling that I needed to get on with my life before some other untoward event cut it short. In this I think I was much like servicemen returning from war who, having experienced frightening and life threatening situations, were more than ready to finish their education and settle down to making a family. I did not want to wait for anything and had a strong feeling that time was not on my side.

In April or late March, when all that could be done for my feet had been done, I went home. It was too late for me to be admitted into spring quarter at Stanford and as I was still on crutches I had little prospect of gainful employment while I waited for summer school. A few weeks later I traveled down to Stanford to see Jack, Frank Gordon, other friends in the Sigma Chi house and to enroll in summer school

During the week I was there, I had a chance to go out with Diana who at the end of the evening pressed me to tell her what I thought about the future of our relationship. I think I would have made a different decision had we had the least sort a sexual connection, but at that point the attraction of Karen in that way was too strong. I was not willing and perhaps not able to wait for such a closeness to develop with Diana. I was in too much of a hurry to get on with Life as I currently depicted it in my mind. I told her the truth that I admired her immensely, loved her as a friend but was not able to make a commitment to her at that time. I felt saddened about it because I admired and cared for her so much, but I felt I just could not wait for our relationship to mature and returned to Medina and the family home to await the start of summer school.

Karen and I now slipped slowly into a more active sexual relationship which seemed a vital need to me at the time. I was thinking less about future adventures and became totally caught up in the need for close contact with a woman. I am certain Freud would have had a lot of fun with my screwed up thinking, but that is where I found myself in the spring of 1949.

I attended summer school at Stanford and met a friend of Jack's at the house by the name of Blair MacDonald. Blair was from Carmel where his family owned the Monterey Sand Company. A transfer from Menlo Park J.C., he was a great athlete, lithe and very strong and totally committed to outdoor activities, like hiking, fishing, skiing and tennis. We became close friends, sharing all sorts of adventures, until he died in an auto accident in 1998 at a very great personal loss to me and many others.

Summer school was interesting. I liked my courses, especially one in Russian History. The weather was great in Palo Alto and Rosotti's Beer Garden beckoned us more often than was good for the studies, but this diversion notwithstanding, my grades remained good. I went with Blair a few times to Carmel, where his folks had a beautiful home up the Carmel Valley and we occasionally took women out on double dates.

I went home at the end of summer quarter and while there Jack and I decided to buy a car together. After looking around we purchased a used 1948 Ford convertible. It was black with a gray top, red leather seats and white sidewall tires. As was the style in those days, we dropped the rear end about four inches, put on "flicker discs," the latest rage in fancy hubcaps and installed rear fender skirts. How we loved that car. It was soooo cool! Jack and I traded around on who got to use it when, but we often had one of our parents' cars to use in the evenings so had no trouble working it out. When it was time to go back to Stanford Jack was committed to driving a girl friend down in her car so I was to drive the new beautiful black convertible.

We were to meet in Weed, California, and drive together from there, but I got in four or five hours ahead of him, so to kill time and feeling like a little manly adventure, walked into a small bar and ordered a tequila. I drank this in the traditional way using salt and a piece of lime. It went down so well I ordered another … and another … and another. This was on an empty stomach and somewhere along the way the lights just went out. I don't remember how I got to the car and was probably lucky I did not get mugged, but the next thing I knew Jack was pounding on the window of the car where I had locked myself in and passed out. On top of that I had thrown up in front of the seat on the floor.

Jack was rightly disgusted with me. He and his friend uprooted me from the car and with an arm over each of their shoulders, helped me into a motel and to bed, leaving me there to continue their trip to school. I awoke next day with the mother of all hangovers, a headache, dizziness and an upset stomach. I got up once to start out, but was so dizzy I had to go back to bed. Three hours later I was able to make it to the car, but the drive later that afternoon was pure misery. I did not feel really well for at least two weeks. This experience with the alcohol helped educate me in the price I would pay for stupidly drinking to excess.

When fall quarter started I was in my brother's pledge class in the Sigma Chi house. For me the whole thing was too much like a high school fraternity and I found it stupid and silly. I felt very much past that time in my life. I managed to get sideways with one of the "brothers" who challenged me to trade hacks using a wooden paddle. I had been down that road big time in the Revelers, so I said, "Sure, any time." After dinner everyone gathered around to watch the fun and he went first as the challenger. When it was my turn, I loaded up from halfway across the room and really took out all my frustrations on his poor backside. I was never challenged again, nor was I forced to do some of the dumb things pledges are often made to do. It was as if the older members somehow understood that I was past putting up with such antics.

Fall quarter was a bummer for me. I was in several courses taught by teaching assistants I just did not like. One was statistics. To that point I had never come across a teacher who could create a more tangled web out of a fairly simple explanation. The more he talked, the more confused I became. I felt lucky I was graded a D, the only thing saving me from failing was the President of the prior year's freshman class, who was a great guy, but who managed to skip a few too many classes and was given the F for his trouble. But I was fast becoming fed up with Stanford.

At that time the Korean situation was getting tense, and Jack and I, both wanting to fly and already classified 1A, just cannon fodder in the draft, we decided to explore the possibilities of signing up for flight school. We had understood it was a three-year hitch and thought we could handle that as the price of learning to fly and we went together to meet with the Air Force recruiters. We learned it was a four-year minimum contract, we would need our college degrees and the best way to go, they advised, was to get into the Air R.O.T.C. at the University we were attending. This would practically guarantee getting into flight school as an officer. I felt four years was too long a time for me and I could not picture myself walking around some campus dressed in a uniform, but Jack took to the idea and when he enrolled at the University of Washington he joined the R.O.T.C., graduated and went on to the Air Force flight school for training and became an F86D fighter pilot, an outcome over which I had the mixed emotions of pride in his accomplishment and jealousy that he was flying and I was not.

At the end of the fall quarter I decided to leave Stanford. I did not particularly like living in the Fraternity, although it was a great bunch of boys, but I knew the pledge hazing was going to get crazy in the next quarter leading up to initiation, and feeling I was way beyond such nonsense, I decided to transfer to the University of Washington for winter quarter. I seemed to be spinning my wheels at Stanford, never really feeling at home and a bit disappointed in the courses I had taken as a sophomore. Also getting back closer to Karen was on my mind. She was now a freshman at the University of Washington and living in the Chi Omega sorority on campus as a pledge. Jack decided to transfer from Stanford along with me and we both moved home to Medina.

Neither Jack nor I had intentions of moving into the Sigma Chi house at the University of Washington, even though we had been invited to do so, electing instead to live at home and commute from Medina. We enrolled for winter quarter and the courses I selected in history and literature turned out to be excellent. They were taught by full professors, a huge difference from my experience at Stanford. I found that I had developed an insatiable appetite for literature, poetry, history and philosophy, so when I finished my second year I declared Literature as my major with History as a minor. I never stopped to think about the practicality of such a degree, but as 1950 arrived I knew I wanted to be totally immersed in the world of ideas and art and history and to this day I have no regrets for this choice, because these interests have added immeasurable pleasure and understanding of the human condition to my life.

As for Karen and me, we had a heavy-duty affair going on and we were not thinking clearly about any of that. In early February Karen let me know she had missed a period. To say I was aghast and frightened by what this portended would be the understatement of the century. I was in a terrible turmoil on how to deal with this black scourge overtaking me. We waited another week and still no change and I knew I had to act, even if it turned out Karen was not pregnant. Karen was becoming frantic about what to do and when we talked it over, I told her that we had to break this news to her parents and I would take the responsibility of telling them, and of course, I would talk to my mother and dad as well.

When I told my parents about our potential problem, they were highly disgusted with my stupidity and thoughtlessness. It was beyond their belief that I could have done something so incredibly dumb. They were very concerned that this situation, if true, would hurt our family's reputation and they were most interested in trying to shield Karen, who might end up as a daughter-in-law, from any scandal. They called my Uncle Ed, Chief of Staff at St. Jude's Hospital in San Francisco, to ask if he could organize the testing to be sure about the pregnancy, if Karen and I were sent down there. All of this was arranged and it was left for me to speak to Karen's parents, John and Jessie.

I would have gladly taken a beating rather than have to face these two nice people and was somewhat afraid that I might indeed get one from her father. We arrived at their home in the late afternoon, Karen taking her mother upstairs while I stayed below to speak to her father. I realized the revelation of our dilemma would be a big blow to her father when I took a chair facing him in their living room. In addition I knew I had taken advantage of his good will towards me and been altogether deceitful. He had been reading a newspaper and when I started to talk with him, he continued to look at the paper and not towards me, as if he had a premonition of what I was going to tell him.

I said, "I have something important to talk over with you," and without waiting said, "We think Karen is pregnant and we need to find out for sure."

He was silent for a time and without looking up from his paper, he finally asked, "Do your parents know about this?"

To which I replied, "Yes, I told them yesterday."

He said, "I can imagine they would like to give you a good beating." No doubt thinking he would like to do the same thing as well. "And what did they say to you?" he asked.

I answered, "They were angry and disappointed at my lack of responsibility," and added, "I'm very sorry this has happened, but I love Karen and I want to marry her," which was more than a white lie, but under the circumstances I knew no other way to make the best of the situation. I reiterated again how sincerely sorry I was for what had happened and that I really cared for Karen, all of which was true. I told him we wanted to go to California to find out for certain and after that, there really was not anything else that could be said and I left him a silent and saddened man and I was deeply ashamed at what I had wrought.

Karen and I flew to California the next day, staying with my aunt and uncle. While riding somewhere in the car alone with Aunt Marion, she said to me, "What a stupid thing to go and do. You better learn to keep your zipper up!" I promised I would, knowing full well it was already too late.

When the test came back it was positive. I had escaped once before but this time it was not to be. We were sitting in Uncle Ed's office and after giving us the bad news, he said, "You have two choices. I can send her across town and get this taken care of, or you can get married." I was a bit offended by the "send her," instead of using her name. That made me feel protective of Karen, but the truth was there was nothing in the world I wanted less to do than get married, except for one thing; after having gotten Karen pregnant, I could not face my parents if I elected to send her to some abortionist to get out of the problem and pain I had made for everyone. I felt my only possible redemption, and the only way I could make it up to Karen's and my parents, would have to come through me taking responsibility for her and the baby that was coming into our lives. With this in mind I stated to Uncle Ed, "Karen is not going to go across town, we'll get married."

And that is what we did two days later with help from Aunt Marion who went with us to a Justice of the Peace in Marin County. Coming back to the city, I called the Palace Hotel for our one-night honeymoon and being the callow youth I was, got all flustered when the room clerk asked me what kind of bed I wanted for our wedding night. I think I mumbled something to the effect that anything would do. A bit exasperated, he informed me that they had many kinds of beds, double beds, single beds and would I please just choose whatever I preferred. I finally blurted out, "A double bed would be OK."

When we walked into the lobby of the hotel a few hours later I could not help feeling that all eyes were on us and probably wondering what a couple of kids, aged twenty and not yet eighteen, could possibly have been thinking to get themselves married. We had solved a pressing current problem, but there was not much joy in the change of status to a married couple. However, I was determined to try hard and make it work. After all, Mother and Dad had married young and had made a great success of it, so maybe we would as well.

Thus it was that Karen and I started our married life. Based on a major mistake and an immature sense of married love on my part, and on her side, perhaps a love based on my willingness to marry her when I could have walked out. Mother sent out announcements that we had been married in early January so Karen would not be embarrassed with a baby coming in less than nine months, although I am sure everyone who received the notice suspected what had happened.

We found a small apartment for $45 a month above a little store in Montlake, close enough for me to walk to the University. Having scheduled morning classes so that I could take an afternoon job, I applied through the University's job service center and found work at the University Central Stores, a warehouse, run like a hardware store, holding all of the tools, piping, fittings and supplies used in the maintenance of the great number of buildings on campus. I was paid $1 per hour, and earned $20 to $30 a week. This kept the wolf from the door and I went straight through the last two years of school without a break.

I was busy with school and work as Karen grew the baby and on October 10, 1950, the time came and I took the day off to be with her in the hospital. In those years they did not believe in letting fathers into the delivery room, so I sat in the waiting room with both Jessie and Mother, both about to become grand-parents, and several other men who had been through it before. I was worried and anxious at the thought of what Karen was going through and the realization that I was the cause of any pain or trouble she might incur plagued me. Happily, without too lengthy a labor, Karen gave birth to our son Bill, named after my father and we were very happy to have him.

Karen seemed to take to the role of mothering a baby, and fairly bloomed. She seemed happy about the whole experience and quickly became devoted to Billy. I was busy trying to keep my grades up and work, but tried to help out with the baby when I was there. I knew how to cook and sometimes could help in that way, and often tended to Billy in the night helped Karen get some needed rest. I have often thought about this choice, put to us so inelegantly the year before, to "go across town," or have the baby, and when I think about the fine young man that came into our lives by taking responsibility for our actions I am immensely gratified for the choice I made.

While I was busy with school and work, the larger world backdrop was a very risky cold war developing between the Soviet Union and the United States, both armed with nuclear missiles, and both trying to proselytize their views to other countries of how the world should work. This came to a head in 1951, with the attack by North Korea upon South Korea in an effort to impose the North's communist dictatorship on the South. This was seen as a direct challenge to America and much of Western Europe, the general perception being, that if it succeeded, a lot more countries would come under communist, and therefore Soviet, control.

I was 21 and this would have been "my" war, but the happenstance of getting married in 1950 changed my draft status to 3A and I was never called. But I was intensely interested in the war's progress, since the stakes were high. I soon became very disheartened by the political control of the war, instead of letting Gen. Douglas MacArthur, the Supreme Allied Commander, prosecute it from his vantage point of military expertise. This appeared to me very different from what had been the case in WWII, where the idea was to win it completely, not strive for only a political solution. To maintain the status quo we left over 50,000 young Americans dead. One of these was Alfie and Amy Davis's older brother, a West Point graduate in a class that was almost totally lost in the war.

My agitation grew until I began to get stomach pains and other symptoms and one day these got to the point where I called Dr. Berge, my doctor for years, to get his advice. His answer was simple: "Try not to go crazy over things you have no control over and cannot change." I took his recommendation to heart throughout the rest of the war, even the proceedings of Truman sacking Mac-Arthur, my hero. Later I watched the famous speech by MacArthur delivered to a joint session of Congress on TV, an extraordinary event.

During that summer, the final quarter of my senior year, we got a job house sitting on Mercer Island for some friends of my parents. Situated on the shore of Lake Washington it was a wonderful place for Karen and the baby to spend their days playing on the grass near the lakeshore. I took a swing shift job at Boeing paying me $1.51 an hour. My classes ended at noon, I studied until 3 in the afternoon, drove to the Boeing plant to start work at 4 PM, which lasted until 11:30 PM and arrived home each night after midnight.

Working for Boeing was interesting. I was in the transportation department working as a swamper on a small flat bed electrically powered truck, moving casting dies, airplane parts and miscellaneous items, between departments throughout the plant. I was urged to join the union, but refused on the pretext that I would soon be gone when school ended. This did not placate the union members in the department, and occasionally I was given a rough time from them for working too hard, and they complained, making them look bad. The driver of my rig weighed 325 pounds and was strong as an ox and when he saw me strain a bit to lift something and put it on the truck, if he thought it was over the 50 pound limit for a man to lift, he would get off the truck, pick up the offending box and hold it straight out with his arms and moving it up and down for about 10 seconds to determine if the weight was over the limit, before putting it back down on the floor and directing me to leave it where it was. In this manner lifting the package twice but moving it nowhere.

By 11 PM you could not find a person in the transportation department working. They were all hiding out smoking in various utility shacks and storerooms near the main building making sure that the next shift would get whatever work they did not complete. The waste by these kinds of actions must have been colossal and the anti-company attitudes made me into a real believer in causes like the "Right To Work," a movement my father had been very active in support of, that made joining a union not a prerequisite to getting and holding a job. I could only imagine how difficult it must have been to run any company in the face of a determined union shop.

These were long days for me, but we were saving some money, partly because we were not paying any rent for the summer months. At the end of the quarter I still was short three credits to get a diploma, but I did not want to go back for another quarter of school, preferring to take the final three credits by correspondence and get started working. I had been thinking of returning to Alaska to trap with Lou, and the more I thought about it the more the idea appealed to me.

I was so enamored with Alaska and had such great memories from my trips in 1947 and 1948 working with Lou that I was certain Karen would love it also and it would be a great experience for us to look back on in later years. Even though she was again pregnant, she did not try to argue me out of it, so I contacted Lou Anderton to see if he would take me on again for trapping. I had another reason, maybe more compelling than trying to make money trapping, and that was the need for some sort of redemption by proving I was able to handle the winter weather trapping and that my earlier experience and frozen feet had not frightened me off or stopped my notion of living successfully in the out-of-doors.

I heard from Lou that he would like us to come and that we should be up there by October. He planned to have us stay with him in his cabin, as it was the largest in the tiny settlement and when he and I were out trapping, Karen and Billy would have the place to themselves. I was also sure that Harry Sutherland and Joe Davis, who would be in cabins nearby for the winter, would make sure they were all right when I was away.

In August of 1951 I signed up for a three credit correspondence course through the University which I needed for graduation, and started to collect the things we would be taking to Alaska. I also had heard that there were Alaskan car buyers who were looking for people to drive their cars up to Alaska for them. After considerable exploration I found a truck driver who had purchased a new Lincoln Continental in Seattle and needed a driver. When I made contact with him, he agreed that we would drive his car to Anchorage at the same time he was driving a loaded tractor trailer back there himself. This was magical good news. A brand new Lincoln to drive up the Alcan Highway to Alaska. For a car lover like me, nothing could have sounded better.

I gathered up my gun, a Winchester 270, a new Rollicord reflex camera (a poor man's Rolliflex) and film, my binoculars, new warm clothes for Karen and Billy, my moccasins, a cradle I made that could be hung from the cabin ceiling, sleeping bags and other stuff. The car was completely loaded down when we started out.

The prospect of making this drive was exciting to me. I had heard a great deal from those who had done it shortly after the war and had wanted this adventure for myself. The Alcan highway in 1951 turned out to be a gravel road from Dawson Creek north for about 1500 miles and turned out to be a challenge for tires and contending with the dust and potholes. However, the route was through beautiful scenery the farther we went and the roadhouses that we passed about every 50 miles were each distinctive and interesting stops for us. But it was a long drive and I was pressing to get there as quickly as possible since our money was running out rapidly and this meant we drove for long hours each day. Karen, after a few days, was not feeling too well and when we arrived in Whitehorse, in the Yukon, she was really ill and ended up miscarrying the baby.

We lay over the next day for her to rest, but she wanted to move on the following day. It was 300 miles to the Yukon/Alaska border and seven hours later we pulled into the Canadian Customs and Immigration office, to show the gun, camera and binoculars, which I had declared I was taking to Alaska. I walked into the office, leaving Karen and Billy in the car, and faced a single official who did not seem very interested or friendly, but nevertheless I stepped forward, said "Hi, I'd like to check the things on my custom form through, as well as the car." He looked at the papers for a minute, shoved them back at me, and said, "You can't take the car through, because you don't own it."

I was shocked and said, "What do you mean? When I came into Canada, customs knew it was not my car and that the owner was coming behind me in a truck. He has all the papers for the car with him and should be crossing maybe tomorrow or the next day."

"I don't care about that," he answered, not even looking at me, but continuing to fuss with the papers he had been working on when I came in. "You cannot take the car across without the papers, and that's that!"

I said, "look, we've come 300 miles, my wife is ill and we have to get her to some decent medical help. I've got a gas tank leaking (which it was from a small hole punched in it on a rough spot in the highway) and we can't go back to Whitehorse now."

His answer to that was, "I don't care what problems you've got, that car cannot go through, so just turn around and come back with the owner!" turning once again to shuffling papers. I had always had trouble dealing with officious petty government employees and this one truly took the cake for blatant lack of concern. I was beside myself. I didn't know what to do and walked outside to the car. I got in and told Karen that I had just been dealing with the worst son-of-a-bitch I'd ever met and he was not going to let us through. She was deflated by this news and I knew she was not feeling well at all. I looked at the border gate swung open at the time, and trying to collect my wits, I turned and started to drive slowly back down the road, my mind racing and churning in rage. After going several hundred yards I thought about the lack of other people around the office, the open gate and no visible patrol car and instantly knew what I was going to do. I said, to no one in particular, "Screw him!" made a U-turn and hit the accelerator and we blew through the border crossing at 70 mph and into Alaska.

We were five miles from Scotty Creek Lodge, the very place I had been taken after freezing my feet in 1948 and I kept one eye in the rear view mirror to see if they had sent the Mounties after me. Five minutes later I pulled up to the road-house. We went in and I called the Alaska State Patrol to ask some advice on what to do, explaining our situation. The man I talked to was not very concerned. He said, "You're through the border now and inside Alaska, so you don't need to worry. They are not coming after you here." That was very good news and I began to calm down. We continued on our way toward Tok Junction where we stopped for the night. The next morning I drove past Copper Center and we arrived in Chitina around noon. I got a room for Karen and Bill in the only hotel and then drove to Anchorage to deliver the car, staying at Harold Curtis' home that night.

Two days later Karen and Bill and I climbed aboard an old Norseman airplane for the 120 mile flight into Chisana, landing there around midday, with the entire population: Lou Anderton, 59; Joe Davis, 65; Harry Sutherland, 72; and N.P. Nelson, 85; on the dirt airstrip to greet us. We spent the rest of the afternoon getting our stuff into the cabin and arranging things so Karen, Billy and I had a small room to ourselves. Karen told me many years later that with her first sight of Chisana she was overwhelmed with feelings of despair that she would be almost alone in that tiny place and frightened by the isolation it offered.

There was a lot to be done and Lou and I began right away making plans for the trapping ahead. We discussed the options and what fur bearing animals to go after. I had been told about trapping martin in the wooded areas east and north of Chisana in the Beaver Creek watershed. This sounded better to me than returning to the White River, since the terrain was easier, the traps smaller and easier to handle and the value of the pelts high. However, the horses were still grazing out along the Chisana River bars and Lou felt it was a better plan to take them over to the White River to set up several camps before the snow came and

Karen, Chisana 1951

then to make our trapping headquarters at a place named Horsefelt, a single cabin set in a large open area. There was ample grass for the horses during the winter and we would be able to look at them often to make sure they were doing all right. I deferred to his judgment on this, as I knew he had the experience to make the right choice.

Leaving Karen and Bill in Chisana, Lou and I set out with the packtrain a few days later and spent the next several weeks preparing the necessary camps and waiting for enough snow to fall so that I could hike back to Chisana and bring out the dog team. I talked with Lou about this forty mile walk back to town and he told me that someone had done it in 11 hours many years before. When we got a few inches of snow and it appeared that there would be more coming over the next week, I prepared to go back to town. I wanted to try to set a record time for making this hike from Horsefelt to Chisana, so I decided to go very light, without a rifle because of its weight and just a few sandwiches and dried fruit along with a jacket and parka in a rucksack.

The trail essentially followed Francis Creek up grade for about 24 miles and then over a low pass near Porky Point and into the drainage to Johnson Creek about 8 miles further on at Bonanza, where Harry, Joe, and N.P. had their gold claims and another 8 miles down stream from Bonanza to Chisana.

I started out at daybreak as I knew it would be dark long before I got to Chisana and set a fast pace in the two to four inches of snow that covered the landscape. When I was about 15 miles from Horsefelt, I came on some very fresh looking grizzly tracks that came in from the right and meandered here and there along the trail, but generally going in my direction.

Soon I came to a place where the bear had lain down in the snow near the trail, which looked very fresh and I began thinking about a grizzly looking for a place to den up and maybe being a bit grumpy about the change in the weather. The trail at this point was above timberline so there were no trees to climb, and I was fervently wishing I had a gun with me. The tracks meandered off the trail to the left but in a half a mile came back in from the right. Now I began to get real nervous and I stopped every now and then to look behind myself to make sure he would not come up from the rear. I came to a second place where the bear had lain down and this looked fresher than the previous spot. I knew he had to be close and I just plain did not want to meet up with this bear out in the open under any circumstances. This went on for several miles, but finally the tracks angled off to the left and I did not see them again and began to relax.

It was dark by the time I hit the summit and I was feeling the strain of trying to complete the journey in under eleven hours, starting to assert itself. The trail was easier going downhill, but by the time I arrived at the Bonanza cabin, with eight miles yet to travel, I was aware that I was greatly fatigued. I had set the hike up as a personal test and the last miles into town had been hard even though the slope was downhill. My muscles were stiffening up and looking back now, I suspect I was dehydrated in a major way, having had almost no water all the way. When I arrived at the cabin in Chisana, 10½ hours after leaving Horsefelt and leaned on the door I was totally played out. I knocked and Karen opened the door, very much surprised to see me and seeing I was really tired, helped me to a chair and asked if I wanted to eat. I asked for a can of fruit and she opened a large can of grapefruit section is light syrup which I devoured immediately. I asked for another can and went through half of it, I'm sure mainly slaking my thirst and then within 15 minutes I had a major distressed stomach, complete with cramps and bloating and spent a very uncomfortable night.

A few days later and a few inches more snow allowed me to hook up the dogs for the first time since spring. They were really wild with excitement and to make sure they did not run over Harry who was going to hold Pat, the lead dog, I tied the sled to an eye bolt in a corner of the cabin. I got Pat into his harness, and then one by one started hooking up the rest of the team. By this time they were jumping up in the air and hitting the towline in unison to get going and as I got Bingo, the last one hooked up, and was in the process of tying his collar chain to the sled, the dogs lunged into the towline and broke the rope tied to the cabin, knocked poor Harry flat and took off at a dead run, with me leaping for the handle bars and dragging myself upright to get onto the sled where I could use the brake. I looked back and saw Harry standing up, shaking the snow off of and knew he was all right, so I hollered at the dogs to go faster, but within 200 yards they were fagged out. I could see it would take a few days to get them in shape for the trip back to Horsefelt.

During the time I was in Chisana, I started working on the correspondence course and was able to prepare a few lessons for the plane to take out and mail. Five or six days later I left with the dogsled for Horsefelt. I worked on the lessons at night whenever possible and also started writing some poetry which was pretty bad, but I continued to try to do this while out on the line, motivated partly because I was lonesome being away from my wife and child for two to three weeks at a time.

After returning to Horsefelt with the dogs, Lou and I settled into the routine of working the traps all the way to the White River and along Beaver Creek. We were out of fresh meat and we both were looking for opportunities to hunt. On one trip I made over to the White, the trail left Rock Lake and in two miles went through a narrow cut between some mountains that rose up about 4000 feet on each side and I noted that some sheep had been moving from one side to the other. I kept this in mind and on the return trip the next day I saw that a small band of sheep had crossed to the north side shortly before I had arrived. It was a good opportunity to get some fresh meat so I tied the sled to a tree, took out my 270 Winchester and took 11 shells, six of which I put in the gun and started to climb up the steep slope of the mountain.

Karen and Billy in Chisana

Near the top I climbed to point about half way up the edge of a small basin that was about 75 yards across at the bottom, but with shear sides all the way around the bowl. I knew I was close to the sheep but had not seen any when all of a sudden a small bunch took off running in the basin. I shot several times across the basin at one ram that was climbing up the steep side without hitting him and then saw directly below me another ram running across the bottom of the basin and I was almost shooting straight down at him. I missed with one shot and then hit him with the next and he went down.

I left that ram and started to run on up to the top of the ridge above the basin, where the other sheep were heading, thinking I would get another chance to shoot on the ridge. I was puffing when I got there and had to reload, and then several sheep came into view about 100 yards away right on the ridge. This was as easy as shooting in a gallery so I took my time, lined up on a ram, and pulled the trigger. Nothing happened. I shot again. Again nothing. I could not figure what was wrong. I tried to remember everything about shooting I could, before I shot again, but when I pulled the trigger, again I missed! I had one more shell to go and it also hit only air. I could not believe what I had just done. Shot 11 times and had one hit! It was beyond me what had gone wrong, but when I started back down I knew I had a sheep down and no shells to finish him if he was alive.

When I descended to the bottom of the basin where all the action had started, I came over a small rise and the wounded ram, twenty yards away, jumped up and ran angling downhill. I could see that the bullet had broken his right front leg at the elbow and this was the reason he moved downhill. He went about 150 yards and lay down and when I again got too close, up he went running, but always downhill. I figured that if I could herd him down part way, I would be a lot closer to the sled where I could get more shells and hiking back up to kill him would be easier, so as long as he went down I stayed on his tail. Each time he jumped up and ran though, the distance of the run was shorter and the closer I could get to him before he took off again. After four or five such efforts he went out of sight over a drop off. I kept going in the direction he was moving towards a steep slide where the shale dropped almost vertically down to a small swale about 15 feet below. Reaching the point where I could see down into this swale, I stopped, since he was right there, resting. Instead of running, he turned his head to look at me and I thought that I could maybe take him with my hunting knife and save a long hike to the sled and back up.

I was about 1500 feet above the sled trail and from the side of the mountain I could look north over to Rock Lake and beyond, and to the south I could see the White River in the distance. For some reason, Prince Valiant popped into my mind, perhaps from a drawing I remembered in the comics, of him overlooking a vast Nordic expanse from a mountainside and ready to do battle with some awesome creature. I knew Prince Valiant would not have hesitated to finish off the animal even though this thought sort of scared me not knowing how strong or quick the ram would be. But back then, thinking of the adventure of it and what a story it would be to tell later, I determined to try to kill the ram even if I was to lose a few teeth in the struggle. I took my hunting knife out of its scabbard on my belt, and frightened or not, launched myself down the slide, hardly touching the shale it was so steep and landed on top of the ram. He struggled for a moment but I grabbed a horn and pulling his head back, cut his throat.

I was really elated about this adventure, even though killing the ram had turned out to not be a very big contest. The ram's horns were full curl and even on both sides, a real trophy of 39 or 40 inches and I hated to leave the head on the mountain, but it would be easier to pull the carcass down the mountainside without the head, so I cut it off right there. After gutting him I then cut an opening between the Achilles tendons and the leg bones and working my fingers into these slots and grasping the two leg bones I started down towards the sled pulling the animal behind me.

In late October of 1951, when we returned to Chisana for our first time since moving our trap line over to the White River, the mail flown in by a bush pilot contained a letter from my father informing me that he had purchased a ranch in the East Kootenay region of British Columbia, at Lake Windermere, and asked if I would be interested in coming back and going to work for him there.

Lake Windermere is twenty miles north of the headwaters of the Columbia River and about twenty miles South of Briscoe B.C. where Dad had helped me get my first summer farm job in 1943. My first reaction to Dad's letter was great surprise since I had not heard a single word about such a possibility before but this led to a second feeling that just loving the area was not a great reason to buy a ranch with the intent of developing a cattle operation. I also had, I must admit, a little flash of irritation at not having been asked my opinion about where a ranch should be, especially since my parents were asking me to go there to work. I knew enough from my summer ranching experiences to be concerned about running cattle on timber range and where there was little or no winter grazing available.

At this time of my life I did not want to work for my father. I was fully intent on building my own future and really wanted to make it on my own. I had some pride in having supported my family through the last two years of college and I felt there was a possibility to make it in Alaska and at the same time have some real adventure to boot. So I wrote Dad declining his invitation to go to the ranch, explaining that I thought Alaska would provide me with some opportunities and that I wanted to finish the trapping season with Lou, who was counting on me.

Karen hauling ice For water

A few days after that Lou and I were headed back to Horsefelt. We stopped for the night 16 miles out at Porky Point, the highest point between the two cabins, where we maintained a tent right out in the open, treeless, tundra-like expanse. We kept two heavy Woods 3-Star sleeping bags on wooden platforms, firewood and an "airtight" heater that could be used for cooking as well as heating. This camp had been set up as an emergency stop on the route since above timberline there was no other shelter to be had. That night was clear with magnificent Northern Lights and we heard a wolf pack running Caribou and howling like crazy for several hours. It was right out of a Robert Service story poem. The next day we made Horsefelt after passing through where the wolves had been playing under the Northern Lights, seeing tracks all over the place but no kills.

The following day I went alone to the White River and spent the first night at our Ptamigan Lake tent. The dogs were very uneasy that night and I was certain that the wolf pack we had heard two days before had followed our trail to the camp. The dogs kept whining and I had a gun handy, and each time I went outside to calm them, I used a flashlight to see if I could pick up any eyes lurking in the woods but saw none. The next morning I left camp with the dog team and the trail led across Rock Lake several miles from my last night's camp. When I stopped to rest the dogs, I looked back across the frozen lake and there came a pack of six wolves following our sled trail. I tried a shot and knowing they were a long way off for the 22 cal. rifle I had along to kill anything I found in a trap, I aimed three or four feet over the closest one. I missed, but they turned off our trail and headed into the woods on another angle. How I wished I had my big gun since each wolf was worth about $60 with the bounty and the pelt, but wanting to lighten what I knew would be a very heavy load on the return trip, I had left it at Horsefelt.

As we worked the line day after day, I was becoming more concerned that we were not going to do well with the trapping in the area we were working and Lou finally decided that we ought to move the entire trap line down the Beaver Creek. I agreed with this idea and we started on this project around December 10th. It was going to take some hard sledding to relay the various camps and gear 50 or 60 miles north and I was the one who would handle the dog team to get this done. We had about three heavy sled loads of gear that would require at least ten days to move. This was all new country I had never been in so Lou and I would move a load to the next stop and the following day I would go back for another load while Lou set traps in the new area.

I had plenty of time while relaying our camps to think more and more about the probabilities of making any money trapping with Lou. I also thought about my new set of responsibilities looking out for Karen and Billy. The enjoyment I had found in the two hunting seasons and the three months spent trapping with Lou when I was a teenager no longer applied. I now had a family to look after and that was my primary obligation, regardless of what Lou's and my relationship had been before. I had to make some money to support my family and I would rather have taken a beating than call on my parents to bail me out of a financial difficulty now that I was supposedly a family man.

Contributing to this problem was the fact that Lou, for some reason, found it hard to accept Karen and our son Bill, then one year old. I can only assume that having a woman and child in his cabin, with confusion over the daily routine of cooking and cleaning Lou was not used to while living alone, created for him some unexpected changes in his routine and adversely affected his acceptance of Karen into his domain.

Harry Sutherland and Billy, 1951

I struggled with this dilemma for several weeks in early December while we were relaying our various camps down Beaver Creek to the new trapping site. I finally made up my mind that continuing to trap with Lou was not going to work out. Telling him this was one of the hardest things I have ever had to do in my life. I simply dreaded the moment when I actually had to say the words aloud, and I rehearsed what I would say over and over in the week before I could bring myself to do it. I loved and respected Lou like a surrogate father, and would not have hurt him for anything, but I felt it was an impossible situation for me to continue. We were going to go broke trapping if things did not change dramatically and my reason told me that there was no prospect of a change to be had.

I remember exactly when and where Lou and I were when I told him. We were holed up for a few days in an ancient flat-roofed cabin, actually a forest hut, which was named Buhldoff Cabin and was located at the confluence of Buhldoff and Beaver Creeks. The cabin was located in the 50 foot wide logged off boundary line separating the Canadian Yukon from Alaska, probably built using logs from the very trees cut down to delineate the border. We had spent several nights there while I went back and forth relaying our gear. Lou had told me that, years before, one traveler who stopped here had his dog team attacked by a wolf pack, a very rare occurrence.

It was a low-ceilinged cabin about 12' by 18' and we had to duck low to get in the front door. Small windows on either side of the door provided little light so most of the light came from a kerosene lamp that cast flickering shadows as we moved about the room. We were soon to head back to "town" for Christmas and I simply had to tell Lou of my plans before we started back. I was just returned from several very hard days of solo travel with the dogs. The weather had been very cold, the overflow on Beaver Creek deep and scary, (I still had some unanswered questions about my feet and their ability to handle the cold) the sled was heavy and as I climbed into my sleeping bag that night I just blurted out, "Lou, I've decided not to come back out trapping after Christmas."

There was a long silence while Lou stared at the floor, not moving, and then he answered, "I wish you had told me that before. I told George Neydengast, who wanted to come, that you were going to trap the winter with me."

Then almost in tears, I said, "I'm really sorry Lou." I felt sick about letting him down and sicker that the relationship I had with Lou when I was younger had been lost and irrecoverable with my marriage. Later I told Lou that I would help him after Christmas with the moving of the trapline, but I would be taking my family "outside" after that. I could see that my need to get work was imperative, but I was still not ready to take a nine-to-five job in a city.

We were going to town around December 20th and Lou asked if I would hunt on the way back to try to take some fresh meat into town for everyone while he spent a few more days in Horsefelt. He would come with the dog team later and if I killed anything, I should pull it out to the trail and leave it for him to bring in with the sled. He thought the best chance was to hunt sheep around Teepee Mountain, one of the areas we usually had seen sheep when we passed by, to and from Chisana. I agreed to this plan and on the 20th started out at daylight with my rifle, a knapsack with a few sandwiches and raisins and extra sox and moccasins.

Buhldoff cabin

I hiked at a fast walk the 15 miles to the turnoff point to Teepee Mt. and crossed the gently upward sloping flat to the base of the mountain. Teepee got its name since it was shaped like an almost perfect pyramid with one steep front face parallel to the trail I was on and the other two sides out of sight behind this front wall. I approached the mountain, which was small by any standard, rising maybe 2000 feet to its peak and climbed half way to the top up one edge of the pyramid. There were signs of sheep all over the place so I traversed the face using the myriad of sheep trails, still not seeing any game. When I got close to the other side of the face I began to hear the hollow banging sounds, like two wooden clubs being hit hard together, of rams fighting. I still did not see any sheep and when I came to the end of the face I started down, as it was now about 1 P.M. and I had only two more hours of daylight to use for the remaining miles to our camp at Porky Point.

As I descended this ridge almost to the bottom I heard another fight going on and then saw a small herd of ewes and rams moving up the backside of the mountain. I worked my way back up a draw facing the mountain and picked out a couple of ewes that were in range and killed them. It was now 2 P.M. as I gutted them and when that was done, I began to drag them down the draw to the main trail where Lou could pick them up. I could only take one at a time and it was extremely hard work as their dense hair acted like Velcro sticking to the low brush I had to drag them through and over. I pulled until I could not hold my grip on their legs any longer, or my thigh muscles would just start to burn from the exertion and I would then have to stop and rest. It took a full hour to get the two sheep down to the trail.

Porky Point camp

It was now almost dark and I had only covered about 16 miles up the trail. However, I had climbed up and down a mountain as well with still another eight or nine miles to go to make Porky Point and I was completely worn out. I hiked the next four miles to Carl Creek in the moonlight under a beautiful Aurora Borealis, the temperature around—25°F and dropping in the clear night and stopped there for a rest. I was standing, but resting some of my weight on a snow covered hummock while I ate half of my last sandwich, feeling very much alone and terribly tired. It was really beautiful with the moonlight reflecting off the snow and the Nutzotin Mountains backdropped in waving drapes of green shimmering light to the north, but under the circumstances I could not appreciate it the way I might have. I was beginning to have a small gnawing of fear about my feet with the temperature falling and being so fatigued. This was dangerous and I had to get to Porky Point, where there was safety. I started the last five miles up to the pass at a very slow pace, my legs feeling like lead, and when I arrived at the tent I was so tired I did not make a fire but just crawled into the big Woods 3 Star sleeping bag in all my clothes and went to sleep to a very restless night.

At daylight I got up and ate the last half sandwich and started down the trail to Bonanza, eight miles away. Even though I was going downhill, I was still so tired that it took me four hours to get to Bonanza. Needing some food to recharge my batteries I went into the cabin looking for something to eat. All I found was cornmeal left from the stash we kept there for feeding the dogs, and a sack of brown sugar. I cooked up a big bowl, liberally spreading the sugar on top of the mush and ate it like a starving man. I rested in the cabin for about thirty minutes while the food took effect and then started down the last eight miles to Chisana. I made these miles in two hours, having regained my strength with the food and in places I actually jogged along. What a change from the morning hike into Bonanza before I ate and was able to restore some energy. I arrived in the early afternoon, elated to be back in some semblance of civilization and to be with my wife and child again.

Waiting for me in Chisana was a letter from Dad containing Christmas greetings along with another request that I reconsider my decision about the ranch. He added that he would feel better knowing a family member was there, and laid out his thoughts on what the ranch could become with good management. It was a bit of a "full court press."

I wrote him back after Christmas, that although I did not think I wanted to commit to him about the ranch, I was willing to go take a look at it and that we would be coming out as soon as I could help Lou reorganize the trap line, settle my account with him and make arrangements for a plane to come and get us.

The next few weeks saw the end of my work with Lou, and Karen and I began to pack up to leave for the outside. Although Karen had become very fond of old Harry, she was excited to finally be getting back to civilization. When the plane came in we loaded our things, said our goodbyes to Lou, Harry, Joe, and N.P. and clambered in. We taxied to the north end of the gravel runway, did a run-up of the engine and started our takeoff roll back towards town. When we lifted off, I saw the small group of friends still on the field waving to us as we passed over them and the few cabins several hundred feet below. As we climbed out towards the Wrangle Mountains I had my last look at Chisana, a tiny cluster of cabins in a great expanse of forest, rivers and mountains and was saddened by the prospect that I might never come this way again, a place that held so many meaningful memories for me.

Ranching Years

*Wherein our hero moves to Canada to become a cowboy,
raises a family, and makes a grave decision*

In February 1952 we arrived in Seattle and I met with Dad to explore what his purpose was in buying the Elkhorn Ranch. I soon found out that his reason for buying the ranch was not, as I had guessed, to be close to good hunting. Dad explained to me that what had prompted his purchase was the income tax burden he was laboring under. Without deductions, he explained, and a tax rate around 70%, it was almost impossible to build capital. With the help of a tax accountant it was decided that a ranch property could provide an opportunity to charge costs of the operation as personal deductible expenses. This meant that Uncle Sam was really a partner in funding the costs of building a ranching business.

Also, the cattle could be depreciated as an expense over a five-year period, under the "basic herd" rules. This meant the costs in buying cows to stock the ranch would be an important tax consideration. The ranch property was set up as Elkhorn Ranch Ltd., a Canadian corporation, owned by Mother and Dad, and it was leased to Elkhorn Ranch, a private cattle company also owned by my parents. After learning that the main thrust of the decision was to try to build family financial assets, I began to think quite differently about the prospect and could see why my father might want me to go there.

Soon thereafter I left Karen and little Bill at her parents and drove alone, the 600 miles to the Ranch. The route there was via Spokane, up the Idaho panhandle to cross the Canadian border at Kingsgate, then following highway 93 north through Cranbrook to Lake Windermere, about 150 miles north of the border. I was familiar with part of the beautiful valley formed by the Rockies on the east and the Selkirks to the west in which the ranch was situated, from having worked in the summer of 1943 about 30 miles north of Windermere. The valley formed by both mountain ranges lay at 3000 ft. on an axis basically north/south creating a conduit for the Columbia River which flowed almost 200 miles farther north to Mica Creek before turning south to join first, the Kootenay River, and then the Snake River on its way to the Pacific.

On arrival I presented myself to Vaughn DuBois, the ranch manager and was put up for a few days in a small cabin near the main house, from which I could explore the layout, meet the people working there and discuss the job and future outlook with Vaughn.

The land had been purchased and the buildings constructed in the mid 1920's by the Canadian Dominion Government as an experimental farm with the goal of demonstrating to the mainly English farmers settled in the valley, what crops and livestock could be grown and how to do it. After operating it for about 10 years, government officials came to understand that the knowledge they had gained had no application anywhere else in Canada except this small valley. In other words it was not a paying deal to continue the project and the property was sold to private owners.

The property ultimately came into the possession of a partnership that included Vaughn DuBois, Dix Anderson, who also worked there, and several other investors not involved with the ranch. It was being run as a dude ranch when Dad purchased it, and both Vaughn and Dix were licensed guides who contracted big game hunting trips each fall as part of the operation. There was almost no livestock, only the riding horses for the dudes, some packhorses used for hunting, a team of mules and a few cows to milk.

The ranch, about 300 feet above the Columbia River at Lake Windermere, was a square section of land with about two thirds of the acreage flat except for a wooded hill sloping up behind the barnyard and corrals filling in the northeast third. The main gate to the ranch was on the Highway 93, which from Lake Windermere, continued north to meet the Trans-Canada Highway at Golden, 90 miles away. The largest cultivated fields were located along the highway. The town of Lake Windermere was about 1½ miles west of the ranch and consisted of a primary school, a small hotel and bar, a general store with a country post office and maybe 35 or 40 homes scattered around on small plots of land on, or near, the lake.

The weather was generally nice with an occasional mountain storm coming in over the Selkirk Mountains to the west. The elevation seemed to limit high temperatures and there were few days reaching into the nineties, and even during hot weather the evenings were always cool and pleasant. With only twelve inches of moisture per year, six of which fell as snow, we continually irrigated with sprinklers during the growing season, since without water nothing would grow. In the winter it was fairly mild as well, with the temperatures ranging between freezing and—10ºF, with an exceptionally cold day dropping to—30º. Rarely was there snow deeper than a foot on the ground and the blizzards that were common on the east slope of the Rockies almost never came into the valley.

The Dominion Government constructed first class buildings when they developed the experimental farm. There was a horse barn with 10 stalls, used to manage and care for the teams of horses then used in the farm work and beyond the stalls a milking parlor with stanchions for our milk cows. Baled hay was stored in the hayloft on the second floor and could be dropped through openings to the stalls and milking parlor below. The building had a concrete floor, as did all of the main farm buildings, including a barn with grain silo and hayloft, built for the dairy herd the experimental farm maintained, a small creamery building for processing the milk, a shop, machinery sheds and root cellar. The corral system as rebuilt by Vaughn and Dix was well laid out and very strong.

A 100,000-gallon water tank at the end of a half-mile long aluminum flume from Windermere Creek, which the property bordered on the north, supplied the domestic water for the eight homes and two small cabins on the property. The flume crossed the many hollows and depressions between the creek and the tank on wooden trestles often 20 feet in the air, something that had to be walked whenever the flume broke or became dammed or frozen. This at substantial risk to the person, usually myself, who was charged with restoring the water flow.

The ranch included 230 Acres of land suitable for cultivation, although much of this land had not seen a plow for years. Oats were grown in a rotation with an alfalfa/grass mix, mainly to support the twenty-five head of horses but all the cultivated land would have to come into production to meet the buildup of the herd. The business plan called for 500 cows, with the main product being calves sold at weaning time in mid-November.

Vaughn told me that they had made arrangements with the Forest Service for permits to graze cattle from May 1st until Oct 31st, and it looked like there was enough Crown Range available to handle more than 500 head. They had already purchased 100 head of yearling steers in Calgary with the intent of bringing them to the ranch by early April and put them onto Crown Range May 1st to graze the summer, mainly as a test to see how good the grass was, planning to sell them in the fall. They planned to buy 100 cows the next month to start the basic herd, but as luck would have it, hoof and mouth disease broke out in Alberta and no cattle could be moved from Alberta to B.C. There was nothing else to do but find grazing for the steers south of Calgary and postpone buying the cows for a year.

I talked to Vaughn about the job. He told me the going salary was $250 per month, we would have a rent free house, milk, a vegetable garden plot and all the deer and elk I was willing to hunt. He laid out the daily work schedule: in the barn at 6 AM each morning to milk the cows and separate the milk, feed the horses and prepare any equipment to be used during the day. This usually finished by 7 AM when we went for breakfast. The day's work started at 8 AM and ended when it was done. This was the routine on the days that did not include riding chores such as moving cattle, which often started at 5 AM or earlier. Work was six days a week and Sunday off, except for chores, unless work was needed to be done, which I was soon to find out there usually was. However, this was not unexpected and sounded fair to me as a start.

I felt Vaughn was a little cool towards me, but I could understand this, since having the owner's son there would not make his life any easier or his job any more secure. In this last observation he was correct.

The decision on taking the job was at hand. I needed steady work, Karen was pregnant again, and this was far enough away from Dad that I thought I could work for him with the few times he would be at the ranch. I felt somewhat secure in the knowledge that in the agricultural aspects of the job, I knew more than my father. The job also met the criterion of not being a nine-to-five job in Seattle, one of my prerequisites. After listening to the plans for the business, looking the ranch over, seeing the house we could move into rent free, and seeing the wonderful scenery of the valley and nearby mountains, I left for Seattle, telling Vaughn that I was interested and would let him know within the week. When I arrived home, Karen and I talked it over, and we agreed that I should take the job.

After this decision was made, to my surprise, I became greatly interested and excited in what lay ahead. I had a strong feeling that I could be successful at ranching, although at the same time I knew there were countless things I did not know and skills that I would have to acquire. I also knew I was going to have to prove to Vaughn and the other men working there that I was not afraid to work and I was certain they would test me on that point immediately and hard.

Some weeks later, at the end of February, we arrived at the ranch late in the day, after many hours of driving, unloaded our stuff from the truck and fell into bed. The next morning I was in the barn at 6 AM for my first lesson in the chores to be done every day which continued with little change for the next ten years. I shared the chores with Dix Anderson, a good-looking man of 32 years, lean and hard and a bit smaller than me, with a cheerful personality. He knew the ranch and the work expectations and over the years we grew to respect each other and become good friends. This relationship instilled in each of us a strong sense of being unwilling to let the other down in relation to the work. I think that in the eight years we worked together, neither one of us was late to the barn for chores more than a few times. We took a certain pride in this fact and I know this contributed to the mutual regard between us.

When I reported for work after breakfast on that first morning, Vaughn, as I expected, had a special job for me that I was sure he had saved for a good long while, probably because he and his compatriots who had owned the place before, definitely had not wished to do it themselves. He handed me a pick and shovel and directed me to a tractor and manure spreader, and for the next two weeks I cleaned out an old building and adjacent area used many years for raising sheep and hogs. The manure was two feet deep, packed hard, and required the pick to break it out and the shovel to load it into the manure spreader.

The only respite from this labor was the act of spreading the hard won manure on the field when, at least for a few minutes, I got to sit on the tractor seat while emptying the spreader. I tried to take all this with good grace, as I knew it was a test of my determination to stay and willingness to do hard work, but I felt very isolated from the other employees working at the ranch during this process. However, at some point the last load had been spread and I moved on to the other types of work at the ranch. I felt a much higher level of acceptance by Vaughn, Dix and the other hands and knew I had passed the initiation test.

Starting that spring most of our effort went to bringing back into cultivation the hayfields that had not been worked for years. The soil, hard and sod-bound and loaded with rocks, required plowing, heavy disking and harrowing to get it ready. That year we planted oats on the newly opened areas and an alfalfa-brome-grass mix in the fields that had been in oats the prior year. This continued to be the crop rotation we followed during the years I was at the ranch. We began the installation of a sprinkler system, which in time I got to know only too well. Fences were put back in shape, some new equipment was purchased, the corrals were improved and the irrigation system of ditches fed from Windermere Creek were renovated to serve all the new fields coming into production.

That first summer was very busy, but since there were hardly any cattle on the ranch it seemed more like a farm. However, I did get a little riding in. I was assigned a dark sorrel mare named Ruby who was docile and easy going. Vaughn was an excellent rider and although I had ridden horses a lot, Vaughn taught me quite a bit about managing a horse and getting it to do exactly what I wanted. He could get his horse into a very fast walk and keep it there, something I could never accomplish with Ruby. I would slowly fall behind and have to kick Ruby into a trot, which always evoked Vaughn's silent disgust, shown by a shake of his head. I felt a bit better by seeing that no one else could get what Vaughn got from his horse, and I liked to believe it was the horse not the rider that was at fault. This idea made me feel a lot better even if not true.

In the fall of 1952 it was decided that since there were no cattle on the ranch to winter feed, I could leave to attend Washington State College in Pullman (it was quite a few years before it would be called a University), to take some courses in Agronomy, Agricultural Economics, and beef cattle science. This was the last time I attended formal schooling other than short courses or seminars at WSC, which were offered each year in ranch management, supervision or breeding. I enjoyed the beef husbandry course, which was scientific but practical and used a great thick book by professor Ensminger who taught the course at WSC.

This introduced me to modern methods of cattle raising, very different from the old ways of doing things on the range. Everything was aimed at efficient meat production instead of using cattle as a reason to play "cowboy". These concepts were reinforced in me by attending the annual Beef Cattle Short Course at WSC, and I became convinced over the next few years that we needed to take steps to improve our product. This had to wait until the ranch was stocked and I had a chance to put into place the newer methods.

At the time I started fall semester in Pullman, Karen was in Seattle for the birth of our second child, Susan. There were some difficulties after the birth that necessitated the baby staying in the hospital for several weeks, so Karen, Billy and the new baby did not join me until late November. I moved out of the dorm I had shared with two veterinary students, Gordon Wimpenny, a veteran airman from the war in the Pacific, with whom I continued a friendship during my years at the ranch, and Jason Otter, who later set up his practice in Idaho, to live with Karen and the little ones in a small apartment in downtown Pullman.

When the semester ended in late May we returned to the ranch where I again entered into the day-to-day farming routine. I had purchased several textbooks on beef cattle management and spent my lunch hours and evenings reading these books cover to cover. I was determined to learn as much as possible about the business I was entering with the idea of making it a success. I knew enough to see that the methods currently being used were not up to date and I also knew that Vaughn did not know much about modern cattle raising, although he knew plenty about horses.

By this time most of the crops were planted and 100 head of pregnant cows were to be purchased from the Calgary auction ring, along with some yearling steers that were to go to rented pasture on the Kooteney Indian Reserve, a ten-mile stretch of prime land between the highway and the Columbia River. Several of the pastures, those of Moises Michel, and Joe Jimmy, were directly across the highway from the ranch and cattle grazing there were visible from the ranch. Four or five purebred Hereford bulls had also been purchased and put with the cows, but Vaughn and Dix usually did the riding work, and my education as a farmer, to the exclusion of raising cattle, seemed destined to continue with little opportunity to ride and spend time with the livestock.

These cows were not put out on public land controlled by the B. C. Forest Service, and referred to in Canada as "Crown range", as they did not arrive until late summer. This rangeland to be allotted to the Elkhorn Ranch began about twenty miles south of the ranch to the west of the highway and lay between Dutch and Findley Creeks, a range about 15 miles long and 10 miles wide. This was all timber range, mainly Jackpine, Tamarack and Aspen, not too brushy, with many open meadows and plenty of water. It was usually not hard to find the cattle and move them about as required but as with all such forestland there were places with downed timber and thick brush where herding cattle was difficult. It was easy to become frustrated in such a situation and finally in desperation, be compelled to sink spurs into the horse and just crash through everything. This was hard on horses and riders, but often got the attention of the cow. That is when a hat and chaps came in mighty handy.

The business plan was to stock up to five hundred head of commercial cows, breed the yearling heifers, and sell weaned calves as the main crop. The intent was to buy good purebred Hereford bulls and try to improve the quality of the herd over time. We intended to grow the hay for winter-feeding and use leased spring and fall pastures to reduce the feeding days. Vaughn organized these leases, with the fall pastures on the Fairmont Hot Springs land near Dutch Creek and the Kootenay Indian Reserve. The spring pastures were a section of land across Windermere Creek on the north, adjacent to the ranch, and a few other fields close by the ranch on the Reserve.

During this second summer we completed installation of the sprinkler system adding aluminum pipe and diesel powered pumping units to irrigate the additional acreage being cultivated. This was all portable pipe in 20 foot lengths with the main header lines 6" in diameter, and the laterals in 4", 3" and 2" to compensate for the line friction loss and to assure equal pressure at each sprinkler head. The power units were fed from 55 gallon barrels of diesel fuel that had to be constantly refilled from the fuel storage tanks and hauled into position next to the power units. They ran about 20 hours a day and seemed to suck an ungodly amount of fuel. When changing from one barrel to the next, the usual procedure was to start a siphon by mouth, to get the lines full so the fuel would flow from the barrel. Naturally, if one does this often enough one will get many a mouthful and I guess I drank more than my fair share of diesel fuel, thus developing my lifelong aversion to the smell of diesel.

Unlike the large automatic sprinkler systems of today, our pipe had to be moved by hand. Sprinkling started in mid April and ended in October and it entailed moving the two lines twice a day unless we got behind and went to three moves. These changes took at least an hour if nothing went wrong, but many nights after dark I was walking the lines with a flashlight to find a connection that had broken. We carried two lengths at a time, using the two-foot long riser that carried the sprinkler head, to rotate the pipe to uncouple the latch and to carefully reconnect it to the coupling at the end of the line being laid out. We moved the lines 60 feet each time and this established a sufficient overlap of water to compensate for changing wind conditions.

This work was relentless because we received very little rainfall in the summer growing season, and I lost at least 10 pounds in weight each summer. The compensating factors were watching the crops grow, the wonderful fresh air, the smells from mown hay and the nearby forests, the small calves coming in the spring and the always inspiring natural beauty of the valley. To this day, many years after I have left the ranch, the sight of a lush field of emerald green alfalfa has struck me as a vision of pure beauty, especially if situated in a summer dry landscape.

After my first two years working on the ranch, Dad decided I probably could run it about as well as Vaughn and offered me the chance to take over as manager. I suspect that he felt that what I didn't know I could learn faster if the responsibility for everything was mine. I was sure that my knowledge about the more modern techniques of beef cattle raising were better than Vaughns', but I also knew that he had knowledge of a great many more practical things about year around ranching than I did. I was acutely aware that I would be scrutinized closely by the ranch hands working for me and by other ranchers in the valley, who I'm sure were surprised by this fairly rapid management change at Elkhorn Ranch. The change would be effective on January 1st, 1954.

Immediately upon my taking over the management, the company faced its first major dilemma. The 100 head of bred cows that had been purchased from the Calgary stockyard auction and brought to the ranch the prior Fall were now getting close to calving. In the very first week of my tenure as Manager, one of these cows aborted her calf and in a day or so two more did as well.

We called in a veterinarian from Creston who tested the three cows in question and soon found that they had Brucillosis, which is a highly contagious bovine disease. The herd was quarantined at the ranch by the B.C. Department of Agriculture and before the outbreak was over, 23 cows had dropped their calves. This was a severe blow since we could not turn infected cattle onto Crown Range for fear they might transmit the disease to the deer and elk population. This meant we had to test all the cows so we brought the vet back to blood test and vaccinate the herd. To maintain the identity of each tested animal we put a numbered ear tag on every cow. When the results came in we shipped all positive testing cows to Calgary and sold them. We then received permission to turn the rest of the cows onto Crown Range and we did not have another outbreak during my tenure at the ranch.

On January 16th, I turned 24 years old and in the first few months as manager I was excessively worried about how the men working on the ranch, almost all of them older than I, would relate to their new boss. The process I used to allocate the work was to meet with the hands in the barnyard at 8 A.M. and parcel out the various jobs on the day's agenda to the individuals I wanted to handle them. I started out making sure that I took on all the hardest, dirtiest work rather than direct one of the other employees to do it. I just hated to send someone off on a hard job for fear they would think I was unwilling to do it myself. In about the second week of agonizing over this issue, I had to tell one of the men that his job was to dig fence post holes most of the day. I said something like, "I really hate to ask you to do this and I'll try to make it up to you later, but would you mind going up on the hill and digging the post holes …?"

He interrupted me with, "Bill, for God's sake, just tell me what you want me to do, and I'll do it. You're the boss, so don't beat around the bush. If there's work to do we'll do it. You just make it harder on all of us by worrying about it."

I was really surprised with the feeling of exasperation I noted in his voice, but I realized he was right and that I had made the whole process more difficult for the men. I said, "I'm sorry, and thanks for telling me this," and after that delegating the work went much easier for me.

The next important thing I learned was that I needed to be prepared with the day's work plan before I arrived in the barnyard. On a few occasions I arrived without a plan and tried to ad-lib my way through soon realizing this was easily recognized by the men. After a couple of glaringly poor performances I made certain to have the plan set before I went to bed each night. These were simple management skills Father was also trying to help me with, but I was a quicker learner when it was our employees teaching me in the daily working environment.

In late January, Vaughn and his family left and Karen and I moved into the "Manager's house", which, with more bedrooms, fit our growing family much better than the two bedroom home we had used the first two years. A portico attached to the house over the three steps leading up to a large front door covered the driveway and was supported on the outside by two large pole columns set on concrete bases. The interior walls were finished and had about four layers of wallpaper and numerous paint jobs applied over the years and we added our own decorating ideas with a new layer.

On the first floor was a kitchen with dining area and an electric stove with a wood or sawdust burning unit attached so that if the power was out we could still heat the kitchen and cook. Off the kitchen was a ten-foot-wide porch running the full width of the house with a couple of long tables with benches and enough space to feed a large summer crew during haying season. Also on the first floor were the living and dining rooms, both with fireplaces, and the master bedroom and bath. We put the kids in the upstairs bedrooms. The basement held a sawdust burning furnace that heated the water, sending much of it to a myriad of heating radiators located in each room. There was a washing machine but no dryer, so the clothes were hung on clothes lines outside. Even in the winter they dried in the cold low humidity air and most ladies claimed that the sunshine would whiten the linens. Whether or not this was true, the open air made the laundry smell fresh when brought inside after drying.

Trying to deal with veterinarians at 150 miles distance I found to be expensive and difficult. One could not afford to call a vet for every little thing that happened to an animal, as the trip in from Creston cost more than the animal was worth. Therefore, it seemed natural that I should learn all I could about animal health, diagnosis and practical surgery. To this end I called upon Gordon Wimpenney, my vet friend from WSC. Gordon loved to hunt, and I needed to know how to do some things in veterinary medicine, so we exchanged skills. Gordon would come hunting for a few days, and then spend some time showing me how to do certain procedures, or I would go to his clinic in Rosalia, Washington, and travel with him to the ranches or farms that he visited professionally. On one trip up to hunt I hired Gordon to teach me to pregnancy test the cows by doing the entire herd. He would test a cow and then I would check the same cow as he explained what he had felt. Sometimes the poor cows were tested three times before I let them out of the chute. In this way I learned almost for free and he hunted for free.

During my attendance at several Beef Cattle Short Courses at WSC, I believe the single most important thing I learned about beef cattle breeding was from a lecture by Tom Lasater, the Texas stockman that created the "Beefmaster" breed. This was a cross of Brahma, Hereford and Shorthorn breeds. He taught a simple theory requiring an understanding of what the product was we were selling, and to the degree possible, to cull only for that one character trait. In our case it was weaner calves and their weight at the time of sale was the single most important factor in how the business would do. This meant we should undertake to do everything we could to improve the weaning weights of the calves. This goal became my mantra at the Elkhorn.

Moving cattle into barnyard near corrals, horse barn and shop.

As part of the upgrading effort to improve both the quality of the herd and the weaning weights of the calves we started regular pregnancy testing of all cows and bred heifers in November 1956 and continued this practice each year. This allowed us to get rid of all dry (non-pregnant) cows and yearling heifers so as not to feed them through the winter. We also shipped any cows that it appeared would be calving very late. These late calves being younger at weaning, would weigh less at sale time, but the cost to maintain the cow was the same for a small as for a large calf.

Me, with a set of newly purchased purebred bulls.

To increase the size and uniformity of the calves we also began a breeding management program. The goals of this plan were to begin calving earlier in the spring, thus adding to the weaning weights in the fall, and to compress the calving period so that all calves would be about the same size at weaning. We turned the bulls out earlier in the season and each year shortened the time they were with the cows. To do this we kept riders out on the range through the breeding period, their job being to assure that every cow was bred as early as possible. This meant keeping bulls from congregating where several bulls would be breeding the same cow and missing others as they came into heat.

In my early years on the ranch we bred our yearling heifers to purebred Hereford bulls, but after losing several young cows in calving and my having to do a few caesarian sections, we changed to black Angus bulls. These calves were smaller, especially in the head, and our birthing problems with the heifers practically went away. These animals required real attention during calving and they had to be separated from the main herd and kept in a nearby field so that we could easily look at them several times each day. From that point, using horses, we cut out those that were within one or two days of calving and moved them into a pen where we could catch them if they needed our help in the calving process. We visited this pen once or twice each night to make certain we would be available to assist if necessary.

My first caesarian operation was performed on a two-year-old heifer in the middle of the night in the calving pen we set up in the old sheep shed. I had gotten out of bed several times to watch her efforts, and finally, at around 2 AM, seeing no progress being made, ran her in the shed, put a rope on her, and with Dix to help, got her on her side. We tied her so that she could not get up or kick, and I examined her. I figured that we could use a calf puller to assist the birthing, but when I got my hand into the birth canal I could tell the head of the calf was just too big to pass through the pelvis. I knew then that we would lose both her and the calf unless I succeeded in a caesarian section. I was determined to try to save at least one of them so gathered the instruments and anesthetics I had collected from Gordon Wimpenny just for this eventuality, along with hot water, soap, nylon monofilament and piles of clean cloths.

I understood, in general, how to do this procedure, but did not have a foggy notion of what problems might occur during the surgery, and how I would cope with them if they did. I figured even if the heifer did not die from shock, or loss of blood, I might cut some nerve I didn't see and she would never walk again. But this had to be done so I shaved, washed and disinfected her belly where I was to cut. I then administered an anesthetic with a syringe, for a two-foot long incision along the midline of her belly. I was very anxious not to hurt her, but determined I was not going to let her have a long and painful death.

With nothing to lose, I placed the scalpel at the top of the incision line, pushed it down hard and drew it straight back about 20 inches, watching her hide part with the pressure of the calf. Dix's eyes bugged out as he watched. I knew he thought I was killing the animal and that it would have been simpler to just shoot her.

Next I cut through the inner membrane lining to expose the uterus. Taking another breath I cut a long incision down the length of the uterus, which was about half inch thick which exposed the calf. I recall vividly seeing the red and white Hereford hair markings on the calf, which struck me, seeing this for the first time as incongruous that this calf was still inside the cow. I tried to be very careful not to cut the calf which was pressed tight to the wall of the uterus. As the uterus opened, fluid and blood spilled out and working as fast as I could, I gently pulled the calf out, trying not to tear the uterus. I saw that the calf was already dead so I cut the umbilical cord leaving the placenta inside the uterus.

I then started the longest part of the operation, which was to close up the gaping cuts in the uterus, membrane and the midline of her belly. Using large needles and 20 pound test monofilament fishing line, the only suture material I had, I spent the next hour and a half getting the sewing job done. I hoped nothing would come undone. As it turned out, the heifer lived and I shipped her to market in the Fall with strands of monofilament hanging out below her belly, something I hoped the auctioneers would not see.

Continuing our efforts to improve the herd we began to cull all wild or hard to handle cows. We found out very soon that like humans, calves learn from their mothers. Wild cows invariably raise wild calves and their crazy behavior created tension and fear in the rest of the herd. With weight being the critical issue in every animal we sold, it made sense to have docile cattle that could be handled in a quiet manner. And if the cattle were docile there was no need to play "cowboy" using ropes and rough handling. Modern methods always aimed at keeping the anxiety of the animals as low as possible.

When it was necessary to do stressful things to an animal I began to use tranquilizers procured through Gordon Wimpenney and smuggled up from the States. These drugs had a very calming affect on any animal being worked on and I used them often when we shipped cattle to Calgary, a trip that was very stressful for them.

In 1956 we bought the Tegart ranch whose properties cornered with our own. This 1000 acre ranch consisted of 150 acres of cultivated fields and ran a 350 head commercial cow herd, using Crown range adjacent to ours. Bob Tegart was a tough man in his late 50's whose father had immigrated from Texas many years before and started ranching in the valley. Bob had grown up on a ranch and remained a rancher his whole working life.

Bob had raised a large family, mostly boys, who were maintained in a bunk-house on the ranch. Alfie, one of the sons, told me once that the way their father got them going in the morning when they were teenagers was to open the door to the bunkhouse and greet them with "Let go your cocks and grab your cups, cof-fee's on!" I knew some of the boys well, as they were near my age, but most of them did not have an interest in the ranch or even in riding horses, preferring to work in the woods as independent sawmill operators, cat skinners, or as commer-cial truckers. Perhaps Bob's rough and tumble early morning greetings helped form their antipathy to the ranching life, but I also suspect he was a hard task-master on his sons and their lack of interest in working with him on the ranch may have been the main reason Bob ultimately decided to sell the ranch.

I had approached Bob several times with the idea of his selling the ranch to us, and after quite a few meetings with him over several months, he said he'd like to proceed. I notified Dad who arranged to come up from Seattle with Ed Coon, our advisor from the Spokane and Eastern Bank, over a long weekend to try to close a deal. It was a rather comical negotiation with Ed representing our side in the talks with Bob. The main risks to closing the sale were two: first, just getting Bob to finally make the deal after much hemming and hawing and mind chang-ing over the three days of talks; and second, keeping Dad away from him which everyone knew would kill the deal immediately.

Father was terribly frustrated not to be allowed to, as he described it, "just go over and tell Bob what the deal was and get him to sign up." He had a very hard time understanding that Bob was selling not only the ranch, but the only way of life he had known since he was a child. Bob knew very well how dramatically his future was to change after the sale and this required much sympathy and patience on our part, while Bob worked his way through his personal agony. Ed was a master at this sort of negotiation and could talk the line of a country boy himself. He knew when to kick rocks and suck straws and wait for Bob's process to keep unfolding. Dad just didn't have the necessary patience and I doubt if he really understood how hard a decision it was for Bob to make, but with Ed skillfully handling the negotiating, a deal was finally struck Sunday afternoon.

We took over responsibility for the 350 head of cattle and 150 acres of irri-gated cropland the next day. The deal included the right of the Tegarts to use the house for one year or until they found another place to live. Since the cattle were already out on the range there was not much to do with them until we got the farm work organized. The crops were well into the growing season so we started bright and early Monday morning to change the sprinkler lines at the Tegart ranch.

When we arrived and started up the equipment, Mrs. Tegart came out to watch how everything was done. From the look on her face we knew she was not at all happy with our methods. This process went on each morning when we arrived and became very disconcerting to me and to the crew. On about day three she began to criticize how we used the tractors, how we moved the pipes, how we parked the equipment after use and every other nit she saw that was in the least way different from how Bob and she liked to do things. They were very protective of their farm equipment.

On the next Sunday, one week from the purchase date, I sent a crew over to change a sprinkler and in half an hour they were back to tell me that Bob had kicked them off the ranch, saying the deal was off and he was taking over again. I was very concerned, confused and alarmed about how to handle this situation since my experience with the law was limited to getting married and receiving traffic tickets. However, I called our barrister who had written the purchase and sale agreement and he assured me that the deal could not be revoked by the Tegarts. I asked him to call Bob and explain this fact, so that I could send the crew back to work.

My worry now was how to deal with a very tense and unfriendly situation with the Tegarts. I was concerned that things might get physical and I wanted to build a relationship with Bob and reduce the chance that I would get punched in the nose over some minor problem. We needed to use Bob's experience and his inputs on the many details of the ranch systems, equipment and practice, so it was very important to at least gain a working relationship with him. In time this was accomplished and we enjoyed a cordial working relationship for many years although I was sure he saw me as just a kid who did not know much about raising cattle.

In the Spring, after most of the cows had calved, we moved the herd to Crown range where the most southerly portion was a four-day cattle drive. Our method to induce the cows to make that long journey was to separate them from their calves which we loaded into our stock truck, and using up to six riders, with the truckload of calves at the head of the column bawling for their mothers, we slowly herded the cows along the road. There were always some tight spots where cows not hearing or smelling their calves tried to go back to where they last nursed, necessitating some short but hard riding by the cowboys.

There were three or four sets of corrals along the way where each night we could unload the calves and make sure they were with their mothers, feed the cows and leave them corralled over night. We always left someone to guard them to make sure they were in the corral in the morning. If they escaped, they would be spread out along the highway, climbing through fences into someone's field, or dispersed over a part of the range that was not on our permit. Since these days could be very warm we started early, arriving in the barn to feed the horses around 3:30 am, out of the ranch by 6 am, and on the trail by 7 or 8 am.

Me and Ruby on the Findley Creek range

Moving this herd down the highway made for some interesting traffic problems. Although we would have liked to let the cars through as soon as they arrived at the rear of the herd, this always pushed the cattle off into the brush and timber on each side, necessitating additional riding and wear and tear on the horses. Usually we waited until several cars were queued up, and then, signaling the lead driver to follow close behind our horse, one of us led the line of cars through the herd, with the least disruption possible.

Winter feeding from bobsled

One time moving the cattle down the highway south of Canal Flat, a driver of a car became very irate and quite abusive to Tom Watson, one of our cowboys who had been a rodeo hand in Alberta and was riding a horse known to be very light behind, in other words, he had a propensity to kick. Tom soon led the car through the herd while the driver continued his tirade and then before the car was fully clear of the animals, Tom rode close up beside the car whose driver had the window down, leaned over towards the driver and said, "Are you finally satisfied," to which the driver replied, "Hell no I ain't!"

Tom wheeled the horse, whose rump was now facing toward the car, to go back to herding, stuck him with a spur whereupon the horse kicked, driving a sharp-shod hoof deep into the metal of the door just beneath the open window and the driver's head. Tom looked back surprised, saw what had happened and said, "Well maybe you're satisfied now," and trotted away. The driver, aghast at how close he had come to meeting his maker, did not answer but accelerated out of there without even looking back. I thought for sure we would hear from the

Mounties, but the call never came, nor did we hear from the driver about the car damage.

Fall was a busy period. We had to complete the haying by mid September, work the fields we wanted to fallow over the winter and fix the fences wherever we intended to hold the cattle when they came in for the winter. All sprinkler and other equipment was stored away to be worked on during the winter and the final hay bales loaded. We usually got in a few days' hunting for ourselves, since we never killed from the herd for meat.

Around mid October snow would begin to drive the cattle out of the higher country and some small bunches would begin to be seen grazing along the highway from Findlay Creek, always moving slowly towards the ranch and the fall pastures we leased on the Kootenay Indian Reserve and Fairmont Hot Springs, near Dutch Creek. Here the cattle found excellent feed until the snow was almost a foot deep. This usually was towards the end of November, when we moved all the cattle to the home ranch and began to feed every day from the hay we put up each summer.

From October through December, riding and working the cattle was the chief occupation. A typical day would begin in the horse barn around 5:30 with feeding, grooming, and checking their shoes to make sure all four caulks were there, screwed in solid and not bent over. We usually saddled up, leaving the cinches loose as they munched on their hay and oats and then went in for a quick breakfast. We used our 2 ton 1956 Chevrolet truck with stock racks which had room enough for four horses and some bales of hay, or if necessary, two horses and a portable loading chute in case we had to load a cow for some reason. Leaving as close to 7 am as we could, we would be riding by 8-8:30 in the morning depending on how far away the jump off point was.

In this time before the invention of Polar Fleece, we dressed in long underwear, jeans, wool shirt and wool jacket or lined jean jacket. We always wore chaps and carried a yellow slicker, just like Marlborough Man, tied behind the saddle. And of course, felt cowboy hats were a necessity. If it was cold we blanketed the horses for the road trip to the jump off point.

Although most of the cattle came out of the lower hills on the range and began to congregate along the highway, they kept slowly moving towards the main ranch on their own. We were riding every day to gather them up along the road and herd them into pastures and off the highway to avoid the possibility of an accident on slippery blacktop. It was also hunting season and a fat calf was sometimes too great a temptation for a hunter to pass up, so making our presence known to hunters as we rounded up the cattle probably reduced this activity. We did lose a few head to hunters each year, evidently by those unable to distinguish between a real elk and a poor cow with ELK branded along the ribs. This made for a few cartoons in the Cranbrook newspaper each hunting season.

In mid November we began the separation of the herd into various groups, such as; old or dry cows to be shipped; bred yearling heifers; heifer calves we intended to keep for breeding the next year and the sick or injured that would be tended to at the main ranch. We weaned the calves from their mothers and began shipping all cattle we did not plan on feeding through the winter. The route used to go to market was north on the highway 16 miles to the turn off at Radium Hot Springs, up the Kootenay River valley in Kootenay National Park, through a pass in the Rockies that led to the valley of the Bow River and Banff National Park, and leaving the mountains behind entering the foothills on the East slope of the Rockies another sixty miles to the Calgary stockyards where they were sold at auction.

I made many trips over the mountains in our 1950 Chevrolet 18 foot truck, loaded with 12 or 13 cows. It was a five-hour trip and after a long day's work sometimes it was just too hard for me to stay awake driving and I had to stop for an hour's nap. I went through the No Doze pills with regularity. One night on the return trip, too tired to continue, I pulled over near the east gate of Banff National Park and went to sleep. An hour or so later I was awakened by a raucous chorus of bugle sounds, whistling and snorting. I got out of the truck and found myself in the middle of a large elk herd that had moved into the grassy open area where I had parked. They were in the middle of rutting season and in bright moonlight it was amazing to see the bulls fighting to keep their harems intact, the cows and younger bulls being run around by the larger animals.

During these late fall days of hard work, the cowboys and I seldom returned to the ranch before dark, but we accomplished what we needed to in several weeks, gathering most of the herd together. Later in December, after we had a good count on the cattle, there were always a few missing, either dead or stranded, entailing more days of riding into country where we knew pockets of feed might be. To cover the ground easier I learned to fly in 1959 and using the airplane to locate the strays saved many hours of cold riding.

One of the awful areas to work cattle was in the Kootenay River bottoms just south of Canal Flat, with a thick tangle of trees, downed timber and brush. I had been told some cattle had been seen in this area and one day I set out to get them with Joe Jimmy, a good horseman who worked as our summer rider on the Find-lay Creek range. Joe was a Kootenay Indian of some renown due to having climbed up a tree after a cougar and killed it with his hunting knife tied to a long stick. A large man with a huge Mexican style mustache, Joe was riding Ruby and I was on Boxcar, a large gelding I had bought at a horse auction the year before. Boxcar was fairly well broke and I was still riding him with a hackamore. He weighed about 1200 pounds, was beautiful with straight legs and an rump like a quarter horse, and incredibly strong, accelerating like a rocket when needed, but I had not used him much on the range and never in rough country like the Kootenay bottoms.

The plan was to bring the cattle up from the river to the highway about 2 mi. south of Canal Flat, then move them down the highway and over the Kootenay River bridge and into our corrals on the edge of town. It was an overcast day with about six inches of snow on the ground enabling Joe and me to track the cattle rather easily. It turned out to be a group of about six cows and a couple of calves, from the Tegart herd. This was the first year rounding up the Tegart Ranch cattle, and this small group was wild and crazy. We finally got them moving towards the highway at a trot and when they got there, instead of turning to follow it into Canal Flat, they broke into a run across it and into the jackpine on the other side intent on getting away from us.

Joe was ahead of me as we tried to head the cattle. We were in a full run to get around them, dodging this way and that through the small jackpine. In about 100 yards, Boxcar zigged when he should have zagged, almost ran head on into a tree but at the last instant cut right and the tree slid down his left side and hit my left leg with such force that it threw it back over his rump. I was instantly in a 90 degree position from vertical in the process of leaving him when I smashed into an 8-inch diameter tree that caught me full across the chest, stripping me from the horse that had not broken stride. I hit so hard that my legs wrapped around the tree and I hung there for a second before falling in a heap to the ground at the base of the tree.

I was stunned for some time from the blow and I didn't hurt much during that time lying in the snow, but I sensed that I had been injured. Finally when the pain did come, surprisingly it felt like I had a harpoon in my back, not in front where I had hit. I could not move or get up, but wiggled around so I could get my back against the tree and just lay there in the snow waiting for Joe to come back, as I knew he would, when he saw Boxcar running without a rider.

As I had expected, in about 15 minutes Joe came backtracking, leading Boxcar. I told him I was hurt and that if he could help me get to the road we could flag down a car to take me to the hospital in Invermere. As Joe helped me to stand, he looked up at the tree and pointed out there was bark off the trunk where I had hit. I was lucky because if it had been my head or my throat it might have been my last ride.

I staggered to the road with Joe's help where he flagged down a car going north, asked the driver to get me to the hospital in Invermere and helped me into the back seat. The pain was really gut wrenching by this time and because I could not tighten any muscle in my body even to keep myself on the seat I slid slowly to the floor where I was when they opened the door at the emergency entrance to the hospital an hour later.

Removing my jacket and multiple layers of shirts and long underwear to see what damage I had sustained was agonizing. They gave me a shot, waited a few minutes and tried again but it just hurt too much to raise my arms or move anything. Finally they gave me another shot and that made things easier. The X-rays showed that I had broken my sternum and several ribs on both sides. They thought I might have punctured a lung but this did not turn out to be so. In any event I spent the next two weeks in the hospital, worrying about the work going on and trying hard not to sneeze, cough, or laugh.

As I improved and my spirits lifted, laughing became the most painful and hardest thing to stop, especially when friends came in to see me and brought their malignant sense of humor just to watch how I reacted. The harder I tried not to laugh the more difficult it became to suppress it.

One funny story I had told to me was about Gordon Wimpenny who loved hunting more than anything in life. He had been scheduled to come up for a deer hunt before I had hurt myself and since no one had told Gordon that I was in the hospital he came along as planned. When driving his car just north of the border and still south of Cranbrook, a coyote started across the road ahead of him. Never one to miss an opportunity to shoot at something he slammed on the brakes, grabbed his old 30.30, jammed a shell in and in his excitement to work the lever action to place the shell in the magazine, accidentally shot a hole through the floorboards, narrowly missing his own foot, but blowing the corner off one head of the engine. He and his car had to be towed into Creston for repair, but after several days in Creston, he continued his trip to the ranch to see me. The entire escapade had been reported to me before he arrived at my bedside.

My children warned Gordon that under no circumstances was he to make me laugh since he had the reputation of being a really very funny person and they were sure that this latest episode of his would probably kill me if he tried to relate it. Needless to say, when he came to the hospital to see me, he opened the door to my room very slowly and just stuck his head inside the room to get the lay of the land. When I saw him he had a stupid grin on his face and I started to laugh and pretty soon I was laughing and crying from the pain and humor of everything.

The few cows that had led me to hug that jackpine with such vigor were finally corralled a week or so later in Canal Flat by Joe and several other riders and then moved to the corral at the Tegart ranch. In this first year of dealing with the Tegart cattle we were finding out that many of them were wild, indicating that they had been handled hard or not handled at all and the herd had never been culled for this miserable trait. There were many cows not bred and the cowboys speculated they were so skittish the bulls wouldn't try to catch up to them, preferring to stay with the cows who seemed to appreciate their attentions.

After my release from the hospital I went to view these particular cattle in the corral and decide what to do with them. A few were really snuffy and agitated when I stepped into the corral. These backed up still facing me and began to paw the ground and snort the way a bull might do and then to my great surprise one actually charged me and sent me jumping up the corral logs. This was the first time I had ever seen a cow intent on running a person out of a corral. It did not take long for me, sitting on the top rail of the corral, to decide what to do with this bunch. They would be off to Calgary as soon as I could arrange the truck.

That evening I called Kenny Tegart, a nephew of Bob's, a commercial hauler with a new truck, who agreed to take this load over for us in a few days. When the time came we added a few other cows to make it a full load, but even with these more docile additions it was exciting trying to load them without sustaining bodily injury ourselves. We finally got them into the chute and up the ramp to the truck, placed the stakes of the tailgate into the deck openings and latched it down.

Among this group were three very ugly cows and one wild, dry (not nursing a calf) three-year old heifer that was big and fat, but had never had a calf. I did not bother to pregnancy test any of these cattle, but culled them because of their nasty temperaments. We told Kenny to enjoy the trip, but advised him if a cow fell down to think twice before getting inside the truck to try to help it up. I don't think he needed this admonition after seeing the wild behavior of these cows.

I thought we had accomplished a good stroke of business when I went to bed that night but around eleven o'clock the phone rang, dragging me out of a deep sleep. It was Kenny and I could barely believe what he then proceeded to tell me. The cows in their agitation had somehow gotten the tailgate stakes out of the pockets, freeing the bottom of the tailgate from the deck, and three of them had fallen out of the truck in the Park somewhere on the flat twenty mile stretch along the Kootenay River. I could not believe such a thing could happen. Our cows in Kootenay National Park! I could only imagine how the Forest Service would view this little event

Kenny was calling from Kootenay Crossing where there was a B.C. Forest Service outpost complete with a ranger and corrals. He had off-loaded the rest of the cattle, thinking we could bring in horses the next day and drive the three cows that escaped up the highway to the corral. As it turned out the three cows that had gotten out were the dry heifer and the two wildest cows so the prospect of an easy cattle drive with that bunch, in snow over a foot and a half deep, was highly improbable. I decided we might do better to find them one by one as they were separated from each other by about five miles and when we captured each one, load them right in the middle of the highway using the portable loading chute.

Bright and early the next day, I saddled Tom and Kenny Newhouse, a rider on the ranch, selected Highpockets, a very tall thoroughbred. We loaded the chute, threw in some baled hay, and headed into the Park. It was very cold, around—10°F when we left the ranch and much colder than that inside the Park along the river. Kenny told me it was 50 below zero at Kootenay Crossing although I never confirmed that. But it was cold enough for cowboying.

We drove up through the Radium Hot Springs canyon and then down onto the Kootenay River. Kenny met us there, indicating that the first cow had fallen out at the beginning of the flat. Parking the truck in the right lane of the highway, we pulled out the loading chute, unloaded the horses and started looking for cow tracks. We soon found some that we followed as they meandered through the timber, but due to the deep snow, did not go far from the road. Within ten minutes we succeeded in finding the first cow and she turned out to be the one that had run me out of the corral a few weeks before.

We tried to herd her back to the road but she kept turning on the horses trying to butt them in the belly, so I roped her and mostly dragged her out to the road with Ken hazing from behind on Highpockets. We came out onto the highway about fifty yards from the truck and the waiting loading chute. She kept charging the horse while I tried to kick her in the head to keep her from knocking us down on the snow-covered road. She flat refused to be herded and since we were getting nowhere fast, I called to Ken Tegart to come over and get in front of her to see if maybe she would chase him to the ramp. He did not cotton to this idea very much, but I promised I would not let her catch him, though I allowed as how he might have to run as fast as he could to stay ahead.

It worked like a charm. As soon as the cow realized Kenny was right behind her she wheeled around and with her head down charged after him. I still had the rope on her with a couple of dallies around the horn, so I paid out enough rope so that when she had a good head of steam going, her nose was about three feet behind Kenny's butt and with all her snorting and squealing trying to catch him, Kenny had a frightful inducement to run like hell for the ramp. He reached it and ran up into the truck with the cow right behind him, but she fell on about the third step, two thirds in the chute and one third, her hind end, still outside. Ken and I jumped off the horses and grabbed her tail so she couldn't slide back out. Since she could not turn around in the narrow chute we were able holler and use the electric stockprod to move her up and into the truck. Talk about feisty!

We left the chute where it was and drove to Kootenay Crossing to unload her into the corral with the other cows. This left two to capture, one of which was close to Kootenay Crossing so we rode out, quickly found her and drove her into the corral. Kenny loaded these up and left once again for Calgary. We drove back along the river and spotted the big heifer. We threw her half a bale of hay which we knew would hold her overnight, planning to return the next day and try to move her out of the park on foot with two horses. She was only a few miles from the canyon and we figured if we could get her into it, she could not get away from us until we hit the valley. We then started back to the ranch, stopped to load the chute and headed out of the Park.

As it happened, we did get her out of the park the next day, but she was wild and almost impossible to handle, going at a fast trot down the highway in the canyon, shying at each passing vehicle, her tongue hanging out, and blowing snot as she shook her head in anger at all she passed. Once down in the valley we finally lost her in the thick timber five miles south of Radium, and gave up trying to get her into a corral farther south. I figured she would probably die over the winter, and good riddance! But late the next summer when we were riding on the Horsethief Creek range, looking at the 125 head of yearling heifers we had put there, I couldn't believe my eyes but there she was, having survived the winter and fat as ever. She did not escape the roundup that fall and went to her comeuppance, again in Kenny's truck, to the Calgary stockyard where she was soon hanging by her heels in a meat refrigerator. A fitting end to a crazy wild heifer.

Father tried to come to the ranch two times each year, once in the spring and again during hunting season in the fall. These were very short visits, usually over a weekend and this meant that Dad and I had to sequester ourselves in my office to go over the items he had on his list. The list was usually long, as he tried hard to educate me in management skills, which, by the time he left, I came to believe I sadly lacked. There was not much time remaining for him to deal with those things he felt I was doing right and after a few meetings where all the shortcomings of the prior six months were brought to my attention, I began to dread these visits. As each one of these meetings came closer I began to get very tense, worrying about all the possible things Dad might want to talk over. Much as I loved my father, I never much relished "discussions" with him and understand clearly why my kids feel the same way when I feel I need a chat with them.

In thinking back on those occasions now, I think Dad recognized how hard I was working and that I knew more about raising cattle than he did, so he spent his time trying to help me understand that if I did not learn to think clearly about certain aspects of the business, I could work myself to death and still not achieve the results we hoped for. Tough as these meetings were for me, I slowly began to better understand budgeting, planning, decision making and communications, especially with him. Because I very seldom called him to talk over a plan I had decided upon, he was trying to let me know that I might benefit from discussing things with him on a more regular basis. I did not take to this idea very well since I did not want to have to get permission from him for every operational plan I had, figuring two meetings a year was about all I could handle. But over time I found it easier to discuss new ideas relating to the future of the business with Dad, but I always felt a certain constraint in his willingness to put in the capital that my ideas usually seemed to require.

At the end of the fifth year of ownership in the ranch, when the basic cow herd had been fully depreciated, Dad sold a 50% interest to Norton Clapp, which started the depreciation all over again and happily for me I began to report to Al Link, Norton's real estate manager. This made relations with Dad much easier and I am sure he was relieved with this change, but he remained a stickler for meeting the budget and doing proper planning.

In the last five years of my time on the ranch we pregnancy tested all the cows after weaning their calves, to make sure we did not feed any that were not going to calve again in the spring. All unsettled cows were shipped, no exceptions. Pregnancy testing is a very messy, one might say, shitty job. It entails palpating the uterus through the wall of the colon. This necessitated using a special rubber glove that covered the entire arm to the shoulder with a rubber strap that went around the neck to hold it in place. In mid November the weather could be freezing but when your arm was up to your shoulder inside the cow, it was nice and warm. In the cold weather I used to build up what seemed to be twenty pounds of frozen cow flop all down my coveralls and on my knee high rubber boots and I kept a container of warm water to clean the arm after each test.

Gordon Wimpenny had trained me in this art and with practice I was able to tell not only whether the cow was pregnant, but about how far along she was. This was important, since the earlier she calved, the larger the calf would be in the fall. I tested around five hundred cows each fall, the whole process taking two to three days with four or five ranch hands and horses working the cows into and out of the chutes. When I was done testing a cow, I called out where she was to go since we separated the yearlings and the two-year-olds, needing special feeding or attention, from the older cows. The cowboys worked the corral gates and moved each cow from the chute to the pasture or pen set up for each group. After testing all the cattle were located in their respective pastures for winter feeding.

Pregnancy testing, coupled with keeping a high ratio of bulls to cows, constantly shortening the breeding season, and using summer riders to move the bulls around to compress the calving period, in a few years produced calves looking like peas in a pod. Also buying good quality bulls, culling for disposition and fertility and calving earlier each year, gave results that started to be noticed by the buyers responsible for filling orders for the feedlots each fall and I began to get calls asking to come over to visit and inspect the herd. Soon we were selling our calf crop directly from the ranch, due to demand for our quality. A story about the Elkhorn Ranch appeared as a lead article in the Canadian Cattleman magazine in 1959, a monthly publication going to all cattlemen in Canada. It described our programs aimed at improving quality of the calf crop, in-house veterinary work and how we handled the cattle to remove stress and increase weight.

We bought most of our registered bulls from the purebred auctions in Calgary or Kamloops, but sometimes I went directly to some of the ranches that raised purebred Herefords to find what I wanted. Of course, those bulls were all fitted for the shows and looked magnificent in every way. Fat, clean and curried, they probably had never been far from a barn and feed trough. You had to try to look under the fat to judge the real conformation of the animal. It did not take long to learn that this beauty was only skin deep and when these young two year old bulls returned to the ranch after their first breeding season on the open range, they were shadows of their former selves. Many a lewd comment was offered as to the reason for this great change.

Over the years while I was trying to build the herd and calf crop, Karen and I were also building a family. When we arrived at the ranch we already had one child, Bill, (William VanGorden) born in Seattle in 1950. A daughter, Susan, also born in Seattle, arrived in the Fall after starting the ranch job, but Christopher John following in '53, and Ann Louise coming in '55, were born in Invermere. I had always thought that having a large family would be fun and interesting and I admit to paying little attention to family planning until my fourth child. They had come along and that was good enough for me. However, after four I was ready to call it enough, as I could see how hard financially it was going to be to support a big family on a ranch manager's salary. And then despite the good intentions, David Kergan came as a surprise, born, appropriately, on April Fool's Day 1957.

Of course, my salary did increase over time and with each raise Dad was very fond of letting me know if I complained it was hard to get by on such a salary, that with the house, milk and butter (if I milked the cows) and plenty of game to hunt, my pay package was really very good and certainly comparable to living in the big city. I had started work in 1952 at $250 a month and ended it ten years later paid $1000 per month. I could live on this salary but really could not save anything to speak of, even when the Christmas gifts from Mother and Dad were mostly clothing for the kids. This feeling of poverty became increasingly important to me over time and along with my worries concerning the quality of the children's schooling, the lack of an intellectually stimulating social life, led me to reconsider if the ranching life would be the best for the family in the long run.

About this time five years into my marriage, I really began to wonder if I would ever be able to build a nest egg of any significance. Would I ever live to see 10,000 dollars back to back? I admit to having a terrible feeling that no matter how I worked I could never make it happen, and this became, for a while, a terrible weight that I was carrying with me. My relations with Dad were a bit strained as well, feeling that I might never please him, no matter how hard I struggled.

My sister Jan was visiting the ranch with her children, Philip and Roshanna, during this rather down time of mine and one day she accompanied me on the seven mile drive to Invermere on an errand. On the way I was talking about Father, saying that I wished I had had a different sort of relationship with him that might have given me a better self image and ability to achieve a happier financial circumstance, or some such complaint I don't well remember today. What I do remember was the real life-changing response I received when Jan, turning towards me said, "You know, you can't spend your life complaining about what someone else may have done that has made your life more difficult than you would like. You can change your own life tomorrow, since only you are responsible for your own actions and outcome. Not anyone else!"

Hearing this was like a slap in the face! It made me realize that I had allowed myself to wallow around in self pity, looking elsewhere for the source of my problems instead of in the mirror every time I shaved in the morning. The truth of the statement had an amazing affect on me that almost instantly raised the weight off my back and somehow made me believe that I could make it happen, given a little time and a little luck and I would try never again to blame others for the shortcomings in my life. I do not think after that drive to Invermere with my sister that I ever again allowed myself to blame another person for my moments of unhappiness or pain.

The lack of intellectual or artistic culture in the valley surprised me, having come from the city. From our arrival in 1952 until about 1955, not a single boy graduated from Invermere High School, the new school serving about 50 miles of the valley in both directions. These youngsters opted to go to work in the woods, or take small jobs in the various towns, since they could earn $1.25—$1.50 per hour and that was enough for them to get by. I doubt there were many parents of these highschoolers that had finished high school themselves and almost none that had gone on to a university degree. As for the girls, mostly they went to nursing or clerical school after high school, took office jobs, or got married within a few years of graduation. One of the worries I developed with my own kids was that their typical response about their grades at the end of the year was, "Well I passed." That seemed to be the universal criteria used by parents of their school mates to determine if they were doing okay in school.

There was a small movie theater in Invermere, but no arts organizations at all. One radio station in Cranbrook, CFCN, served the entire valley and played country western music around the clock. This was okay by me as I loved it, but if you wanted to hear any classical music you had to buy the records. There was no TV, or stereo sound, and for quite a few years we were on a party telephone line. From Mother and Dad we inherited a tape player, which used large reels of tape, and seemed very advanced to us then, but most people had old 78 rpm clay records until the plastic 45s' came along and a few years after that, the plastic 33 rpm HiFi records arrived on the scene.

In those days there were strict regulations governing purchase and consumption of alcohol. Indians could not go into the bars but they could always find someone willing to buy the booze for them to take to the Reserve for a party, and to my knowledge the Mounties never went there trying to stop them. A few years after our arrival, Indians were allowed into the taverns and this is where most of our ranch paychecks were cashed. We had made a big mistake in not buying the White House Hotel and its bar, for had we done so, we would have just circulated our money over and over.

I hired a lot of Indian labor and got to know the men very well and more than once I found an Indian laying on the kitchen floor on a Sunday morning, no doubt having come over for an advance on his next week's work but too drunk to accomplish his goal. Many a Monday morning one or two of these men would show up ready to work, looking absolutely terrible from having been on a big drunk the whole weekend and nevertheless would put in a day of hard labor without complaining at all. I truly had a great respect for them and counted many as good friends. I also was invited occasionally to parties held in their homes on the reserve. These shindigs were well lubricated with beer and usually turned quite wild with Indian dancing and chanting finally taking over. During such times one could feel the built up resentment towards their life in the white man's world and get a glimpse into the earlier strength and power their own traditions still held for them, even though deeply buried to make their current lives bearable.

Unescorted women were not allowed in the bars either and the bars had two rooms, one for men and the other for couples. Saturday nights were a good time to stay at home if you did not want to get into trouble. Invariably there were fights every Friday and Saturday night. In cases when the Mounties were called to quell a disturbance, they usually had to fight the person they were trying to arrest in order to get them to jail. Invermere usually had only two Mounties and they had to be tough to survive. When there was a dance, it was a high probability there were going to be some fist fights. There was a group of miners, many of whom were recent immigrants from Europe, who just loved to tangle with the loggers or the Indians, or anyone else for that matter, whenever they had too much to drink.

In the winter of 1959 I realized some Indians were coming into our barnyard at night and stealing gas from the large above ground fuel tank, because the tracks showing this transaction would show clearly in the snow the morning after. One New Year's Eve, right after Midnight, I saw a car drive in with just the parking lights on. I waited about 5 minutes, got in my car and with the lights off drove over towards the barnyard. When I came around the corner and could see the barnyard I turned on my headlights and instead of stealing gas, which I thought they were up to, they had jacked one of our cars up and were stealing a tire. I drove right up behind them and jumped out determined to put a stop to the stealing.

I saw it was Tony Fisher and Charley Lewis and their two squaws. Charley ran to their car and climbed in and I just marched straight up to Tony and without slowing down or saying anything, punched him as hard as I could right in the jaw. He was a big man over 200 pounds and my blow merely knocked him back a couple of steps and his hat went flying off. He raised his arm, I thought to come after me, but he was only trying to grab his hat. He caught it and in one motion turned running around the front of the car to jump into the driver's seat. I gave them hell and said they would hear from the Mounties, I was so angry they would steal from the ranch. Tony got to spend the winter in Ocallala prison, and around Christmas I received a letter from him, asking if he could get an advance on his pasture rent to buy cigarettes, which of course I sent him and there were no hard feelings at all when he came home. This incident stopped the Indian pilfering at the ranch.

There were a few highly educated people who had migrated into the valley from Britain, Russia, or eastern Canada. We enjoyed seeing these folks in order to have conversations from time to time about something other than the most mundane observations on driving trucks, running a bell mill, putting up hay, the weather, or the pet dog. We managed to find some well educated and interesting people there, and made some good friendships. But I continued with a concern related to our children's education.

There was also a latent anti-American bias in Canada in the 1950's. Even though their dollar was 5% higher than the U.S. dollar, we were still seen as having too much impact on Canadian culture, and Canadians resented the fact that most big-ticket items a family needed to buy, cost considerably more in Canada. Anti-American comments were seldom directed at me, since I was a Landed Immigrant working there, but I heard the occasional comment and quietly resented it. This attitude survives to this day in Canada, since I suppose, although we are great friends, we will still always be competitors and lovers of our own respective countries.

I think there were many advantages to raising kids in a ranch environment rather than in a city. Our property formed a huge playground where we could turn the kids outside every day when they were not in school. It was healthy for them, and there were all sorts of interests they could cultivate. Of course, hoeing the vegetable plot was not one of their favorites, but riding horses, driving trucks and tractors and driving the team of black Percherons that pulled the bobsled to feed the cattle in the winter certainly were. Watching the diverse things going on in the fields or in the barnyard with the livestock, left the children with happy memories from their days on the ranch, even though Ann, David and Fletcher were very young when we finally left for the city. Of course, raising children in the 1950's was a much simpler proposition than just a few years later, but even then I suspect the opportunities to get into trouble were less in the country than in the city.

There was little time for family activities on the ranch because the work often was seven days a week and sometimes very long days. However, we tried to limit Sunday work to chores only, to the extent possible, so that other family experiences such as picnics or swimming in Lake Windermere or Radium Hot Springs could be enjoyed. One advantage was that I was in the home for most meals and had plenty for interaction with the children.

During those early years of marriage I was fully engrossed in the work of the ranch. I assumed Karen would handle the household and kids by herself, except when she cooked for the hands in the summer haying season. I never slowed down to find out what she felt about her life, even to ask her how she liked living in the country and the ranch life in particular. The truth is that we were not communicating well about important aspects of our marriage. Without asking her, I tended to assume the major role in making decisions, somewhat on the order of what I had observed with my parents. For her part she never offered to tell me what was really on her mind. I assumed she would like to have a horse to ride, but it turned out that was not an interest of hers. She seldom came to the barnyard if there were things going on, but it never entered my head that she might be suffering from being cut off from her own friends and family in Seattle, or was becoming overwhelmed by an increasing number of kids to look after.

I thought I was proving my commitment to the marriage through showing Karen that I was willing to work very hard for our family, but I now suspect that my effort was not read this way by Karen, who perhaps needed some other manifestation of my commitment to her. I don't know because she never told me, and I did not ask. But I could feel a slow separation and at least in me, a resentment developing between us. This, coupled with another thought I had squirreled away and carried as baggage in my mind was that I had made a huge sacrifice to her in getting married in the circumstances we had found ourselves, when I could have easily said, "No." That thought, with all its immature reasoning and self-serving evidence, crawled around in the back of my mind, making it easy for me to be critical of Karen's efforts in mothering the children and being the homemaker. Looking back, it is hard to understand why we communicated so poorly to each other about the most important decisions we made and our real feelings. Without this ability to discuss our needs openly, we had little chance at growing closer over time and this pattern finally proved fatal to our marriage.

I had a very close call in the summer of 1956 which could have made my marriage problems seem very small. One of the scourges parents most feared was a child contracting Infantile Paralysis, a disease that reared its ugly head each summer in many countries and left badly crippled children in its wake each time it struck. The Salk vaccine had been used a bit in 1955, but not in Canada and an outbreak of polio hit the southern part of the valley in Cranbrook and Kimberly and within a week or so cases began popping up in Invermere. As it turned out it was not young children being hit, but adults and I was one of around ten cases that ended up in the hospital.

Polio for me was like having a bad fever with tremendously aching muscles, especially in the legs and arms, but when told that I was not suffering from a summer flu but actually had polio, I was truly frightened that I might end up crippled. As it turned out I was not affected that way and made a full recovery, but my friend Sandy Dobbie, who entered the hospital at the same time as I, was not so lucky. I walked out of the hospital, but Sandy came out in a wheelchair and never walked again. It was a good lesson to remember that when things seems hard and we tend to feel a bit sorry for ourselves, there are always others worse off, and indeed, it is better to feel grateful for what we have and to think about the positive aspects in our lives.

As I knew all of the other ranch owners in the local area, through helping each other with the livestock at times, being a member of the local Board Of Trade, (similar to the Grange in the U.S.) and sharing common problems with them, we developed an interest in reviving the rodeo as part of the Fall Fair put on at The Crossroads near Invermere. The Crossroads, was misnamed since it was actually a "T" formed by the road to Invermere intersecting highway 93 about six miles from the ranch. The fair grounds sported a set of corrals and four or five bucking chutes all somewhat in disrepair and a small grandstand, all that was needed to put on a rodeo.

We decided to repair the livestock corrals, bucking chutes and calf roping chute in time to bring rodeo back to the Fair that September. Everyone contributed to this work and a committee was formed to plan and carry out the show. Bob Tegart was elected President of the newly re-formed Lake Windermere Rodeo Association and he selected the help he needed. We developed a plan to have calf roping, bareback and saddle bronc riding, a wild horse race, wild cow milking and kids' calf riding.

Of course we needed livestock to carry this program off. The Elkhorn agreed to provide the calves and try out several horses for bucking. Some of the smaller ranchers, who were also hunting guides and outfitters, had strings of packhorses that ran loose all summer and most had only been packed and not ridden. These horses were often of Clydesdale blood, crossbred with some kind of thoroughbred stock. They were long-legged but heavy set and looked like they might "turn the crank" when a flank strap was put on.

One summer weekend we drove our horses over to the fairground corrals to see which ones could buck. I took Ruby, our versatile 15-year-old mare that everyone rode and several others, but I did not want our good horses used for this purpose. We had a group of young guys who wanted to try their luck on bucking horses and I tested one of the bareback horses that afternoon. We found out that we had a great group of bucking horses that tended to be better than the riders by a country mile. Even Ruby bucked pretty well for an old nag but I felt a little guilty at using her in such a way.

When the Fall Fair opened we put on a pretty good little rodeo, but it dragged on interminably. Nothing was organized, and Bob, the headman, simply sat on his horse in the middle of the arena without paying the least attention to what was going on back in the chutes and corrals. It looked like pure grandstanding to me and led to a very inefficient program. I was sure we would have to do much better in the future if people were going to pay money to come and see it.

I tried my luck in calf roping, bareback bronc riding and the wild horse race. I didn't get bucked off my draw in the bareback event, but did not win a prize either and in calf roping, I missed. The wild horse race was fun. We had selected five two-year olds, that had never been touched, and they were all to be let out of the chutes at the same time. The team would win whose horse, with rider, got to the other end of the arena first.

The teams consisted of a "shank-man" whose job it was to hold the fifteen foot long halter shank and stop the horse which would be coming out of the chute scared stiff and going full tilt; an "ear-man" whose job it was to help the shank-man and after the horse was stopped, go up the shank, grab an ear, fold it in half, put it in his mouth and bite down very hard until the horse stood still enough to saddle; and the rider whose job was to saddle the horse, and get up and ride him wherever he went, which was hopefully in the direction of the finish line. I chose as my teammate the two biggest, strongest young guys I knew, who had come up from Sckookumchuck Prairie sixty miles away to see the show.

There was total chaos when the chutes opened. The horses came out all together, rearing and jumping and whinnying in absolute fear, crashing into one another and the contestants and to avoid getting kicked or knocked down in the melee, men were jumping in all directions in the dust cloud that rose up and engulfed the front of the chutes. Some of the shank men were knocked down and were then dragged on their bellies by their horses until they got them under control again.

Me, coming out of the chute during the Fall Fair Rodeo

My two teammates were very good. They had our horse stopped in half a minute and the instant the ear-man had his mouth full of ear, I threw the saddle on, pulled the cinch tight raveling the end of the latigo around the horn to hold it in place and jumped on. My team helpers let go of the ear, tossed me the halter shank and ran back so one was on each side at the rear end to get the horse going in the right direction. Hollering, they slapped the horse on the rump to get it in high gear. I didn't think it needed the slap on the rump as it just ducked its head and started bucking straight ahead. I thought we were going to win but somehow I lost a stirrup, then got forward, and next thing I was flying through the air to land in a big belly flop in the six inches of dust that made up the arena floor. I had a mouthful of it, but could not suppress a laugh as I tried to spit it out. It had been a very exciting sixty seconds and great fun even though I did not win a silver buckle.

After the fair was over, I practiced calf roping on Sundays using Tom, a pretty good all-round cow horse. I got better at it and competed in amateur rodeos as far away as Cranbrook, but really did not have the time to practice enough to be very competitive. I continued to ride bareback broncs at the Fall Fairs and I was just smart enough to know that I would never be really good at it, although I did not get bucked off the times I rode in competition. I got bucked off a few times practicing, always hoping that what I learned would help me later on.

I was President of the Rodeo Association the next year and was determined to run a much more efficient show than had been the case in our first attempt. One change I made was to run the program from the announcer's tower directly over the chutes where I could see what was going on in the corrals and chutes. I became a dictator, keeping the crews going in the right directions, loading the proper animals and trying to have each event ready to go when the prior one was completed. It worked like a charm and we completed the program in half the time as the prior year. Afterwards, I was invited to stay on as President for another year.

It was not so good for Bob Tegart though, as he had to work around the corrals handling the livestock and midway through the show he got kicked by a horse that broke his leg severely, putting him on crutches for a few months. This was an unusual condition for a double-tough man like Bob.

One of the outgrowths of our success, especially in the quality of our bucking stock, was to initiate a spring saddle bronc-riding event. Feeling pretty positive about the quality of the horses, we called it The North American Amateur Saddle Bronc Championship. We wanted the six best amateur riders we could find to come and sent invitations to the cowboy who won the amateur event at the Calgary Stampede, the British Columbia amateur champion, and the amateur champions from Washington, Oregon and Idaho.

It was to be a $500 entry fee for each rider, very high for that time, and a winner take all prize, meaning several thousand dollars after some costs were taken out. Each rider was required to ride two horses and they were graded on each ride, the rider with the highest total points would win. The scoring was done exactly as was done in the professional rodeo circuit. It turned out that even though these riders were very good and most would turn professional in the next year or so, the horses were much better. Out of twelve rides at our first spring rodeo, only five made it to the whistle, a ten second ride. The cowboys were flung off right and left and it appeared that the horses were beginning to relish the sport themselves. We carried on the event the next spring with about the same result, with some of the same riders plus any new champion.

Word began to get around the rodeo world about the quality of our bucking horses and later that summer, Kenny McLean, a famous B.C. cowboy and a Rodeo Cowboy Association champion bronc rider himself, came to our valley to investigate. He represented Butler Brothers, one of the largest livestock contractors to the professional rodeo circuit. He was to check the horses out to see if any met their criteria and to buy them for the company if they did. The horses were to be tested at the fairgrounds one evening with Kenny McLean looking on while another rider would ride each one for $10 a head. I was not able to see this action, but heard about it early the next day. It turned out that the cowboy riding for mount money was thrown and killed by one of the horses. Getting kicked in the head by a twelve hundred pound horse is definitely not beneficial to one's health, but this almost never happens in bronc riding, although the risk is always there. The horses lived up to expectation and Butler Brothers bought a truckload. One of these horses went on to the National Finals Rodeo in Las Vegas in 1959, in its first year on the circuit, this selection designating it as one of the top bucking horses in RCA competition during the year.

Several years later when we were living in Bellevue, Washington, I saw the National Finals Professional Rodeo, coming from the Cow Palace in San Francisco on TV, and one of the cowboys that had bucked off several times in two years at our spring rodeo was riding as one of the top cowboys that year in the RCA. He got bucked off in the finals as well, so I never did have a strong feeling for his skill, but he had won enough money to be in the top group of professional riders nationally and invited to the finals.

We abandoned the spring saddle bronc championship after the sale of the string of good horses. From then on we concentrated on the Fall Fair rodeo. One event we did not have, while I was involved, was a cutting horse competition. In this event the skill of the horse in handling a cow was paramount. In fact, the rider was not supposed to direct the horse at all, just hang on and let the horse make the cutting decisions with the reins slack at all times. Of course, on the ranch, things often turned rodeo like, in the normal course of ranch work.

Tom was a pretty good cutting horse. He was from a quarter horse sire, and was fairly fast and agile. He was smart as well. In the spring when we had to cut cows out of the herd in order to bring them into the barnyard for calving, I would lay the feed out in a long line in the field where we were holding the cows for winter feeding. This would get all the cows strung out in a line eating and I could ride the line and look to see which ones I needed to bring into the yard. I put another few bales of hay several hundred yards away but closer to the barnyard, where I would take the cows after they were cut from the herd. In this way they would stay with the feed while we continued to cut more animals out and not attempt to come back across the field to rejoin the herd.

When I selected one I would direct Tom to her and we would cut her out of the bunch and drive her over to the other pile of feed. Naturally they did not want to leave the feed or the safety of the herd, so it was quite a challenge for a horse to keep them from getting back to the herd. Tom appeared to really enjoy this work. He seemed to know he could beat a cow and they would soon be head to head, Tom's ears flat back on his head in anger and when the cow made a move to either side to run around us, he was quick and aggressive in cutting her off. Once he got her turned around and headed the direction he wanted he usually would try to bite her on the rump for good measure.

After the first cow was moved over all I had to do was show Tom the cow I wanted next, let the reins slack, maybe hook him gently with my spurs and he would do the rest. He became really very good at this and along with his calf roping skills became one of the horses that built a reputation with other Valley ranchers and horsemen.

One winter day when Dix and I were working a group of heifers that we had put across the highway in a pasture leased from Joe Jimmy, an unfortunate incident occurred that slowed me down for a time. We were trying to cut a few of these heifers away from the group and drive them through the gate that led to the highway. From there we intended to take them a quarter mile up the highway to the ranch gate and into another paddock close by the barnyard. Both of our horses were sharp-shod as the ground was still frozen and things seemed to be going fine until I had to make a fast turn to head a heifer and on a hard icy patch Tom became airborne and down we went.

When we hit the ground my left foot was somehow at a wrong angle and I instantly felt a quick stab of pain and knew I was hurt. Dix had seen it happen and rode right over to help. Tom was okay, but I told Dix I thought my ankle might be broken he immediately pulled my boot off. I could see the swelling come up until there was a knot like a large egg on the outside of my ankle. If Dix had waited another few moments, I'm sure we would have had to cut the boot off. My ankle was indeed broken and for the next few weeks I was in a plaster cast and had to direct the ranch operations from a pair of crutches. This was not too easy and I went through two casts before the doctor laid the law down with dire warnings to behave myself and let the break heal properly. With this admonition I tried to stay a bit removed from any action in the barnyard and my ankle came out good as new.

Summertime was all about preparing the fields for planting, doing the sowing of either a bromegrass/alfalfa mix, or oats to be cut for green feed, fertilizing the hay fields, cleaning up irrigation ditches, picking rocks from the fields, setting up and changing the sprinklers starting in April, watching the cattle on the range, cutting, raking, baling and stacking the hay and repairing all fences. The days started early and most often ended late. The work was steady and sometimes extremely hectic, such as when we went to three-times-a-day sprinkler changes. More hands were needed during summer, especially for haying and most of these extras were from the two Indian reserves near the ranch. We generally fed lunch to the crew on the back porch of our house and often served up to fifteen men with huge appetites. Karen was a good cook and I'm sure the men ate better at the ranch than when at their own home.

A young girl was hired each summer to help look after the children when Karen had a large crew to feed. One of these was Suzanne Blake, a teenage girl from Calgary, whom we met in 1957 when she was working for the Skookum-chuck restaurant up the highway from the ranch. She was not afraid to work and appeared to be a very responsible girl, mature beyond her years. She left the restaurant to work for Karen for the balance of the summer. She had an innate understanding of what work around the house was needed to be done and I was very impressed with her and her way with the children.

On hot days Karen often made up Kool-Aid or iced tea and sometimes accompanied with cookies or tarts, delivered these treats to whatever field we were working in to give a cold refreshing drink to the men. Her work was, like mine, never ending during the summer and with four young children always demanding attention, in some ways mentally harder to cope with than mine. By 1956 it appeared that with four children to look after and the ranch life in general to deal with, Karen was not coping too well. She visited a doctor in Invermere who felt she was depressed and anxious and prescribed a tranquilizer for her to take. This drug was one of the first anti-anxiety drugs to come along and was called "Milltown." Of course there was little known about various mental states at that time, but the drug seemed to help for a while.

However, we never needed to worry about the kids keeping busy. There was just too much exciting stuff for them to become bored. I very seldom heard any whining such as, "what can I do now?" or "there's nothing to do." Usually they were out of he house right after breakfast, either following me around or headed for the barnyard where there was always something going on and they would not come back until chow time at noon, and again just before supper. During the summer vacation they were back outside after dinner until dark on most evenings, unless it was bath night.

I did not try to contain our children to any special area for safety reasons, but tried instead to educate them as to what was dangerous, how to move around the livestock and how to avoid being run over by a piece of farm equipment. I figured they would take their lumps occasionally and that would be a learning lesson. There were a few close calls but happily, and perhaps luckily, none of them was ever seriously hurt. But things could happen very fast sometimes and when you least expected them to. Once I was inside the corrals on the Findlay Creek range where we had herded a few bulls prior to loading them to take back to the ranch. I was not watching as several bulls started to fight and suddenly one bull put the run on another, who in his effort to get away, just missed hitting me by inches and the force of his collision with the corral wall, shattered a gate made of 3" planks into pieces. I would have been badly smashed if he had hit me in his blind effort to save himself.

One day when I was walking across the barnyard I happened to look up and there was Suzie, about four or five years old, on the roof of the horse barn walking between the two roof cupolas that were about forty feet apart and twenty five feet in the air. They were set so that she had to walk a line that was about two feet up from the edge and on a steep slope. My heart almost stopped, but trying not to alarm her, I looked up at her and said, "That's not a very good place to be young lady, so you better climb back in that next cupola." She smiled a big charming smile and said, "OK Dad," as if it was nothing out of the ordinary. I walked casually over towards the barn until I was directly under her in case she fell, but I'm not certain I breathed until I saw her grab the window frame of the cupola and climb inside to continue playing in the hayloft.

Another heart stopper happened on a spring day when our youngest child, Ann was just a toddler. We were holding some two-year-old heifers in the barnyard for calving and one of them had had a very rough birthing time and was wild and snuffy when anyone came near her or her calf. Karen had brought Ann over to the barnyard and in a few seconds of her mother's inattention, she wandered across the yard and happened to walk too near this calf for the mother's comfort. At this, the young cow let out a bellow and charged right at Ann, skidding to a stop two feet away with her nose close to the ground, pawing and bawling. I took off running towards Ann who at the same time opened her mouth and let out a scream, grabbed her by one arm on the run and swept her away. I don't know why that young cow stopped instead of knocking Ann into the next county, but perhaps when she got right up close to Annie she realized it was a small human and not the dog, that the day before, went barking close to her calf and had received a similar attack. Who knows, but it certainly got my adrenaline going.

Most of the children loved to ride horses. We had one big old dappled gray named Granger, who would carry three kids at a time. He stood still for everything and even when the youngsters crawled around, under and about his legs, he never moved. Getting him into a trot took some energy, but usually Sue had a long branch she used as a quirt and this proved to work well. One day while riding around the yards of some of the employee's houses, the kids had Granger going at a good clip when he went under a clothesline that caught Sue, the lead rider, under the chin and swept them all off. There ensued a mighty yowling as Sue had a painful rope burn across her neck.

One summer day when no other rider was available and thinking this might be a good time for me to do something with my eldest son, I asked Bill, who was then about eight years old, if he would like to go riding down near Dutch Creek with me. He was a little tentative, so I said he could ride Tom, as I trusted Tom to behave with a child on his back, so he finally said yes. We loaded the horses in the truck and drove down to Dutch Creek to move some cows to another location on that section of range. All was well until we got into some very rough country, with steep draws and more than enough brush and we were having difficulty moving the cattle. Bill was little help in a situation like that and in my frustration I gave him a very hard time when he could not get Tom into the right position at the right time. This took all the joy out of the day for Bill and killed any budding interest he had in horses. In a stupid and thoughtless act, I had done to him, what Mr. Gay had done to me many years before when I was learning to ride and I still feel remorse at my actions towards my son that day. It is one of those days I wish I could have another chance at.

On the other hand, Bill's real interest lay in the equipment. As soon as he was able to reach the clutch and brake pedals on our large truck by standing and hanging onto the steering wheel I let him drive in the fields while I fed the hay off the back for the cattle. When he was nine I taught him how to drive the tractor and a perfect day for Bill was to be shown a forty-acre field and told to disc or harrow it. Driving out early in the morning he was content to work all day at the job, often coming back with dust encrusted all over his face. He seemed to thrive on this work so we let him do it. My big fear was having him tipping over on a side hill, so we kept him on the flat as much as possible.

But he was not afraid, either because he did not know at what point a tractor could tip over, or assumed he would not get into that situation. I learned later that Bill and Phil Geiger's son Darrell, would sneak a tractor out the back gate and drive it up the Mount Swansea Road behind the ranch, turn around and come down at full throttle in road gear. Had I known this, Bill would have been grounded for sure, as I cannot think of anything more dangerous to do. Anyway he lived through it and I know the memories of his adventures and interesting times while living at Lake Windermere, are stored in his memory forever.

Sue was different from Bill in that she loved horses and riding and since she was naturally fearless, she became very good at it. I often asked her to take a horse and do something useful like moving a cow somewhere or running horses out of a field where they did not belong. I could count on her getting the job done, even when she was a little tyke. Sufficient strength to open and close a gate by herself was her only limiting factor.

Excepting turning the crank on the milk separator and other lighter chores, the other children were a bit too young to be very helpful, but their lives outside the home, in the open air, were full of interesting things to do. I taught the eldest three to milk cows and although this was usually Dix's and my chore to do, they would help. One of our older Ayrshire cows, Fernie, having been originally purchased in the town of the same name a few years before we came to the ranch, was a favorite. The kids thought she was great and she took all the abuse they gave her in learning to milk.

Unbeknownst to the children, when she grew too old and not even worth shipping to Calgary, I took her to the local butcher in Invermere, to be converted into mostly hamburger, for that was all that could be done with the meat in her old skinny condition. Later in the week I took delivery of the meat and soon thereafter we had hamburgers for dinner. After everyone was happily munching their burgers, I asked the kids if they knew what they were eating and how special it was. They shook their heads and said, "No, so tell us," so I casually said, "These exceptionally fine burgers are called Fernieburgers," and when that sank in all hell broke loose. There were howls of "how could you do that to Fernie," much mock gagging and as I remember even some tears, but in a few minutes they were all back to eating Fernie who had given her last full measure of devotion to our family.

Wintertime's foremost chore was feeding the cattle every day from mid November until late March when green grass began to appear. By mid March we had many calves and since most of the older cows did not have calving problems, we moved them across Windermere Creek to the 640 acre Kimpton pasture. We gathered them together in a long line by feeding them high protein pellets each morning off the back of the truck and we could drive slowly down the line, looking at each one yet to calve, for any signs of a problem. All I had to do was honk the horn when we entered the pasture from the highway and even the cows quite far up one of the draws would hear the horn and come running back out onto the flat of the dirt airstrip that was on the property. Usually when we arrived there were not many cows to be seen as they were off grazing, but all the calves would be lying around with their chins flat on the ground, their front hooves mostly curled up under their chests and their faces pure white from the cleaning job done on them by their attentive mothers. Watching over the calves were always a few baby sitting cows standing around chewing their cuds.

In the winter it was possible to take some time off and the family generally got in a few days skiing fifty miles away at Kimberley with the kids, or even a week to Seattle to see our families and friends. It was a much slower pace than summer and fall and the day's work seldom exceeded eight hours, not counting chores. Feeding the cattle consumed most of the morning since the bales were loaded by hand on the bobsled and then pitch forked off in some semblance of even distribution. There were almost eight hundred head and it took a lot of bales. The balance of a typical winter day would be repairing equipment, maybe shoeing a horse, welding in the shop or repairing tack.

Although there was snow on the ground it was never deep and the weather was generally dry. It was easy to get around in the winter for visits or attend parties and the valley folks always socialized more in the winter when our friends had more time with the tourist traffic gone until the next summer. Going to a dinner party in the valley was always fun, but many parties on a weekend lasted until early morning. Often, about 4 AM, long after I wanted to get home for a little sleep, the women would all go to the kitchen and make up a huge breakfast, thus we would get back to the ranch just in time to do the barnyard chores.

Several months after Karen started taking Milltown's I began to notice that things were not getting done around the house. This trend grew worse over time, until I found that the kids were not getting fed on a regular schedule. I talked to

Karen about my concern and soon I realized that she was taking many more pills than had been prescribed. I tried to get her to understand that this could not continue, that she was failing to look after the children properly and was probably doing some kind of harm to herself as well. For short periods, I could get her to use the proper dosage and things would improve a bit, but then she would slowly regress back to the former state.

I was unable to cope with this kind of problem and there were no psychologists available for her to see, or for me either, for that matter. I did not know how to help her at the time and was losing my ability to deal with the situation at all, coming to the conclusion that it was a problem that only she could solve and I expected her to deal with it. However, nothing did change and my resentment continued to grow and our marriage entered a phase I can only describe as very troubling, frustrating and full of countless concerns, especially about the children. And it continued downhill into the spring.

Six months later, at 5:30 AM, on a beautiful early summer morning, I was up at the head of an alfalfa field situated in a downward sloping and curving coulee in order to change the sprinkler. I had just shut down the power unit pump at the top of the field and everything was quiet. Only the sound of birds in the nearby woods and the wonderful smell of the Jackpine forest intruded into the scene I beheld. The sun had just appeared over the Rockies to the east, sending shafts of yellow sunlight into the coulee, bringing out the solid emerald green of the lush alfalfa growing there. It was a sight that could have graced any calendar carrying photos of the natural world. I looked out on this wonderful scene with my mind registering the fact of how beautiful the landscape was, I knew it rationally, but I could generate not a shred of feeling from the vista. I was so wound up in worry about what was happening to Karen and my marriage, the children and how Karen's problems were affecting them, that everything my senses registered seemed to be more dead than alive. This beautiful morning view might as well have been painted in grays and it failed to touch my heart in any way. This sudden realization that I was losing my ability to get any joy out of my life truly shocked me. I contemplated this strange dichotomy for a few moments longer and then the transformational thought came to me, *"I can't live this way any longer or I'm going to die!"*

In that instant I knew that I was going to act. I started to change the sprinkler feeling a great load fall from me and an hour and a half later was back at the ranch house. Finding Karen, I said to her, "I've thought a long time about our family problems and I'm sorry, but this morning I've made a decision that I want to end our marriage. I can't live any longer the way we are and I can't continue to worry about the kids and try to manage the ranch. I want to end it now. I'll help you in any way I can, but it's over."

I had been blunt, no doubt hurtful, but I think deep down Karen must have felt some relief, because she agreed with me right then and there and showed no outward remorse whatsoever. She had not been happy, evidently for a very long time, did not enjoy the ranch life, and was overwhelmed by the children. And I did not know how to help her. So the die was cast and a change, the nature of which was still unknown to me, would once again bring a new chapter to the story of my life.

The Cowboy Life

Our cowboy takes a slow ride through a green pasture,
delighting in spring sunshine, clean-scrubbed calves,
and finds a Badger hole

He stepped from the kitchen onto the back porch, letting the screen door slam shut behind him and walked down the steps, thinking he should fix the door to close easy, and turned towards the barnyard gate. The walk from the big house to the horse barn, past the cow barn with its silo and down the slope the fifty yards to the gate and another fifty to the door to the horse barn, afforded a perfect view east to the Rocky mountains, etched against a cool springtime blue that arched over the Columbia valley, coming to rest on the ridgeline of the Selkirks to the west. The look of the sky assured a warming sun, even though it was early April.

The older cows had been moved to the Kimpton pasture a mile north of the ranch as was the practice each spring in mid March, or as soon as the snow was off on the flat and the bottoms of the coulees that wound in curves up through the low wooded hills rising from the flat. They were still fed pellets each day off the back of the truck and after a few days of honking the horn when feeding started, the cows would come streaming out of the coulee or off the hills on a run when they heard the horn.

This was a ride he looked forward to. It would be easy, no urgency, no rough riding, just a ride alone with Tom and himself for a couple of hours. He wanted to look at the herd for any possible problems; a cow with an udder not sucked, a calf with the runs or a separated pair that for some reason were not bonding. He knew he would find them all out in the open when he got there, since they had been fed about an hour before. The calves, mostly dropped within the last three weeks, would be laying around or trying to suck while their mothers ate and before they wandered off looking for new grass on the southern slopes of the hills.

He opened the barn door and stepped inside and was hit with the familiar odors of horse, hay and manure, mixed into the pleasing aroma that greeted him each morning on opening the door. He walked past the stalls on either side towards the one Tom was in and as he took his first few steps inside, the horse raised his head, looked at him and gave a soft nicker. There were no other horses in the barn although the three milk cows that he had helped milk at 6:00 AM were in their stanchions, still eating the last of the alfalfa he had fed them. He walked past the horse and opened a side door and then the stanchions to release the cows that then moved through the door to the outside barnyard. He took the remaining alfalfa and threw it out the door after them so they could finish it.

He turned back towards the horse, grabbed a curry comb and walked to the stall laying his hand gently at first and then firmly pushing on the horse's rump and said, "over boy," as he moved up the left side to the horse's head. He straightened the horse's forelock and scratching the base of both ears at the same time ran his left hand down Tom's face to the soft nose stroking gently. He then took the comb and starting high up on the neck right behind the ears began the hard rhythmic brushing always working back and down and along the belly and finally ending at the hooves. When the left side was finished he went to the other side and went though the same procedure. He noted that more winter hair was coming out and never ceased to be amazed at how much dust and grit seemed to lie embedded under the hair that no matter how hard the brushing, the hair would continue to offer up more.

As he worked, he remembered four years earlier when Tom, then a yearling stud colt, by lineage half quarterhorse and half something else, backed out of the horse trailer. When they brought the colt out for him to inspect he was surprised to see that it was crème colored in its winter coat, with whiter mane and tail, a white blaze down his nose and three white stockings. It was, to him, a fine looking animal with an intelligent alert eye and not too skittish. He had the owner walk him around while he inspected him from all angles and satisfied with what he saw paid the hundred dollars asked.

He had brought him back to the ranch, named him "Tom" for the cowboy who told him about the Q Ranch. He kept Tom close to the barnyard that first summer so that in the evenings he could work with him until he was without fear of being touched and easy to handle and mainly gentled. The next summer he broke him to ride as a two year old, with no problems. He determined to use only a hackamore instead of a bridle and bit, to make sure the horse would work cattle with his head down and not risk someone jerking on the bit and ruining his mouth. He kept him away from the rest of the horse herd until completely used to being ridden, but turned him out after that to the hilltop pasture with the herd so that he might produce a few foals the next spring.

Now the horse was five years old, had produced some fine looking foals, was docile and easy to handle and was developing into a good cow horse. More than that, the man had developed a true affection for the horse. Tom was always ready to do whatever was needed and had never let him down. There had been some very long hard days of riding, some of it in the rough country along the Kootenay River bottoms, or up in the hills above Findlay and Horsethief Creeks. Lots of miles together he thought, and a trust had grown between them.

He had had great affection for other horses before Tom, but with Tom, and perhaps because he had raised him, it was really love. They had experienced much in the few years they had been together that a feeling of certain trust had developed in the man. The horse was willing to go into any kind of rough terrain and had never faltered or irretrievably lost his footing, something the man could not say about some horses he had ridden.

It took a good horse to manage the problems with the herd that could and did arise on the timber range the ranch leased from the Crown for summer grazing. Some of the problems were not easy to deal with, but Tom was eager, responsive, sure footed and willing and they had been through enough together that he had a feeling they understood each other perfectly.

When he had worked both sides back to the tail, he changed brushes and began to straighten the tail hair and sort out the matted areas working slowly trying not to pull too much hair until the tail was loose and flowing. He then leaned against the horse to move its weight off the side he was working, and pulling on the fetlock of a hind leg received a bit of help from the horse in lifting the rear hoof up to look at the shoe. He was grateful to have a horse that did not mind his messing around with its feet. Using a hoof trimmer he cleaned out around the frog of the hoof and checked to see if the shoe was tight and all four of the screwed in bolts in place. He did not want to have the horse go down on some frozen spot unseen below the surface.

After all the hooves and shoes were inspected he reached for the saddle blanket that was lying bottom side up on top of the saddle which straddled the wall between the stalls. He laid it on the horse making sure it was forward enough on the withers and centered evenly. The horse continued to chew as he lifted the saddle pulled the two cinches and offside stirrup up onto the seat and put the saddle solidly on the blanket. He shook it by the horn several times to make sure it was positioned well and them dropped the cinches over and then the stirrup and reached under the belly of the horse to grab the front cinch ring and hook it into the holder on his side. He pulled the cinch latigo enough to make the saddle secure and then attached the rear cinch loosely.

He removed the halter from the horse, leaving it tied to the manger, and took the hackamore off the nail it was hanging from and with his left hand slid the bosal over Tom's nose, pulled the headstall over the ears and straightened his forelock. He then tied his lariat to the right side of the saddle near the horn, tied his slicker behind the pommel and then left the stall to put on his spurs. He had always liked his spurs and later when he left the ranch they were the only things he took that would remind him of these years. They were long shanked so it was easy to touch a horse without moving, just turn his heels in and the horse knew he was being commanded. They had big rowels, but dull so as not to inadvertently hurt a horse when things were happening fast.

He backed Tom out of stall onto the cement floor slowly because it was slippery with him sharp shod. He never enjoyed seeing a horse go down unless it wanted to roll or lie down to rest, but it happened sometimes and it paid to not take chances. He led him outside by the lines into the sunlight and after a few yards the horse shook his head and sneezed hard pulling back on the lines. "Come on Tom, wake up!" he said to the horse, who seemed to be a bit reluctant to go anywhere.

He led the horse past the shop and opened the barnyard's north gate and went through saying "Come on Tom move your butt," and when the horse was through, shut the gate. Turning to Tom he said "Are you going to be lazy all day?" and took the cinch latigo in his right hand, shook the saddle horn with his left hand to make sure the saddle was still set right and pulled the cinch in tight. He brought the back cinch up to touch the horse's belly, put his left foot in the stirrup, saying "Easy now," and swung up into the saddle. "Let's go boy," he said, touching the horse's sides. Tom immediately became alert, ears forward and they started in a fast walk up the road towards the Windermere Creek crossing and the Kimpton pasture.

The narrow road led north to the creek along side several cultivated fields and was mostly used to move sprinkler pipe or farm equipment to and from the fields. A small irrigation ditch on the left side of the road showed a trickle of water and was part of a network of irrigation ditches that moved water out of the creek from April until October.

He felt good. He ran his right hand along the horse's neck under the mane and patted him several times. The sun was beginning to warm through his lined jean jacket and he began to hum the melody to 'Streets of Laredo' ... doing the words in his head, ... "*As I walked out in the streets of Laredo, as I walked out in Laredo one day, I saw a young cowboy all wrapped in white linen, wrapped ... *" He began to relax into the rhythm of the horse and was looking around at the panorama of the mountain ranges on both sides of the valley, still showing snow above timberline and whose ridge lines seemed to converge in the perspective of distance northward down river. Suddenly, several prairie chickens broke cover in a blast of whirring wings and cackles and the horse jumped sideways startled by the rapid movement and noise. "Easy now!" the man said, the adrenalin hitting, himself startled by the birds that had intruded so sharply into his reverie.

Once again settled, he lifted the lines and touched the horse moving him into a trot. He liked to ride standing up in the stirrups with a hand on top of the horn for balance and to reduce the shaking and the horse moved easily under him. In a half-mile they came to a gate in a barbed wire fence and he had to dismount to use the lever to release the gate keeping the lines secured in one hand. Once open he led the horse through and shut the gate.

They crossed a hay field that curved gently to the right and finally narrowed into a point between the hills on the right and the creek on the left side. It had been disked in the Fall for replanting in the Spring and had been used until recently as a winter feed lot for the cows now over on the Kimpton pasture. It showed only brown dirt now with the remnants of hay worked over by the cattle and was studded everywhere with the drying cowpies from the cattle fed there during the winter.

The trail led steeply down from the field to the creek below. He stopped the horse and without dismounting tightened the cinch a notch before starting down. He kept his weight fully on the stirrups and leaning back moved with Tom as he picked his way down, slipping every so often with the steepness. Each time Tom skidded he sat further back on his haunches until his rear hooves were almost touching his front ones. In this manner they came to the bottom and then forded the creek.

Going up the other side was easier but when they reached the top the horse was breathing hard and the man got off to open the gate into the pasture. He decided to walk for a ways to rest the horse and led him out onto the long expanse of flat pasture that gently fell away to the north from the bench above the creek bed. From there he could see the cows a quarter of a mile off still working the ground for pellets that had been fed a short time before.

The pasture was beginning to show signs of green and the small plants were starting to form buds that in a very few weeks would be in full bloom. After the five months of winter, spring was always an enchantment to the man. The feeling was heightened by the yearly arrival of calves and foals, the long missed warmth of the sun still low in the sky and in this, his twenty fifth year, the expectation of the impending birth of his fourth child.

He remounted and they walked into the herd slowly taking their time so as to not disturb either the cows or their calves and moved around and though them inspecting each one in passing. Most of the calves were lying down in a cluster a little ways removed from their mothers, their heads down with chins flat on the ground as if to be unseen from whatever it was their instinct told them they should hide. He marveled at how white their heads were. They always looked scrubbed as if they had just came home from a laundry somewhere that specialized in Hereford calves, but he knew that it was the mothers constantly licking and cleaning them up.

After a half hour of trying to note all the details he wanted to remember about the cows on that day, he turned the horse away toward to hills that rose from the flat. They entered a low coulee that led up from the flat and then moved higher through the sparse fir and lodgepole pine until they broke out on top of the flat hills. He was looking at the grass trying to estimate how long before they could quit feeding pellets and figured it was at least another week to ten days depending on the weather.

Some time later as they came down into the coulee the cows were already moving up off the flat. They came looking for grass without their calves left where they had been sleeping, but still tended by several cows that stayed behind. He was always amazed at this behavior from the cows who usually were so attentive, but the need for new green grass was urgent to them, possibly because they understood the connection between the grass and their milk production.

He decided then to ride over the flat part of the pasture to check the north end and inspect the fence line along the road bordering the pasture on the West. In the center of the flat running north and south were the tire tracks of the airplanes that used the field and were hangered in a very rustic barn near the road

He started to follow the wheel tracks northward and realizing that it was very smooth decided on an impulse to put a little bit of excitement into this otherwise simple ride and see just how fast Tom could run. He put him into a trot and then into an easy lope and after maybe a hundred yards leaned forward and low and put the spurs hard into the horse's side. He was amazed at the power this generated and Tom was now in a flat out run.

Leaning far forward with his head just over the horse's ears and using the length of the lines as a whip, he laid the ends hard on his rump and got the last bit of speed that was in him. He knew the horse was giving all he had and the excitement of the run gave a real adrenaline rush, but suddenly in full stride, Tom's left foot went deep into a hole and instantly the horse's rear end changed places with the front end slamming into the ground and propelling the man, like shot from a cannon, low through the air until he hit the ground sideways rolling over and over to a stop.

Lying there dazed for a few seconds and concerned with possible damage to his own body, he suddenly realized that Tom had probably been badly injured and was instantly heartsick. He knew without looking that from such a fall the horse would probably have a broken leg or neck and have to be destroyed, but when he did look back from the ground where he was lying, he was amazed to see the horse get up and shake himself and appear to be all right. He began to search his own body for injuries but soon realized that they had both been very lucky. He had hit the ground with so much forward speed and with the ground sloping away, had rolled over and over to a stop, that he didn't have a scratch.

He got up looked around for his hat, found it twenty feet away, and walking back to Tom said, "Jesus, you're not supposed to run into a god dammed hole you dummy," and began to pat the horse's neck and straighten his forelock and hackamore and let the relief swell up in him. He saw that the saddle had survived as well with nothing broken which was major good luck. Still somewhat excited he said, "you're lucky I'm not going home to get a gun to put you out of your misery you stupid son of a bitch, you almost killed me!" But as soon as he said it he was hit with the guilt of knowing it had been his idea, not the horse's. He felt both front legs down to the hoof and finding nothing amiss gently lifted the left one that had gone in the hole to see if it was sore or sprained. Miraculously everything seemed OK.

He walked past the horse then to see what they had gone into and quickly saw that it was a badger hole, greater than a foot wide and the bottom over a foot deep. The horse's hoof had come down on the far edge which had broken away letting the hoof drop in the hole. He walked farther on past it and then turned back to see how it looked from the direction they had come and saw that it was partially hidden by some tufts of grass around the edge and not easy to see coming from that direction.

He walked back to the horse and picked up the lines, rubbed the horse's ears and turning back the way they had come said, "Come on now," and began leading Tom slowly back up the airfield towards Windermere Creek. His head was full of what had just happened. He could not get out of his mind the feeling of astonishment and relief the way it turned out. He knew that had the horse been hurt it would have been a long time before he would have gotten over the guilty feeling that just for a lark he had ruined his favorite horse.

As they walked up the pasture he looked over at the cows and saw that some were beginning to come down off the hills towards their calves. Looking south past the creek and on past the ranch and the Indian Reserve he could see the beautiful mountains fading southward toward Montana. It was always beautiful, he thought, when you took the time to look.

When he got to the fence and passed through the gate, he turned the horse one more time in both directions looking at how he moved his legs, and satisfied again there was no damage, mounted up and turning the horse to the trail back, said to Tom, "Let's go home."

Searching for Avalon—An Interregnum

Our hero contemplates memories, small birds, life on the wild side, and the value of a good woman

As I sit here in Mazatlan writing at the computer this morning, with the door open to the sun dappled patio, I can see a Cinnamon Hummingbird attacking the red-flower feeder with gusto and as I watch his efforts to drain the tank I am reminded of Maurice, a young French Canadian of 18 years, who walked up the highway and entered the ranch gate in 1955 and asked if he could have a job. Maurice was strong, built like a weight lifter, but his muscles were more probably from the only kind of work he had ever done in his young life, hard physical labor. He was uneducated and functionally illiterate at least in English, thus we described him as the farmhand with the size 5 hat and 19 inch neck.

One day Maurice and I were working on a piece of machinery in the barnyard and I asked him to get a wrench from the shop, which he did directly. He could take orders. In a moment I heard a holler from the shop and Maurice came running out exclaiming that there was a hummingbird inside. He was not about to go back in for any wrench, believing that the bird would attack and spear him with its long beak. I could not help but laugh at the incongruity of this hyper-muscled young man frightened of a hummingbird so I went in and single hand-edly, trying to impress the incredulous youngster with my bravery, caught the poor terrified bird and brought it out to show Maurice he did not have to worry further about eye-spearing hummingbirds.

It is surprising to me how many forgotten memories continue to float up like this one, from my personal memory banks, sometimes triggered by a small bird, other times by a smell, or a sky color of a certain hue, reminding me of some feeling or place from long past. A hint only, but enough to suggest a similar sky once long ago when I was alone on a trail in Alaska, or possibly a quick scene or spoken word that reminds me of a sadder time demanding to be reexamined. So it is now, trying to remember the events and feelings associated with the separation of Karen and myself, and all that this upheaval meant to our family.

◆   ◆   ◆

In the days following my announcement to Karen that I wanted a divorce, my greatest fears concerned the children. I was determined that I would keep them with me, since it was obvious that Karen was not able to manage them herself and I did not have enough money to hire help for her in Seattle. At the ranch I could get help and had a house large enough to keep them all together in a healthy and safe environment. I could not bear the thought of being separated from them and I don't know to this day what I would have done if Karen had said she would fight to keep the children. Nor did I want to see the children split apart, although I knew that David, still a baby, would have to stay with his mother for a time. Luckily for me, and I think for the children as well, Karen did not try to keep the children, perhaps realizing that she simply was not capable of doing it at that time.

I talked with my parents, telling them of my plans, which included moving things along as fast as possible. With their help, my cousin, Ann Bruck Moore, agreed to take Karen to her home in Reno, where she could get a special out-of-state six-week divorce. In that summer of 1958, Karen then 26 years old, taking David, went to Reno and started the divorce proceedings. There had been no talk of reconciling, nor of counseling, nor any real arguments between us about money or the children, all of which I think indicated that somehow Karen must have felt a great burden being lifted from her. On the other hand, not a year has gone by since that time when I have not asked myself about my own culpability in the downfall of the marriage. I am certain that had I been more mature many of my assumptions and actions would have been different, but whether the final outcome would have changed I doubt very much.

After the divorce Karen went to her family in Seattle and entered secretarial school preparing for the job she was going to need. When she graduated from the school she became a legal secretary, work she continued for many years, and ultimately married David Noble, an insurance agent.

After having lived the prior eight years with a mate, not having one quickly brought to my attention a certain hunger for female companionship, natural enough in any 28 year old single male, especially one that felt a bit robbed from enjoying the ladies since his sophomore year in college. Being, I guess, of the marrying kind, I was soon thinking about finding a new mate for me and a mother for the children, but I was also determined to make the most of my bachelorhood and catch up for all the years I had missed by marrying as a mere boy.

I kept my eyes open for every opportunity that came my way and with a reliable housekeeper looking after the children I began to get less and less sleep, making the rounds so to speak. I became intimately knowledgeable with both Indian reserves where there were some fine looking maidens; a beauty who worked in the bakery in Invermere; a gal who lived in Cranbrook but who came to help a time or two when Else was not there; and an 18 year old of French Canadian and Cree blood that absolutely got my pulse rate moving. She had two sisters who were older and also beautiful, but Shirley Ann was striking, resembling not so much a classical beauty, but carried with her, enough to turn heads, a Cher-like sexual aura. She definitely was not a girl you would take home to mother, but she had my number until her family moved to Revelstoke.

Looking back now, I suspect that I presented a ridiculous sight to my friends in the valley and precipitated a huge amount of gossip, but at that moment I could not have cared less since I was fully involved in the chase and enjoying my new freedom. However, at some level way deep down I sensed I was again acting like a 19 year old and not a responsible father of five children, but until I became serious about a particular woman I was unable to slow down.

One winter night when the children were away, Shirley Ann and I were asleep in my bed at the ranch. Her mother, returning towards their home from a night in the bars of Invermere and maybe suspecting Shirley Ann was there with me, came into the ranch house which was always unlocked, looking for her.

We awoke with a start hearing her mother talking to herself as she approached down the darkened hallway, and could tell she was drunk and on the warpath. Shirley Ann, recognizing the trouble coming our way, pulled the covers over her head trying to hide as her mother burst into the bedroom. Unfortunately I was not wearing the bottom half of my pajamas so I stayed put, trying my best to calm down her mother from my prone situation. This turned out to definitely be a position of weakness and she would have none of it and in an instant grabbed the covers from under my chin and jerked them right off onto the floor.

Shirley Ann let out a shriek but at least she had my bottoms on, and although bare on top, enjoyed a much better situation than I faced. So with nothing more to hide I jumped out of bed to try to usher Momma Bear into another room in the house. Calming down an inebriated Cree Indian woman trying to protect her daughter is not for the faint of heart, but using both cajoling and threatening words and finally offering her a drink if she would settle down, I was ultimately able to put her into a bed upstairs. In the early morning Shirley's mother looked bad but was at least manageable and I took the two of them home hoping there were no people around to gawk at this grotesquerie.

With Karen leaving I had to have help in the house if I were to continue to run the ranch properly, so I called Christine Blake, whose daughter, Suzanne, had worked the prior summer for us, to see if she would allow Suzanne, then 17, to work for the summer taking care of the kids and cooking. Suzanne was willing, her mother and father agreed to this, and Suzanne arrived shortly after she got out of school for the summer.

Suzanne was a beautiful and intelligent young woman, surprisingly mature for her years. She had a strong will backed by good common sense and when I talked with her, her gray-green eyes never wavered the slightest from looking me squarely in the eye, almost to the point of being disconcerting. She seemed to understand some of the trauma my children had been going through and went out of her way to do things with them. Bill, at 8 years old, was suffering the most from the loss of his mother, as Karen had doted on her firstborn, but the younger children took to Suzanne immediately, remembering her from the previous summer. They promptly named her "Big Sue" to differentiate her from Susan who was then 6 years old.

As the summer went on I began to appreciate Suzanne's many attributes in managing the children. She seemed to understand when to play with them and when to be firm and there was never confusion as to what she wanted from them. We settled into a way of living that summer which seemed to work for all of us and I strove hard to take enough time from work to enjoy evening or Sunday outings as a family. As the children began to bloom under her care and attention, I could see how great it would be for them if I could find a person they could really care for as a stepmother. We all enjoyed having her around that summer but when fall arrived Suzanne left for Calgary to attend Mt. Royal College and work for her father in his electrical contracting business.

Knowing when I hired her that she would have to leave for school in the fall, I had advertised in Vancouver for a "mature" live-in housekeeper, and finally hired Else Heiberg, a tall Norwegian woman who, although she claimed to be 56, I suspected might have been a bit older than that. She was truly a character who had lived a most interesting life as I learned bit by bit during her time with us.

Suzanne at a family picnic 1958

Mrs. Heiberg arrived with all her personal belongings stuffed into multiple suitcases in September 1958 and stayed with us for the next year and a half. She was tall and big-boned, slim, with the largest hands I had ever seen on a woman. She was a heavy smoker, her face beginning to sag, especially around the eyes, which gave her a bit of the look of a person fond of drink. She was not a great cook, but I helped out as I could, and her version of bringing up children was definitely to brook no back-sass, demand reasonable manners, make them do their chores, and administer corporal punishment as required, all areas where I was perhaps a bit soft because of the trauma they had been through. She was a big change from Suzanne, a change the children did not particularly appreciate.

Else was good to them though and did her best to win them over. Her background was cosmopolitan in the extreme. It was hard for me to believe, seeing her in her present circumstances, but she had been an actress of some success before WWII, married her Director, some 29 years older than she, and had lived in notable affluence prior to the war. One day after she and I had become better acquainted, she pulled out her scrapbook full of photos and memorabilia from her days as an actress. I was truly dumbfounded when I saw how really strikingly beautiful she had been as a young woman, as well as an actress of noteworthy accomplishment. She described to me their home in Oslo, the walls covered with French impressionist artworks, the life they led before the war, the parties they threw, the drinking they did, the art world they moved in, and it all sounded very avant-garde and glamorous.

But the war had come and with it the German occupation of Norway, the closing of the theaters, two of which her husband owned, and the struggle to raise her three children during that time. The occupation lasted the better part of five years, and times were very difficult with countless shortages of food, clothing, fuel and many necessities of life. A few years after the war ended her husband died leaving her in the unaccustomed position of dealing with the family finances, a job she was remarkably unready for. She explained to me that when she needed a little more money she just took a painting off the wall and sold it, until one day there were no more pictures to sell and her accountant confirmed that she was broke and would have to get a job.

I'm sure all of this was most difficult for her since she could not get over thinking of herself as an intellectual aristocratic grand dame. But facts were facts and she decided to come to British Columbia where her son was, taking a housekeeping job with the family in Vancouver that owned the Vancouver Sun newspaper. Even though she was reduced to becoming a housekeeper she never ceased to express opinions or make comments that let me know that she tended to look down her nose at how life was carried on in our rural valley. But I understood how much she needed to hang on to some of her past and was never offended by her more denigrating comments.

Once again we settled into a routine that carried over the winter, and as Else and I got to know each other, she began to talk to me about her eldest daughter, who was recently divorced from her husband, the leading pop singer in Norway. She had pictures of her children and this daughter was very nice looking and I could tell that Else was rather openly trying her best to play matchmaker. I was not yet ready to entertain such a proposition and conjured up a picture of Else and her daughter taking over the management of me and my children. Her other daughter was a different matter altogether. She was drop dead beautiful, single, and had gone to Sweden as a movie starlet. I rationalized that with the youngest one as a mate, I might be able to put up with Else's histrionics, but she made it clear that only the eldest was suitable for me, a pronouncement I took with somewhat poor grace.

During this period the ranch was building a reputation among the buyers in Alberta, I was running the Rodeo Association and competing, getting more time in the airplane, and still was working long hours on the ranch. I was definitely not gaining weight. David was returned to me so all five children were together, and other than me being alone and running around, Life was good. But during this new chapter in my life I had drifted to my more wild, testosterone driven side, and was taking more chances, being less discreet and more emboldened in my actions.

One night I was working on making out with a young woman who asked me to go buy us some beer. Down to the Whitehouse Bar in the Windermere Hotel I hurried and when I entered saw it was chockablock full of Indians from the Kootenay Reserve, most of whom I knew well. I bought six bottles of beer at the counter and on the way out was called over to a corner table near the door by several Indians who worked for me off and on. I wanted to get out the door as fast as I could to get back to the real business of the night, but I also did not want to hurt their feelings, so I sat down with them still clutching my bag of beer.

While I was talking with them, a young Indian named Michael Michel walked over and made some comment to me and at the same time leaned forward and slowly swung his hand across the table and lightly slapped me open-handed on the side of my face. Everyone in the place saw this mock insult and without even thinking, and in the best Lonnie Austin style, I came out of my chair and in a single movement, dropping the bag of bottles from my right hand where several shattered on the floor, came up full force and hit him straight in the jaw. The blow sent Michael reeling backwards, where, in the classic tradition of a western movie bar fight, he slammed into a table in the center of the room that went down in a crash, along with him and several others sitting there, beer and broken glass all over the place.

The bartender let out a roar and jumped from behind his counter at the same instant all of the Indians in the place sprang to their feet, shouting and waving their arms, clamoring to fight me. Michael, unable to get up, crawled towards me on his hands and knees, still shaking off the blow determined to redeem himself in front of all his friends and relatives. I just stood still waiting for whatever was next and Michael arrived at my feet about the same time the bartender did. The bartender, whom I knew well, trying to stop an impending free for all, pushed Michael away, who was then using my legs to climb to a standing position to better continue his comeback effort, and ushered me out the swinging doors holding my sack and remaining bottles of beer, to the sound of multiple threats shouted at my back. Nothing more was heard from any Indians about this altercation and the next time I saw Michael he was friendly as could be.

This behavior was not at all normal for me since I would go a long way to avoid a fist fight and truth be told I did not want to continue the brawl in the pub with Michael. But I went back to the ranch with a certain heightened sense of machismo countered only by a feeling that I could have just swallowed my pride and walked away instead of hitting out. I badly needed the calming hand of a good woman.

One good woman I knew was Suzanne, and as my interest in her continued to grow over the fall I stopped in to see her and her parents several times when in Calgary on ranch business. Right after Christmas, Suzanne graduated from Mt. Royal College and took a job as a nanny with Maryann and Jack Fleck who rented two houses on the ranch as headquarters for his Emerald Christmas Tree Company. They had met Suzanne when she worked for me and persuaded her to go to their home in Bellevue for the winter, then staying with them at the ranch until she went on to college the next fall. I was able to visit Suzanne once on a winter trip to Seattle and was able to see her often in the evenings after our work was done when she returned to the ranch with the Flecks. We finally realized that our feelings were the real thing and I proposed getting married and she agreed. We knew it was going to be a tough sell, but we drove to Calgary and made our case with her parents.

They were properly aghast at the thought of their 19 year-old daughter marrying a man not only almost eleven years older, but also the father of five children. Not exactly what most parents want for their daughters. After much discussion, and I can only dimly imagine what the family meetings were like for Suzanne when I was not around, I very reluctantly agreed with them that Suzanne should go off to Washington State College for her freshman year. It was understood that if Suzanne still felt like getting married after being away from me for the school year, they would not stand in the way. Of course, they assumed that once at WSC she would meet many other young men and the idea of marrying the boss of the largest ranch in the valley would fade away. I also thought this was a high probability, but it was the only fair thing to do for Suzanne, although I hated every minute she was away in what I considered to be a world of temptations, if not a den of iniquity.

With the possibility marriage coming nearer I began to focus on what I could do to improve my financial position. During the early spring Jack Fleck and I talked about a venture he was interested in starting in Mexico with a business acquaintance of his and he asked if I would like to join in with them, even as a minor partner. It appeared to me that Mexico might provide the opportunity to get rich as we would be going in on the ground floor in a huge agricultural exporting industry starting up there. I agreed and later in the spring Jack, Mike and I flew to Mexico City to sign a partnership agreement between Cornucopia S.A. de C.V., our new company, and a Mexican company that would share in the venture. I also began thinking about what I could do with the ranch to change the business model to increase revenue as well as my salary. All of this was consuming my mental energies at the same time I was worrying about my relationship with Suzanne.

By then I was truly committed to her, my running around came to an abrupt halt, but my jealousy at the thought of all those other men around her grew into a huge cloud hovering always close at hand. I knew WSC, the fun and games that went on there and I was almost beside myself if I called at night and she was not there to answer. This feeling grew over the school year and I doubt that our relationship could have survived even one more quarter apart. But finally she was home, still feeling our mutual commitment to each other was intact and we began to prepare for the marriage. My idea was to get straight to any Justice of The Peace and get married with no fanfare, but of course, Suzanne and her mother would have none of that nonsense.

Our wedding was planned for June 18th, in Calgary, but several weeks before the big event we had to get a marriage license and find a minister who would marry us. Suzanne and her family were members of the Anglican Church with its notoriously tough position on divorce. We met with the Minister one afternoon who ushered us into his small office where he began to fill out the necessary forms. In questioning us it naturally came out that I was 30 years old, while Suzanne was 19, and I was divorced with five children. I could see his growing discomfort and then he asked me about my religious affiliations. I told him about my Episcopal confirmation at age twelve, and singing in the choir, and then, instead of keeping my mouth shut, but wanting to be very honest, said, "But I don't believe much of what I was taught and am not active in the church."

With that, he dropped his pen and clasped his hands in front of him and said to us in a very pious manner, "You know, God, at this very moment, is more real to me in this room than you are, and under these circumstances I cannot in good conscience perform this marriage." This was a big blow to Suzanne, although she already knew the heathen I was, but for me I could not believe the nonsense I had heard the minister say. I stood up, forced a, "Thank you for your trouble," and we walked out into the sunlight. I was furious, and was determined not to go through such an episode again. Suzanne wanted to try one more time and suggested we go to a nearby Unitarian Church she knew, a more liberal sect by far, but she did not know the minister. I said, "Okay, but only one more try, if they won't do it we get married in a civil ceremony at your city hall."

The United Church Minister was younger and I immediately had a glimmer of hope. He turned out to be a very nice and understanding man who said he would be happy to marry us. We acquired our license and on the eighteenth of June, with both families and many friends, and with all of my children in attendance, we were married. Christine and Guy Blake put on a fine reception, complete with large meal and many toasts to Suzanne's and my future good fortune and we left in my 1956 Mercury 2-door hardtop for a week's honeymoon at Lake Louise in the Canadian Rockies. I'll never forget our arrival at Chateau Lake Louise when we entered the lobby around five o'clock in the afternoon. All the guests, mainly older folks, were seated listening to a piano concert, and we had to march in front of them with rice still falling from our hair and clothes, and obviously looking like the newlyweds we were. It was very embarrassing but funny none-the-less.

We lasted until the day before our scheduled stay was to end and then abruptly decided to head back to the ranch. I let Suzanne drive and at one point looked at the speedometer noting that she was doing 110 mph, a big smile on her face, as we tooled down the beautiful open highway towards Eisenhower Junction where the road turned west towards the Columbia Valley and her new home. Life just seemed about perfect with a new chapter about to be lived.

Suzanne and Me camping trip, Kootenay Park 1960

Once at the ranch we settled into married life. Suzanne, now stepmother to the children, began the process of building her new relationship with them. A major change was in creating a secure, steady and loving atmosphere in the home and Suzanne was gifted in this endeavor. Suzanne and I were on the same page when it came to how the children would be raised and we very seldom disagreed over such issues. She was probably more determined than I as far as making the kids perform their chores, have good manners and do what they were told. Her presence lifted a huge load of worry off my back, which allowed me focus on the job at the ranch and begin to think more long term about what I wanted to accomplish for the family. Big Sue was interested in the goings on at the ranch, relished the ranching life, the occasional horseback rides we took, the picnics in that beautiful valley and I believed everyone living on the ranch liked and respected her and enjoyed her addition to the ranch scene.

Guy Blake, Suzanne's father, became quite ill with heart trouble in that first year of our marriage, requiring a serious operation for an aortic aneurysm. He survived the operation but the problem was not completely cured and he occasionally suffered great pain. During one of Guy's and Christine's visits to the ranch he had an attack in the night and all that could be done for him was to give him an injection to control the pain. I went to their cabin, very confident of my ability to administer a shot, having done hundreds of them on heavy-hided cattle. Guy handed me the syringe with the thinnest needle I had ever seen, but when I tried to demonstrate my skill in painless injection, to my embarrassment, I immediately bent the needle at a 90° angle. He was hurting badly and not wanting to wreck the second needle he offered up, I slowly shoved the needle in, knowing that whatever pain I was inflicting paled into insignificance to what he was already suffering.

In that first year of our marriage, the only thing to mar our happiness was the worry about Suzanne's father and we drove to Calgary to see him on a few occasions but on the anniversary of our first year together, June 18, 1961, Guy passed away at age 58, not living long enough to see his granddaughter, Mary Fletcher, born four months later.

One looming family issue was the difficulty we were having in living on my salary. Trying to make ends meet each month was difficult and I began to think about my ability to stay on the ranch if I could not find something to enable me to earn more money. I was ready to look at all options, including leaving the ranch, which would be a blow to Suzanne I knew, but something had to change. The opportunity to invest in Cornucopia, to develop an agricultural business in Mexico, seemed to me to be an exciting solution to this pressing problem, and the planning continued for the startup of operations in Mexico.

Old Mexico

Wherein our hero meets some wicked pistoleros and
macho hombres, pays a mordida, and finds the beauty
of Mexico in its people, its flowers, and its pueblos.

In the early summer of 1958 a car drove through the Elkhorn Ranch gate and turned up the rise to the ranch manager's house where I was living and a man stepped out. I saw that his car carried Washington plates so assumed he was a friend of Dad or of Norton Clapp, just stopping by to say hello, but he was friend of neither, and maybe not friend to many. He introduced himself as Jack Fleck, the owner of the Emerald Christmas Tree Company. He was from Bellevue, he said, and was interested in buying the Christmas trees that were on Elkhorn Ranch property. This was a totally new idea for me as I was only dimly aware of Christmas tree cutting activity in the Columbia Valley, although each October I had seen heaps of trees at several of the tree company yards where trees were sorted by size and type for shipping to the states.

Interested in increasing the income of the ranch, I invited him in to talk about it. By the end of an hour's conversation, I had found Jack to be a very engaging person, of good humor, irreverent of most things, a total entrepreneur, rather like a used car salesman, smart as hell, always knowing what side of a deal he was on, and full of energy. He also told me he was looking for a rental home he could use each fall, but was willing to pay for one for the entire year. He had heard we had a house available, and this, probably more than the limited supply of Christmas trees on the ranch, was what had brought him to my door. (Jack was always ahead of me on any deal we did together.)

When I showed him the house he jumped on the terms I offered, leasing it for a full year. We next walked around the wooded part of the property looking at the trees, and then drove over to the Kimpton air field section we leased, to see what tree potential was there. One of Jack's pitches was long term management of the Christmas tree lands, including fertilization programs to increase yields over time. Within several weeks I had committed the Elkhorn's trees to Emerald, and in September, Jack and his wife, Mary Ann, a tall and elegant woman, moved in and set up their Canadian office on the ranch.

I got to know the Flecks very well. Jack was a bounder, a diamond in the very rough, but exceptionally quick witted and Mary Ann maintained a queenly toleration of Jack's verbal and other excesses. I found the pace of the Christmas tree business to be very fast compared to how a ranch seemed to plod along with the changing seasons. After the tree operation's first year, Jack talked to me about using our 18 foot stock truck for hauling trees out of the woods, and the proposal appealed to me as another way to make extra money for the ranch in the next tree season. So in the second year of our association, after most of the stock hauling was done in the Fall, I pulled the stock racks off the truck and began hauling trees for Emerald.

Jack and I became good friends. He was brash and loud and exuded confidence, all traits that I lacked and in a way he became an unwitting mentor for me. I watched how he operated wishing I had the balls to be more like him, but it just was not in me. On the other hand he could use people in ways I could not and it was this character trait that made many people dislike and distrust him. But he was terribly interesting to be around.

Jack was selling his trees into the southwestern United States: Texas, Southern California, Arizona, and even into Mexico. One of Jack's customers was a fresh produce business in Houston, Texas, run by his friend, Mike, who interested Jack in investing in a company to grow vegetables in Mexico for export to the States. Mike was already importing fresh produce from Mexico and saw a great opportunity to get in early in this new Mexican agricultural scene. Jack started talking to me about it, always emphasizing the huge profit potential from such a venture. The original idea was to get together with some Mexican growers in a partnership located somewhere in the state of Sinaloa, near Culiacan or Los Mochis, where the Mexicans would do the growing and we would do the selling and distribution in the States. We had many a laugh over how it was to work and if any potential money concern developed, the stock answer was "we'll plant another row of beans!" That became a phrase we used many times, and I should have recognized we would have one very huge farm if we planted all the rows of beans we joked about needing to get rich.

In the early Spring of 1960, Jack and his friend Mike put a tentative deal together with a Mexican produce company named Fruitilandia SA de CV, whose head office was located in Mexico City. However, instead of growing vegetables in Culiacan, we were going to grow cantalope and watermelon in an area of southern Michoacan, near the city of Apatzingan. Jack invited me to join their project by investing in the American marketing and distribution company they planned to form. The name of the company was to be Cornucopia, Inc. and Jack provided plenty of visions of it becoming a "horn of plenty" for investors. The logo was designed as a cornucopia horn spilling out all sorts of fruits and vegetables, but when we eager investors looked at this picture, we saw only an unstoppable flow of dollar bills spewing forth from the horn and into our pockets.

I was planning on being married for a second time that June, and wanting badly to enhance my meager financial worth, I hurried to tally up what I could possibly put into the venture. When I had looked in all crannies and emptied all pockets, so to speak, I came up with the grand total of $4000 which I took to Jack. To say he was mildly surprised at my pitiful offering would be an understatement, but since he had asked me without demanding a minimum entry level, he graciously accepted my money and invited me to go with him and Mike to Mexico City and finalize a contract with Fruitilandia. He offered to pay for my ticket, and a week later, away we went.

Mexico City was for me a wonderful experience and I was totally taken with the city. The broad boulevards, punctuated occasionally by beautifully landscaped turning circles called "glorietas," usually centered with a statue of a famous man of Mexican history, horns constantly blaring, millions of taxis, gave the impression of constant movement and energy flowing within the city. The light blue sky, colorful gardens, tall sophisticated buildings, engendered a feeling of European elegance, with people hurrying along the sunny streets, businessmen and very beautiful women with a certain vitality and pride expressed in the way they moved. And maybe most of all, the constant humming of Spanish conversation, a language of exotic rhythm and melodic expressiveness. I was excited to be there, to see and experience the city, if even for a few short days.

We met with our lawyers on an upper floor of a tall building. Their office was ponderously heavy with dark wood paneling exuding a, we got here because we are very good at what we do message, to all new clients. Our particular lawyer was an American named Sidney, who was from Texas and very bright and confident. He was also bilingual which was a necessity in putting together a deal between Mexicans who did not trust, or particularly like, Americans, and Americans, who just did not want to get screwed. Anyway, after a few sessions and many hours of work with Jack, Mike and me, a contract was signed. It was a full inch thick of fine print, perhaps with the idea that if every single possible point was covered the deal would actually work. The basic idea was that Fruitilandia would lease and prepare the land, hire the people and grow the melons, and Cornucopia would finance the payroll, sell and distribute the melons in the United States, and we would split the revenue, each getting half. We shook hands with Miguel and Ruben, representing their family business, Fruitilandia SA de CV and flew back to Canada.

In September, Jack had hired a young man he met at the Berlitz language school in Seattle on the basis that Carlos, a Colombian was naturally fluent in Spanish, and had sent him to the growing area in Apatzingan to look after our interests. This proved to not be the smartest move Jack ever made, because the Mexicans hated Carlos, who was lacking much empathy for Mexican culture and feelings, and more than once, wounded our Mexican partner's famously fragile pride. By the end of November, after investing over $100,000, including my measly piggy bank amount, we had not seen melon number one! Things appeared to be going from bad to worse as the growing season moved on, and finally Jack asked me to go down to Apatzingan to try to sort things out.

The plan was for me to take a leave from the ranch for two months after the herd was in from summer range, had undergone pregnancy testing, and all shipping of livestock to market had been finished. I would then go on the payroll of Cornucopia. I cleared this plan with Dad and Al Link, Norton's real estate investment manager. I was leaving my foreman, Phil Geiger, in charge. Phil's mother-in-law agreed to come and live in our ranch house to look after the four younger kids and with Suzanne, my freshly minted new wife and my eldest son Bill, who was 10 years old, we flew to Mexico City. Carlos picked us up and we drove the 275 miles through Morelia and Uruapan, then out of the mountains into the lowland heat and Apatzingan. We drove into the main plaza and up to the entrance of the Posada Del Sol, the only reasonable hotel in Apatzingan, to start rebuilding relations with the brothers running the melon growing for Fruitilandia and Cornucopia.

Apatzingan was a small city located in the low land west of the Sierra Madre Occidental, but inland from the coastal mountains that rose to a height of 2000 meters. It was about sixty miles from the sea, as the crow flies, in an area well suited to growing winter melons and other vegetables that could handle the rocky soil. It was hot and humid by day and warm and humid by night and the plants grew as if they liked it well. In typical Mexican fashion, the town was laid out around a square central plaza surrounded by small shops and the hotel. Different kinds of palm trees, ficus, jacaranda and bougainvillea provided shade in the plaza, pools of color contrasted against the light colored buildings, and were home to all kinds of lizards, birds and insects. The small stores and shops had roll-up steel store fronts that opened at 8 A.M., shut at noon, re-opened again at 3 or 4 P.M. and finally closed at 8 P.M. Unlike the custom in many larger cities in

Mexico, the afternoon siesta in Apatzingan was alive and well and all of the stores observed it.

The Posada del Sol, Apatzingan, Sinaloa, Mexico 1961.

The small reception desk of the Posada Del Sol, manned by the hotel manager, Felix Ocampo, was located thirty yards inside a wide foyer which was entered through a large portal from the sidewalk. Two stores, one on either side of the foyer, had rollup doors opening into the foyer, as well as onto the sidewalk outside on the plaza. One of these was a coffee shop and the local meeting place for many growers and landowners, as well as the place many men spent time at chess and baccarat. The three story hotel was built around an inner patio restaurant open to the sky. We took a room on the second floor with windows that opened towards the plaza, across the street below.

The next morning we were awakened about 4:30 A.M., long before daylight, a scene repeated every day of our stay in the Posada del Sol, by the rustling sounds of people waking up, soft voices drifting up through our window open to the plaza, indicating the beginning of a work day for the peones sleeping outside below us. Soon the two-wheeled cooking carts of the women vendors could be heard rolling into the square, followed by the aroma of tortillas and frijoles being prepared for the men, and by 5 A.M. the whole square was a cacophony of sound punctuated soon by the shifting gears of trucks arriving to load the men and take them to the fields.

Almost all of the peones wore baggy light tan cotton pantalones, white long-sleeved shirts that were cut square and never tucked in, huarachis on their feet, and a straw sombrero, clothes well suited to the hot and humid weather, and many carried serapes folded over their shoulders. I was fascinated watching the men being loaded into the flatbed trucks with their four foot stock racks, until every square foot of the truck floor had a person standing on it. No one could have fallen down, they were so tightly packed, and I often thought of the terrible scene that would follow if one of these trucks had an accident.

The days were hot, usually above 90°F, and very humid, and while the night-time temperatures might drop to around 80°F, it still remained humid. The heat was the most difficult thing to deal with and we all looked forward to the bit of cooling we felt after the sun went down. In this southern latitude dark descended suddenly like a book being closed. No lingering sunset to be seen, just a rapid transition from daylight to a gold and purple twilight, to night, and around 6 P.M. when we usually returned to the Posada del Sol from the fields or the empacadora it was well after dark. The evenings were lovely and tropical, the pace slower, the palms reflecting the light of the many shops around the town, and often the wafting sounds of a mariachi band playing near the plaza could be heard. The townspeople came outside to congregate in the plaza or to walk around enjoying the relative coolness after the hot sun-drenched day.

Since the stores stayed open until 8 P.M., many people waited until after the heat of the day to shop, and later many young people and married couples walked around the square, often with the single senoritas, most often accompanied by a dueña, going in one direction, and the younger men walking in the other direction, passing and flirting with one another as they circled the plaza. On the sidewalk, sitting with their backs to the now closed store fronts, were the *peones* back from the day's labor in the fields, with the vendors always nearby to feed them. Later on in the evening, these men would wrap up in their serapes, slide down full length across the wide concrete sidewalks, lying side by side around the plaza and along the streets that led into the plaza, sleeping with their heads next to the steel rollup doors of the shops, like giant burritos in an almost endless row.

In those days it was thought that there were only two kinds of girls in Mexico. This was especially so in a rural town like Apatzingan. The good ones had eagle eyed parents or a dueña with them constantly, and the other kind were plentiful in the many cantinas in town. No women wore pants and especially not shorts. At the local public park and outdoor swimming pool there were no bikinis, only full bathing suits. When a girl was out of the water, she was always wrapped in a large towel. This made getting into the water an interesting project. The young women would sit on the side of the pool and sort of slither into the water, shedding towels like a snake might shed his skin. It was a slow wriggling ballet. Once in the water it seemed all concern about appearance was gone and they just had fun playing in the pool.

Mexico is a Catholic country, but it seemed to me that this affected the women much more than the men. I could understand why women might require the solace of religion, since they were forced to live in a very male dominated society. Machoism was an important attribute of Mexican males, and this in part was why the men were so delighted when their wives produced an offspring, especially a male child, and is one of many reasons for the rapid population growth rates in Mexico. This was aided by Church doctrine of course. Every population center, even the tiniest town, had a church. In Apatzingan, the church was a block from the plaza, and we could see its tall spires from quite a distance. It was different though in one major component: it had no roof. Evidently it was a work in progress, but while I was there over two years I never saw any work being done. I drove past this church many days in the very early morning, just after daylight, and never once failed to see a few old women dressed in black, sitting in the pews, alone, with their black mantillas covering their heads, in solemn prayer. The scene seemed to exude a fume of resignation and sadness.

picking cantaloupe near Apatzingan

The melon fields were often quite distant from town and the unsurfaced roads off the highway were rough, winding and rocky and wound through low undulating country covered with scrub trees, brush and low cactus. The fields of rocky soil were located near a source of water for irrigation. Once the land was cleared, thatched roofed open storage rooms were erected for tools and chemicals, and another palm frond covered lean-to served as a residence for a watchman or guard. Once the field was planted, a few women set up cooking areas under other thatched roofs, to make tortillas, frijolis, y arroz, to sell to the 'peones' who did the work. The workers' jobs were split into three main categories; the field laborer, or peon; a fumagador, the worker that applied chemicals to the plants and was paid a bit more than a peon; and the irrigador, paid the highest, was responsible for managing the surface irrigation of the crop. Some of the men stayed at the field continually, but others went into town after work where they were picked up each morning and returned to the fields around 6 A.M.

The first thing I noticed at breakfast the day after our arrival in the hotel was that many men were carrying pistols in holsters attached to their belts. An important man, a large grower or landowner, had an armed pistolero with him as a guard. Apatzingan, it seemed, was a very "Western" place, and it turned out that the guns were not always for show. One reason some of the men were armed was that in those days the 'raya,' or payroll, was paid in cash rather than with checks because almost none of the workers could sign their names to a check, or get it cashed even if they could. This meant that every Friday morning Carlos and I went into the bank with the payroll numbers and walked out with two canvas bags of real money. This we had to transport out through the boondocks to the fields where the men were to be paid at the end of each week. We carried a pistol in the car, but it would have been a simple thing for just a few people to rob us. Although we felt a little concern about our safety, I never heard of a payroll being taken. Perhaps the reason for this was that justice was rather swift in southern Michoacan back then, and a theft would probably end up with the bandido getting shot rather than taken to trial in Morelia. Nevertheless, a payroll must have been a temptation since the prevailing wage was 12 pesos per day, or about ten cents per hour. One payroll must have been worth a year's pay to a farm laborer.

We parked our car directly in front of the Posada del Sol, and the day after our arrival, a small, 13 year old Mexican youngster named Enrique approached me and asked if he could guard our car. I said he could if he would wash the windows each morning and I agreed to pay him. Enrique stayed nearby, or in the car, all night. He was a budding entrepreneur to say the least, and always had some gimmick to offer me in exchange for a few pesos. One morning when I came outside the hotel, Enrique approached me with a major grin on his face and extended one hand curled into a fist with the palm up. I asked what he had and with great delight he opened his hand and there sat a small scorpion with its tail right up in the air ready to sting. Enrique laughed and a moment later he popped the bug into his mouth and closed his lips. I was aghast at this spectacle! He then opened his mouth and stuck his tongue out and there was the scorpion standing in the middle of his tongue poised to strike. With that he grabbed the scorpion with his fingers and held it out for me to take, an opportunity I found very easy to forego. Enrique, who had enjoyed himself immensely, then showed me that he had pinched off the tip of the tail where the stinger was, but even this new evidence did nothing to move me to take the scorpion in my hand. I had a good laugh and gave Enrique five pesos for his wonderful circus act.

Although one of the problems with the melon venture was poor relations between the Fruitilandia people and our manager, Carlos; it was also apparent that the payroll was stacked with a myriad of cousins, uncles, nephews, and shirt-tail relatives of the family owners of Fruitilandia, brought in from all over Mexico to participate in the Gringo's payroll. After a few weeks I was able to get things smoothed out a bit, and more melons began arriving into the packing shed where Fruitilandia was grading and packing the melons before shipment. As the season moved on, more and more melons were being harvested, packed and shipped to Laredo, where Jack Fleck had his sales office. We were still financially underwater though, and I was sure that some of the crop was continuously being sold out the back of the field to other buyers who were congregating in Apatzingan as the main part of the crop came in. These clandestine sales generally occurred during the night, with a buyer's truck being loading up and cash exchanging hands right then.

One morning I went to a field with one of the Fruitilandia men, a relative of some sort, and as we inspected the harvesting operations, he said, "I was offered $10,000 pesos to kill Carlos, but then we decided not to do it." I asked why they would want to do such a thing under any circumstances, and he said, "We didn't like him and he made things more difficult with all his questions and interfer-ence." As we continued talking, I tried to explain that we all could do well if we worked together instead of trying to get an advantage over one another. I told him that we believed melons were being sold to other buyers, breaking our agree-ment and creating a feeling of distrust. I think this conversation made clear to him our concerns and I am sure that it was passed on to the Fruitilandia owners.

We still felt very insecure, believing that our partners not only had "put it to us" but would find it even more to their advantage to divert melons to other buy-ers as the harvest increased. I spent my time trying to build the relationship, and perhaps in some ways I did help, but when I left at the end of February, I felt there was still a chasm of distrust between us and Fruitilandia. I was sure they would try to take advantage of us any way they could, and perhaps this made them feel some concern about getting paid, since the sales revenue came first to Cornucopia in Texas. To assure Fruitilandia was receiving its proper share of the revenue stream, Ruben was sent to Laredo to verify all invoices and payments.

When Suzanne, Bill and I headed back to the ranch, Carlos, his wife, and Walter, a Canadian youngster working for Jack, were still in Apatzingan to see the final melons shipped. Jack told me we were down about $60,000 dollars at the time the last eight carloads, fully loaded and iced, rolled out of Apatzingan headed north. He was determined to see these get to Laredo as it was our last chance to ensure that Fruitilandia share some of the loss with us. Relations had gotten so testy Jack was very concerned that the Mexicans might try to divert these cars to another destination. But several days later, when they passed north of Hermosillo, it was assured they would cross the border into Texas.

It was then Jack, determined to use the leverage of the revenue from the last shipments in making the final settlement with Fruitilandia, called Carlos and told him to pack up and get the three of them out of town without anyone knowing. So at 2 A.M. they quietly loaded their car and took off for Uruapan and parts north. When they had gone about fifteen Kilometers, the rear view mirror showed lights from another car coming up fast behind. It caught up to them, followed very close for a minute and then pulled out to pass. When it was beside them, a man, gesturing with a pistol in his hand, motioned them to the side of the road. At this point Carlos, his wife, and Walter were kidnapped at gunpoint by several men hired by Fruitilandia, taken back to town and held under tight security.

The next morning in Laredo, Ruben came into Cornucopia Inc.'s headquarters with a pistol in his hand, walked into Jack's office and over to his desk and while waving the pistol in Jack's face said, "We've got your people, and we intend to kill them if we don't get paid." According to Jack, he just looked a long time into Ruben's eyes and then casually said, "Well, go ahead and kill them, but then you get nothing!" Jack was not easily intimidated, especially when it was someone else's life at stake. This, I think is called a "Mexican standoff" and it was hardball on each side, with repercussions that would reach into the next year. After five days our people were let go. In the meantime, Jack sold the melons and when the money came in we held out from Fruitilandia's share what he felt was a fair amount to cover the excess payroll and stealing that had gone on. We still lost around $30,000 on our first venture in Mexico.

In spite of the difficulties, including the loss of money, I began to think of how I might spend my summers managing the ranch in Canada, and my winters in Mexico, managing Cornucopia's operations. This lifestyle idea very much appealed to me and seemed to hold promise of a chance to vastly increase my income, if only we could figure out how to get things right in the produce business. We were sure of one thing though. We would not ever go into another growing partnership with Mexicans we did not know and would have to find another way to get into the Mexican fruit and vegetable export business.

The following year, Jack and Mike decided to expand the operations of Cornucopia Inc. to include strawberries with the melons. This meant the season would be lengthened several months as well, and Jack asked if I would go to Mexico for six months to manage the procurement and shipping of strawberries, and when that was finished, go back to Apatzingan where a deal had been put together with an empacadora to buy all of the melons brought by the farmers to the packing shed that graded U.S. #1 or #2. And I was to do the grading. This was a cleaner deal, and without a growing risk. We would pay for what we got. I was very excited to get back to Mexico, but this time I would be taking the whole family. Suzanne was expecting a baby in mid October, so we settled on leaving around the first of November, to return in April. Cornucopia would pay the rent of a house in Mexico City, and all company expenses, and we would pay our personal costs.

During the summer of 1961 I found my thoughts more and more turned to a life other than ranching. I was a bit burned out from the work load, a bit bored by the lack of cultural opportunity, a bit worried about the kids' schooling, and very concerned about where I was going financially. I began to visualize myself at the end of a ranching career with no retirement plan other than the possibility of having half the ranch passed on to me, and even this was not a slamdunk since Dad had a partner and many things could occur that might eliminate that potential. I needed a way to earn more money at the ranch and began to think how that might be accomplished, but in the interim, the opportunity in Mexico was welcome.

We drove our hand-me-down station wagon from the ranch in Canada to Mexico City, where we took a couple of rooms in the old Geneve hotel, in the Zona Rosa, the tourist shopping center in the city. We began immediately to search for a rental house. Jack had a contact in the city named Joe Gutirrez, who was being paid for services rendered to Cornucopia Inc., including helping me in any way I needed. He was a very nice person who worked for the Missouri Pacific railroad, and since we anticipated all the rail cars loaded in Apatzingan would be shipped through them, he was happy to help. Joe advised us to look in the San Angel area out on Boulevard Insurgentes near the University, which we did, and found Elena Braniff, an eccentric and aristocratic woman who happened to have a home for rent. It had a walled in garden with broken glass imbedded into the top layer of cement, a wrought iron gate complete with padlock, and three stories of bedrooms and baths. It was perfect for us and we took a six month lease.

We hired two young sisters as housekeepers, and an Indian woman, Maria, to help with the children and cooking. We enrolled the oldest four children into the American School, which entailed taking them back and forth from home each day. Suzanne had her hands more than full with all the children and our baby, Fletcher. The kids seemed to thrive in the new environment, and as they lost their fear of meeting other Mexican children when playing outside, were soon running all around the neighborhood. There was lots to see and do in Mexico City and we used our Sundays to visit the many museums and the big archaeo- logical site near the city at Teotihuacan. Mexico City was beautiful at night as Christmas approached, with lights festooned everywhere, and the Boulevard Paseo de Reforma was like a multicolored lighted river drawing us into the heart of the city.

The strawberry growing area was northwest of Mexico City about 350 km. near Irapuato. Another young man, hired by Cornucopia, had been sent down from Texas to watch the harvesting of the berries in Irapuato throughout the sea- son. He had little experience in handling produce as fragile as stawberries, there- fore I made quite a few trips to Irapuato myself, sometimes staying for a few days, while we organized the picking and handling of the berries. Later on, I went to check the quality of the berries being picked and ensure that they were kept cold until they reached the Mexico City airport for shipping.

I spent the first three months working out of our home in San Angel. My operational job was to manage the airfreight shipping of the strawberries. Most of the time I was at the Mexico City airport reserving space on jets flying to the east coast of the United States, verifying ETA's at the destination points, organizing shipping manifests and export documents, making sure the loads were organized as per the customer orders which came to me from the Laredo office, and check- ing on how the product was handled from arrival to departure. This included supervising the handling and loading of the planes and often to help with the loading, which was done by hand, this before the time of wide body containers that could be packed in a warehouse and then transported to the jets. There were a few times when we heard back from our buyer, that the product looked more like strawberry jam when it arrived at its destination, due to luggage falling on the boxes.

One day while I was at an airplane helping to load, a very large man approached me, flashed an immigration badge, and asked for my passport and work permit. I handed him my passport but all I had was a tourist card to go with it. He looked at them and then at me, and as he pocketed my documents, said, "You're in a lot of trouble. You cannot work in Mexico without a work permit. It is against our law. You have to come downtown with me now. You will be expelled from the country!" I couldn't believe my ears. I could not leave the family alone in Mexico, but he was rapidly walking me out towards the parking lot. At one point in this march to destruction, we passed a bank of telephones and I said, "I have to make a call before I go another step!" He said to make it fast and I grabbed the phone and called Sydney, our lawyer at Goodrich, Dalton. By some miracle he was there and I told him my predicament. Sidney said, "I need to talk to the man, so put him on", and I handed the phone to him. I did not hear what was said between them, but when the phone was handed back, Sidney said, "You are coming down here to the office. I'll be waiting."

When we announced ourselves in the waiting room at Goodrich, Dalton & Requelme, Sidney and a Mexican lawyer greeted us, and Sidney took me into his office, while the other lawyer took the official with him. I sat down and said, "What's going on Sidney?" He answered, "Just wait a minute and you'll know." In a few minutes the phone rang and Sidney listened and then wrote something on a notepad. He handed it to me and it was the number 1500. I looked at Sidney, not understanding, and he said, "You are paying a mordida of 1500 pesos, and you will be off the hook, and free to go." The money was paid then and there, and I walked out a free man, went back to working at the airport, and was never bothered again. This was my first experience with the mordida system which at that time was endemic in Mexico. It was very common within the customs, immigration and police officialdom, and permeated the whole society as well. It allowed the wealthy to get away with almost anything. This type of corruption was promulgated by the very low salaries and wages paid to bureaucrats at all levels.

The strawberry business went quite well. Cornucopia was possibly the first produce company to use the new Boeing 707 jets serving Mexico City for moving perishable commodities quickly to distant destinations, such as New York, Chicago, Boston and Philadelphia. Of course, occasionally the weather interrupted our perfect plans, and a shipment once landed in Halifax instead of Boston due to inclement weather. I doubt Canadians, in 1961, had ever before seen a fresh strawberry in December, which must have created quite a stir.

When the melon crop started to come in I had to leave Mexico City and the family to work in Apatzingan. Walter, the 20 year old Canadian boy, still working for Jack even after being kidnapped the year before, drove to Mexico city and then the two of us went in the Cornucopia Volkswagen bus to Apatzingan, where we had arranged a very different system from the prior year. This season we would buy all the #1 and #2 grade melons coming into an empacadora owned by Adolpho Barrigan. I would grade the melons, and when I was away, Walter would do the grading for me. In this way we avoided the growing risks, and having partners that could steal from us. We would visit fields of various growers to verify quality prior to picking and help convince growers to use Adolpho's packing plant.

Adolpho was a man of 55 years, not too tall, round faced and slightly rotund, with hair just turning to silver. He had a friendly countenance and demeanor, and I liked him immediately. He became my mentor, and one morning after my first two weeks in Apatzingan, he said to me, "Guillermo, I am no longer going to speak in English with you, we are going to converse in Español! Esta Bien?" This surprised me but he explained that the sooner I began to use Spanish full time, the quicker I would learn the language. In this he was very perceptive and I understood he was doing me a favor because he liked me and we were getting along very well together. He actually reverted to English when he was telling me a complicated story or just chatting at a meal, but we tried to do all business discussions in Spanish.

I enjoyed my time in Apatzingan, except for the length of time between my visits back to Mexico City to see the family. This could be as long as three weeks, as it was a 300 mile drive, unless I flew with the small twin Beechcraft G17 that made trips between the two cities. In the interim, Suzanne's widowed mother, Christine Blake, came to stay with Suzanne and the kids in Mexico City which was a huge help to Suzanne struggling with five children and a new baby. Maria, in an effort to help Suzanne and show her the proper Indian method of handling a baby, insisted on wrapping Fletcher up with her arms at her sides so they were totally immobile. Fletcher surprisingly took this in stride, and made no struggles to free her arms. She was trussed up like a mummy when her grandmother arrived, who took one look at that situation and immediately unraveled the baby from her cocoon, clucking at how awfully she was being treated and that ALL babies had to wave their arms about in order to grow right! Only Maria was unhappy about this turn of events.

packing shed scene; packing crates with melons

packing shed scene; loading rail cars.

One day Adolpho told me about a strike going on at one of the other empaca-doras. I could see men lying around doing nothing, but all seemed calm. He told me that there had been occasional labor trouble because there were several unions vying to represent each packing plant. I asked what kind of trouble he had seen, and how the unions tried to organize. He said the last big struggle had been set-tled with guns and knives. The workers of one empacadora simply attacked the workers in the one they wanted to take over. Adolpho said men were killed in the melee that ensued.

The packing plants were located in a line, each separated from the next by at least 100 yards, and all located alongside the railway siding where cars were placed for loading. The plants were mostly open sided steel frame sheds with high ceilings in which a variety of activities were carried out. The melons were packed in wooden crates assembled from stacks of precut wood pieces. It was a regular manufacturing line, starting at the stacks of wood and ending at the packer's table. The packers were men of all ages, who filled the crates with melons of dif-ferent sizes. There were, for example, 24, 36, and 45 packs, based on how many melons of a certain size could be put into a single standard crate. The packers worked next to the bins that held the graded melons rolling off the three grading belts ten feet above the packing area.

The melons were delivered from the field in trucks which unloaded into a holding bin at one end of the three grading belts moving to my right as I faced the first belt. When the door was lifted from the bin the melons began to roll onto the #1 grade belt. The #2 belt was close enough so that I could easily place a melon on it, and the #3 grade belt, on the far side of the #2 belt, was in range to toss a melon from where I stood grading. I was after a top quality pack, and I graded pretty tough. Most of the time I graded a grower's melons without the grower being there, but there were several who always watched me grade to make sure I did not downgrade his melons too much.

After several weeks grading in the packing plant, Miguel, one of the growers, a 40 year old, well built man with a big Mexican mustache, who always watched his melons being graded, took his usual place ten feet down the belt from me. Just before the melons were to start down the belt, with a great theatrical flourish, he pulled out his pistol, an awesome automatic, and laid it on the wooden frame between himself and the #1 belt. Everyone in the plant saw this gesture, and all were waiting to see what would happen. I suspect it wasn't often that a gringo was being intimidated in front of them, and it certainly broke the monotony of their work that morning, as it did mine.

Miguel lived near Nueva Italia, a little town 40 Kilometers outside Apatzingan, on the road to Uruapan. Nueva Italia had been a huge hacienda owned by a wealthy family, but was broken up by President Cardenas in a program of land redistribution, becoming one of many small pueblos to arise around the country from this process. A cantina and bar were built along the highway and several weeks earlier, Miguel had gotten muy borracho and for the fun of it had pulled his famous pistol and shot out all the glass behind the bar. He was duly apprehended for this rowdiness and thrown in jail until he sobered up, then paid his mordida and walked away. I liked him because he exuded a certain energy, had an easy smile, and was reasonably friendly, except when I graded his melons. He felt I graded too tough, begrudged my throwing any of his melons off the #1 belt, and scowled the whole time his melons were being graded.

All eyes were surreptitiously on me as the melons started to roll. After a few minutes of grading I took a melon off the #1 belt and put it on the #2 belt, but when it got in front of Miguel, he nonchalantly picked it off the #2 belt and put it back on the #1 belt. This was it! The test I had anticipated coming some day had arrived, and I if I did not handle it well, the consequence would be losing my ability to get the grade we needed from then on. My mind exploded with the realization I had to act. I didn't know what to do, and Miguel said not a word, acted like everything was just fine, looking straight out over the people working in the plant, but with a slightly supercilious smile on his face.

It seemed like an hour, but in a few seconds an inspiration came to me. I stepped off my grading platform, went past Miguel and caught up to the offending melon twenty feet farther on, and chucked it into the #3's. With that, everyone laughed and let out a collective breath, and I walked as calmly as I could back to my position and started grading. I never looked at Miguel, except from the corner of my eye, as I needed to know when to duck if he was planning to shoot me, which I greatly doubted. A few minutes later he put the gun away and it never came out again. I knew for certain I had passed an important test and when I told Adolpho, he thought the whole thing extremely hilarious. Actually I did too, but only after it was over.

I was reminded of an interesting incident when Suzanne, Bill and I were on our way back to the States the year before. We had stopped for a late lunch in a hotel in Uruapan and the only other people eating in the large dining area were two families sharing a long table. The two husbands were at either end of the table, and the wives and many children were seated along the sides. When they were finished the waiter handed la cuenta to one of the men to be paid. The other husband said, "No, yo pago," (I'm paying). The other replied, "No YO pago!"

and after several more 'yo pagos' from each of them, at ever increasing volume, they both jumped to their feet and were soon shouting at the top of their voices, "No! YO PAGO!" The wives and the kids reacted like they were at a tennis match as they turned their collectives heads trying to watch the 'yo pagos' flying back and forth, as the two males became really heated up. I felt it was fortunate that neither carried a gun, as it looked to us that things were fast getting out of hand. Suzanne and I were amazed at this spectacle of machoism, and it must have ruined the nice time the two families had been having. The Mexican male pride was a thing to behold when it was challenged, and was the cause of many unfortunate actions with really awful outcomes.

However, most of my days in Apatzingan were full of grading melons when the trucks arrived with a load, trying to stay cool when there was no air conditioning in any of the buildings, taking meals in the hotel, meeting with Aldolpho, and buying a wonderful concoction made from shaved ice, any fresh fruit you desired, and sugar syrup, all blended into a fabulous cooling drink, thick as a shake.

One afternoon I came back to the hotel and saw that there were two gendarmes with rifles standing one on either side of the entrance to the foyer, and another inside near the front desk. I asked Felix, the manager, what was up, and he told me that two men had engaged in a duel with pistols, right in the foyer. They got into a dispute, maybe over a game, as they had been together in the coffee shop when things erupted. One had been struck and knocked down, but got up and ran out through the kitchen, and the other had not been hit. Muy machismo!

Walter and I occasionally went to a cantina on a weekend evening, for a drink and to watch the scene. There was always wild, loud music, some dancing and a pretty girl trying to sit on our laps every two minutes. It was a place a man could get into a lot of trouble and I tried hard to have fun without the trouble. It was like a great Western movie scene, really outrageous and fun to have a margarita and watch all the action. I could see how things could get out of hand pretty easily in that atmosphere, and it did with one of the managers of another empacadora. He was a big, burly, laughing young man, about 35 years old, with lots of black hair and a swarthy complexion, noted for his wildness, drinking and whoring around. He was in a cantina one night drinking, and got into a row with one of his employees from the packing shed who happened to be there and was very drunk, and ended up shooting the man in the cantina.

I did not witness this piece of Apatzingan history, but the shooter also had a room across the hall from our room, and when I got to the hotel, there were two armed guards at the bottom of the wide steps leading upstairs, and two more men outside his room. The empacadora manager kept to his room until his brother arrived from Mexico City to try and sort things out. Felix confided to me that the newly arrived brother was the smart one of a fairly prestigious family, whereas the brother sent off to manage the packing operation in Apatzingan was the black sheep of the family. This I could believe. The manager was quickly smuggled out of town to Mexico City, while the remaining brother stayed to attempt a financial settlement the family of the wounded man could accept. Ultimately, after a week of negotiations, a deal was struck, and the manager returned to his job.

One day in a field of melons with the brother who had come from Mexico City to settle the shooting, I was talking with him about the incident and I posed the question to him, "If it had been your brother that was shot and badly wounded or killed, how would you deal with the person that did it?" He was a University of Mexico graduate, and an intelligent businessman, but he answered simply, "I would have had to kill him, that's our way." This episode showed me just how deep the machismo culture ran.

I had become a friend of Blair Doig, a 60-year-old Californian, manager of a large melon growing and packing operation outside Apatzingan. We met one morning in the coffee shop and he told me they had lost one of their irregadores during the prior night. Asked what that meant, he explained a field worker had found the body of the man, but without its head, which they finally found about 100 feet away. Someone had used a machete to do the deed. When I asked Blair why this happened he speculated that it probably was a family feud or vendetta, or love triangle of some sort. This was long before drugs became the major reason for bloodshed. Like most of the shootings, nothing was ever heard about a trial or a sentencing of the perpetrator. It seemed that the families settled such disputes in their own ways.

During one period of two weeks I tallied 14 killings or shootings. It was really Western, like in the movies, but nevertheless I felt relatively safe. I did wonder about one thing, which was that Jack Fleck refused to come to Apatzingan in that second year. Instead, he would call and arrange for me to drive to Uruapan to meet with him. The reason for this became very clear to me one night when I came back from the packing plant. As I pulled up to the front of the hotel, right in the middle of town with many people around, I looked up from the car to see Walter standing on the elevated sidewalk with a 45 cal. automatic shoved into his chest. Attached to the fist that held the gun, was one of the pistoleros that the Fruitilandia people had used the year before. He was a large man and very drunk. Walter's eyes were big and round in his white face as I got out of the car. Walter was my responsibility to get home to his mother in one piece, and much as I didn't want to do it, I climbed up the two high steps from the street to the sidewalk, which put me right next to Walter, and asked the pistolero, "Que es su problema? Que paso? Por que habla con mi amigo, el es solamente un muchacho?"

With those words nothing changed in the drunken pistol holder's expression, but the gun was now poked into my chest instead of Walter's. A 45 cal. muzzle looks to be an inch in diameter when it is pointed at you; just huge, and I knew very well what could happen if by accident it went off. He started talking as he listed from side to side, as if he were standing up in a canoe, and in a drunken doggerel said, "I'm gonna kill me a gringo … I wanna kill a gringo…. got beat up in Eagle Pass…. dumped across border…. fucking pendejos … no one do that me…. damn cabrones … I'll get them…. what they did me…. gonna kill that sonavabeech Jack Fleck…. paid $10,000 pesos … he comes to town…. I get him….", and on and on. I just kept talking to him and I finally got it into his drunken head that, one, I was not Jack Fleck, two, I liked Mexicans, and three, we could talk about it in the morning when he was sober. Finally he put the gun back in its holster, and lurched slowly away down the sidewalk.

Walter was very shaken by the whole incident, so after washing up I suggested we go around the corner and have a hot chocolate before turning in. The little café was run by a grandmotherly looking woman helped by a young daughter. There were three booths on each side against the walls, with the kitchen in the back. We walked in and took the first booth on the right, with Walter looking out to the street and my back to the door. We ordered our chocolate, always laced with cinnamon and crème which tasted great, and a few minutes later we were enjoying ourselves and laughing about our recent experience. When about half done, I saw the look on Walter's face change as the door opened and in stepped the same *pistolero*, but this time with a partner. They went past our booth and sat down on the other side, next to the kitchen counter. The *pistolero* had not seen us, but sat with his back to the kitchen facing me, and when he finally looked up and saw me, he reached down and drew the pistol which he aimed right at me and said, "Vaya gringos! Y pronto!"

With that, Walter jumped up to go but I caught his belt and said, "Sit down, we'll go when we choose, so finish your chocolate, or we'll be run out of town by this jerk." To the man with the gun I answered, "Si señor, en una momento cuando nuestros chocolate estan terminado." Seeing some obstinance in that reply, the pistolero repeated his order, accentuating it by cocking the hammer back and then pulling the trigger. There was a click, and I think I levitated a bit in my seat as the hammer was stopped by the safety. By then I was pretty sure he was not going to shoot us or he would have already done so, but he continued to amuse himself with cocking and pulling the trigger with the pistol all the time pointed at us and I was worried that in his drunkenness he might just make a mistake and either Walter or I would have a hell of a hole in us. We drank the last half of the chocolate faster than the first half, paid the bill and with a final "Muchas gracias y Buenos noche," to the proprietress, we left, grateful to once again have survived a potentially ugly scene, and walked to the hotel in the warmth of the night.

I now knew why Jack did not come to Apatzingan. He had gotten the word somehow, and was not about to test the truth of the threat. As for myself, aside from the heat, I loved Apatzingan. I enjoyed the people and found the place wild and romantic, with a tiny hint of danger thrown in. I was learning the language a bit, working hard, and making new friends. Apatzingan was full of interesting people, including experienced gringos working the melon deals for companies in the States, as well as friendly shop owners, and I found the ordinary people in town to be always courteous and helpful. The Posada del Sol served a perfect limonada that helped restore me at the end of a hot day but I especially loved it when darkness fell each day, and I could feel the unrelenting heat dissipating as the stars came out, forming a beautiful tropical ambiance, accentuated with the tall palms growing everywhere, and often the sounds of a single guitar or a maria-chi band heard faintly in the distance.

For some time, I had been having trouble with Jack sending money to me to cover company expenses, both in Mexico City and Apatzingan. I was becoming frustrated because I was not aware of the cause, and I knew it would have a bad business result as the buying pressure for the melons was increasing. We had to pay the general market price for our melons, and if we refused to pay this price the melons would go to another empacadora. I was on one of the only two public telephones in the town almost daily with Jack, trying to get directions and warn him that we had to meet these competitive challenges or end our buying. But as the weeks went by I could see we were being slowly pushed out, and finally Jack told me that we would have to end our buying.

I said my farewells to Adolpho Barrigan and Felix, the hotel manager, and went back to Mexico City to prepare the family's departure back to the ranch. We drove to Laredo, where I met with Jack, and it was then that I heard he had put Cornucopia Inc. into a pineapple buying venture in Veracruz that had not gone well. The losses in pineapples ate up all the profit in strawberries and mel-ons, and we owed money to several people. I was really disappointed and rather angry at this turn of events. I had not been made aware of these decisions, but as I was a very junior partner, there was no obligation for Jack to have discussed company plans with me. Also I did not ask, but assumed erroneously, that my investment and personal friendship might have merited his consulting me, even without a requirement to do so.

During a stop in Seattle on our way to the ranch, Jack directed some of Cornucopia's creditors to talk to me about their unpaid invoices. Never having been in the loop of Cornucopia's office management, or having any knowledge of the accounts, I was not able to be of any help to the callers, but I did take the heat for whatever their complaints were. I was terribly upset that Jack would use me this way, to try to avoid dealing with these people himself, and when I left Seattle for the ranch, our paths never crossed again.

I learned a few things from this Mexican venture, some very positive and some negative, but instructive. The hard lessons concerned getting into a risky venture without knowing anything about the business, and trusting that the people who purported to know would chart a direction for the venture in a way beneficial to me, even without my being a participant in the decision making process. I let my fascination with being in Mexico substitute for making certain the business was on a safe financial basis. I felt my small investment precluded me from insisting on being in the management loop, and I also believed that Jack's and Mike's experience in the produce business gave me all the security I needed. I was too eager to participate in what I concluded would be a great adventure, to take the few simple steps that might have helped produce a different result.

Even so, the positive benefits were many, especially a few things I learned about myself. I came away believing that I had proven some management skills: an ability to build good personal relationships; and leadership in motivating people in very difficult situations, both capacities that would come into play often in the future chapters of my life.

One of the reasons I had invested in the Mexican venture was that I had been unable to create a secure, long-term financial situation at the ranch that provided an opportunity to build assets for my family over time, and looking ahead, I could not see any change in the offing. I also felt that there had to be more challenge in my life than managing the ranch under its current business plan. I had hoped that the Mexican venture would provide both to me, along with sustaining my adventurous impulses enough to keep me interested in a dual life of Canadian ranching summers and Mexican produce winters. However, it was not to be.

In thinking about this chapter in my life many years later, maybe most important to me long term was to have found Mexico and in so doing, I created a lifelong connection with that country that has added immeasurably to my storehouse of adventures as interesting and exciting as I could ever have hoped for. Through these experiences, I developed a great affection for Mexico, for its infinite variety, for its culture and beauty, for its latent opportunity and for the Mexican people whom I have come to respect immensely in their struggle to improve their lives. I feel the tapestry of my own life story has been colorfully and richly embroidered by my early experiences in Old Mexico and count myself as supremely lucky to have been there then, and to have shared a long relationship that continues to this day.

When I returned from Mexico to the ranch in late March, I immediately fell into the routine of the spring work. We had the fields to ready for planting, cows to move to Spring pasture, summer riders to hire, equipment to receive final repairs, two year olds still to calve out and the sprinklers to get ready to start pumping by mid April. It was good to get back, to ride Boxcar and Tom, and after work occasionally take an evening ride with Suzanne, who I sensed could settle into the ranching life forever.

Although I had hoped in vain to make some money in the Mexican venture, I was still looking for a change in my life that could deliver a better financial outcome. I had pride in what I had accomplished at the Elkhorn in developing a commercial herd recognized by buyers for its high quality, but the financial returns were just not to be found in commercial cow/calf ranching. Notwithstanding the romantic aura of the cowboy, the physical action, the cows and horses and the healthy outdoor life, I was ready to reshape my future to fit the obvious reality of the need to build some financial security for the family, and this took precedence over my more youthful desires to live an adventurous life.

With this in mind and because I also loved the life at Lake Windermere, I made the effort to find a scenario that would make it financially possible for me to stay at the ranch. During the summer of 1962, I worked with an idea to change the business plan of the Elkhorn. In thinking about many possibilities the ranch assets might be turned to, I came up with a plan to reduce the number of commercial cows from 750 to 350, consolidating the herd on one range and cutting related costs significantly. To make up for this reduction in numbers, I proposed that we buy 100 head of purebred Hereford cows which would be maintained on irrigated pastures on or near the ranch and in this way transform the Elkhorn into the breeding stock business, where the return per head was many times higher. This would be a very significant change and I was confident that in time, with the resources we had, we could develop a top purebred herd and make some real money.

I put together a business plan and sent it off to Dad and Norton. Suzanne and I agreed that if they turned it down we would leave the ranch. This change would require at least a $100,000 investment that I believed would be recovered from increased revenues and profit. In my cover letter sent with the proposal, I indicated that without this change Suzanne and I had agreed we would have to leave the ranch, but if they approved, I would commit to staying at least ten years to assure success of the new venture.

Within a week I received a negative answer. They did not want to invest in a new venture in which I did not have any experience. Although I argued that we would have to hire an experienced herdsman in any case, that I already knew how to promote the new side of the business and that I had some knowledge of pure-bred herds, the competition and what it would take to be successful. The answer was still "no." I immediately sent a letter indicating I would be leaving the ranch at the end of September and would prepare Phil Geiger to take over as permanent ranch manager, a role he had filled on a temporary basis while I was in Mexico.

During the summer, I made a trip to Seattle to confer with Father, who was about to leave on his and Mother's first expedition to Iran. He wished to discuss family matters with me in case something happened to them. In their absence I was to be in charge of making decisions on his Living Trust, and any other matters that might come up while they were away. They also offered the use of their home until they returned, so that Suzanne and I would have a place to stay while we looked for our own house. This was a great help to us during what we knew would be a rather stressful period.

Dad asked me what I intended to do when I returned to live in Seattle, and I confessed I had no idea but felt confident that I could find something interesting. I was planning on talking to Al Link to see if there was anything in Norton Clapp's real estate empire that might afford an opportunity. Dad said he would talk to a few people as well, to let them know I was returning and would be looking for a job. He left me with a few names on a list that I might call.

On the way back to the ranch, I stopped at the U.S. Immigration and Customs offices at Kingsgate, where we would be crossing the border with all our stuff. I wanted them to know of our plans, especially to avoid a problem with the moving van taking our furniture to Seattle, since Suzanne, the children, and I would not be crossing at the same time as our goods. We got things set as far as I could tell, and all seemed ready for our return to America.

Everything was now in place for the change in lifestyle except my head. I knew I had to make the change for the benefit of the family, especially the children, whom I could picture drifting through school and never having a really first class education with all that might mean to them. I did not want to picture them aspiring to nothing more than going to work in the woods, or driving cattle trucks as their life's vocation. For me it was different. I had the management job at the largest ranch in the Columbia Valley and maybe over time I could have come to actually own it. I needed a higher income and a new challenge, and without that, even the management job did not fulfill my personal needs. But to leave it all behind was very difficult. I knew deep inside that this break had to be made final and complete and I felt that any time spent dwelling on my experiences at the ranch would probably negatively impact whatever new job I might take. I would have to stay focused on my new career and life and hope that sometime in the future I might yet again have a ranch and a horse as good as Tom to ride.

I had invested ten years in the ranch and the closer the time came for leaving, the harder I found it to cope with the impending loss. When I thought about it, which was all the time it seemed, the pictures that were etched in my memory and constantly projected in my mind's eye, were of the alfalfa turning the brown dirt of a field to lush, sweet smelling emerald green, riding my horse in the evening, seeing the graceful backlighted water arcing from the irrigation sprinklers as the sun dropped low in the west, the all-pervasive perfume of new mown hay, the wonder of watching a newborn calf get to its feet and begin to nuzzle its mother, or simply stopping to take in the beautiful and peaceful grandeur of the wide valley wrapped protectively by the mountains.

Much as I loved most of what I had been associated with at the Elkhorn, especially the horses, I knew I could not afford to take Tom with me. I finally concluded the best path to follow would be to rid myself of all things that reminded me of the ranch and the life I had been living and really make a total change. This meant selling Tom, the horse I brought to the ranch as a yearling, my saddle which had been specially ordered by me from Hamley's saddlery in Pendelton and smuggled back into Canada in the back of a pickup covered in dust, my hackamores and other riding tack, my chaps, and even my rope. I decided to take with me only my spurs and the cowboy boots I was still wearing. Both these items are hung at the cabin in Bliss Landing as my only reminder of my days as a cowboy.

Tom had a good reputation as a cow horse and his offspring were all fine looking horses, so I soon found a man in Ft. Steele who wanted a stud and I sold him. When they loaded him into the truck, I patted his neck and rubbed his ears and then just walked away without watching him taken out the gate. I traded my saddle to the ranch for $300 and left my chaps for $30 as well. As I let each item go, it was like doors which opened to the memories attached to the things themselves were closing one by one, until much of my ranching past was driven from my consciousness. What other memories I held, I forced from my mind and turned to look only ahead to the future of a new life, as yet undefined, but toward which I was inexorably moving.

I also had two stock dogs, English Shepherds I had brought in from a breeder in Cedar Rapids, Iowa. They were smaller than border collies, brown with wide white collars and white feet. I bought the male first and trained him to help work the cattle in the brushy areas. We named him Brownie and he became a big help working the cattle. I then bought a female several years later with the idea of breeding the pair and selling the pups. We named the bitch Brownie II for some unknown reason, but perhaps because the children continued to use the name. When she had her first litter, she became very protective and would put the run on any adult who came too close.

Old Brownie had been injured so that most of the time he went about on three legs and I did not plan to take him to the States. I gave both my brother, and my long time friend, Les Snapp, pups from the first litter and they turned out to be great pets and also very protective of their children. I was still undecided on Brownie number two, but one day a buyer from Alberta arrived at the ranch to discuss a cattle purchase and when we were done talking and he walked towards his car, Brownie two did a perfect "heeling" job, nailing him right at the ankle and tearing his fancy cowboy pants. Watching that episode determined that I would take neither of them to the States and after thinking about alternatives finally decided to put them both to sleep.

This I did with the help of Gordon Wimpenny, who was visiting me at the time for some out-of-season hunting. I decided to do the procedure in my office, and as we prepped each dog, Gordon kept asking me, knowing the finality of the procedure, if I really wanted to keep going. I kept answering in the affirmative and as I petted them, Gordon put the needle into a vein just above the paw and as they looked up into my eyes as calm and trusting as could be, Gordon slowly pushed the plunger on the syringe and the light just went out and they sagged down completely relaxed. I had killed many animals in the past, from chickens to elk, but in the act of killing these two dogs I did something that did not sit easy on my conscience. Afterwards, the question of alternatives kept coming back to me. Was there no other solution? Did I really have no other choice? Well, of course there were other choices, but it had seemed to me they all carried risks to the two dogs and in the case of Brownie II, to people she might injure. I have thought about it with a nagging doubt over the years, but it is history and cannot be changed. It is best to try to forget such things after sufficient penance is made.

In the weeks before leaving, I visited with my many friends to say farewell. This was difficult as we had a multitude of fine acquaintances with whom we had shared many experiences, but I hoped that we might continue to see them from time to time. It was very hard for the children, as it was the only life they had known and they would be leaving the only friends they had. For most of them this had been their home since birth and they truly loved the open and exciting life they had led on the ranch.

In early October we began serious packing, organized with Bekins to move the furniture left in the house to storage in Seattle. There was no room for any luggage with six children and two adults in the Pontiac station wagon, so with Phil Geiger's help, I built a large two-wheeled trailer in the shop, to be towed behind the car when we moved, to carry our personal things needed until we found a house of our own to buy or rent.

Finally, on October 12th, 1962, with Suzanne, one-year old Fletcher, and the five other children, we hit the road early in the morning for the long drive towards our new life. I had, and I know that Suzanne shared with me, a multitude of anxieties about what the future would bring into our lives. I had absolutely nothing lined up, but I was confident I would find an opportunity where I could make a contribution. I was looking ahead, not back, and was more optimistic than apprehensive at what the future might hold for me.

Horses

Wherein our now, somewhat more mature hero,
Is left to only reminisce about all the pretty horses

From a very young age, maybe from the ubiquitous statues of famous men on horseback in many towns or from my first recollected "up close" horse, Sir William, a thoroughbred race horse at my great grandfather's small ranch in Walnut Creek, California, I was in some wonder of horses. They seemed to me to be so large and powerful, and almost endowed with magical powers of speed and flight. I found it easy to enjoy the concepts of unicorns or of the flying horse, Pegasus. These pictures stimulated my fantasies and when I was around nine or ten years old I jumped at the chance to learn to ride.

There is, I think, in all humans, an emotional response in seeing a well-formed horse with a refined head and wonderfully expressive eyes. Large, lustrous eyes that show as broad a spectrum of basic emotion as the human eye does, and when we look into them, seem to lead us into the very core of one of nature's beautiful creatures. The form so balanced, the musculature so well defined and whether standing still, calmly walking, or flowing over the ground in a graceful and powerful run, an awe inspiring sight.

Like so many things in life, we all have moments that seem to encapsulate the essence of something, like a man's relationship with a horse, and when I think back on doing things with a horse, these images always come to mind. It may be about sitting on a hillside resting, with your horse standing quietly at your side, looking out over a beautiful landscape you have been riding through, or swimming your horse in deep water, or sitting in a corral just watching a horse you are breaking getting used to a saddle, or riding drag moving a herd of cows over the range. These images define the essence of a man's affection for his horse and the companionship they share in the act of riding.

Naturally, the reality of riding, especially as a cowboy or packer, is far removed from these bucolic scenes. But the scenes described actually existed in my past, only they were a small part of the workaday cowboy life of my experience. But these calm memories come back to me still, when I think of all the horses I have

345

been around, and these pictures in my mind blot out the reality of the wind, the rain and snow, the long tiring days, the branches slapping my face, the falls, the dust and sometimes the difference of opinion between me and the horse adding to the effort needed to just get the day's work done.

But in the end, It is the horse that gets you through the day, out of the tight spot, who does the brunt of the work, who doesn't fall when by all natural forces he should, walks calmly into deep water and who continues to keep the cows moving in the right direction. At day's end, no matter how tough it was or how angry you became with the horse, you remember these things, and as you unsaddle and begin to brush him down you can't help saying "good boy" and patting his neck and stroking his soft muzzle.

My sister, Georgann, was already becoming an accomplished rider by 1941, and was very excited about horses at that time of her life. She went on to enter many shows around the Northwest and had a room full of ribbons won at these events. This encouraged me to try riding so one Saturday I started going to Gay's Academy where they taught, under the dictatorial tutelage of Mr. Gay, three- and five-gaited English riding.

I was started, as most probably are, on a very reliable old horse in the arena, learning to sit properly, hold the double reins correctly, and post when the horse was at a trot. This was all right with me, although I thought posting looked silly and I was eager to get out of the arena and onto some of the trail rides they could still do in 1941 Seattle, out 15th Avenue, north of the University. This somewhat open area is long gone, taken over by housing and urban bustle now, and it is hard to visualize what it was like before time removed the open space, woods and trails, and left me with only dim and sketchy memories of the area.

I do however, remember some of the horses and one in particular I hated. His name was Challenger, and he had what I later came to call a hard mouth and high head. I found out to my sorrow that if you pulled on the reins hard his head would snap back and one time when he did this he hit me in the mouth with the top of his head and split my lip. He was very hard to hold at the speed I wanted as he paid no attention whatsoever to the use of the reins as a braking mechanism. What seemed to keep him in a proper pace was his need to stay with the other horses.

One day after having been riding for maybe four or five months, and feeling pretty good about my skill, we went on a trail ride. I was riding Challenger, and for some reason the horses developed into two groups, with Mr. Gay and the more advanced riders slowly putting distance between themselves and we beginners. When the lead group were well out of sight ahead I began to have trouble controlling Challenger, who was intent on catching up to the leaders. The trail came to a steep ravine and when we started to descend into it, Challenger took off at a run down the ravine with me hanging onto every piece of leather and hair I could find to grab. I was terrified both of falling off and staying on. There was no escape. He ran up the other side of the ravine and along the trail at a flat out gallop and there was nothing I could do. It was like my worst nightmare coming true.

In a hundred yards more the trail opened up into a wide gravel road in a direct line towards the riding academy, but a quarter mile ahead was 15th Avenue, which even then was a busy arterial highway. I knew Challenger had no intention of stopping for traffic and we were going to hit that busy arterial at a full run. Luckily for me, the other riders with Mr. Gay were clustered next to the road waiting only for a clearing in the traffic so they could cross, when they heard my howls. As soon as Mr. Gay saw me coming he also realized that the horse might not stop at the road and jumped off his horse and placed himself between the highway and the line Challenger was galloping on, waving his arms and hollering "Whoa, whoa"!

This slowed my horse enough so that Mr. Gay could grab the reins and stop him. I had been totally terrified during this run-away and had felt completely out of control of the horse. Irrespective of these feelings, Mr. Gay delivered a terrible tongue lashing for my inability to handle the horse. I was mortally embarrassed and angry at his response to what had been an awful and frightening experience for me.

This incident killed, in the space of a few minutes, all the interest I had in riding horses, and I cared not a whit if I ever got on another horse. As it turned out, I did not get on another horse until 1943, when at thirteen I had my first summer job at a small farm in eastern British Columbia. I was not eager even then to ride, but since there were several horses, and our boss encouraged me, I very tentatively began again to ride and soon my enjoyment with horses returned, but perhaps a bit more cautious than before.

My life with and around horses revolves mainly with the specific animals I have known well. In Alaska there was Tim, a lanky buckskin with two white stockings and a white blaze on his forehead who turned out to be my favorite to ride while working with a pack string as a wrangler. Also Brownie, a short coupled, small, brown all over horse, always half broke, who bucked me off one day in a low mountain pass when I tried to get on holding the halter shank of the packhorse I was leading, and as I went through the air, the packhorse went to bucking over the edge, spreading grub, pots and pans down the mountain side.

Boxcar during training.

The Roan, a proud-cut red roan gelding, bought as a pack horse, still believed he was a stud, and I had to ride him from Valdez to Chestochina to bring up the rear of the horse herd we were moving to the Chisana River. He never stopped jigging for 160 miles, worrying about the three mares which Lou had tailed together and was leading, getting too far ahead of him, until in desperation Lou sold him to get him out of the string. I know many think a prancing horse is pretty, but if you have to ride one that far, you soon come to the conclusion that you could kill with no remorse

At the ranch there was Ruby, a dark sorrel low built mare, picked for me to ride when I first arrived at the ranch. She was fifteen years old, docile but responsive and we had many miles together until I got my hands on some better horses.

Tom, a yearling stallion I bought for $100, was the first horse I broke from start to finish, in an attempt to end up with a good all-around cowhorse. In this I was successful, and the horse came to exemplify for me, the bond that can exist between a man and a horse. He became the best known horse in the Columbia valley, and sired some good foals.

Another memorable horse we broke was High Pockets, a very tall four year old thoroughbred type we acquired with the purchase of the Teagart ranch. He had never been ridden when we got him, I think because Bob Teagart was too old to take on a project like High Pockets, the older Teagart boys were all in the woods or driving trucks, and the youngest son, who was interested a bit in horses was too young. He was to be a formidable challenge, and I left him to Tom Watson, an experienced bronc and bull rider who worked for the ranch, and was more experienced and a better rider than me to do the task.

Boxcar was unforgettable, named because of his square bulk and red color, a very large and beautiful bright sorrel horse who just felt turbocharged powerful when he accelerated. He was solid red except for two rear white stockings, and I bought him cheap at the Highriver, Alberta horse auction as a very green broke, obviously hard to handle four year old, that fought the bit and had a high head. No one was enthused about bidding the price up, so I took him on as a project at 200 dollars. He was built like a quarter horse, was an axe handle across the rump and very powerful and exciting to ride. I broke him, as with Tom, using only a hackamore, hoping that I could make a cowhorse out of him and repair his mouth, as he could get very excited when warmed up.

There was also Toby, one of the mules in a team that was on the ranch when I got there. He was, as they say, "light behind" and I was warned early on to be careful around him because if you startled him, you might get your head kicked off. I was very cautious when working with Toby as he frightened easily, a fact I was to find out for myself later on.

There are many other horses that crowd into my memory, perhaps more transient because I did not have long term relationships with them. Their names are lost to me now, but I remember one on the Y Cross Ranch near Horsecreek, Wyoming, that Mr. Davis, the owner of the ranch gave me to ride with the warning to be careful about cinching him too tight and to walk him around a bit before mounting, otherwise he had a propensity to rear up and "go over back-ward". I was given to understand that I could get myself killed easily if this occurred with me in the saddle. It was brought home to me one day as I led him out of the barn, humped up and walking rather stiff legged, and with one snort he reared up and over he went crashing down on the saddle. I never forgot the admonition after that performance and made sure I walked him around enough to get rid of his hump before mounting him.

Tom working in the corrals.

But he turned out to be a good horse for me to build up some riding skills, which Mr. Davis helped me with. Skills that had more use on a cow ranch than my past experience at the riding academy and the farm in Canada, neither of which had livestock to work. A neighbor of the Y Cross was King Merritt, one of the first serious breeders of Quarterhorses, a breed which has become famous for their skill in cutting, calf roping, steer wrestling and even barrel racing due to their quick acceleration and speed for short distances.

The cattle ranches around the Y Cross in 1944, were still managing cattle in the old ways. This meant using horses for all aspects of handling cattle such as roping on the range if needed, cutting cows, branding calves and working other horses. This meant that the quality of the horses as working stock horses was really important. This is why King Merritt and other ranchers were running horse breeding operations that would not only provide better stock horses for their own use, but create another source of income.

One Sunday afternoon, Mr. Davis took me along with some of the crew to watch Mr. Merritt geld all the yearlings that were not wanted to grow out as stallions. A circumstance, you might say, where not making the cut actually got you cut. The way they did it was to run the yearlings into a round corral, one at a time, get them running around the wall of the corral where they were roped by the neck. The roper took several dallies around the hitching post and another roper would catch the two hind feet and they would stretch the animal out on his side where he could be worked on.

We watched from outside the corral, staying out of the way of the horses and ropers, and then went inside and close up to watch the actual cutting procedure. After about eight or nine had been done, there was only one more, the best of the lot, a beautiful black horse with a few white markings. They moved him into the corral and got him running around to the left. Mr. Merritt or one of his brothers, got the lariat ready and casually turning with the running horse laid the rope easily over his head and tried to stop his run by getting a dally around the hitching post.

The black, with the rope tight, right behind his ears, in his effort to get away ducked his head a bit and ran into the only spot in the sixty foot wide corral wall that was not seamless, the four or five inches next to the gate. He hit with such force and in such a position that it broke his neck, and down he went. We were all appalled that this beautiful animal lay dead from such a fluke accident. I had already been amazed that they were not going to save this horse as a stud since he was the standout of the group in my mind, and then to lose him altogether was extra sad. We drove back to the Y Cross in a very somber mood.

On another day I was at the Merritt ranch, a new neighbor who had recently bought the adjoining ranch had been asked to come over and discuss a common problem between the two operations. This man was from the East and knew nothing about how things might be done in the west. The problem was that he had a Palamino stallion, and had put it in a pasture adjacent to the field the Merritts ran their Quarterhorse brood mares. They were pretty blunt with the neighbor, telling him that they better not find his stallion in that field again or there would be trouble. This was all pretty exciting, and definately western, to a kid of fourteen.

A couple of weeks later I heard that the neighbor had returned the Palomino stud to the forbidden pasture, and King and his brother just saddled up, rode over, team roped it and castrated it on the spot. As far as they were concerned the issue was taken care of. I never heard if there were any repercussions from the episode, but I doubt it in those times.

When I arrived at the Elkhorn Ranch eight years later, I was very impressed with their horse corral set up. There were no cattle to speak of since it was operated as a dude ranch and hunting outfit. But they did have about twenty horses and a team of mules. Vaughn DuBois was a good horseman and he built the corrals so that breaking horses could be managed with the least damage possible to both horses and men.

The corrals were constructed from eight to ten inch diameter fir logs. These were stacked to at least seven or eight feet high to discourage even the most crazy horse to try to jump out, although they told me that once the mule Toby had tried to do just that. The large corral was a 50 foot diameter circle with a hitching post off center for dallying ropes, and two large swinging gates about eight feet wide, one that led to the barnyard and the other that opened into a much smaller round corral 20 feet in diameter, but the same height, without a center hitching post as it was too small for any roping work.

This design allowed a lot of opportunity to break horses without always worrying about getting bucked off, and was much easier on the animals as well. The general idea was to use the smaller of the two corrals for the initial work with the horse, such as getting used to a human in close contact, 'flagging' the horse to make it understand that a blanket or slicker would not hurt him, saddling for the first few times and always the first couple of rides. It was almost impossible for a young horse to buck you off in such a confined area. Two jumps and they were into the wall and the circle was too small for them to run fast in it.

Once the horse got used to the basics, you could move into the large corral and it was seldom at this point that a horse would take off running which often would lead to a saddlebronc ride with no upside. You would not win a buckle if you stayed on and could teach the horse a very bad habit if you went off.

Boxcar was one of those exceptions. The day I thought he was ready for the large corral I opened the gate and seeing the great open space on the other side of the gate, after being in what must have looked like a tiny round box to him, he charged through at a dead run making one round at top speed and then ducking his head and began bucking. I bailed off for the top rail to avoid the possibility of getting bucked off or smacked into the corral logs, or having him fall due to the footing in the corral and the leaning position he had to maintain to counter the centrifugal forces from his speed. So back into the small corral for a few more sessions we went and the next lesson in the large corral went as planned.

Boxcar came from thoroughbred blood and I knew he would tend to be flighty and quick to get worked up. I used a hackamore which is a headstall that does not use a bit in the mouth, but a braided rawhide nose 'bosal' which ended under the horse's chin in a small ball which was where the reins attached. The idea was to not have to jerk on the horse's mouth by using a bit when first starting out the training, which could easily make the horse raise his head up instead of keeping it low when working cattle. A horse with his head up cannot see the critter it has to handle, and all good stock horses work with their heads down eyeball to eyeball with the cow.

I rode Boxcar every day I could, missing only those days when the nature of the work was more than he was ready for. He continued to progress and began to learn about cows and really was a pleasure to ride because he felt so powerful when he accelerated. He soon developed into a very responsive horse, easy to handle and light on the rein. I continued to use the hackamore with him still fearful about putting him on a bit. Since the incident in the corral he never tried to run or buck, so my confidence in taking him out on the range became complete.

About two years later, I was riding Boxcar on the east side of Columbia Lake to check up on 100 head of cows we had on this narrow piece of range between Dutch Creek an Canal Flat, 25 miles to the south. I had unloaded him at the Fairmont Hot Spring corral and rode the few miles down to the north end of the lake. I planned to ride the range down to Canal Flat where I would be picked up by one of the other cowboys working on the Dutch Creek side of the Lake. I rode south between the lake and the hills to the east and did not come on any of the cattle so I knew they were all congregated on the south half of the range.

About half way down the lake was a high bluff with a shear wall falling into the water. A steep trail climbed up and over this barricade, which made me think it might be interesting to see if I could get Boxcar into the lake to swim around the wall instead of climbing up the trail. I had never before had him in water above his knees and I did not think I could get him to go in, certainly not without a major test of wills, but much to my surprise he just walked in calmly, without any hesitation and kept going until he was swimming. Totally unconcerned.

He was so strong I was able to pull up my legs and put my feet behind the saddle and I did not even get my boots wet. We swam about twenty feet out from the rock wall and it must have been at least 150 yards until we could find a place to get out onto the shore. When I looked into the water it was a very deep blue and I could see the face of the rock wall down about thirty feet below the surface, until it disappeared into the blue depths. It was certainly one of my most memorable riding experiences, and created a special bond between Boxcar and me.

In 1962 I spent an extended time in Mexico and left the ranch in the hands of the ranch foreman, Phil Geiger. Phil was competent in many areas but not noted as a horseman in the sense that he was raised on a ranch and ridden all his life, but he was competent enough around horses to get the riding jobs done. But I don't think he was aware of how quickly certain horses could be spoiled by the wrong rider. Such was the case with Boxcar.

Phil let some young hand ride Boxcar one day when they were working cattle along the road. The rider could not resist showing off for the cars that passed by to make them think he was a real cowboy riding a very difficult to handle animal. To do this he kept jerking on the bit and at the same time spurring him. The effect was that the horse wanted to run, but was kept from doing so by pulling roughly on the lines and this set the horse to prancing in place.

When I came back in the Spring from Mexico and got on Boxcar he was a totally different horse. His head was up, he was nervous and flighty, and had been ruined as a stock horse by a drugstore cowboy. I was disgusted that this had been allowed to happen, but it was too late. I tried to work him again with a hackamore, but he was not going to be the same horse I had come to care so much about.

For almost fifteen years horses were an important part of my life. I found horses, like dogs, easy to love. They became, in my mind, like good friends. They seldom let me down and seemed tolerant of my screwups, although had they been able to speak, I would have, no doubt, received an earful at certain times. They could, especially those poorly trained or with bad habits, quickly bring me to the peak of exasperation and anger.

By refusing to get into water in order to cross a creek or small river, being unwilling to go into some rugged or steep terrain, unreliable to let loose and catch again, hard to load into a trailer, generally being frightened by anything new or startling and of course, kicking or biting, were behaviors that could rapidly bring a string of curses and a hard use of spurs or quirt. In my book, the work was just too hard to tolerate a poorly trained horse making it harder. Having said that, there were many times when although things were going from bad to worse, the humor or outright funniness of the situation made us laugh and helped us get through a tough day.

The second Fall I was at the ranch I decided to go deer hunting, up Windermere Creek behind the ranch. Dix and Vaughn told me to ride Ruby and take the mule Toby, to pack. I left at daylight and rode about five miles up the creek where there was a gate and a short piece of barbwire fence that had been put in to hold horses from going back down to the valley. We went through the gate and I closed it behind me just in case, and continued up the small steep valley another two miles. From there I could see the alpine slide area I wanted to hunt so I tied the horses and started up the mountain.

This was in the low mountains that led right up into the Rockies and it was a beautiful but very steep climb up to the slide area. I worked my way up to the ridge where I could look westward back down to the Columbia River valley and the ranch and traversed it only a short way when I saw a large mule deer buck fifty or sixty yards below me. It was an easy kill and I dressed it out cutting the head off and quartering the rest to make a good even pack. A half hour later I was on my way down to get Toby and bring him up to the kill site.

After another arduous climb up with the mule, I turned him sidewise to the steep slope and began to get his rigging ready to load the meat. He did not like this deal at all. He could smell the meat and I could tell it might be tricky to get him loaded without some sort of confrontation. I carefully took one quarter and put it in the downhill side pannier and then the next chunk into the uphill side. His eyes began to roll around showing mostly white, and he was twiching all over. I picked up the next quarter and as I walked with it around his rump to the downhill side to put it on top of the first piece, I saw that I had inadvertently moved the deer's head, which I saw roll over and stop, hesitating for a moment against a small rock, and then gravity won out and the head broke loose to tumble down towards Toby. I stood still, unable to move, and watched in fascination, the head with its blank staring eyes, roll right under Toby's belly and down the mountain side.

That was it! He went straight up, wheeled, and in a run headed down, the meat flying off in arcs down the mountainside. I could not believe it. I was going to have to walk back down to the bottom and back up a third time, or leave the meat for the bears to get. Resigned, I started down picking up and moving the meat to where I could easily load it again and on reaching the bottom saw that Toby had disappeared. I got to Ruby and rode back down the trail and, naturally, found Toby calmly standing by the gate in the fence as if I should open it for him so he could continue homeward. If the gate had been open he would have already been at the ranch munching hay in his stall.

I angrily grabbed his halter shank and back up the valley we went, and after tying Ruby once again to a tree, climbed back up the mountain with me cursing him every time he lay back on the shank to protest. I felt like I was dragging him up, but finally we were there. I gathered the rest of the meat, bringing it down to the lower loading site, to join the pieces he had unloaded so unceremoniously. I finally got him loaded and led him back down the slide to the bottom. I Got on Ruby and started down the trail to the ranch reaching it without further incident.

Although the whole process went from being a short easy hunting trip to a much harder one, I couldn't help but laugh at the look in Toby's eyes as the deer head rolled towards him. It was all very funny afterwards, and Dix and Vaughn thought it was hilarious, but of course they did not have to climb the mountain three times.

Tom was the first horse I trained from the ground up. I bought him from the Q Ranch in the very southeastern corner of Alberta, on the recommendation of Tom Watson, a cowboy working for us who knew the ranch and its horses. I was looking for a Quarterhorse stud to upgrade our string of cowhorses. When the colt arrived I was surprised to see he was a palamino, but almost white in color. This changed over time into a light, somewhat dappled gold color with a white main and tail, and three white feet. He had a small but wide head and very intelligent eyes with a white blaze down the center of his face. He was halter broke and already pretty docile to be around.

I spent the first summer just fooling around with him and getting him used to me. I kept him away from the other horses because I did not want him injured if he got excited around the mares. I was not too sure when I could expect to see some sexual interest starting to manifest itself, so took no chances. By Fall I had him used to the saddle. In the Spring when he turned two I started to ride him, using a hackamore and in the small corral. After two sessions we moved to the large corral and soon went out and rode around the ranch. I gave him no work to do but lengthened the rides to an hour or so and then turned him out with the mares on the hill pasture behind the barnyard for the rest of the summer. I was not sure what, if anything, would accrue from his being with the mares, but the following Spring three or four of the mares produced nice foals.

His real training with the cattle started early the next Spring and soon I could see that he liked this. He became very intense when turning a cow and seemed naturally to keep his head low and interested in taking a bite out of any cow that annoyed him. I began to rope off of him as well, and set up a small calf roping run just outside the barnyard on the lane that led to the fields, which was fenced on both sides. So turning, pulling his hind legs up under his belly and skidding to a stop, backing up to keep a rope taught and not getting excited when the rope went under his tail were learned by Tom as a three year old.

He was stronger and bigger as a four and five year old, and by then was a fairly accomplished stock horse. I used him several times for calf roping in amateur rodeos and he was a better roping horse than I was roper. I lent him to some of the other ropers to use as well since he was the best around. He was very intelligent working cows, and this showed especially when cutting out or separating one group from another or heading a cow that tried to turn away from the direction we needed it to go. All in all he turned out to be a great horse for me, and in his spare time produced a bunch of good horses for the ranch.

Over the years that I rode Tom, my affection and respect for him continued to grow. I liked to think that his did for me as well, but who can really know how a horse feels towards his master. I do know that he often whinnied when I walked into the horse barn and often would reach out with his nose as if to ask for a treat or pat. He was a joy to be around all the time and even though he was a stud he did not harass the geldings anytime he was on the job or in the truck.

I know that my experiences and the subsequent relationships developed in those ten years with Tom, Boxcar, Ruby, Tim, High Pockets, even Toby the mule, and the other horses at the ranch or in the distant past, whose names I cannot now recall, are the memories that come back to me now and fill me with pleasure. The horses we rode at work or at play, exemplified for me the essence of ranching and greatly lessen the memories of the hard and unending work that accompanies ranch life.

When I decided to leave the ranch in 1962, I realized I had to put this interesting and sometimes exciting part of my life totally aside since returning to the city, would surely create a paradigm change in my life. I knew the next chapter in my life's odyssey would require me to be totally focused on whatever enterprise I became involved with as I tried to build a new life in the city, and constantly being reminded of the freedom and variety of my ranching experience would make this change more difficult than I already expected it to be.

For a time I had thought seriously about taking Tom with me to the city as I could almost not bear to part with him, but I finally realized that I had to give it all up to get it completely out of my mind. I delayed until the last possible moment and then with much resolution to make the complete change to a new life, I sold Tom, the horse I unabashedly loved, to a rancher at near Ft. Steele; the saddle I had specially ordered from Hamley's in Pendleton, Oregon; my blanket; my ropes; bridles and hackamores; and even my chaps, I sold to the ranch for $500 dollars. I made only two exceptions and these were my boots, which I was still wearing, and my spurs, which I spent so much time selecting ten years before, and would have no future use for. But I had to take something, and for some reason, I could not bear to think about someone else riding with these spurs.

I felt a great loss as I closed this chapter in my life, knowing not where the next chapter would take me, but I was determined to try to prove myself in whatever lay ahead. I came away wanting nothing to remind me of the cowboy life and I was determined to stay away from horses and keep those memories buried. It was fourteen more years before I ventured to ride again, this time on a short packtrip near Bozeman, Montana. I left for this trip with me feeling a certain trepidation about getting on a horse again, but when I put a foot in the stirrup and swung aboard, it was like I had never been away from horses I felt so at home, back in the saddle again. It started the horse and ranch juices running at flood tide and I was so excited I began to look at the possibility of a small horse ranch as a vacation site. Finally, I beat those strong impulses back down, but it was a close call.

I now remember this part of my life as the perfect way to have spent the decade of my twenties, even though it probably put me ten years behind in experiences that might be more useful in the city and I found right away that not too many employers were interested in a young man who only knew one end of a cow from the other. But I still think positively about a time when hard physical work was usually a pleasure, the body could stand the banging around it had to take working with livestock, and I was able to saddle up and ride a good horse over much of that beautiful valley.

My boots and spurs are still my only possession from those times so long ago, and sometimes when I look at them hanging in our cabin at Bliss Landing, they remind me of my days as a cowboy and of the beautiful horses I shared so many experiences with and I feel full with the memories of it all.

Return to Civilization

Wherein our hero, forsaking the cowboy life, returns to the city,
buys a job, makes an investment and turns into a mushroom farmer

I knew it would be a hard day, but I did not expect the problems that occurred. First off, we had not gone three miles from the front gate of the ranch when I heard an intermittent scraping sound of metal hitting pavement with every unevenness in the highway. I stopped to check what was causing the problem and found to my dismay that the frame of the trailer had cracked. Disgusted, I turned around and went back to the ranch shop, where Phil and I strengthened and re-welded the frame. This cost us an hour and of course the kids were already starting to ask how long the trip would take, when could they eat and could we wait another day before leaving.

When the repair was finished we started out a second time on the first leg of the journey, 150 miles to the border at Kingsgate. After stopping for lunch in Cranbrook, we arrived at the border around noon. Suzanne and I marched into the U.S. Customs and Immigration office with all the papers I had been told I needed, congratulating myself that I had had the foresight to inquire several months earlier to make sure everything was ready for our move back to the States, allowing our entry to go without a hitch. Presenting myself confidently to the agent at the counter, I flourished our documents and said, "It's been a long morning, but here we are, and very happy to be coming back to the States." After he looked at everything he said, "Well, you and the children can go, but your wife can't!" I was dumbstruck and I'm sure my jaw dropped wide open. I must have almost shouted back, "What do you mean she can't go? I informed you months ago we were moving, and there was no problem then?" "I'm sorry, but she's a Canadian citizen and she can't move to the United States without a visa!"

I could not believe it! I thought we had planned everything correctly, except for one thing: we had assumed erroneously that since she was married to an American citizen, she could move to the States. In true bureaucratic fashion, the official simply turned away as if this was a closed discussion. "Look", I said, "I've got six young children in the car and one is a baby. Do you expect us to just turn around and go back! We have nowhere to go back to. The house is empty!" His answer to that exclamation was, "Well, I don't know anything about that, but you can't go through." I was fast getting into a rage and was having a lot of trouble containing it. I hated these types, none of whom, it seemed to me, could have made it in the real world were it not for their government jobs, and it seemed to me they all relished an opportunity to use the power they had to abuse the public who paid their salaries.

I had to get out of there before I said something like what I was thinking, which might have created a much bigger problem than I was already facing, so I walked outside to try to cool off and get my brain in gear. I did not know the immigration laws, except cursorily, but I thought there must be a way to let us go through on some basis. Suzanne and I talked for a while about our options, none of which looked good, but we agreed I should try to work the problem more calmly than I had been doing and to remain deferential to the agent at all costs. This was hard for me because I really felt like punching him in the jaw.

I went back in and in the nicest voice and manner I could muster, I began to talk to the officer. I pled the case of hardship on the children, the effort I had made in the summer planning with immigration about our impending move and that I could not believe there was absolutely no way to be allowed through, even if only temporarily. This spiel jogged either his sympathy or his memory, I'm not sure which, but in the end he said, "Well, she could go in as a visitor or tourist for thirty days, but if she cannot get her visa by then she has to leave."

When I heard this It was like a great load had been lifted from me, but in thinking about the level of anxiety he created made me so angry I said, "I appreciate your telling us this, but why didn't you tell us that when we first arrived, instead of putting us all through this agony?" He didn't answer that and after a few minutes merely pushed the tourist card over towards me, shrugging, and said to Suzanne, "Sign here!" This episode had cost us almost an hour and five years' worth of mental anguish and I was ready to murder anyone associated with governments anywhere. They were all the same as far as I could tell.

We made it to Spokane without further incident, and stopped for supper at a restaurant. As we walked in, all eyes turned to see this very young mother, carrying one baby, and trooping along after her, five additional children and me bringing up the rear. I could fairly hear their minds asking, "How can that young girl have all those children", or "Are they really married?" I felt like some kind of lecherous old man for either having spawned all these kids, or taking on this young wife and subjecting her to mothering the lot of them. This had not ever occurred to me while we were living on the ranch, but now back in the city, I could see that we presented a very different looking family from the norm.

We left Spokane around five in the afternoon and by the time we made Sprague, Fletcher started to cry. There seemed to be no way to get her to stop and finally after everyone had taken a turn at soothing her, we were resigned to listen to her screeching until she keeled over into sleep. Unfortunately, this did not happen. She stood on the front seat between her mother and me, facing the kids in the back and squalled all the way to Bellevue, where we arrived at Mother's and Dad's at eleven that night, in the middle of the famous Columbus Day Storm of 1962. This storm carried winds up to 100 mph and of course trees were bowled over and the power went off, and stayed off for the next three days. It had been a very long and arduous day to say the least and I figured things just had to get better from then on, and of course, they did.

In spite of no electricity, we had a Coleman two burner stove making some cooking possible, but there was no heat in the house until the power lines were repaired, and no hot water. So much for civilization! However, things returned to normal in a few days and we started house hunting in earnest. We found a home for $42,000, in Woodridge, a suburb of Bellevue, with enough bedrooms and bathrooms to handle a family of eight people and finally put together a mortgage we could afford. I was 32 years old and this was the first home I had owned and the first long term debt that I had incurred. It was a little scary especially since I did not as yet have a job.

Finding work was the next order of business. I met with Al Link to explore possibilities in their real estate business and he directed me to Jim Clapp, Norton's son, who was developing Newport Shores, a fancy priced property where each lot had its own dock and access to Lake Washington. I was very intrigued with the possibilities and after looking at it felt I could help in the marketing end, but they either didn't need me or didn't want me and I didn't ask which. Jim, however, did have something he thought I might be interested in, which were fixed base operations at several airports in California and Nevada. Jim had a Piper Aircraft distributorship which owned or leased these operations with the idea of selling Piper airplanes to the base operators for their flight schools, sales and charter flying work. Three of these were available for me to look at if I was interested.

Because I was only a low flying time private pilot with a Canadian license, I would have to get a U.S. private, commercial and instrument license before it would make much sense to try to take on such an operation. I called my brother Jack, now out of the Air Force, to ask if he might consider joining with me in a partnership to pursue an aviation business career. I figured he could do the flying while I worked on my ratings and I could manage the office. He was interested and a week later we flew to San Jose, were met by one of Jim's managers and visited the base operations over the next few days. On the last leg, as we flew commercial in a Lockheed Electra to Reno, I noticed a trail of white smoke coming from an outboard engine. The volume of smoke increased and in a few more minutes the propeller stopped, was feathered and we continued on three engines. When we came into Reno for a landing, I could see all their fire trucks lined up on the side of the runway, but the landing was normal. I wondered if this was some sort of omen as to what we might expect in the aviation business. In the end, although we both were interested, we decided it was too big a business risk for us to take on with our limited capital.

I next met with Bill Pratt, a broker with United Pacific Corporation, an investment firm in Seattle. Bill was also on the Board of Directors of Physio-Control Corporation, a very small company developing medical electronic equipment and he informed me that they were looking for someone to come on as Vice President and General Manager to support Dr. William Edmark, the designer of the equipment. The deal that was offered was for me to buy 10 shares of Physio common stock for $3500 and take a job that would pay me $500 per month for about half time work, with the possibility that it could transition into a better paying full time job in the future. I was to manage the company's income stream from a licensing agreement with American Optical Co., producing about $100,000 per year on the first machine Physio developed and patented, an electronic heart rate monitor named the Cardiometer. Electronics was plain magic to me and words such as *analog, digital, transistor, resistance, plethysmography, capacitor, or impedance,* I understood not at all, but figured I could manage the money coming in and somehow make a contribution to the business. In effect, I bought a job, and hoped development of new machines would take the stock value up in a future that could afford to pay me more than the meager amount I agreed to start with.

Dr. William Edmark, who was a Cardiologist and heart surgeon, as well as an electronic genius, had a healthy understanding of what high tech medical equipment could do in the operating room if it could only be developed. Although he had a full calendar with his practice, he managed to get into the office almost every afternoon to meet with Jack Howard, the electronic technician who built most of the various internal parts, to discuss the design issues and testing required over the next few days.

Physio-Control in those days of 1963 was a "skunk works" in every sense of the word, or what is now euphemistically called a "development company," meaning it probably had a very short life expectancy and carried a very high risk investors would lose any money they put in. It actually was a one room electronic lab with a couple of offices and reception desk, located at 4711 Brooklyn Avenue, in the University District. It might just as well have been in a garage somewhere similar to the birthplace of many a notable company and the burial ground for thousands never heard of since they died in infancy.

It was staffed by Doctor Bill when he could leave his day to day medical practice to pop in, Jack Howard, the electronic tech, a Secretary/Receptionist, and myself. The little money we had coming in was being totally reinvested in Bill's newest effort, a machine to measure blood pressure with a finger cuff for on-line monitoring of intensive care patients. Bill's enthusiasm was contagious and everyone strove to improve the concept machine to the point of public demonstrations as fast as possible. I tried to be helpful and to deal with outside issues including the Board of Directors. I liked Bill Edmark and we became good friends and collaborators in a short time.

Bill and Mary Edmark introduced me to many of their friends, most of whom were constructing successful careers in a variety of occupations. This enabled me to build a network of new friends and to set the stage for becoming involved in the community through volunteer work with non-profit organizations.

Within a year the company had two technicians, had farmed out circuit board and other manufacturing services to several local companies and I had gotten my salary up to $1000 monthly and was working full time. The negative to all this "progress" was we were also eating up our cash flow at a faster rate. Sometime in the winter of 1963-64 Bill Edmark and I flew east to Buffalo and Rochester to demo the "Pressure/Pulsometer" to some docs. We arrived on a very wintry night and the next day put the machine through its paces on some actual patients. The results were not super, but nevertheless, the doctors were very impressed with the potential. The machine was so sensitive that it was difficult to get constant blood pressure readings unaffected by the various movements of bedridden patients. Bottom line, we had a machine that was not quite yet ready for demonstration, much less for manufacturing and sale. So back to the lab we went to deal with these issues.

The Board of Directors was growing very discouraged with the slow progress on the Pressure/Pulsometer and with the expenditure of the entire revenue stream from the licensing arrangement with American Optical. In other words, we were not paying any dividends. We had a very tough Board meeting where all the outside Directors wanted to give up on the effort and just "clip coupons" from the licensing fee income stream. I pled the case that we had come a long way to this point, that we had the makings of a successful machine, but that we needed some additional capital invested to buy time to perfect it. It turned out I was convincing enough for the Board to consider starting down a path towards refinancing, but I was wrong about our ability to perfect the Pressure/Pulsometer.

We needed a capital infusion and unable to do a public offering, we decided to raise money through a private placement and started talking to potential investors.

In the meantime I had a call from my father who was very aware of the high risk in making Physio-Control into a profitable company, much less a worthwhile career for me. He had received a call from Kline Hillman, a fishing buddy of his, about a business that his son-in-law, Paul Voinot, wanted to buy. He explained to Dad that he would only loan the money to make a down payment on condition Paul find a partner to invest with him in the business. Kline had called Father knowing that I had some experience in agriculture wondering if I would be interested in becoming Paul's partner. If I was, then he would loan the required money to Paul.

I had met Paul Voinot years before when he dated my sister Jan several times, most notably as her escort to the infamous Christmas Ball. He was a very high quality young man, was married to Margy Hillman and had several beautiful daughters. Paul evidently suffered some trouble getting lined out in a vocation, and at age 36 had been unable as yet to build a viable career. As for myself, I had taken one vocation as far as I could and was trying to get started in a totally new one and thus we were not unlike career-wise. We both hoped the investment we were contemplating would prove to be successful and long lasting, which at that time in our lives we both badly needed.

The company in question was the Ostrom Mushroom Company, a small mushroom growing and packing business located in the Lake City district of Seattle. Paul, in his job at Safeway, had become interested in the Ostrom Company and had talked several times with Cameron Ostrom, the originator and owner of the business, who wanted to sell it as he was then around 65 years old and thinking about retiring. The deal was to buy the business, but not the underlying real estate, for $125,000 plus the inventory value of finished goods in the warehouse, which would be paid over the term of the contract. We were to pay Ostom $25,000 down with the balance paid over five years. This meant both Paul and I would each initially put up $12,500. Paul also had worked out an arrangement for Mr. Ostrom to consult with us for a year, to help us learn mushroom growing and processing, which we considered absolutely necessary if we were to survive.

This opportunity sounded interesting to me as I could see the financial crisis growing at Physio-Control. But before I would consent to the investment, I wanted to talk to some people, other than Mr. Ostrom, who were experienced in the mushroom business. This meant a trip to Pennsylvania where 80 percent of the total U.S. production was grown and where Penn State University carried on research in all aspects of mushroom growing and processing. Paul and I developed a list of names of top figures in the business, including Ph.D's in mycological sciences, as well as businessmen managing some large operations and made arrangements to go east to meet with them.

At Penn State University we met Dr. Leon Kneebone, a plant pathologist and consultant to the industry and Dr. Edward Lambert, famous for many improvements in cultivation techniques and spawn development. It was easy to see that they could hardly take us seriously as we were absolute neophytes who knew nothing about the business and were asking them if we should buy this tiny mushroom farm in Seattle. Their unqualified assessment was that we should not make the investment. They explained in some vivid detail that it was a difficult business with many risks to growing and the market was already beginning to feel pressure from Taiwan imports at very low prices. Also, no one we visited with knew the Ostrom farm, but they felt it was too small to be viable, even if it was well designed and enjoyed high yields, neither of which seemed to be the case, as we learned after our visits to several large farms in the Kennett Square area south of Philidelphia.

These farms clearly demonstrated to us what successful operations looked like, at least in 1964 Pennsylvania. After listening to all the negative observations about the industry and recognizing the Ostrom farm did not measure up in many physical aspects to the farms we had seen on our trip, we felt that the Northwest market, with its reduced competition and Ostrom's high product reputation, would be enough to lead towards a profitable business. We decided on the trip home to buy the business, notwithstanding the negative comments we had encountered, counting on the special factors about Ostrom's to carry the day. In other words, blind optimism in the face of the negativism of the experienced folks in the industry.

Paul and I agreed that the business could not support two full time working owners, so I planned to stay at Physio while Paul took over the full time management of Ostrom's. I would visit the farm several times a week, and spend Saturdays helping out and learning what I could about the business. With the help of

Tom Foster, the attorney we hired to put the deal together for us with Cameron Ostrom, we soon had signed the necessary papers. I cashed in some old war bonds that had been accumulating interest for many years in order to make my half of the down payment. We also signed a partnership agreement backed by $65,000 of "key man" life insurance, to cover the unlikely event of one of our deaths and made our first premium payment on that policy, thinking it was a lot, especially considering we would have the annual premium cost for many years ahead. Thus it was in October of 1964 Paul Vionot and I laid our money down and purchased Mr. Ostrom's mushroom farm.

Back at Physio, Bill Edmark continued to work on debugging the machine and trying to interest people in investing in the company. In early 1965, he introduced me to Ray Dilling, CEO of Interface Mechanisms, the company working in the electronic field of barcode readers, the systems now used universally to designate and control product inventories and sales. Ray knew some investors from his own financing efforts at Intermec and soon he brought Bagley Wright around to talk to Bill. At this time it became obvious that there would be no place for me in an expanded and refinanced Physio-Control. Investors would have to feel very secure about the management of the company and an ex-cowboy was not exactly their idea of what would be needed at Physio-Control. I made it clear that I understood this fact very well and was prepared to resign whenever another manager was hired after the refinancing was done.

Three months later in March of 1965 while the refinancing efforts at Physio appeared to be coming toward conclusion, I received the startling and painful news that Paul had been diagnosed with lung cancer. It was unbelievable that such a thing could happen. We had just bought the company and Paul was so excited about the future. It was a terrible blow to him, but he tried hard to deal with it and I never heard him complain. This meant I would have to spend more time supporting Paul in the daily management of the mushroom business, while also trying to keep Physio on an even financial keel. With the advent of summer, Paul's condition required that he be hospitalized and I had to rely on some of the Ostrom staff to keep things going until the refinancing of Physio was accomplished, and a new manager took over.

While Paul fought his private battle with cancer, Physio was reorganized. Bagley Wright brought some other investors with him and Hunter Simpson, then regional manager for IBM, agreed to come on board as President and CEO. Bill Edmark and I were to remain as Directors along with some of the men who were putting up the new money. Ray Dilling became Chairman of the Board. The rest of the Board was made up of Bagely Wright, Tedrowe Watkins, and Hunter.

One of the big stumbling blocks was that doctor Bill was going to have to give up control of the company. He was obliged to sell a large block of his stock to the new investors. This created a major heartburn for him and he was very reluctant to take this step. Unless he agreed, the deal was going to come undone and I was asked by Ray and Bagley to talk with him as a friend, to help him understand how important this move was if he wanted to finance the business properly and enable it to continue.

One of Bill's business heroes was Dr. Land, the inventor of the Polaroid camera, who had been able to retain control of his company during the initial financing stages. Of course, this had made him a millionaire many times over and Bill was having a hard time understanding why he could not get a similar deal. Finally I asked him if he wanted to be a part owner of a business that could be very successful and make him a lot of money, or the whole owner of a worthless business. As I was very optimistic about the field of medical electronics, I encouraged Bill to think of the values he could create for himself, even with a smaller percent of ownership. I know this was a very hard decision for Bill to make, but the reality of the situation finally brought him around, the investment was completed and Hunter took over as CEO of Physio.

In September, six months after he had been diagnosed, and slightly less than a year from the time we purchased the mushroom company, Paul, at thirty seven years old, became the third heavy smoker I knew to succumb to this disease. With the funds from the $65,000 life insurance received by the company at Paul's death, I paid off the bank loan covering the loss on the first year's operation and purchased Paul's stock in the company, as required by the partnership agreement. In so doing, in 1965 I became the sole owner of The Ostrom Company and embarked, on my third career, to be a mushroom farmer.

Epilogue

The Joy of Rummaging

Looking backward at my life has brought about an interesting thought concerning time. I had always felt, when studying history, that the Civil War and World War I were about as far removed from me as the Battle of Waterloo or even the Roman Empire and I found it hard to empathize with the people who lived in those times. It just seemed too long ago to allow a personal human connection, something besides the dry words of other people, other times. But on closer inspection of my own life I have come to realize that, in a way, my life encompasses the lifespan of every person I have known and touched. By this new rationale, in being fortunate to know my great grandfather Poppy, born in 1845, I actually knew someone who was 14 years old when Lincoln was President and the Civil War began. Just three generations in my family, up to my own, and continuing this thought, only several more to the days of the Revolution and Washington, Jefferson, Adams and Madison. This realization has helped me to understand that only a short time has passed since the Civil War was fought, when thousands of men the age of Poppy had perished or suffered greatly in it. It is perhaps for this reason that the history of the great western migration of America has seemed so real to me and my family, and maybe increased our abilities to better feel and understand the struggles, the pain endured, or losses incurred by our forebears who helped construct the world we now live in.

And so we are arrived where the tale of my youth is coming to a conclusion and the road to maturity beckons. My travels back in time, rummaging around in the chapters of my personal story, have been very enlightening to me and even at times, entertaining, eliciting many a chuckle or outright laugh at my youthful foibles. I must also admit, sometimes a few tears, from more painful and poignant memories that seemed to float into my consciousness unbidden, dredging up some deeply buried sorrow from my past. And much about me that I did not discern at the time of the doing, has been made more apparent through the process of remembering.

I see myself more clearly now as the conflicted personality I was and perhaps still am to some degree, worrying about self image, fearful of embarrassment or rejection, anxious to not being chosen last, but at the same time feeling some pride in things tried, and occasionally, even things accomplished. I just never could settle on which trait would dominate and maybe this was good, since when too high a level of hubris seemed to rule for a time, I was always brought back to reality through some youthful excess or failure. Perhaps this is how it is for everyone but of course when we are young, and wrapped in the web of our own existence, we are certain that no one else can feel love or disappointment, joy or pain, as strongly as we do.

There is no doubt that my family history, especially the example of the adventurous life led by Poppy, and the exciting tales of ancient heroes that books brought into my life, induced in me an overly romantic vision of what was possible. I was slow in growing past this dream of how I could shape my life outside the norm, because I could not visualize how to prepare myself to be successful at it. It was all about *the adventure* and I struggled to avoid what I saw as the "nine to five life story," mundane career choices open to me that all appeared to be repetitive and lacking in anything more exciting than the country club.

But ultimately, kicking and screaming, I was dragged to the reality that it was time to get serious about my life in an economic sense. This understanding induced me to seek new, and I hoped, interesting work and maybe more important, find the freedom to build my own career or business in my own way. This prospect I looked forward to with optimistic enthusiasm.

I cannot help but feel truly blessed with good fortune having now taken a detailed look back at the story of my growing up, the wonderful supporting family and friends I had as important actors during this period of my Life Play. The fact that the backdrop for this play was America coping with depression and then war, the war's unsettled aftermath and our nation still remaining the beacon of hope for the world, has given me a sort of inner strength when I think of this heritage, of being a part of this wonderful experiment in a new kind of human culture.

Our country is surely far from perfect, but certainly it is a model for mankind to build upon, since it best answers our human aspirations towards the freedom of thought and action in realizing our personal dreams. And when I think about it, where else could I have played at being a dilettante Don Quijote for as long as I did?

But life is a continuum that we must live and the world beckoned to me with all its hard realities. So with a young wife and six children and no job, it was time to get serious and leave the windmills alone. But the challenges were there, only they were different; no longer the snowy trail, the horses to break, the cattle to manage, or the senoritas flirting; all replaced by a need to learn how to build a company and make it excellent, educate the children and try to form a semblance of a productive and contributory life.

◆   ◆   ◆

It was difficult to leave the romantic outdoor life for the reality of the city, but we will leave the story of that transition to later chapters in this tale, which may disclose if our hero can fulfill his own personal aspirations and perhaps even give something back in return.

We are about to witness what the management books call a paradigm change come into his life with the decision to leave the ranch and seek his fortune elsewhere and we will find out if the inevitable spin-outs on the curves of his life's story will shake his fundamental optimism.

Will he continue to move ahead still needing to look towards the western horizon, still believing in the promise of America, still gazing outward to the spiral of the Milky Way on a clear bright night? And will he continue to believe that his Avalon lies always just over the horizon line and if he finally arrives there, joy and fulfillment will enter into his and his family's life? Or will he finally learn that his Avalon is already within himself if he would only take the time to look?

I hope you will come along with me and perhaps we shall see if there is an answer to his youthful ending phrase....

"All that happened seemed a...."

978-0-595-43087-

0-595-43087-2

Printed in the United States
99800LV00003B/73-114/A

9 780595 430871